中国政府白皮书汇编
（2023 年）

人民出版社　　外文出版社
FOREIGN LANGUAGES PRESS

目　　录

新时代的中国网络法治建设

（2023 年 3 月）

携手构建人类命运共同体：中国的倡议与行动

（2023 年 9 月）

新时代党的治藏方略的实践及其历史性成就
（2023 年 11 月）

第二部分　英文版

China's Green Development in the New Era
（January 2023）

China's Law-Based Cyberspace Governance in the New Era

(March 2023)

A Global Community of Shared Future: China's Proposals and Actions

(September 2023)

The Belt and Road Initiative: A Key Pillar of the Global Community of Shared Future

(October 2023)

Development of China's Distant-Water Fisheries

(October 2023)

CPC Policies on the Governance of Xizang in the New Era: Approach and Achievements

(November 2023)

第一部分　中文版

新时代的中国绿色发展

（2023 年 1 月）

中华人民共和国
国务院新闻办公室

前　言

绿色是生命的象征、大自然的底色,良好生态环境是美好生活的基础、人民共同的期盼。绿色发展是顺应自然、促进人与自然和谐共生的发展,是用最少资源环境代价取得最大经济社会效益的发展,是高质量、可持续的发展,已经成为各国共识。

几千年来,中华民族尊重自然、保护自然,生生不息、繁衍发展,倡导"天人合一"是中华文明的鲜明特色。改革开放以来,中国把节约资源和保护环境确立为基本国策,把可持续发展确立为国家战略,大力推进社会主义生态文明建设。

中共十八大以来,在习近平新时代中国特色社会主义思想指引下,中国坚持绿水青山就是金山银山的理念,坚定不移走生态优先、绿色发展之路,促进经济社会发展全面绿色转型,建设人与自然和谐共生的现代化,创造了举世瞩目的生态奇迹和绿色发展奇迹,美丽中国建设迈出重大步伐。绿色成为新时代中国的鲜明底色,绿色发展成为中国式现代化的显著特征,广袤中华大地天更蓝、山更绿、水更清,人民享有更多、更普惠、更可持续的绿色福祉。中国的绿色发展,为地球增添了更多"中国绿",扩大了全球绿色版图,既造福了中国,也造福了世界。

作为世界上最大的发展中国家,中国秉持人类命运共同体理念,坚定践行多边主义,提出全球发展倡议、全球安全倡议,深化务实合作,积极参与全球环境与气候治理,为落实联合国2030年可持续发展议程,推动全球可持续发展,共同构建人与自然生命共同体,共建繁荣清洁美丽的世界贡献了中国智慧、中国力量。

为全面介绍新时代中国绿色发展理念、实践与成效,分享中国绿色发展经验,特发布本白皮书。

一、坚定不移走绿色发展之路

中国顺应人民对美好生活的新期待，树立和践行绿水青山就是金山银山的理念，站在人与自然和谐共生的高度谋划发展，协同推进经济社会高质量发展和生态环境高水平保护，走出了一条生产发展、生活富裕、生态良好的文明发展道路。

（一）坚持以人民为中心的发展思想

以人民为中心是中国共产党的执政理念，良好生态环境是最公平的公共产品、最普惠的民生福祉。随着中国现代化建设的不断推进和人民生活水平的不断提高，人民对优美生态环境的需要更加迫切，生态环境在人民生活幸福指数中的地位不断凸显。中国顺应人民日益增长的优美生态环境需要，坚持生态惠民、生态利民、生态为民，大力推行绿色生产生活方式，重点解决损害群众健康的突出环境问题，持续改善生态环境质量，提供更多优质生态产品，让人民在优美生态环境中有更多的获得感、幸福感、安全感。

（二）着眼中华民族永续发展

生态兴则文明兴，生态衰则文明衰。大自然是人类赖以生存发展的基本条件，只有尊重自然、顺应自然、保护自然，才能实现可持续发展。中国立足环境容量有限、生态系统脆弱的现实国情，既为当代发展谋、也为子孙万代计，把生态文明建设作为关系中华民族永续发展的根本大计，既要金山银山也要绿水青山，推动绿水青山转化为金山银山，让自然财富、生态财富源源不断带来经济财富、社会财富，实现经济效益、生态效益、社会效益同步提升，建设人与自然和谐共生的现代化。

（三）坚持系统观念统筹推进

绿色发展是对生产方式、生活方式、思维方式和价值观念的全方位、革命性变革。中国把系统观念贯穿到经济社会发展和生态环境保护全过程，正确处理发展和保护、全局和局部、当前和长远等一系列关系，构建科学适度有序的国土空间布局体系、绿色低碳循环发展的经济体系、约束和激励并举的制度体系，统筹产业结构调整、污染治理、生态保护、应对气候变化，协同推进降碳、减污、扩绿、增长，推进生态优先、节约集约、绿色低碳发展，形成节约资源和保护环境的空间格局、产业结构、生产方式、生活方式，促进经济社会发展全面绿色转型。

（四）共谋全球可持续发展

保护生态环境、应对气候变化，是全人类的共同责任。只有世界各国团结合作、共同努力，携手推进绿色可持续发展，才能维持地球生态整体平衡，守护好全人类赖以生存的唯一家园。中国站在对人类文明负责的高度，积极参与全球环境治理，向世界承诺力争于2030年前实现碳达峰、努力争取2060年前实现碳中和，以"碳达峰碳中和"目标为牵引推动绿色转型，以更加积极的姿态开展绿色发展双多边国际合作，推动构建公平合理、合作共赢的全球环境治理体系，为全球可持续发展贡献智慧和力量。

专栏1　碳达峰碳中和政策与行动

碳达峰碳中和"1+N"政策体系：《关于完整准确全面贯彻新发展理念做好碳达峰碳中和工作的意见》《2030年前碳达峰行动方案》共同构成中国推进碳达峰碳中和工作的顶层设计，与能源、工业、交通运输、城乡建设、钢铁、有色金属、水泥等重点领域、重点行业碳达峰实施方案，以及科技、财政、金融、标准、人才等支撑保障方案，共同构建起碳达峰碳中和"1+N"政策体系。

碳达峰十大行动：《2030年前碳达峰行动方案》部署开展能源绿色低碳转型行动、节能降碳增效行动、工业领域碳达峰行动、城乡建设碳达峰行动、交通运输绿色低碳行动、循环经济助力降碳行动、绿色低碳科技创新行动、碳汇能力巩固提升行动、绿色低碳全民行动、各地区梯次有序碳达峰行动等十大行动。

二、绿色空间格局基本形成

中国积极健全国土空间体系，加强生产、生活、生态空间用途统筹和协调管控，加大生态系统保护修复力度，有效扩大生态环境容量，推动自然财富、生态财富快速积累，生态环境保护发生历史性、转折性、全局性变化，为经济社会持续健康发展提供有力支撑。

（一）优化国土空间开发保护格局

国土是绿色发展的空间载体。中国实施主体功能区战略，建立全国统一、责权清晰、科学高效的国土空间规划体系，统筹人口分布、经济布局、国土利用、生态环境保护等因素，整体谋划国土空间开发保护，实现国土空间开发保护更高质量、更可持续。

实现国土空间规划"多规合一"。将主体功能区规划、土地利用规划、城乡规划等空间规划融合为统一的国土空间规划，逐步建立"多规合一"的规划编制审批体系、实施监督体系、法规政策体系和技术标准体系，强化国土空间规划对各专项规划的指导约束作用，加快完成各级各类国土空间规划编制，逐步形成全国国土空间开发保护"一张图"。

统筹优化国土空间布局。以全国国土调查成果为基础，开展资源环境承载能力和国土空间开发适宜性评价,科学布局农业、生态、城镇等功能空间,优化农产品主产区、重点生态功能区、城市化地区三大空间格局。统筹划定耕地和永久基本农田、生态保护红线、城镇开发边界等空间管控边界以及各类海域保护线,强化底线约束,统一国土空间用途管制,筑牢国家安全发展的空间基础。

加强重点生态功能区管理。着力防控化解生态风险,将承担水源涵养、水土保持、防风固沙和生物多样性保护等重要生态功能的县级行政区确定为重点生态功能区,以保护生态环境、提供生态产品为重点,限制大规模高强度工业化城镇化开发,推动自然生态系统总体稳定向好,生态服务功能逐步增强,生态产品供给水平持续提升。

(二)强化生态系统保护修复

山水林田湖草沙是生命共同体。中国加强系统治理、综合治理、源头治理和依法治理,坚持保护优先、自然恢复为主,大力推动生态系统保护修复,筑牢国家生态安全屏障,筑牢中华民族永续发展的根基。

初步建立新型自然保护地体系。自然保护地是生态建设的核心载体。中国努力构建以国家公园为主体、自然保护区为基础、各类自然公园为补充的自然保护地体系,正式设立三江源、大熊猫、东北虎豹、海南热带雨林、武夷山首批 5 个国家公园,积极稳妥有序推进生态重要区域国家公园创建。截至 2021 年底,已建立各级各类自然保护地近万处,占国土陆域面积的 17% 以上,90% 的陆地自然生态系统类型和 74% 的国家重点保护野生动植物物种得到了有效保护。

专栏 2   自然保护地体系

自然保护地是指由各级政府依法划定或确认,对重要的自然生态系统、自然遗迹、自然景观及其所承载的自然资源、生态功能和文化价值实施长期保护的陆域或海域。依据管理目标与效能并借鉴国际经验,中国将自然保护地按生态价值和保护强度高低,依次分为国家公园、自然保护区及自然公园 3 种类型。

国家公园:是指以保护具有国家代表性的自然生态系统为主要目的,实现自然资源科学保护和合理利用的特定陆域或海域,是中国自然生态系统中最重要、自然景观最独特、自然遗产最精华、生物多样性最富集的部分。

自然保护区:是指典型的自然生态系统、珍稀濒危野生动植物种的天然集中分布区、有特殊意义的自然遗迹的区域。确保主要保护对象安全,维持和恢复珍稀濒危野生动植物种群数量及赖以生存的栖息环境。

自然公园:是指重要的自然生态系统、自然遗迹和自然景观,具有生态、观赏、文化和科学价值,可持续利用的区域。确保森林、海洋、湿地、水域、冰川、草原、生物等珍贵自然资源,以及所承载的景观、地质地貌和文化多样性得到有效保护。包括森林公园、地质公园、海洋公园、湿地公园、沙漠公园、草原公园等各类自然公园。

科学划定生态保护红线。生态保护红线是国家生态安全的底线和生命线。中国将生态功能极重要、生态极脆弱以及具有潜在重要生态价值的区域划入生态保护红线,包括整合优化后的自然保护地,实现一条红线管控重要生态空间。截至目前,中国陆域生态保护红线面积占陆域国土面积比例超过 30%。通过划定生态保护红线和编

制生态保护修复规划,巩固了以青藏高原生态屏障区、黄河重点生态区(含黄土高原生态屏障)、长江重点生态区(含川滇生态屏障)、东北森林带、北方防沙带、南方丘陵山地带、海岸带等为依托的"三区四带"生态安全格局。

实施重要生态系统保护和修复重大工程。以国家重点生态功能区、生态保护红线、自然保护地等为重点,启动实施山水林田湖草沙一体化保护和修复工程,统筹推进系统治理、综合治理、源头治理。陆续实施三北、长江等防护林和天然林保护修复、退耕还林还草、矿山生态修复、"蓝色海湾"整治行动、海岸带保护修复、渤海综合治理攻坚战、红树林保护修复等一批具有重要生态影响的生态环境修复治理工程,科学开展大规模国土绿化行动,推动森林、草原、湿地、河流、湖泊面积持续增加,土地荒漠化趋势得到有效扭转。2012—2021年,中国累计完成造林 9.6 亿亩,防沙治沙 2.78 亿亩,种草改良 6 亿亩,新增和修复湿地 1200 多万亩。2021 年,中国森林覆盖率达到 24.02%,森林蓄积量达到 194.93 亿立方米,森林覆盖率和森林蓄积量连续 30 多年保持"双增长",是全球森林资源增长最多和人工造林面积最大的国家。中国在世界范围内率先实现了土地退化"零增长",荒漠化土地和沙化土地面积"双减少",对全球实现 2030 年土地退化零增长目标发挥了积极作用。自 2000 年以来,中国始终是全球"增绿"的主力军,全球新增绿化面积中约 1/4 来自中国。

塞罕坝位于中国河北省北部,距北京市约300公里。20世纪50年代,塞罕坝是黄沙肆虐、鸟无栖地的不毛之地。为改变"风沙紧逼北京城"的严峻形势,20世纪60年代初,中国组建了塞罕坝机械林场,一支由369人组成的创业队伍,开启了"为首都阻沙源、为京津涵水源"的拓荒之路。在"黄沙遮天日,飞鸟无栖树"的荒漠沙地上,几代塞罕坝人甘于奉献、接续奋斗,建成目前世界上面积最大的人工林,创造了荒原变林海的人间奇迹,为京津冀地区筑起了一道高质量发展的绿色屏障,成为中国乃至全世界荒漠治理的典范。

目前,塞罕坝林场森林面积115.1万亩,活立木蓄积量1036.8万立方米,每年涵养水源、净化淡水2.84亿立方米,有效防止水土流失,为京津冀地区高质量发展打下了良好的生态基础。在塞罕坝林场辐射带动下,周边区域生态苗木基地产业以及乡村旅游产业,直接为当地4000多名群众提供就业机会,带动周边4万多名群众受益。塞罕坝林场不仅释放出了巨大的生态效益,也不断影响和改变着周边群众的生产生活,彰显出强大的社会效益。

塞罕坝筑起的"绿色长城"获得了世界赞誉。2017年,塞罕坝林场获得联合国"地球卫士奖";2021年,获得联合国"土地生命奖"。

（三）推动重点区域绿色发展

中国充分发挥区域重大战略的提升引领作用,坚持生态优先、绿色发展理念推动实施区域重大战略,着力打造绿色发展的第一梯队,带动全国经济社会发展绿色化水平整体提升。

推动京津冀协同发展生态环保率先突破。实施京津冀协同发展战略,在交通、环境、产业、公共服务等领域协同推进,强化生态环境联建联防联治。以京津冀地区为重点,开展华北地区地下水超采综合治理,扭转了上世纪80年代以来华北地下水位逐年下降的趋势。

高起点规划、高标准建设雄安新区，围绕打造北京非首都功能集中承载地，构建布局合理、蓝绿交织、清新明亮、水城共融的生态城市，打造绿色高质量发展"样板之城"。2021年，京津冀13个城市空气质量优良天数比例达到74.1%，比2013年提升32.2个百分点，北京市大气环境治理成为全球环境治理的中国样本。

以共抓大保护、不搞大开发为导向推动长江经济带建设。长江是中华民族的母亲河，也是中华民族发展的重要支撑。中国坚持把修复长江生态环境摆在压倒性位置，协调推动经济发展和生态环境保护，努力建设人与自然和谐共生的绿色发展示范带，使长江经济带成为生态优先、绿色发展的主战场。发挥产业协同联动整体优势，构建绿色产业体系，加快区域经济绿色转型步伐。大力推进长江保护修复攻坚战，深入实施城镇污水垃圾处理、化工污染治理、农业面源污染治理、船舶污染治理和尾矿库污染治理"4+1"工程，全面实施长江十年禁渔，开展长江岸线利用项目及非法矮围清理整治。2018年以来，累计腾退长江岸线162公里，滩岸复绿1213万平方米，恢复水域面积6.8万亩，长江干流国控断面水质连续两年全线达到Ⅱ类。

专栏4　长江十年禁渔

2021年1月1日0时起，长江干流和重要支流、大型通江湖泊等重点水域实行十年禁捕，期间禁止天然渔业资源的生产性捕捞。目前，长江禁捕水域核定的11.1万艘渔船、23.1万渔民全部退出捕捞，22.2万符合社保条件的退捕渔民实现应保尽保，16.5万有就业意愿和就业能力的退捕渔民实现转产就业。

实施长江十年禁渔,对于保护生物多样性、修复水域生态功能、保障国家生态安全具有重大意义。禁捕实施以来,沿江各地水生生物资源量显著增加,水域生态功能恢复向好趋势逐步显现。"微笑天使"长江江豚群体在鄱阳湖、洞庭湖、湖北宜昌和中下游江段出现的频率明显提升,20年未见的鳤鱼在长江中游又重新出现;上游一级支流赤水河鱼类资源明显恢复,鱼类物种数由禁捕前的32种上升至37种,资源量达到禁捕前的1.95倍。

发挥长三角地区绿色发展表率作用。加快长三角生态绿色一体化发展示范区建设,率先探索将生态优势转化为经济社会发展优势、从项目协同走向区域一体化制度创新,依托优美风光、人文底蕴、特色产业,集聚创新要素资源,夯实绿色发展生态本底,打造绿色创新发展高地。

推动黄河流域生态保护和高质量发展。把保护黄河作为中华民族发展的千秋大计,坚持对黄河上下游、干支流、左右岸生态保护治理工作统筹谋划。开展全流域生态环境保护治理,推动上中游水土流失和荒漠化防治以及下游河道和滩区综合治理,黄河泥沙负荷稳步下降,确保黄河安澜。坚持以水定城、以水定地、以水定人、以水定产,走水安全有效保障、水资源高效利用、水生态明显改善的集约节约发展之路。沿黄地区在保护传承弘扬黄河文化、发展特色产业上积极探索,培养壮大新产业新业态,推动生态、经济价值同步提升,让黄河成为惠民利民的生态河、幸福河。

建设美丽粤港澳大湾区。以建设美丽湾区为引领,着力提升生态环境质量,探索绿色低碳的城市建设运营模式,促进大湾区可持续发展,使大湾区天更蓝、山更绿、水更清,打造生态安全、环境优美、社会安定、文化繁荣的粤港澳大湾区。

（四）建设生态宜居美丽家园

城乡是人们聚居活动的主要空间。中国把绿色发展理念融入城乡建设活动,大力推动美丽城市和美丽乡村建设,突出环境污染治理,着力提升人居环境品质,打造山峦层林尽染、平原蓝绿交融、城乡鸟语花香的美丽家园。

建设人与自然和谐共生的美丽城市。中国把保护城市生态环境摆在突出位置,推进以人为核心的城镇化,科学规划布局城市的生产空间、生活空间、生态空间,打造宜居城市、韧性城市、智慧城市,把城市建设成为人与自然和谐共生的美丽家园。坚持尊重自然、顺应自然,依托现有山水脉络等独特风光推进城市建设,让城市融入大自然,让居民望得见山、看得见水、记得住乡愁。持续拓展城市生态空间,建设国家园林城市、国家森林城市,推进城市公园体系和绿道网络建设,大力推动城市绿化,让城市再现绿水青山。2012—2021 年,城市建成区绿化覆盖率由 39.22% 提高到 42.06%,人均公园绿地面积由 11.8 平方米提高到 14.78 平方米。大力发展绿色低碳建筑,推进既有建筑改造,建筑节能水平持续提高。

打造绿色生态宜居的和美乡村。中国将绿色发展作为推进乡村振兴的新引擎,探索乡村绿色发展新路径。积极发展生态农业、农村

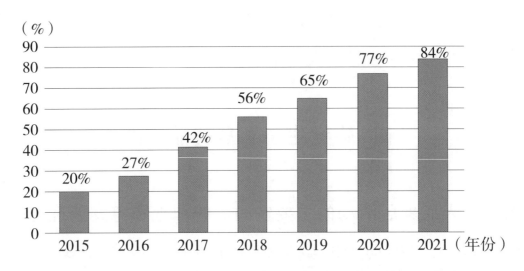

图 1 2015—2021 年中国城镇当年新建绿色建筑面积占比

电商、休闲农业、乡村旅游、健康养老等新产业、新业态,加强生态保护与修复,推动农业强、农村美、农民富的目标不断实现。持续改善农村人居环境,完善乡村公路、供水、供气等基础设施,推进农村厕所革命,加强生活垃圾、污水治理,开展村庄清洁行动,全面推进乡村绿化,持续开展现代宜居农房建设,越来越多的乡村实现水源净化、道路硬化、夜晚亮化、能源清洁化。加强传统村落保护利用,传承优秀传统文化,提升乡村风貌。广大农村生态美起来、环境靓起来,丛林掩映、果菜满园、满眼锦绣,呈现山清水秀、天蓝地绿、村美人和的美丽画卷。

专栏 5 完善城乡环境基础设施

中国高度重视环境基础设施建设,着力补短板、强弱项、优布局、提品质,健全污水收集处理及资源化利用设施,大幅提升生活垃圾分类和处理能力,推进固体废物、危险废物、医疗废物安全有效处置,推动环境基础设施一体化、智能化、绿色化发展,构建集污水、垃圾、固体废物、危险废物、医疗废物处理处置设施和监测监管能力于一

体的环境基础设施体系,形成由城市向建制镇和乡村延伸覆盖的环境基础设施网络。截至 2021 年底,城市和县城污水处理能力达 2.47 亿立方米/日;城镇生活垃圾焚烧处理能力超过 77 万吨/日,城镇生活垃圾无害化处理率接近 100%。

持续打好污染防治攻坚战。环境就是民生,青山就是美丽,蓝天也是幸福。中国坚持精准治污、科学治污、依法治污,以解决人民群众反映强烈的大气、水、土壤污染等突出问题为重点,持续打好蓝天、碧水、净土保卫战。区域联防联控和重污染天气应对成效显著,全国地级及以上城市细颗粒物(PM$_{2.5}$)年均浓度由 2015 年的 46 微克/立方米降至 2021 年的 30 微克/立方米,空气质量优良天数比例达到 87.5%,成为全球大气质量改善速度最快的国家。工业、农业、生活污染源和水生态系统整治加快推进,饮用水安全得到有效保障,污染严重水体和不达标水体显著减少,2021 年全国地表水水质优良断面比例达到 84.9%。全面禁止洋垃圾入境,实现固体废物"零进口"目标,土壤环境风险得到基本管控。蓝天白云、繁星闪烁,清水绿岸、鱼翔浅底,人们呼吸的空气更清新、喝的水更干净、吃的食物更放心、生活的环境更优美,切实感受到生态环境变化带来的幸福和美好。

三、产业结构持续调整优化

中国坚持创新、协调、绿色、开放、共享的新发展理念,以创新驱动为引领塑造经济发展新动能新优势,以资源环境刚性约束推动产业结构深度调整,以强化区域协作持续优化产业空间布局,经济发展既保持了量的合理增长,也实现了质的稳步提升,开创了高质量发展的新局面。

(一)大力发展战略性新兴产业

实施创新驱动发展战略,把科技创新作为调整产业结构、促进经济社会绿色低碳转型的动力和保障,战略性新兴产业成为经济发展的重要引擎,经济发展的含金量和含绿量显著提升。

科技创新投入力度逐步加大。全社会研发投入由 2012 年的 1.03 万亿元增长到 2021 年的 2.80 万亿元,研发投入强度由 1.91% 提高到 2.44%,已接近经合组织国家平均水平。企业研发投入力度不断加大,占全社会研发投入比例达到 76% 以上。截至 2021 年底,中国节能环保产业有效发明专利 4.9 万件,新能源产业有效发明专利 6 万件,分别是 2017 年底的 1.6 倍、1.7 倍。2011 年至 2020 年,中国环境技术发明专利申请总量接近全球 60%,是全球布局环境技术创新最积极的国家。

新兴技术成为经济发展重要支撑。人工智能、大数据、区块链、量子通信等新兴技术加快应用,培育了智能终端、远程医疗、在线教育等新产品、新业态,在经济发展中的带动作用不断增强。数字经济规模居世界第二位,"十三五"期间(2016—2020年),信息传输、软件和信息技术服务业增加值年均增速高达21%。互联网、大数据、人工智能、5G等新兴技术与传统产业深度融合,先进制造业和现代服务业融合发展步伐加快,2021年,高技术制造业、装备制造业增加值占规模以上工业增加值比重分别为15.1%、32.4%,较2012年分别提高5.7和4.2个百分点,"中国制造"逐步向"中国智造"转型升级。

绿色产业规模持续壮大。可再生能源产业发展迅速,风电、光伏发电等清洁能源设备生产规模居世界第一,多晶硅、硅片、电池和组件占全球产量的70%以上。节能环保产业质量效益持续提升,形成了覆盖节能、节水、环保、可再生能源等各领域的绿色技术装备制造体系,绿色技术装备和产品供给能力显著增强,绿色装备制造成本持续下降,能源设备、节水设备、污染治理、环境监测等多个领域技术已达到国际先进水平。综合能源服务、合同能源管理、合同节水管理、环境污染第三方治理、碳排放管理综合服务等新业态新模式不断发展壮大,2021年节能环保产业产值超过8万亿元。各地方积极探索生态产品价值实现方式路径,都市现代农业、休闲农业、生态旅游、森林康养、精品民宿、田园综合体等生态产业新模式快速发展。

（二）引导资源型产业有序发展

中国持续深化供给侧结构性改革，改变过多依赖增加资源消耗、过多依赖规模粗放扩张、过多依赖高耗能高排放产业的发展模式，以环境承载力作为刚性约束，严控高耗能、高排放、高耗水行业产能规模，推动产业结构持续优化。

化解过剩产能和淘汰落后产能。在保障产业链供应链安全的同时，积极稳妥化解过剩产能、淘汰落后产能，对钢铁、水泥、电解铝等资源消耗量高、污染物排放量大的行业实行产能等量或减量置换政策。"十三五"期间（2016—2020年），累计退出钢铁过剩产能1.5亿吨以上、水泥过剩产能3亿吨，地条钢全部出清，电解铝、水泥等行业的落后产能基本出清。

坚决遏制高耗能、高排放、低水平项目盲目发展。提高部分重点行业土地、环保、节能、节水、技术、安全等方面的准入条件，对高耗能行业实施差别电价、阶梯电价、惩罚性电价等差别化电价政策。对高耗能、高排放、低水平项目实行清单管理、分类处置、动态监控，严肃查处违法违规建设运行的项目。水资源短缺和超载地区，限制新建各类开发区和高耗水项目。

（三）优化产业区域布局

综合考虑能源资源、环境容量、市场空间等因素，推动相关产业向更具发展条件和潜力的地区集中集聚，优化生产力布局，深化区域间分工协作，加快形成布局合理、集约高效、协调协同的现代化产业发展格局。

推进原材料产业合理布局。统筹煤水资源和环境容量等因素，在中西部地区规划布局了若干个现代煤化工产业示范区，深入开展煤化工产业技术升级示范。在沿海地区高水平建设一批大型石化产业基地，推动石化行业安全、绿色、集聚、高效发展。

深化各地区分工协作。充分发挥各地区比较优势，依托资源环境禀赋和产业发展基础，探索建立和完善利益共享机制，强化东部和中西部地区之间多类型、多机制产业分工协作，形成协调联动、优势互补、共同发展的新格局。通过产业转移和地区协作，在破解产业发展资源环境约束的同时，为东部发展高新产业腾出空间、促进中西部欠发达地区工业化和城镇化进程，增强了区域发展的平衡性和协调性。

四、绿色生产方式广泛推行

中国加快构建绿色低碳循环发展的经济体系,大力推行绿色生产方式,推动能源革命和资源节约集约利用,系统推进清洁生产,统筹减污降碳协同增效,实现经济社会发展和生态环境保护的协调统一。

(一)促进传统产业绿色转型

将绿色发展理念融入工业、农业、服务业全链条各环节,积极构建绿色低碳循环发展的生产体系,以节能、减排、增效为目标,大力推进技术创新、模式创新、标准创新,全面提升传统产业绿色化水平。

推进工业绿色发展。持续开展绿色制造体系建设,完善绿色工厂、绿色园区、绿色供应链、绿色产品评价标准,引导企业创新绿色产品设计、使用绿色低碳环保工艺和设备,优化园区企业、产业和基础设施空间布局,加快构建绿色产业链供应链。按照"横向耦合、纵向延伸、循环链接"原则,大力推进园区循环化改造,推动产业循环式组织、企业循环化生产。全面开展清洁生产审核,积极实施清洁生产改造,大幅提高清洁生产整体水平。全面推进数字化改造,重点领域关键工序数控化率由2012年的24.6%提高到2021年的55.3%,数字化研发设计工具普及率由48.8%提高到74.7%。截至2021年底,累计建成绿色工厂2783家、绿色工业园区223家、绿色供应链管理企业296家,制造业绿色化水平显著提升。

转变农业生产方式。创新农业绿色发展体制机制,拓展农业多种功能,发掘乡村多元价值,加强农业资源保护利用。逐步健全耕地保护制度和轮作休耕制度,全面落实永久基本农田特殊保护,耕地减少势头得到初步遏制。稳步推进国家黑土地保护,全国耕地质量稳步提升。多措并举推进农业节水和化肥农药减量增效,2021年,农田灌溉水有效利用系数达到0.568。大力发展农业循环经济,推广种养加结合、农牧渔结合、产加销一体等循环型农业生产模式,强化农业废弃物资源化利用。统筹推进农业生产和农产品两个"三品一标"(品种培优、品质提升、品牌打造和标准化生产,绿色、有机、地理标志和达标合格农产品),深入实施地理标志农产品保护工程,全国绿色食品、有机农产品数量6万个,农产品质量安全水平稳步提高,优质农产品供给明显增加,有效促进了产业提档升级、农民增收致富。

提升服务业绿色化水平。积极培育商贸流通绿色主体,开展绿色商场创建。截至2021年底,全国共创建绿色商场592家。持续提升信息服务业能效水平,部分绿色数据中心已达世界领先水平。升级完善快递绿色包装标准体系,推进快递包装减量化标准化循环化,引导生产商、消费者使用可循环快递包装和可降解包装,推进电子商务企业绿色发展。截至 2021 年底,电商快件不再二次包装率达到 80.5%,全国快递包装瘦身胶带、循环中转袋使用基本实现全覆盖。推进会展业绿色发展,制定行业相关绿色标准,推动办展设施循环使用。全面实施铁路电子客票,推广电子发票应用,大幅减少票纸用量。在餐饮行业逐步淘汰一次性餐具,倡导宾馆、酒店不主动提供一次性用品。

(二)推动能源绿色低碳发展

中国立足能源资源禀赋,坚持先立后破、通盘谋划,在不断增强能源供应保障能力的基础上,加快构建新型能源体系,推动清洁能源消费占比大幅提升,能源结构绿色低碳转型成效显著。

大力发展非化石能源。加快推进以沙漠、戈壁、荒漠地区为重点的大型风电光伏基地建设,积极稳妥发展海上风电,积极推广城镇、农村屋顶光伏,鼓励发展乡村分散式风电。以西南地区主要河流为重点,有序推进流域大型水电基地建设。因地制宜发展太阳能热利用、生物质能、地热能和海洋能,积极安全有序发展核电,大力发展城镇生活垃圾焚烧发电。坚持创新引领,积极发展氢能源。加快构建适应新能源占比逐渐提高的新型电力系统,开展可再生能源电力消纳责任权重考核,推动可再生能源高效消纳。截至 2021 年底,清洁能源消费比重由 2012 年的 14.5% 升至 25.5%,煤炭消费比重由 2012 年的 68.5% 降至 56.0%;可再生能源发电装机突破 10 亿千瓦,占总发电装机容量的 44.8%,其中水电、风电、光伏发电装机均超 3 亿千瓦,均居世界第一。

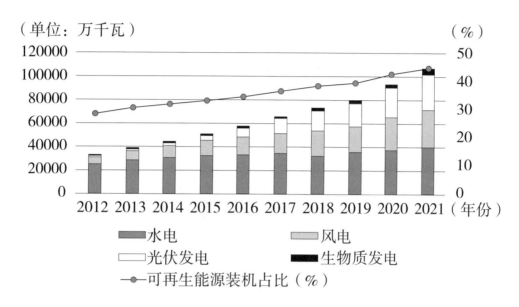

图 2 2012—2021 年中国可再生能源发电装机容量及占比

提高化石能源清洁高效利用水平。以促进煤电清洁低碳发展为目标,开展煤电节能降碳改造、灵活性改造、供热改造"三改联动",新增煤电机组执行更严格节能标准,发电效率、污染物排放控制达到世界领先水平。推动终端用能清洁化,推行天然气、电力和可再生能源等替代煤炭,积极推进北方地区冬季清洁取暖。在城镇燃气、工业燃料、燃气发电、交通运输等领域有序推进天然气高效利用,发展天然气热电冷联供。实施成品油质量升级专项行动,用不到 10 年时间走完发达国家 30 多年成品油质量升级之路,成品油质量达到国际先进水平,有效减少了汽车尾气污染物排放。

2022年2月4日,北京冬奥会开幕。与历届冬奥会不同,北京冬奥会3大赛区26个场馆全部使用绿色电力,意味着奥运史上首次实现全部场馆100%绿色电能供应。

从场馆照明、冰面运维、雪道造雪,到电视转播、计时计分,再到安保安检、后勤保障等,北京冬奥会全面使用绿电,用实际行动践行了申办2022年冬奥会时提出的"可持续发展理念"。为了实现冬奥会绿电供应,中国在北京、张家口等地区建成大量风光发电项目,实施了张北柔性直流电网试验示范工程,将清洁电力引入冬奥会赛场,不仅满足了冬奥会场馆的照明、运行和交通等用电需求,还大幅提升了北京及周边地区清洁能源的消费比重。

中国以举办绿色冬奥会为契机,实现清洁能源大规模输送、并网及消纳,为推动清洁能源发展积累了宝贵的实践经验,彰显了实现碳达峰碳中和目标的信心和决心。

（三）构建绿色交通运输体系

交通运输行业能源消耗大、污染物和温室气体排放多,是实现绿色发展需要重点关注的领域。中国以提升交通运输装备能效水平为基础,以优化用能结构、提高组织效率为关键,加快绿色交通运输体系建设,让运输更加环保、出行更加低碳。

优化交通运输结构。加快推进铁路专用线建设,推动大宗货物"公转铁""公转水",深入开展多式联运。2021年,铁路、水路货运量合计占比达到24.56%,比2012年提高3.85个百分点。深入实施城市公共交通优先发展战略,截至2021年底,已有51个城市开通运营城市轨道交通线路275条,运营里程超过8700公里;公交专用车道从2012年的5256公里增长到2021年的18264公里。

推进交通运输工具绿色转型。在城市公交、出租、环卫、物流配送、民航、机场以及党政机关大力推广新能源汽车,截至2021年底,中国新能源汽车保有量达到784万辆,占全球保有量的一半左右;新能源公交车达到50.89万辆,占公交车总量的71.7%;新能源出租汽车达到20.78万辆。不断推进铁路移动装备的绿色转型,铁路内燃机车占比由2012年的51%降低到2021年的36%。提升机动车污染物排放标准,推进船舶使用LNG动力和岸电受电设施改造,加快老旧车船改造淘汰,2012年以来,累计淘汰黄标车和老旧车3000多万辆,拆解改造内河船舶4.71万艘。

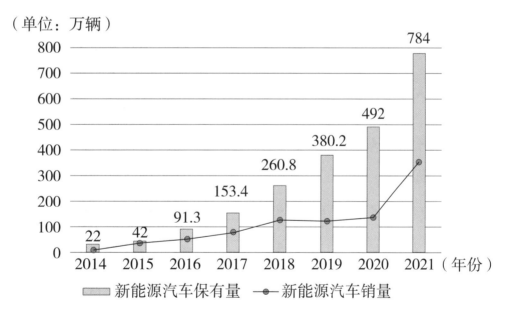

（单位：万辆）

图3 2014—2021年中国新能源汽车销量和保有量

提升交通基础设施绿色化水平。开展绿色公路建设专项行动,大力推动废旧路面材料再生利用,截至2021年底,高速公路、普通国省道废旧路面材料循环利用率分别达到95%、80%以上。持续提升公路绿化水平,干线公路绿化里程达到57万公里,比2012年增加约

20 万公里。推进铁路电气化改造,电气化率从 2012 年的 52.3%上升至 2021 年的 73.3%。深入推进港口和公路绿色交通配套设施建设,截至 2021 年底,主要港口五类专业化泊位岸电设施覆盖率达 75%;高速公路服务区建成 13374 个充电桩,数量居全球第一。

（四）推进资源节约集约利用

作为资源需求大国,中国加快资源利用方式根本转变,努力用最少的资源环境代价取得最大的经济社会效益,让当代人过上幸福生活,为子孙后代留下生存根基,为全球资源环境可持续发展作出重大贡献。

提高能源利用效率。完善能源消耗总量和强度调控,重点控制化石能源消费。大力推广技术节能、管理节能、结构节能,推动能源利用效率持续提升。开展万家企业节能低碳行动、重点用能单位百千万行动、能效"领跑者"引领行动,组织实施钢铁、电力、化工等高耗能行业节能降碳改造,强化用能单位节能管理,推动重点行业大中型企业能效达到世界先进水平。2012 年以来,中国以年均 3%的能源消费增速支撑了年均 6.6%的经济增长,2021 年万元国内生产总值能耗较 2012 年下降 26.4%。

提升水资源利用效率。强化水资源刚性约束,依据水资源禀赋合理确定产业和城市布局。开展国家节水行动,实施水资源消耗总量和强度双控。对高耗水行业实施节水技术改造,推广农业高效节水灌溉。创建节水型城市,推行水效标识制度和节水产品认证,推广普及节水器具,城市人均综合用水量持续下降。中国还将再生水、淡化海水、集蓄雨水、微咸水、矿井水等非常规水源纳入水资源统一配置,有效缓解了缺水地区的水资源供需矛盾。2021年,万元国内生产总值用水量较2012年下降45%。

强化土地节约集约利用。完善城乡用地标准体系、严格各类建设用地标准管控和项目审批,推进交通、能源、水利等基础设施项目节约集约用地,严控新增建设用地。强化农村土地管理,稳步推进农村集体建设用地节约集约利用。建立建设用地增量安排与消化存量挂钩机制和闲置土地收回机制,盘活存量用地。2012—2021年,单位国内生产总值建设用地使用面积下降40.85%。

科学利用海洋资源。严格管控围填海,除国家重大项目外,全面禁止围填海,分类处置围填海历史遗留问题。建立自然岸线保有率控制制度,对海岸线实施分类保护、节约利用,严格保护无居民海岛,最大程度减少开发利用。

提高资源综合利用水平。开展绿色矿山建设,大力推进绿色勘查和绿色开采,提升重要矿产资源开采回采率、选矿回收率、综合利用率,累计建设国家级绿色矿山1101座。实施资源综合利用"双百工程",开展国家"城市矿产"示范基地建设,完善废旧物资回收网络,统筹推进废旧资源循环利用,提升再生资源加工利用水平。2021年,废钢铁、废铜、废铝、废铅、废锌、废纸、废塑料、废橡胶、废玻璃等9种再生资源循环利用量达3.85亿吨。

五、绿色生活方式渐成时尚

绿色发展同每个人息息相关，每个人都可以做绿色发展的践行者、推动者。中国积极弘扬生态文明价值理念，推动全民持续提升节约意识、环保意识、生态意识，自觉践行简约适度、绿色低碳的生活方式，形成全社会共同推进绿色发展的良好氛围。

（一）生态文明教育持续推进

把强化公民生态文明意识摆在更加突出的位置，系统推进生态文明宣传教育，倡导推动全社会牢固树立勤俭节约的消费理念和生活习惯。持续开展全国节能宣传周、中国水周、全国城市节约用水宣传周、全国低碳日、全民植树节、六五环境日、国际生物多样性日、世界地球日等主题宣传活动，积极引导和动员全社会参与绿色发展，推进绿色生活理念进家庭、进社区、进工厂、进农村。把绿色发展有关内容纳入国民教育体系，编写生态环境保护读本，在中小学校开展森林、草原、河湖、土地、水、粮食等资源的基本国情教育，倡导尊重自然、爱护自然的绿色价值观念。发布《公民生态环境行为规范（试行）》，引导社会公众自觉践行绿色生活理念，让生态环保思想成为社会主流文化，形成深刻的人文情怀。

（二）绿色生活创建广泛开展

广泛开展节约型机关、绿色家庭、绿色学校、绿色社区、绿色出行、绿色商场、绿色建筑等创建行动,将绿色生活理念普及推广到衣食住行游用等方方面面。截至目前,全国70%县级及以上党政机关建成节约型机关,近百所高校实现了水电能耗智能监管,109个城市高质量参与绿色出行创建行动。在地级以上城市广泛开展生活垃圾分类工作,居民主动分类的习惯逐步形成,垃圾分类效果初步显现。颁布实施《中华人民共和国反食品浪费法》,大力推进粮食节约和反食品浪费工作,广泛深入开展"光盘"行动,节约粮食蔚然成风、成效显著。

（三）绿色产品消费日益扩大

积极推广新能源汽车、高能效家用电器等节能低碳产品。实施税收减免和财政补贴,持续完善充电基础设施,新能源汽车年销量从2012年的1.3万辆快速提升到2021年的352万辆,自2015年起产销量连续7年位居世界第一。同时,不断完善绿色产品认证采信推广机制,健全政府绿色采购制度,实施能效水效标识制度,引导促进绿色产品消费。推动绿色商场等绿色流通主体建设,鼓励推动共享经济、二手交易等新模式蓬勃发展,绿色消费品类愈加丰富,绿色消费群体持续扩大。

六、绿色发展体制机制逐步完善

推进绿色发展，体制机制是关键。中国加快构建和完善导向清晰、决策科学、执行有力、激励有效的生态文明制度体系，持续提升绿色发展的政府治理效能，为绿色发展任务目标顺利实现提供坚实保障。

（一）加强法治建设

坚持以法治理念、法治方式推动生态文明建设，将"生态文明建设"写入宪法，制定和修改长江保护法、黄河保护法、土地管理法、森林法、草原法、湿地保护法、环境保护法、环境保护税法以及大气、水、土壤污染防治法和核安全法等法律，覆盖各重点区域、各种类资源、各环境要素的生态文明法律法规体系基本建立。持续完善重点领域绿色发展标准体系，累计制修订绿色发展有关标准3000余项。实施省以下生态环境机构监测监察执法垂直管理制度改革，严厉查处自然资源、生态环境等领域违法违规行为。建立生态环境保护综合行政执法机关、公安机关、检察机关、审判机关信息共享、案情通报、案件移送制度，强化生态环境行政执法与刑事司法的衔接，形成对破坏生态环境违法犯罪行为的查处侦办工作合力，为绿色发展提供了有力法治保障。

（二）强化监督管理

建立完善推进绿色发展的目标评价考核制度,严格落实企业主体责任和政府监管责任。摒弃"唯GDP论英雄"的发展观、政绩观,将资源环境相关指标作为国民经济与社会发展的约束性指标,科学构建反映资源利用、能源消耗、环境损害、生态效益等情况的经济社会发展评价体系,充分发挥考核"指挥棒"作用。建立和落实领导干部生态文明建设责任制,制修订《党政领导干部生态环境损害责任追究办法(试行)》《中央生态环境保护督察工作规定》《领导干部自然资源资产离任审计规定(试行)》等党内法规,在生态环境保护领域严格实施"党政同责、一岗双责"、尽职免责、失职追责。开展领导干部自然资源资产离任审计,对领导干部生态环境损害责任实行终身追究。建立中央生态环境保护督察制度,压实生态环境保护工作责任,推动解决了人民群众反映强烈的突出环境问题。

（三）健全市场化机制

中国逐步建立完善政府有力主导、企业积极参与、市场有效调节的体制机制,更好激发全社会参与绿色发展的积极性。创新和完善节水节能、污水垃圾处理、大气污染治理等重点领域的价格形成机制,实施50余项税费优惠政策,引导优化资源配置,支持促进资源节约和高效利用,推动绿色产业发展。建立统一的自然资源确权登记制度,在森林、草原、湿地、荒漠、水流、耕地等领域建立生态保护补偿机制。探索建立生态产品价值实现机制,鼓励支持社会资本参与生态保护修复。在科学合理控制总量的前提下,建立用水权、用能权、排污权、碳排放权初始分配和交易制度,开展全国碳排放权交易市场建设和绿色电力交易试点建设,进一步发挥市场在生态环境资源配置中的基础性作用。大力发展绿色金融,形成绿色信贷、绿色债券、绿色保险、绿色基金、绿色信托等多层次绿色金融产品和市场体系。截至2021年末,中国本外币绿色信贷余额15.9万亿元,绿色债券存量余额超过1.1万亿元,规模均居全球前列。

专栏7　生态保护补偿机制

中国积极建立健全生态保护补偿体制机制,重点领域财政补偿力度持续加大,区域间生态保护领域合作不断拓展,市场化生态保护补偿机制建设取得新成效。

完善财政纵向补偿机制。充分发挥政府落实生态保护责任的主导作用,建立森林、草原等重要生态系统保护补偿机制,加大对生态保护主体的支持。建立健全重点生态功能区转移支付补偿机制,已覆盖全国800多个县。

加强区域间生态保护补偿合作。出台支持长江、黄河全流域建立横向生态保护补偿机制的实施方案,制定洞庭湖、鄱阳湖、太湖流域生态保护补偿的指导意见,推动生态受益地区和生态保护地区、流域下游和流域上游打破区域边界,通过开展污染共治、产业合作等方式建立横向补偿关系。截至2021年底,全国共建立了14个跨省流域生态保护补偿机制。

创新市场化补偿机制。政府和市场协同发力,鼓励和引导社会各方参与生态保护补偿,拓展市场化融资渠道。碳排放权、排污权、用水权等领域的制度体系逐步健全,绿色金融、绿色标识、绿色建筑等支持绿色产业发展的政策体系逐步建立和完善。

七、携手共建美丽地球家园

促进绿色发展、建设生态文明是全人类的共同事业。中国始终是全球生态文明建设的重要参与者、贡献者和引领者，坚定维护多边主义，积极参与打造利益共生、权利共享、责任共担的全球生态治理格局，为人类可持续发展作出贡献。

（一）积极参与全球气候治理

中国坚持公平原则、共同但有区别的责任原则和各自能力原则，坚定落实《联合国气候变化框架公约》，以积极建设性姿态参与全球气候谈判议程，为《巴黎协定》达成和落实作出历史性贡献，推动构建公平合理、合作共赢的全球气候治理体系。提高国家自主贡献力度，将完成全球最高碳排放强度降幅，用全球历史上最短时间实现碳达峰到碳中和，充分体现负责任大国的担当。积极开展应对气候变化南南合作，2016 年起在发展中国家启动 10 个低碳示范区、100 个减缓和适应气候变化项目、1000 个应对气候变化培训名额的合作项目，实施了 200 多个应对气候变化的援外项目。

应对气候变化合作会遇到各种波折和困难，但中国始终是全球气候治理的行动派和实干家。中国将坚定不移推动实现碳达峰碳中和目标,一如既往积极参与应对气候变化国际合作,建设性参与气候变化国际谈判,向发展中国家提供力所能及的支持和帮助,继续为应对全球气候变化重大挑战作出中国贡献。

(二)推进共建绿色"一带一路"

中国始终致力于推进共建"一带一路"绿色发展,让绿色切实成为共建"一带一路"的底色。积极推动建立共建"一带一路"绿色低碳发展合作机制,与联合国环境规划署签署《关于建设绿色"一带一路"的谅解备忘录》,与有关国家及国际组织签署 50 多份生态环境保护合作文件。与 31 个共建国家共同发起"一带一路"绿色发展伙伴关系倡议,与 32 个共建国家共同建立"一带一路"能源合作伙伴关系。发起建立"一带一路"绿色发展国际联盟,成立"一带一路"绿色发展国际研究院,建设"一带一路"生态环保大数据服务平台,帮助共建国家提高环境治理能力、增进民生福祉。积极帮助共建国家加强绿色人才培养,实施"绿色丝路使者计划",已为 120 多个共建国家培训 3000 人次。制定实施《"一带一路"绿色投资原则》,推动"一带一路"绿色投资。中国企业在共建国家投资建设了一批可再生能源项目,帮助共建国家建设了一批清洁能源重点工程,为所在国绿色发展提供了有力支撑。

2019 年 4 月,第二届"一带一路"国际合作高峰论坛期间,为促进共建"一带一路"国家在能源领域的共同发展、共同繁荣,中国与 29 个国家在北京共同发起成立了"一带一路"能源合作伙伴关系。随着古巴、摩洛哥、泰国等国的先后加入,当前伙伴关系成员国数量达到 33 个。

作为能源领域首个由中方发起成立的国际合作平台,自成立以来,伙伴关系充分发挥平台作用,成功策划和举办了两届"一带一路"能源部长会议、两届"一带一路"能源合作伙伴关系论坛等重要活动,为各成员国搭建了双、多边项目合作和技术交流的高质量平台,促成了一系列务实合作;发布《"一带一路"能源合作伙伴关系合作原则与务实行动》《"一带一路"绿色能源合作青岛倡议》等多份重要合作文件,进一步凝聚了各方推动"一带一路"绿色发展的共识与合力;发布能源国际合作最佳实践案例,展示多项清洁、高效、质优的绿色能源项目,成立由成员国政府部门、能源企业、高校智库和金融机构组成的伙伴关系合作网络,推进绿色能源务实合作;组织开展伙伴关系能力建设活动,与各发展中国家共同分享能源绿色发展的经验和成果。

（三）广泛开展双多边国际合作

中国积极推进资源节约和生态环境保护领域务实合作。成功举办《生物多样性公约》第十五次缔约方大会第一阶段会议,以及《湿地公约》第十四届缔约方大会。积极参与二十国集团、中国—东盟、东盟—中日韩、东亚峰会、中非合作论坛、金砖国家、上海合作组织、亚太经合组织等框架下能源转型、能效提升等方面合作,牵头制定《二十国集团能效引领计划》,成为二十国集团领导人杭州峰会重要成果。落实全球发展倡议,推动建立全球清洁能源合作伙伴关系。同时,与印度、巴西、南非、美国、日本、德国、法国、东盟等多个国家和地区开展节能环保、清洁能源、应对气候变化、生物多样性保护、荒漠化防治、海洋和森林资源保护等合作,推动联合国有关机构、亚洲开发银行、亚洲基础设施投资银行、新开发银行、全球环境基金、绿色气候基金、国际能源署、国际可再生能源署等国际组织在工业、农业、能源、交通运输、城乡建设等重点领域开展绿色低碳技术援助、能力建设和试点项目,为推动全球可持续发展作出了重要贡献。

结 束 语

中国已迈上全面建设社会主义现代化国家、全面推进中华民族伟大复兴新征程。人与自然和谐共生的现代化,是中国式现代化的重要特征。

中共二十大擘画了中国未来发展蓝图,描绘了青山常在、绿水长流、空气常新的美丽中国画卷。中国将坚定不移走绿色发展之路,推进生态文明建设,推动实现更高质量、更有效率、更加公平、更可持续、更为安全的发展,让绿色成为美丽中国最鲜明、最厚重、最牢靠的底色,让人民在绿水青山中共享自然之美、生命之美、生活之美。

地球是全人类赖以生存的唯一家园,人与自然是生命共同体。保护生态环境、推动可持续发展,是各国的共同责任。中国愿与国际社会一道,同筑生态文明之基,同走绿色发展之路,守护好绿色地球家园,建设更加清洁、美丽的世界。

新时代的中国网络法治建设

（2023 年 3 月）

中华人民共和国
国务院新闻办公室

前　言

互联网是人类文明发展的重要成果。互联网在促进经济社会发展的同时,也对监管和治理形成巨大挑战。发展好治理好互联网,让互联网更好造福人类,是世界各国共同的追求。实践证明,法治是互联网治理的基本方式。运用法治观念、法治思维和法治手段推动互联网发展治理,已经成为全球普遍共识。

自 1994 年全功能接入国际互联网以来,中国坚持依法治网,持续推进网络空间法治化,推动互联网在法治轨道上健康运行。进入新时代,在习近平新时代中国特色社会主义思想指引下,中国将依法治网作为全面依法治国和网络强国建设重要内容,努力构建完备的网络法律规范体系、高效的网络法治实施体系、严密的网络法治监督体系、有力的网络法治保障体系,网络法治建设取得历史性成就。网络立法、网络执法、网络司法、网络普法、网络法治教育一体推进,国家、政府、企业、社会组织、网民等多主体参与,走出了一条既符合国际通行做法,又有中国特色的依法治网之路。中国的网络法治建设不仅有力提升了中国互联网治理能力,也为全球互联网治理贡献了中国智慧和中国方案。

为全面介绍中国网络法治建设情况,分享中国网络法治建设的经验做法,特发布此白皮书。

一、坚定不移走依法治网之路

中国顺应全球信息化发展大势,立足中国互联网发展实践,将网络法治建设融入全面依法治国战略布局,不断深化对依法治网的规律性认识,在探索中发展、在发展中坚持,走出了一条中国特色的网络法治道路。

——坚持以人民为中心。中国的网络法治建设坚持人民主体地位,凝聚最广大人民的智慧和力量,把体现人民利益、反映人民愿望、维护人民权益、增进人民福祉落实到立法、执法、司法、普法等网络法治建设全过程各方面。切实维护人民群众在网络空间的合法权益,依法加强网络空间治理,充分尊重网民交流思想、表达意见的权利,坚决打击网络违法犯罪活动,构建网络空间良好秩序,营造安全、公平、健康、文明、清朗的网络空间。

——坚持促进互联网发展。依法治网的本质,是为互联网健康有序发展提供保障,而不是束缚互联网的发展。中国将依法治网作为基础性手段,完善数字经济治理体系,提升数字政府建设法治化水平,依法推进数字社会建设,引领、规范、保障数字中国建设高质量发展。坚持发展和安全同步推进,筑牢网络安全防线,以安全保发展、以发展促安全,推动互联网这个最大变量成为社会经济发展的最大增量。

——坚持立足国情。中国的网络法治建设立足中国是全球最大的发展中国家和网民数量最多的基本国情,针对中国网民规模巨大、企业平台众多、产品业态丰富的实际情况,适应法律主体多元、法律关系多样、法律适用场景多变的特点,坚持处理好发展和安全、自由和秩序、开放和自主、管理和服务的关系,深入研究网络法治前沿性、全局性重大问题,运用法治思维和法治方式解决制约互联网发展的瓶颈问题,找出互联网健康发展的中国答案。

——坚持创新引领。互联网因创新而生,因创新而兴,网络法治尤其需要创新。中国全面把握网络空间治理面临的前所未有的艰巨性、复杂性,前瞻性应对互联网新技术新应用新业态新模式带来的风险挑战,推进网络法治理念、内容、方式、方法等全方位创新。完善和创新算法、区块链等新技术新领域规则,努力填补重要领域制度的时间差、空白区,建立网络综合治理体系,创新网络司法模式,以创新引领网络法治实践,全面提升互联网治理效能。

——坚持开放合作。中国的网络法治建设既坚持网络主权,同时广泛借鉴世界各国网络法治先进经验,吸收国外成熟做法,把中国互联网发展置于国际互联网发展的大背景下谋划,形成了既有中国特色又符合国际通行做法的互联网治理模式。积极参与网络空间国际规则制定,开展网络法治领域国际交流合作,与世界各国共同致力于建立多边、民主、透明的全球互联网治理体系。

新时代的中国网络法治建设,立足自身发展实际,借鉴国外先进经验,勇于探索、守正创新,走出一条具有自身特色的管网治网之路,取得了一系列显著成就,为网络强国建设、全面依法治国、党在信息化条件下治国理政作出了重要贡献。

——为网络大国向网络强国迈进提供了有力保障。中国网络强国建设向着网络基础设施基本普及、自主创新能力显著增强、数字经济全面发展、网络安全保障有力、网络攻防实力均衡的方向不断前进,取得重大成就。网民规模全球第一,移动物联网发展实现"物超人",建成全球规模最大、技术领先的光纤宽带和移动通信网络,5G实现技术、产业、应用全面领先。数字经济发展势头强劲,2021年数字经济规模达到45.5万亿元,位居世界第二。互联网新技术在教育、就业、社保、医疗卫生、体育、住房、交通、助残养老等领域深度应用,"互联网+"依法健康运行,形成全球最为庞大、生机勃勃的数字社会。

——推动全面依法治国在网络空间深入实施。中国坚持依法治国原则适用于网络空间,深入实施法治中国建设规划,不断推进网络法治建设,坚持科学立法、严格执法、公正司法、全民守法,深化中国特色社会主义法治在网络空间的实践。网络立法的"四梁八柱"基本构建,丰富和完善了中国特色社会主义法律体系。网络执法不断加强,严厉打击网络违法行为,网络生态和网络秩序持续向好,推动整个社会秩序更加平安和谐。网络司法裁判规则逐步完善,网络案件办理力度不断加大,公平正义在网络空间有力彰显。网络普法深入推进,尊法学法守法用法逐步成为网络空间的共同追求和自觉行动,广大人民群众的法治意识和法治素养全面提升。

——为全球互联网治理贡献中国经验、中国智慧和中国方案。网络空间是人类共同的活动空间,需要世界各国共同建设、共同治理。中国不断探索依法治网的科学途径和方案,在立法、执法、司法、普法一体推进中形成了中国特色治网之道,为全球互联网治理提供了中国经验。中国积极参与全球互联网治理,推动发起《二十国集团数字经济发展与合作倡议》《全球数据安全倡议》等多个倡议、宣言,创造性提出网络主权原则,倡导《联合国宪章》确立的主权平等原则适用于网络空间,贡献了中国智慧和中国方案。

二、夯实网络空间法制基础

法律是治国重器，良法是善治前提。中国把握互联网发展规律，坚持科学立法、民主立法、依法立法，大力推进网络法律制度建设，网络立法的系统性、整体性、协同性、时效性不断增强。

中国网络立法随着互联网发展经历了从无到有、从少到多、由点到面、由面到体的发展过程。第一阶段从 1994 年至 1999 年，是接入互联网阶段。上网用户和设备数量稳步增加。这一阶段网络立法主要聚焦于网络基础设施安全，即计算机系统安全和联网安全。第二阶段从 2000 年至 2011 年，是 PC 互联网阶段。随着计算机数量逐步增加、上网资费逐步降低，用户上网日益普遍，网络信息服务迅猛发展。这一阶段网络立法转向侧重网络服务管理和内容管理。第三阶段从 2012 年至今，是移动互联网阶段。这一阶段网络立法逐步趋向全面涵盖网络信息服务、信息化发展、网络安全保护等在内的网络综合治理。在这一进程中，中国制定出台网络领域立法 140 余部，基本形成了以宪法为根本，以法律、行政法规、部门规章和地方性法规、地方政府规章为依托，以传统立法为基础，以网络内容建设与管理、网络安全和信息化等网络专门立法为主干的网络法律体系，为网络强国建设提供了坚实的制度保障。

专栏1 中国网络立法状况	
类型	**示　　例**
法律	电子商务法、电子签名法、网络安全法、数据安全法、个人信息保护法、反电信网络诈骗法
行政法规	《计算机信息系统安全保护条例》《计算机软件保护条例》《互联网信息服务管理办法》《电信条例》《外商投资电信企业管理规定》《信息网络传播权保护条例》《关键信息基础设施安全保护条例》
部门规章	《儿童个人信息网络保护规定》《互联网域名管理办法》《网络交易监督管理办法》《互联网新闻信息服务管理规定》《网络信息内容生态治理规定》《互联网信息服务算法推荐管理规定》
地方性法规	《广东省数字经济促进条例》《浙江省数字经济促进条例》《河北省信息化条例》《贵州省政府数据共享开放条例》《上海市数据条例》
地方政府规章	《广东省公共数据管理办法》《安徽省政务数据资源管理办法》《江西省计算机信息系统安全保护办法》《杭州市网络交易管理暂行办法》
合计	140余部

（一）建立网络权益保障法律制度

科学构建网络权益保障法律制度，为实现人民群众合法权益的线上、线下全方位保护提供了充分法律依据。

保障公民通信自由和通信秘密。通信自由和通信秘密的保护是确保公民能够自主地在网络空间表达诉求和思想的前提。早在1997年就制定《计算机信息网络国际联网安全保护管理办法》，落实宪法对通信自由和通信秘密基本权利的保护。2000 年制定《电信条例》,规定电信用户依法使用电信的自由和通信秘密受法律保护。2016 年修订《无线电管理条例》,进一步强化无线电领域对通信秘密的保护,实现对这一基本权利在网络空间的全方位保障。

保护个人信息权益。通过民法、刑法和专门立法,构建个人信息权益全链条保护的法律屏障。2020 年十三届全国人大三次会议审议通过民法典,在前期法律规定的基础上,对民事领域的个人信息保护问题作了系统规定。2009 年、2015 年通过刑法修正案,设立侵犯公民个人信息罪,强化个人信息的刑法保护。在网络专门立法中,2012 年通过《全国人民代表大会常务委员会关于加强网络信息保护的决定》,明确保护能够识别公民个人身份和涉及公民个人隐私的电子信息。2016 年制定网络安全法,进一步完善个人信息保护规则。2021 年制定个人信息保护法,细化完善个人信息保护原则和个人信息处理规则,依法规范国家机关处理个人信息的活动,赋予个人信息主体多项权利,强化个人信息处理者义务,健全个人信息保护工作机制,设置严格的法律责任,个人信息保护水平得到全面提升。

守护公民财产安全。持续加大立法保护力度,遏制利用网络侵犯财产权益的行为。2018 年出台电子商务法,规定电子商务经营者销售的商品或者提供的服务应当符合保障人身、财产安全的要求。民法典明确利用网络侵害他人财产权益的行为应当承担相应法律责任。2022 年出台反电信网络诈骗法,为打击电信网络诈骗活动提供有力法律支撑,切实维护人民群众的财产权益。

保障特殊群体数字权利。通过多层次、多维度立法,弥合未成年人、老年人、残疾人等特殊群体的数字鸿沟,使其能够更加平等广泛地融入数字社会,享受数字时代红利。网络安全法规定,国家支持研究开发有利于未成年人健康成长的网络产品和服务,依法惩治利用网络从事危害未成年人身心健康的活动。2019年制定《儿童个人信息网络保护规定》,对儿童个人信息权益予以重点保护。2020年修订未成年人保护法,对加强未成年人网络素养教育、强化未成年人网络内容监管、加强未成年人个人信息保护和网络沉迷防治等做出专门规定,保护未成年人的网络合法权益。2021年出台数据安全法,要求提供智能化公共服务应当充分考虑老年人、残疾人的需求,避免对老年人、残疾人的日常生活造成障碍。

(二)健全数字经济法治规则

不断完善数据基础制度,维护数字市场秩序,规范数字经济新业态新模式,为数字经济健康发展提供良好制度基础,助力经济由高速增长转向高质量发展。

推动构建数据基础制度。注重发挥数据的基础资源作用和创新引擎作用,数据安全法对实施大数据战略、支持数据相关技术研发和商业创新、推进数据相关标准体系建设、培育数据交易市场等作出规定,提升数据开发利用水平,促进以数据为关键要素的数字经济发展。

明晰数字市场运行制度。坚持依法规范发展数字市场，坚决反对垄断和不正当竞争，健全数字规则，有力维护公平竞争的市场环境。电子商务法全面规范电子商务经营行为，明确电子商务平台经营者和平台内经营者责任，要求具有市场支配地位的电子商务经营者不得滥用市场支配地位排除、限制竞争，维护公平市场竞争秩序。2013年修改消费者权益保护法，建立网络购物"七日无理由退货"等制度，强化网络经营者消费维权主体责任。2017年修订反不正当竞争法，增加互联网专条，禁止利用技术手段从事不正当竞争。2021年制定《网络交易监督管理办法》，细化电子商务法有关规定，进一步完善网络交易监管制度体系。2021年发布《国务院反垄断委员会关于平台经济领域的反垄断指南》，并根据平台经济发展状况、发展特点和规律，加强和改进反垄断监管。2022年修改反垄断法，完善平台经济反垄断制度，规定经营者不得利用数据和算法、技术、资本优势以及平台规则等从事该法禁止的垄断行为。

规范数字经济新业态新模式。数字经济新业态新模式快速涌现，在为经济社会发展带来巨大动力和潜能的同时，也对社会治理、产业发展等提出了新的挑战。中国聚焦新业态新模式特定领域、特殊问题，坚持"大块头"立法和"小快灵"立法相结合，防范和化解风险。民法典完善电子合同订立和履行规则，将数据和网络虚拟财产纳入法律保护范围，促进数字经济发展。《网络预约出租汽车经营服务管理暂行办法》《互联网信息服务算法推荐管理规定》《区块链信息服务管理规定》《网络借贷信息中介机构业务活动管理暂行办法》《在线旅游经营服务管理暂行规定》等规范网约车、算法、区块链、互联网金融、在线旅游等新技术新业态，丰富"互联网+"各领域治理的法律依据。

（三）划定网络安全法律红线

网络安全是国家安全的新课题和新内容，成为关乎全局的重大问题。中国通过制定国家安全法、网络安全法、数据安全法等法律，系统构建网络安全法律制度，增强网络安全防御能力，有效应对网络安全风险。

确立网络安全规则。1994年出台《计算机信息系统安全保护条例》，确立计算机信息系统安全保护制度和安全监督制度。2000年出台《全国人民代表大会常务委员会关于维护互联网安全的决定》，将互联网安全划分为互联网运行安全和互联网信息安全，确立民事责任、行政责任和刑事责任三位一体的网络安全责任体系框架。网络安全法明确维护网络运行安全、网络产品和服务安全、网络数据安全、网络信息安全等方面的制度。《网络安全审查办法》《网络产品安全漏洞管理规定》等进一步细化网络安全法相关制度。通过多年努力，初步形成了一套系统全面的网络安全法律规则，以制度建设提高国家网络安全保障能力。

保障关键信息基础设施安全。关键信息基础设施是经济社会运行的神经中枢，是网络安全的重中之重。保障关键信息基础设施安全,对于维护国家网络主权和国家安全、保障经济社会健康发展、维护公共利益和公民合法权益具有重大意义。2021 年制定《关键信息基础设施安全保护条例》,明确关键信息基础设施范围和保护工作原则目标,完善关键信息基础设施认定机制,对关键信息基础设施运营者落实网络安全责任、建立健全网络安全保护制度、设置专门安全管理机构、开展安全监测和风险评估、规范网络产品和服务采购活动等作出具体规定,为加快提升关键信息基础设施安全保护能力提供法律依据。

构建数据安全管理法律制度。立足数据安全工作实际,着眼数据安全领域突出问题,通过立法加强数据安全保护,提升国家数据安全保障能力。数据安全法明确建立健全数据分类分级保护、风险监测预警和应急处置、数据安全审查等制度,对支持促进数据安全与发展的措施、推进政务数据安全与开放等作出规定,以安全保发展、以发展促安全。

（四）完善网络生态治理规范

网络空间是亿万民众共同的精神家园,网络空间天朗气清、生态良好,是人民对网上家园的美好向往。中国本着对社会负责、对人民负责的态度,以网络信息内容为主要规制对象,建立健全网络综合治理法律规范,持续净化网络空间。

规范网络信息传播秩序。面对网络信息治理这一世界性难题,制定民法典、网络安全法、《互联网信息服务管理办法》等法律法规，明确网络信息内容传播规范和相关主体的责任，为治理危害国家安全、损害公共利益、侵害他人合法权益的违法信息提供了法律依据。

打造网络反恐法律利器。坚决依法遏制恐怖主义在网络空间的威胁，刑法、刑事诉讼法、反洗钱法等法律对恐怖活动犯罪的刑事责任、惩治恐怖活动犯罪的诉讼程序、涉恐资金监控等作了规定。2015年制定反恐怖主义法，对网络反恐的对象、措施和机制等作出专门规定。

三、保障网络空间规范有序

严格执法是依法治网的关键环节。中国坚持严格规范公正文明网络执法，加大关系人民群众切身利益的重点领域执法力度，全面保护人民群众合法权益、维护社会公共利益，推动形成健康规范的网络空间秩序，营造天朗气清的网络生态。

（一）保障个人信息权益

伴随数字经济的快速发展，非法收集、买卖、使用、泄露个人信息等违法行为日益增多，严重侵害了人民群众人身财产安全，影响了社会经济正常秩序。个人信息保护不仅关系广大人民群众合法权益，也关系公共安全治理和数字经济发展。中国针对个人信息侵权行为的密集性、隐蔽性、技术性等特点，采取新的监管思路、监管方式和监管手段，加大违法行为处置力度，持续开展移动互联网应用程序（App）违法违规收集使用个人信息专项治理，有效整治违法违规处理个人信息问题。2019 年以来，累计完成 322 万款移动互联网应用程序检测，通报、下架违法违规移动互联网应用程序近 3000 款。通过专项治理，侵害用户个人信息权益的违法违规行为得到有力遏制，个人信息保护意识显著增强，个人信息保护合规水平明显提升，全社会尊重和保护个人信息权益的良好局面初步形成。

（二）保护网络知识产权

加强网络知识产权保护是支持网络科技创新的关键。新技术新应用不断涌现,使得网络知识产权侵权的手段更加隐蔽、形式更加多样、成本更加低廉,执法面临溯源难、取证难、执行难等问题。中国持续探索、准确把握网络环境下知识产权创造、保护、运用的特点规律,通过建立健全监管机制、构建知识产权保护社会共治新格局,推动平台建立知识产权保护合作机制,开展打击网络侵权盗版专项行动等多重举措,持续加强网络知识产权保护。推进线上线下一体化执法,重拳出击,严厉打击网络商标侵权、假冒专利违法行为。常态化组织开展打击网络侵权盗版的"剑网"专项行动、打击院线电影盗录传播集中行动、重点市场版权专项整治等执法活动,严厉打击各类侵权盗版行为,集中整治重点领域、重点市场版权秩序。北京冬奥会、冬残奥会期间,开展冬奥版权保护集中行动,推动网络平台删除涉冬奥侵权链接 11 万余个。经过多年执法,网络知识产权保护环境得到明显改善。

（三）规范网络市场秩序

网络市场快速崛起,对稳经济、促消费、保就业、惠民生发挥了重要作用。中国积极探索与网络市场新业态相适应的执法模式,通过规范市场公平竞争发展、打击不法新型交易行为等一系列行动,助力网络市场健康可持续发展。

保障公平竞争的网络市场环境。随着网络平台企业不断扩展自身的体量和实力,"掐尖式并购"、无正当理由屏蔽链接、"二选一"、大数据杀熟、流量挟持等妨碍市场公平竞争的问题也逐渐凸显。中国积极回应人民群众诉求,在支持网络平台企业创新发展的同时,依法规范和引导资本健康发展,采取多种治理平台竞争失序的执法举措。聚焦大型网络平台价格欺诈、低价倾销等重点问题,通过行政约谈、行政指导、规则指引等多种监管手段,整治垄断和不正当竞争行为。围绕民生、金融、科技、传媒等重点行业,依法审查涉及平台经营者集中案件,防止可能妨碍市场竞争和创新发展的并购行为,引导网络平台企业增强合规意识,规范自身经营行为。通过一系列行动,平台经济市场环境不断优化,公平竞争的行业生态稳步向好,中小企业获得更广阔的发展空间,统一、开放、公平、竞争、有序的网络竞争环境正在形成。

专栏 2　依法查处网络平台企业涉不正当竞争、垄断案件

　　2020 年至 2021 年,依法立案查处电商、网络餐饮外卖等领域 2 件典型的"二选一"垄断案件,罚款 216.7 亿元。2021 年,共查处网络不正当竞争案件 1998 件,罚没金额 1.19 亿元。2020 年至 2022 年上半年,依法审查涉及平台经营者集中申报案件 56 件,依法查处涉及平台企业未依法申报违法实施经营者集中案件 159 件。

规范网络交易活动。让网络交易活动在规范中运行,是营造良

好网络市场环境、维护广大网络交易主体权益的必然要求。开展"网剑行动",集中治理网上销售侵权假冒伪劣商品违法行为,重拳打击网上非法交易野生动植物及其制品活动。严格落实网络平台责任,强化互联网广告监管。针对"直播带货"、微店营销等新型网络交易形式,严管网络招徕渠道,查处多家涉嫌违法网站和平台用户。针对网络传销行为开展专项行动,对网络购物型传销、网络投资理财型传销、网络创业型传销,实施重点打击查处。通过一系列执法,重点领域、重点主体、重点形式的网络交易活动得到有效规范。

专栏 3 "网剑"专项行动

　　2018 年以来,中国连续开展"网剑行动",集中整治网上销售侵权假冒伪劣商品、网上非法野生动植物交易、网上发布违法广告等突出问题。指导网络交易平台删除违法商品信息 182.97 万条,关闭网站 2.39 万个次,责令停止网站平台服务 10.5 个次,查处涉网类案件 11.97 万件,有效维护了消费者合法权益和公平竞争的网络交易秩序。

（四）维护国家网络安全

　　筑牢网络安全防线是实现互联网健康发展的重要前提和基础。中国持续在网络基础资源、重要网络系统、网络数据等领域开展安全执法工作,有效防范化解安全风险,体系化构建网络时代的安全环境。在网络基础资源领域,强化网站、域名、IP 地址等基础资源管理,通过加强技术手段建设、完善预警机制等举措,强化安全保障。

在重要网络系统领域,深化网络系统安全防护,持续监测网络安全威胁,有效防治网络系统遭受大规模服务攻击等重大安全事件。在网络数据领域,提升数据安全保护监管能力,通过建立安全监测体系、实施分类分级管理等手段,强化工业互联网、车联网、5G应用等领域的数据安全执法。

（五）营造清朗网络空间

紧紧围绕人民群众的新期待新要求,规范网络信息传播秩序,整治各类网络生态乱象。聚焦网络淫秽色情、虚假信息、网络暴力、算法滥用等人民群众反映强烈的突出问题,持续开展"净网""清朗"系列专项行动,对传播各类违法违规信息的网站平台,采取约谈、责令改正、警告、暂停信息更新、罚款等多种措施。督促网站平台履行主体责任,依法依约对用户发布的信息进行管理,建立网络信息安全投诉、举报机制,形成治理合力。网络生态持续优化,全社会网络文明素养有效提升,网络环境有效净化。

坚持对未成年人优先保护、特殊保护,构建有利于未成年人上网的良好环境。通过开展"护苗"、未成年人网络环境专项治理等行动,围绕网络违法和不良信息、沉迷网络游戏、网络不良社交等问题进行重点整治,净化未成年人网络环境。加强未成年人网络安全教育,依法惩处利用网络从事危害未成年人身心健康的活动,形成家庭、学校、社会多方位保护合力,营造良好安全的未成年人网络环境。

专栏 4　　“护苗”专项行动
从 2011 年开始,中国定期开展“护苗”行动。一方面,组织执法力量定期检查校园周边重点市场点位,集中清理夹杂“黄暴毒”、宣扬邪教迷信等有害内容的少儿出版物,深层清理网上对未成年人具有诱导性的不良内容。督促网络平台实施“青少年模式”并切实发挥作用,推进重点互联网企业专设“护苗”工作站点。另一方面,培育“护苗”品牌,开展“护苗”系列正面宣传教育活动,打造“护苗”教育基地,推动学校、家庭严格管理学生使用手机等智能终端产品。

四、捍卫网络空间公平正义

公正司法是维护社会公平正义的最后一道防线。中国坚持司法公正、司法为民,积极回应网络时代司法需求,运用网络信息技术赋能传统司法,完善网络司法规则,革新网络司法模式,依法解决新型网络纠纷,打击网络犯罪,保障网络空间主体权益,使人民群众获得更加公平公正、公开透明、高效便捷、普惠均等的司法服务。

(一) 创新网络司法规则

随着互联网新技术新应用新业态的快速发展,网络空间承载的法律关系更为丰富多元,给网络空间司法保障带来了新挑战,需要构建更为完善的网络司法规则。中国及时制定涉及网络知识产权、人格权、网络交易、网络不正当竞争、电信网络诈骗等领域的民事和刑事司法解释。通过审理涉及网络基础设施安全、算法规则、数据权属交易、个人信息保护、网络平台治理等一大批新类型、疑难复杂和互联网特性突出的司法案件,细化法律适用标准,促进裁判标准统一,网络空间规则、行为规范、权利边界和责任义务日益明晰。制定人民法院在线诉讼、在线调解、在线运行规则,细化电子数据证据规则,规范网络犯罪案件办理程序,网络司法程序规则体系逐步建立。网络司法规则的体系化、系统化,为网络司法工作提供了规则引领和制度保障,让网络司法有章可循。

（二）探索网络司法模式

积极探索司法活动与网络技术深度融合的新路径、新领域、新模式,让社会正义"提速"。积极推行大数据、云计算、人工智能、区块链等现代科技在诉讼服务、审判执行、司法管理等领域的深度应用,先行先试构建中国特色的网络司法模式。鼓励各地法院因地制宜,结合当地互联网产业发展情况和网络纠纷特点,探索具有地域特色的新型互联网审判机制。相继设立杭州、北京、广州互联网法院,探索实行"网上案件网上审理"。大力推进数字检察工作,坚持大数据赋能法律监督,系统整合各类办案数据,积极探索构建大数据法律监督模型和平台,努力推动个案办理式监督和类案治理式监督相结合,为新时代法律监督提质增效。网络司法的新模式标志着中国特色社会主义司法制度在网络领域进一步发展完善,逐渐成为中国司法的一张亮丽名片。

> **专栏 5　成立互联网法院**
>
> 　　互联网法院是中国推动司法模式创新的成功尝试。2017 年 8 月 18 日,杭州互联网法院成立。2018 年 9 月 9 日、9 月 28 日,北京互联网法院、广州互联网法院先后成立。互联网法院集中管辖所在市辖区内的网络金融借款合同纠纷、网络侵权纠纷、网络著作权纠纷等十一类互联网案件,推动技术创新、规则确立、网络治理向前迈进。2017 年 8 月至 2019 年 10 月,三家互联网法院共受理互联网案件 118764 件,审结

88401 件,在线立案申请率为 96.8%,全流程在线审结 80819 件,在线庭审平均用时 45 分钟,案件平均审理周期约 38 天,比传统审理模式分别节约时间约五分之三和二分之一,一审服判息诉率达 98.0%,审判质量、效率和效果呈现良好态势。

(三) 维护网络司法权益

中国积极开展网络司法活动,坚决打击网络违法犯罪活动,努力让人民群众在每一个司法案件中感受到公平正义。

强化公民网络民事权益司法保护。依法办理个人信息保护、网络知识产权、网络交易、网络侵权等领域的民商事案件,保障各方主体的网络民事权益。在个人信息保护方面,重点关注处理大规模个人信息的网络平台,对侵犯公民个人信息的网络平台提起民事公益诉讼,通过案件审理明确用户个人信息商业使用的规则和边界,督促网络平台企业合法合规收集使用数据。在网络知识产权保护方面,针对涉及专利、集成电路布图设计、技术秘密、计算机软件等专业技术性较强的案件,探索引入技术调查官制度,逐步构建起维护网络空间公民合法权益的"防护栏"。

加大网络犯罪惩治力度。随着互联网技术的快速发展,传统犯罪加速向以互联网为媒介的非接触式犯罪转变,电信网络诈骗、网络赌博、网络淫秽色情等涉网违法犯罪多发。中国依法办理新型网络犯罪案件。连续多年开展"净网行动",严厉打击群众反映强烈的黑客攻击破坏、侵犯公民个人信息等违法犯罪活动。持续推进"云剑"

"断卡""断流""拔钉"等专项行动,打击套路贷、校园贷、"以房养老"、"投资养老"等电信网络诈骗犯罪,依法惩处为电信网络诈骗犯罪团伙提供互联网接入、域名注册、服务器托管、移动互联网应用程序制作开发、网络支付、引流推广等服务支撑的黑灰产业。完善国家反诈大数据平台和反诈移动互联网应用程序,建设国家涉诈黑样本库,完善快速止付冻结机制、涉诈资金返还机制。坚决打击网络赌博犯罪行为,从严治理网络淫秽色情。网络犯罪治理工作取得明显成效,人民群众安全感有效提升,社会更加和谐稳定。

专栏6 依法惩治电信网络诈骗犯罪
电信网络诈骗犯罪严重侵害人民群众切身利益和财产安全,严重影响社会和谐稳定,人民群众对此深恶痛绝。面对电信网络诈骗犯罪这一全球性治理难题,中国开展全链条纵深打击,取得良好成效。2019年至2021年,全国共起诉电信网络诈骗犯罪12.9万人。2017年至2021年,全国一审审结电信网络诈骗犯罪案件10.3万件,22.3万名被告人被判处刑罚。

探索未成年人网络司法保护新路径。以惩防网络犯罪为重点,依法精准打击"隔空猥亵"等网络违法犯罪,加大对以未成年人为目标的网络诈骗犯罪的打击惩治力度。依法惩戒和精准帮教相结合,最大限度教育挽救涉网络犯罪的未成年人。积极推动网络领域未成年人公益保护,以办理涉毒音视频传播、侵犯未成年人个人信息权益、网络高额打赏等典型个案作为突破口,通过公益诉讼、检察建议、支持起诉、情况通报等多种形式,推动网络平台、社会、政府共同守护未成年人健康网络环境。

五、提升全社会网络法治意识和素养

网络法治宣传教育需要全社会共同参与。中国借助互联网,法治宣传教育的内容、形式、手段不断创新,网民法治观念全面提升,网络平台主体责任和行业自律有效落实,尊法学法守法用法日益成为网络空间广泛共识和基本准则,社会主义法治精神在网络空间得到全面彰显。

(一)拓展"互联网+普法"新模式

互联网日益成为人民群众学习、工作、生活的新空间,成为获取公共信息和服务的新平台,也逐渐成为普法的新渠道、新手段。"互联网+普法"将单向式法治宣传转变为互动式、服务式、场景式传播,专业化的法律术语转化为通俗易懂的生活话语、网言网语,受众的参与感、体验感、获得感不断提升。

充分运用互联网开展法治宣传教育。政府网站、公众号设立普法专题专栏,围绕宪法、民法典、国家安全法、网络安全法等重要法律法规,以及生态文明建设、食品药品安全、个人信息保护等人民群众关心关注的问题,开展网上法治宣传,全面普及法律知识。充分利用中国普法"一网两微一端",加强智慧普法平台建设,宣传中国法治建设实践经验,推送普法信息,引导全社会树立权利与义务、个人自由与社会责任相统一的法治观念,培育遇事找法、解决问题用法、化解矛盾靠法的法治意识和行为规范,引导全体人民做社会主义法治的忠实崇尚者、自觉遵守者、坚定捍卫者。

积极运用网络媒体开展网上普法活动。互联网媒体发挥内容、渠道、资源优势,结合不同群体普法需求,运用图解、动漫、短视频、网络直播、网络音乐等多种形式创作大量网络普法作品,通过论坛、博客、微博客、公众账号、即时通信工具、网络直播、搜索引擎、问答社区等多种渠道向公众提供法律知识,解读法律法规。网络普法打通了普法与群众间的"最后一公里",促进普法更充分地融入市场经营、社区生活、校园学习、乡村建设,法律知识的到达率、普及率、知晓率得到显著提升。

线下普法活动向线上延伸。随着互联网与经济社会生产生活的广泛融合,传统的线下法治讲座、普法基层行动、法律咨询服务、法治文艺展播等普法活动借助互联网不断扩大影响力和覆盖面。学习培训、微视频比赛、互联网法律法规知识大赛等更多"键对键"的线上活动和"面对面"的线下普法相互融合、相互补充、相得益彰,吸引更多人群参与法治宣传教育,让网络法治宣传教育惠及更广泛社会群体。

(二) 普及网络法律法规

宣传普及网络法律法规是网络法治宣传教育的重点内容。网络法律法规全面普及提升了人民群众的网络法治观念,为培育健康向上、文明法治的网络生态环境提供了重要支持。

网络法律法规普及融入网络立法全过程。在网络安全法、数据安全法、个人信息保护法等网络法律法规制定过程中,利用线上线下渠道,通过公开征求意见、研讨论证等方式,广泛听取、充分吸纳公民、法人、其他组织等各方意见。网络法律法规公布实施时,通过召开新闻发布会、答记者问和专家解读等方式解疑释惑,引导公众了解网络法律知识、遵守网络法律法规,为依法治网筑牢群众基础。

在网络执法、司法活动中适时开展网络法律法规普及。围绕利用网络传播违法和不良信息、侵害个人信息权益、电信网络诈骗、未成年人网络保护等人民群众关心关注的问题,发布网络法治典型案事例,集中开展以案释法。通过"中国审判流程信息公开网""中国庭审公开网""中国裁判文书网""中国执行信息公开网"四大平台,公开网络司法案件。民众以更加生动直观的方式了解网络法律知识,社会公众从旁观者变为参与者、支持者、宣传者。

(三)面向重点对象开展网络普法

法律的权威源自人民内心拥护和真诚信仰。中国围绕青少年、互联网企业从业人员等重要普法对象开展法治宣传,引导青少年网民依法上网、文明上网、安全上网,督促互联网企业合规合法经营,提升法律风险防范意识。

加强青少年网络法治宣传教育。青少年是祖国的未来、民族的希望。青少年网民在中国网民中的占比逐步增长。作为互联网的"原住民",青少年是网上学习、交流、生活最活跃的参与者、实践者,其合法权益也更易受到网络违法活动的侵害。中国从保护青少年网络权益,促进青少年健康成长、全面发展出发,遵循青少年身心发展规律,贴近青少年学习生活实际,聚焦网络沉迷、网络欺凌、网络淫秽色情信息等重点问题,通过普法微综艺、儿童普法话剧、网络普法故事广播、网络普法云课堂、学法用法知识竞赛、法治副校长进校园、编写网络普法读本等生动活泼、丰富多彩的形式开展法治宣传教育,逐步形成了政府、社会、学校、家庭相结合的法治宣传教育格局,为提升青少年网民法治意识和网络安全素养提供了全面保障。

专栏7　创建全国青少年普法网

2012 年,中国创建全国青少年普法网,设置影视动漫、法律小故事、看图学法等栏目,为中小学生法治教育学习提供平台。目前,注册学校超过 19 万所,用户数 1.5 亿多。2021 年,通过全国青少年普法网参与宪法在线学习人次达到 83 亿。

强化互联网企业的依法经营意识。互联网企业是推动数字经济健康发展的重要市场主体,守法诚信是其应当遵守的基本行为准则。中国加强对互联网企业的网络法治教育培训,把网络法律法规特别是电子商务法、网络安全法、数据安全法、个人信息保护法、反垄断法、反不正当竞争法等与经营活动、行业发展密切相关的法律法规纳入企业入职培训、日常培训。支持互联网行业组织为互联网企业及

其从业人员提供形式多样的法律宣传教育,鼓励互联网行业组织督促企业坚持经济效益和社会效益并重的价值导向,通过完善行业规范、出台行业标准、发布诚信倡议等方式,引导互联网企业积极履行法律义务和社会责任,依法保护消费者合法权益,维护公平竞争的市场环境。

(四) 强化网络法治研究教育

网络法治教育、网络法治人才是建设网络强国的重要支撑和创新动力。中国面对网络法治实践中产生的重大理论问题和人才需求,初步形成了理论与实践相结合、制度与发展相适应的教育研究、人才培养机制,为网络法治建设提供了智力支持和人才保障。

全面提升网络法治研究能力。高校、科研机构创建网络法治研究新型智库,先后建立多个综合性网络法治研究基地。截至 2022 年 6 月,中国网络法治研究机构超过 90 家。网络法治智库充分发挥"智囊团""思想库""人才库"的重要作用,围绕数据、算法、平台治理等前沿问题开展研究,形成了大量学术研究成果。专家学者深入参与网络法治活动,围绕网络法治重要规划、重大立法、重点改革等加强调查研究,提出建设性建议。

加强网络法治领域人才培养。中国系统整合传统法学学科教育和网络相关学科教育,在设立网络空间安全一级学科的基础上,部分高校开设网络与信息法学、数字法学、人工智能法学等二级学科。高校依规自主开设网络安全与执法等网络法治相关本科专业。组建从事网络法学研究和教学的工作团队,讲授网络与信息安全、法律与人工智能、网络法学、区块链与电子证据、法律数据分析等融合法律知识与计算机科学、统计学知识的跨学科跨专业课程,编写了网络法、计算法、数据法、个人信息保护法等领域的一系列具有前沿性、通用性及实操性教材,培养出一大批兼具法律专业知识和技术背景的复合型人才,为网络强国建设提供了有力的法治人才支撑。

六、加强网络法治国际交流合作

网络空间是人类共同的活动空间。全球推动数字经济发展的愿望相同，应对网络安全风险的挑战相同，加强网络空间治理的需求相同。中国积极开展网络法治国际交流合作，坚持在独立自主、完全平等、互相尊重的基础上，与世界各国一道，共同参与全球网络治理体系变革，促进全球共同分享互联网发展的机遇和成果，携手构建网络空间命运共同体。

（一）积极参与规则建设

中国坚定维护国际公平正义，坚定维护以联合国为核心的国际体系、以国际法为基础的国际秩序、以《联合国宪章》宗旨和原则为基础的国际关系基本准则。支持各国平等参与网络国际治理，制定各方普遍接受的网络空间国际规则。

支持发挥联合国在网络国际治理中的主渠道作用。支持联合国制定打击网络犯罪全球性公约，共提并推动联合国大会通过决议，设立政府间特设专家委员会，并建设性参与公约谈判，呼吁尽早共同达成具有权威性、普遍性的公约，为国际社会合作应对网络犯罪挑战提供法律基础。注重发挥联合国在应对国际信息安全威胁领域的关键作用，与上海合作组织其他成员国共同向联合国提交"信息安全国际行为准则",并于 2015 年提交更新案文。提出《全球数据安全倡议》,分别于 2021 年 3 月和 2022 年 6 月同阿拉伯国家联盟、中亚五国发表《中阿数据安全合作倡议》《"中国＋中亚五国"数据安全合作倡议》,为讨论制定全球数据安全规则提供蓝本。参与推动联合国达成"网络空间负责任国家行为规范框架",明确主权平等、和平解决争端、禁止使用武力、不干涉他国内政等国际法重要原则适用于网络空间,明确应建立全球性、客观的信息技术产品供应链安全标准。拓展与联合国专门机构的网络事务合作,参与联合国教科文组织制定《人工智能伦理建议书》,并与世界知识产权组织在域名规则制定和域名争议解决领域开展广泛合作。

积极参与形成区域性网络治理规则。签署《区域全面经济伙伴关系协定》,与其他 14 个成员国一道,围绕电子认证和签名、在线消费者保护、在线个人信息保护、网络安全、数据跨境流动、知识产权保护等领域形成区域规则,电子商务章节成为目前全球覆盖区域最广、内容全面、水平较高的电子商务国际规则。积极推进加入《全面与进步跨太平洋伙伴关系协定》和《数字经济伙伴关系协定》,参与数字经济领域高标准规则制定。

(二) 广泛开展交流合作

中国始终支持网络法治领域的国际交流与合作,积极开展对话协商、交流互鉴,不断拓展深化平等、开放、合作的全球伙伴关系,以共进为动力、以共赢为目标,共同推进网络国际治理。

开展网络法治双多边对话交流。建立中俄信息安全磋商机制、中欧网络工作组机制、中国—东盟网络事务对话机制、中日韩三方网络磋商机制等对话机制,联合举办"2019中德互联网经济对话""中英互联网圆桌会议""中韩互联网圆桌会议""中古(巴)互联网圆桌论坛""中巴(西)互联网治理研讨会"等活动,与相关国家在网络政策法规和治网实践等方面开展务实交流,及时回应各方关切,平等协商解决分歧。与泰国、印度尼西亚等签署网络安全合作备忘录,加强网络安全政策法规交流分享,共同促进网络安全能力建设。

加强网络安全国际执法司法合作。中国与多国达成网络安全领域合作共识,在打击网络恐怖主义、电信网络诈骗等方面开展深层次务实合作。在打击网络恐怖主义方面,通过联合反恐演习、联合边防行动、警务合作、司法协助等多种形式,不断深化与相关国家交流合作,携手应对威胁挑战,共同维护世界和平和地区稳定。在打击电信网络诈骗方面,开展国际执法司法合作,与多国联合侦办跨境重大案件,取得明显成效。2022年3月至6月,在国际刑警组织框架下,与其他75个成员国共同参与"曙光行动",逮捕犯罪嫌疑人2000余名,拦截非法资金5000余万美元,有效遏制跨国电信网络诈骗活动。

携手保护未成年人网络权益。积极与联合国儿童基金会、国际互联网举报热线联合会等国际组织以及英国、德国、阿联酋等国相关部门开展合作,治理线上未成年人色情问题。加入"WePROTECT终结网络儿童性剥削全球联盟",与全球200多个政府、企业和民间社会组织一道努力打击儿童网上性剥削及性虐待,为儿童创造更加安全的网络环境。

（三）努力搭建对话平台

中国展现负责任大国担当,积极搭建与世界互联互通的国际平台和国际互联网共建共享的中国平台,为世界各国在网络法治领域密切联系、增进了解、促进互信发挥了积极作用。

通过世界互联网大会搭建网络法治交流平台。自 2014 年起,中国连续九年举办世界互联网大会,邀请各国政府、国际组织、互联网企业、智库、行业协会、技术社群等各界代表参加。大会组委会发布《携手构建网络空间命运共同体》概念文件,提出"尊重网络主权,《联合国宪章》确立的主权平等原则是当代国际关系的基本准则,同样适用于网络空间"。发布《携手构建网络空间命运共同体行动倡议》,提出开展数据安全和个人信息保护及相关规则、标准的国际交流合作,推动符合《联合国宪章》宗旨的个人信息保护规则标准国际互认。开展未成年人保护立法经验交流,打击针对未成年人的网络犯罪和网络欺凌,进一步完善打击网络犯罪与网络恐怖主义的机制建设。支持并积极参与联合国打击网络犯罪国际公约谈判,有效协调各国立法和实践,合力应对网络犯罪和网络恐怖主义威胁。

　　2022 年,在世界互联网大会基础上,中国发起成立世界互联网大会国际组织,以搭建全球网络共商共建共享为宗旨,以务实合作推动共享,为全球互联网发展治理贡献智慧和力量。目前已有来自六大洲近 20 个国家的互联网领域机构、组织、企业及个人加入,成为世界互联网大会国际组织初始会员。

　　搭建多形式、多渠道、多层次网络法治国际交流平台。通过金砖国家合作机制、上海合作组织、亚非法律协商组织、东盟地区论坛等多边平台,就网络立法、执法、司法、普法等网络法治建设情况深入交流观点、经验和做法。举办世界互联网法治论坛,发布《世界互联网法治论坛乌镇宣言》,为在网络司法领域分享经验、增进了解、相互学习借鉴搭建桥梁。支持互联网行业组织建立中国互联网治理论坛等国际交流平台,围绕数字包容、数据治理等议题开展交流研讨,促进中外互联网社群增进共识,共同解决互联网行业发展面临的问题。鼓励专家学者通过学术论坛、研讨交流会等多种平台,围绕数字经济、数据安全、人工智能治理等网络法治前沿问题,与国际同行开展学术交流,分享研究成果。

结　束　语

　　中国在互联网发展治理实践中，立足本国国情，借鉴世界经验，形成了具有鲜明中国特色的依法治网之道。在全面建设社会主义现代化国家新征程上，中国将始终坚持全面依法治国、依法治网的理念，推动互联网依法有序健康运行，以法治力量护航数字中国高质量发展，为网络强国建设提供坚实的法治保障。

　　互联网发展红利惠及全球，依法促进网络空间发展和繁荣，符合世界各国人民利益。网络法治既是数字治理的重要方式，也是数字文明建设的重要成果。面对数字化带来的机遇和挑战，中国愿同国际社会一道践行共商共建共享的全球治理观，共同推动全球互联网治理法治化进程，让数字文明发展成果更好造福各国人民，携手构建网络空间命运共同体，共同创造人类美好未来。

携手构建人类命运共同体：中国的倡议与行动

（2023 年 9 月）

中华人民共和国
国务院新闻办公室

前　言

宇宙只有一个地球，人类共有一个家园。

但是，我们赖以生存的星球正面临前所未有的巨大危机——既有已知的，更有未知的；既有可预测的，更有不可预测的。人类文明存亡已是必须面对的现实课题。越来越多的人意识到，相对于物质财富的积累，尤为紧迫的是，要本着对人类命运的终极关怀，找到人类文明永续发展的精神指引。

10年前，习近平主席提出构建人类命运共同体理念，目的就是回答"人类向何处去"的世界之问、历史之问、时代之问，为彷徨求索的世界点亮前行之路，为各国人民走向携手同心共护家园、共享繁荣的美好未来贡献中国方案。

构建人类命运共同体，就是每个民族、每个国家、每个人的前途命运都紧紧联系在一起，应该风雨同舟，荣辱与共，努力把我们生于斯、长于斯的星球建成一个和睦的大家庭，推动建设持久和平、普遍安全、共同繁荣、开放包容、清洁美丽的世界，把各国人民对美好生活的向往变成现实。

构建人类命运共同体理念，着眼全人类的福祉，既有现实思考，又有未来前瞻；既描绘了美好愿景，又提供了实践路径和行动方案；既关乎人类的前途，也攸关每一个体的命运。

10 年来,构建人类命运共同体的理念不断丰富和发展。从习近平主席 2013 年在莫斯科国际关系学院首次提出,到 2015 年在第七十届联大一般性辩论上提出"五位一体"总体框架①,再到 2017 年在联合国日内瓦总部提出建设"五个世界"的总目标②,人类命运共同体理念的思想内涵不断深化拓展。

10 年来,构建人类命运共同体的实践稳步推进。从双边到多边,从区域到全球,这一理念取得全方位、开创性的丰硕成果,共建"一带一路"倡议、全球发展倡议、全球安全倡议、全球文明倡议落地生根,给世界带来的是繁荣稳定的巨大红利,创造的是扎扎实实的民生福祉。

10 年来,构建人类命运共同体的观念日益深入人心。越来越多国家和人民认识到,这一理念符合全人类共同利益,反映了世界人民追求和平、正义、进步的心声,汇聚了各国人民共建美好世界的最大公约数。国际社会普遍认为,人类命运共同体理念超越利己主义和保护主义,打破了个别国家唯我独尊的霸权思维,反映出中国对人类发展方向的独到见解,对于推动各国团结合作、共创人类美好未来具有重要意义。

为全面介绍构建人类命运共同体的思想内涵和生动实践,增进国际社会了解和理解,凝聚广泛共识,更好与各国携手构建人类命运共同体,中国政府特发布本白皮书。

---

① "五位一体"总体框架:建立平等相待、互商互谅的伙伴关系,营造公道正义、共建共享的安全格局,谋求开放创新、包容互惠的发展前景,促进和而不同、兼收并蓄的文明交流,构筑尊崇自然、绿色发展的生态体系。

② 建设"五个世界"的总目标:坚持对话协商,建设一个持久和平的世界;坚持共建共享,建设一个普遍安全的世界;坚持合作共赢,建设一个共同繁荣的世界;坚持交流互鉴,建设一个开放包容的世界;坚持绿色低碳,建设一个清洁美丽的世界。

一、人类站在历史的十字路口

我们所处的是一个充满希望的时代,也是一个充满挑战的时代。站在历史的十字路口,是团结还是分裂,是开放还是封闭,是合作还是对抗?如何抉择,关乎人类整体利益,也考验着各国的智慧。

(一) 相互依存是历史大势

从人类社会发展史看,人类从原始社会一路走来,经历了农业革命、工业革命、信息革命,但无论生产力如何发展进步,都没有改变一个最根本的现实:地球是人类赖以生存的唯一家园。各国有责任共同呵护地球的安全,守护人类的未来。如果为了争权夺利而恶性竞争甚至兵戎相见,最终只会走上自我毁灭的道路。

自古以来,人类最朴素的愿望就是和平与发展。经历过战争和冲突的洗礼,尤其是遭受两次世界大战的浩劫后,世界各国人民珍视和平、扩大合作、共同发展的意识显著提升,人类大家庭的观念更加深入人心,人们对共同体的向往和追求更加殷切。

全球化在世界范围内优化了资本、信息、技术、劳动、管理等生产要素的配置,把一个个孤立的小湖泊、小河流连成了汪洋大海,各民族自给自足的原始封闭状态被打破,市场成为了世界市场,历史也随之成为世界历史。

在信息化日新月异的今天,互联网、大数据、量子计算、人工智能迅猛发展。人类交往的世界性比过去任何时候都更深入、更广泛,各国相互联系和彼此依存比过去任何时候都更频繁、更紧密。全球化不是选择,而是现实,甚至成为一种生活方式。地球村正变得越来越"小",放眼寰宇,地球上最遥远的距离也不超过 24 小时的直飞航程。世界也正变得越来越"平",点一点手机屏幕,就可以瞬时链接到世界的另一端。一体化的世界就在那儿,谁拒绝这个世界,这个世界也会拒绝他。

生活在同一片蓝天下,无论近邻还是远交,无论大国还是小国,无论发达国家还是发展中国家,正日益形成利益交融、安危与共的利益共同体、责任共同体、命运共同体。只有人类整体命运得以关照,每个国家、每个民族、每个人的美好希望才能实现。不管前途是晴是雨,携手合作、互利共赢是唯一正确选择。

(二) 全球性挑战需要全球性应对

当今世界正处于百年未有之大变局,各种新旧问题与复杂矛盾叠加碰撞、交织发酵。人类社会面临前所未有的挑战,不稳定、不确定、难预料成为常态。

和平赤字不断加深。第二次世界大战结束以来,人类社会维持了 70 多年的总体和平,但威胁世界和平的因素仍在积聚。欧亚大陆战火重燃,局势持续紧张,热点问题此起彼伏,军备竞赛阴霾不散,核战争的"达摩克利斯之剑"高悬,世界面临重新陷入对抗甚至战争的风险。

发展赤字持续扩大。全球经济复苏乏力,单边主义、保护主义肆虐,一些国家构筑"小院高墙"、强推"脱钩断链"、鼓噪供应链"去风险",经济全球化遭遇逆流。新冠疫情吞噬全球发展成果,南北差距、发展断层、技术鸿沟等问题更加突出。人类发展指数30年来首次下降,世界新增1亿多贫困人口,近8亿人生活在饥饿之中。

安全赤字日益凸显。国际战略竞争日趋激烈,大国之间信任缺失,冷战思维卷土重来,意识形态对抗老调重弹,恃强凌弱、巧取豪夺、零和博弈等霸权霸道霸凌行径危害深重,恐怖主义、网络攻击、跨国犯罪、生物安全等非传统安全挑战上升。

治理赤字更加严峻。世界正面临多重治理危机,能源危机、粮食危机、债务危机等不断加剧;全球气候治理紧迫性凸显,绿色低碳转型任重道远;数字鸿沟日益扩大,人工智能治理缺位。新冠疫情像一面镜子,折射出全球治理体系这台机器越来越滞后于时代,甚至在一些问题上运转失灵,亟待改革完善。

面对全球性危机,各国不是乘坐在190多条小船上,而是乘坐在一条命运与共的大船上。小船经不起风浪,只有巨舰才能顶住惊涛骇浪。任何一国即使再强大也无法包打天下,必须开展全球合作。各国应携起手来,把"我"融入"我们",共同构建人类命运共同体,才能共渡难关、共创未来。

（三） 新时代呼唤新理念

我们所处的是一个风云变幻的时代,面对的是一个日新月异的世界。传统国际关系理论越来越难以解释今天的世界、无法破解人类面临的困局,国强必霸、崇尚实力、零和博弈等思维越来越不符合时代前进的方向。人类社会亟需符合时代特征、顺应历史潮流的新理念。

"国强必霸"并非绕不开的历史定律。"国强必霸"本质是典型的霸权主义思维,反映的是历史上大国霸权战争的灾难性实践。中国从不认同"国强必霸",我们的历史智慧是"国霸必衰"。中国发展振兴靠的是自身努力,而非侵略扩张。中国所做的一切都是为了本国人民过上更加幸福的生活,为世界人民提供发展机会,而不是要取代谁、打败谁。

"弱肉强食"不是人类共存之道。这一逻辑将自然界的丛林法则简单移植到人类社会,信奉权力至上,从根本上破坏了国家主权平等原则和世界和平稳定。全球化时代你中有我、我中有你,决定了弱肉强食、赢者通吃是一条越走越窄的死胡同,包容普惠、互利共赢才是越走越宽的人间正道。中国一向主张公平正义,坚持在和平共处五项原则基础上同各国发展友好合作,致力于推进国际关系民主化。

"你输我赢"的零和游戏终将玩不转。一些国家抱守零和思维,片面追求绝对安全和垄断优势,这既无助于本国的长远发展,也对世界和平与繁荣构成严重威胁。任何国家都不应盼着别人输,而要致力于同他国一道赢。中国始终把自身发展和世界发展统一起来,始终把中国人民利益同各国人民共同利益结合起来。世界好,中国才能好;中国好,世界才更好。

二、解答时代之问，描绘未来愿景

站在何去何从的十字路口，人类面临两种截然不同的取向：一种是重拾冷战思维，挑动分裂对立，制造集团对抗；另一种是从人类共同福祉出发，致力团结合作，倡导开放共赢，践行平等尊重。两种取向、两种选择的博弈和较量，将深刻影响人类和地球的未来。

构建人类命运共同体，坚持开放包容，坚持互利共赢，坚持公道正义，不是以一种制度代替另一种制度，不是以一种文明代替另一种文明，而是不同社会制度、不同意识形态、不同历史文化、不同发展水平的国家在国际事务中利益共生、权利共享、责任共担。构建人类命运共同体理念，站在历史正确的一边，站在人类进步的一边，为国际关系确立新思路，为全球治理提供新智慧，为国际交往开创新格局，为美好世界描绘新愿景。

（一）确立国际关系新思路

现行国际秩序面临多重挑战，一些国家奉行实力至上的逻辑，恃强凌弱、巧取豪夺、零和博弈大行其道，发展鸿沟加剧，安全赤字加重，结盟对抗、封闭排他的做法与多极化的发展方向背道而驰，与冷战结束后的国际关系走向格格不入。特别是随着一大批新兴市场国家和发展中国家的崛起,现行国际秩序不适应时代发展的一面更加凸显。"建设一个什么样的世界、如何建设这个世界"成为关乎人类前途命运的重大课题。

面对时代之问,中国的回答是构建人类命运共同体。人类命运共同体,就是每个民族、每个国家的前途命运都紧紧联系在一起,应该风雨同舟、荣辱与共、和谐共生、合作共赢。这一理念源于对国家交往关系的合理性设计,源于国际社会的普遍共识和共同期盼,也源于中国的大国责任和担当。

在地球村里,全人类是一个命运与共的大家庭,国与国之间利益交汇、命运交织、休戚与共,越来越成为你中有我、我中有你的命运共同体。人类命运共同体理念超越了集团政治的"小圈子"规则,超越了实力至上的逻辑,超越了少数西方国家定义的"普世价值",顺应时代潮流,倡导全球协作,推动国际秩序朝着更加公正合理的方向发展。

(二) 彰显全球治理新特征

人类命运共同体理念主张世界各国同呼吸、共命运,具有开放包容、公平正义、和谐共处、多元互鉴、团结协作的鲜明特征。

——开放包容。不以意识形态划线,不针对特定的对象,不拉帮结派,不搞排他的"小圈子",海纳百川,有容乃大。主张国际关系民主化,世界的命运应该由各国共同掌握,国际规则应该由各国共同书写,全球事务应该由各国共同治理,发展成果应该由各国共同分享。

——公平正义。世界要公道不要霸道,任何国家都没有包揽国际事务、主宰他国命运、垄断发展优势的权力。要维护以国际法为基础的国际秩序,维护国际法治权威,确保国际法平等统一适用,不能搞双重标准,不能"合则用、不合则弃"。

——和谐共处。各国在求同存异的前提下实现和平共处、共同发展。地球不是国家角力的竞技场,而是人类共存的大舞台。各国发展和而不同,是有差异、多样性的协调和统一,世界发展的活力恰恰在于这种多样性的共存。

——多元互鉴。不同历史和国情、不同民族和习俗,孕育了不同文明。人类文明多样性是世界基本特征,不同文明交流互鉴是推动人类进步的重要动力。我们应当相互尊重,携手推动不同文明在交流互鉴中熠熠生辉。

——团结协作。倡导"计利当计天下利"。关起门来搞建设,只能越搞越穷。从"本国优先"的角度看,世界是狭小拥挤的,时时都是"激烈竞争";从命运与共的角度看,世界是宽广博大的,处处都有合作机遇。单打独斗已无法应对全球性的发展难题,各国通力合作才是唯一选择。

(三) 开创国际交往新格局

中国提出构建人类命运共同体"五位一体"总体框架,包括伙伴关系、安全格局、发展前景、文明交流、生态体系等五个方面,开创了国际交往的新格局。

建立平等相待、互商互谅的伙伴关系格局。联合国宪章贯穿主权平等原则。世界各国一律平等,不能以大压小、以强凌弱、以富欺贫。坚持多边主义,不搞单边主义;应奉行双赢、多赢、共赢的新理念,取代你输我赢、赢者通吃的旧思维。应在国际和区域层面建设全球伙伴关系,走出一条"对话而不对抗,结伴而不结盟"的国与国交往新路。大国之间相处,要不冲突不对抗、相互尊重、合作共赢。大国与小国相处,要平等相待,践行正确义利观,义利相兼,义重于利。

建立公道正义、共建共享的安全格局。在经济全球化时代,各国安全相互关联、彼此影响。没有一个国家能凭一己之力谋求自身绝对安全,也没有一个国家可以从别国的动荡中收获稳定。"弱肉强食"是丛林法则,不是相处之道。穷兵黩武是霸道做法,只能搬起石头砸自己的脚。应摒弃一切形式的冷战思维,树立共同、综合、合作、可持续的安全观。

建立开放创新、包容互惠的发展格局。大家一起发展才是真发展,可持续发展才是好发展。实现这一目标,就应秉承开放精神,推进互帮互助、互惠互利。世界长期发展不可能建立在一批国家越来越富裕而另一批国家却长期贫穷落后的基础之上。应把发展置于国际议程的突出位置,减少全球发展的不平等和不平衡,不让任何一个国家、任何一个人掉队。

建立和而不同、兼收并蓄的文明交流格局。世界上共有 200 多个国家和地区,2500多个民族和多种宗教。人类文明多样性赋予这个世界姹紫嫣红的色彩,多样带来交流,交流孕育融合,融合产生进步。只有坚持弘扬平等、互鉴、对话、包容的文明观,在多样中相互尊重、彼此借鉴、和谐共存,这个世界才能丰富多彩、欣欣向荣。要尊重各种文明,平等相待,互学互鉴,兼收并蓄,推动人类文明实现创造性发展。

建立尊崇自然、绿色发展的生态格局。人类可以利用自然、改造自然,但归根结底是自然的一部分,必须呵护自然,不能凌驾于自然之上。要解决好工业文明带来的矛盾,以人与自然和谐相处为目标,实现世界的可持续发展和人的全面发展。牢固树立尊重自然、顺应自然、保护自然的意识,坚持走绿色、低碳、循环、可持续发展之路。

(四)共建美好世界新愿景

中国提出,推动建设一个持久和平、普遍安全、共同繁荣、开放包容、清洁美丽的世界。从"五位一体"总体框架到"五个世界"总目标,人类命运共同体理念实现了历史视野的再拓展、思想内涵的再深化,为人类未来锚定了更明确的目标、描绘了更清晰的图景。

坚持对话协商,建设一个持久和平的世界,就是告别战争之剑,永铸和平之犁。联合国教科文组织总部大楼前的石碑上,镌刻着这样一句话,"战争起源于人之思想,故务需于人之思想中筑起保卫和平之屏障"。人类历史上由于执迷强国争霸导致战争频仍、生灵涂炭,教训惨痛而深刻,要从思想上拔除这些诱发战争的引信。大国对小国要平等相待,不搞唯我独尊、强买强卖的霸道。任何国家都不能随意制造动荡战乱,不能破坏国际法治,不能打开潘多拉的盒子。要尊重彼此主权和领土完整,尊重彼此核心利益和重大关切,尊重各国人民自主选择的发展道路和社会制度。

坚持共建共享,建设一个普遍安全的世界,就是告别绝对安全,实现安危与共。世上没有绝对安全的世外桃源,一国的安全不能建立在别国的动荡之上,他国的威胁也可能成为本国的挑战。邻居出了问题,不能光想着扎好自家篱笆,而应该去帮一把。越是面临全球性挑战,越要合作应对,共同变压力为动力、化危机为生机。面对错综复杂的国际安全威胁,单打独斗不行,迷信武力更不行,合作安全、共同安全才是解决问题的正确选择。国家之间有分歧是正常的,要通过对话协商妥善化解分歧。只要怀有真诚愿望,秉持足够善意,展现政治智慧,再大的冲突也能化解,再厚的坚冰都能打破。

坚持合作共赢,建设一个共同繁荣的世界,就是告别赢者通吃,共享发展成果。国际社会发展到今天已经成为一部复杂精巧、有机一体的机器,拆掉一个零部件就会使整个机器运转面临严重困难。要坚持经济全球化正确方向,反对任何人搞技术封锁、科技鸿沟、发展脱钩。把全球经济这块蛋糕做大,更要将这块蛋糕分好,让发展成果更多更公平地惠及各国人民,实现真正的合作共赢。

坚持交流互鉴,建设一个开放包容的世界,就是告别文明优越,实现美美与共。这个世界完全容得下各国共同成长和进步,一国的成功并不意味着另一国必然失败。世界上没有放之四海而皆准的发展道路。只有能够持续造福人民的发展道路，才是最有生命力的。各国各民族尊重彼此差异，和而不同。不同文明要取长补短、共同进步，让文明交流互鉴成为推动人类社会进步的动力、维护世界和平的纽带。

坚持绿色低碳，建设一个清洁美丽的世界，就是告别竭泽而渔，永享绿水青山。人与自然共生共存，伤害自然最终将伤及人类。空气、水、土壤、蓝天等自然资源用之不觉、失之难续。工业化创造了前所未有的物质财富，也产生了难以弥补的生态创伤。不能吃祖宗饭、断子孙路，用破坏性方式搞发展。绿水青山就是金山银山。应遵循天人合一、道法自然的理念，寻求永续发展之路，让人人都能遥望星空、看见青山、闻到花香。

构建人类命运共同体为改革和完善国际治理体系提出了中国方案。构建人类命运共同体，并不是推倒重来，也不是另起炉灶，而是推进国际关系民主化，推动全球治理朝着更加公正合理的方向发展。这一重要理念，汇聚了各国人民求和平谋发展盼稳定的最大公约数，画出了不同文化背景和发展程度国家之间的最大同心圆，超越了零和博弈、强权政治、冷战对抗的各种陈旧思维，成为新时代中国特色大国外交的总目标，成为引领时代潮流和人类前进方向的鲜明旗帜。

三、扎根深厚历史文化土壤

人类命运共同体理念基于深厚的中国文化底蕴,源于中国式现代化的道路实践,继承弘扬新中国外交的优良传统,吸收借鉴人类社会优秀文明成果,彰显了悠久的历史传承、鲜明的时代印记和丰富的人文内涵。

（一）传承中华优秀传统文化

中华优秀传统文化是中华文明的智慧结晶和精华所在,为人们认识和改造世界提供有益启迪,蕴藏着解决当代人类面临难题的重要启示,蕴含着丰富的人类命运共同体基因。

中华文化以和合理念为精神内核,秉持"以和为贵,和而不同"的价值取向,追求"和衷共济、和合共生"的高远理想,推崇不同国家、不同文化"美美与共、天下大同"。

中华民族历来讲求"天下一家",主张"民胞物与、协和万邦",遵循"强不执弱,富不侮贫"的交往原则,憧憬"大道之行,天下为公"的美好世界。

中华民族自古尊崇仁德博爱之心,倡导"德不孤,必有邻"的精神追求,坚守"亲仁善邻、讲信修睦"的处世之道,奉行"义利并举、以义为先"的义利原则。

中华民族一向崇尚立己达人之道,"己欲立而立人,己欲达而达人",相信帮助别人就是帮助自己;"己所不欲,勿施于人",不把自己的意志强加于人。

中华民族始终遵循"道法自然、天人合一"的自然观,践行"钓而不纲,弋不射宿"的生态观,体现了对天地宇宙的敬畏和热爱、对人与自然和谐共生的追求。

(二) 体现中国共产党的世界情怀

坚持胸怀天下,是中国共产党百年奋斗积累的宝贵历史经验之一。100多年来,中国共产党既为中国人民谋幸福、为中华民族谋复兴,也为人类谋进步、为世界谋大同,带领中国人民走出了中国式现代化道路,创造了人类文明新形态,为构建人类命运共同体奠定了坚实基础、探索了历史规律、开辟了广阔道路。

中国共产党始终坚持发展自己、兼济天下、造福世界,不仅要让中国人民都过得好,也帮助其他国家人民过上好日子,努力为人类作出新的更大贡献。中共二十大报告擘画了以中国式现代化全面推进中华民族伟大复兴的宏伟蓝图,明确提出推动构建人类命运共同体是中国式现代化的本质要求之一,把中国的前途命运和人类的前途命运紧密联系起来。

中国共产党领导中国人民开创和拓展的中国式现代化,既有基于自己国情的中国特色,也有各国现代化的共同特征。无论是人口规模巨大、共同富裕,还是物质文明和精神文明相协调、人与自然和谐共生,或者是走和平发展道路,都为发展中国家贡献了具体可借鉴的历史经验,为携手迈向人类命运共同体的美好未来,提供了更为健康、更可持续的选择。

（三）弘扬新中国外交优良传统

70多年来,中国外交在国际风云激荡中成长奋进,积淀了优良传统,砥砺了坚韧风骨,铸就了独特精神。构建人类命运共同体,继承和发扬了新中国成立以来的外交理念、战略思想和优良传统,并在波澜壮阔的中国特色大国外交实践中不断守正创新。

新中国成立后,中国坚持独立自主的和平外交政策,提出和平共处五项原则、"三个世界"等政策方针和思想,在国际舞台上站稳了脚跟、赢得了尊重、扩大了影响。改革开放以来,中国提出和平与发展是时代主题的重大论断,倡导促进世界多极化和国际关系民主化,推动建设和谐世界,中国全方位外交取得重要进展。

进入新时代,中国高举和平、发展、合作、共赢的旗帜,全面推进中国特色大国外交,形成全方位、多层次、立体化的外交布局。中国创造性提出推动构建人类命运共同体、新型国际关系、全人类共同价值、共建"一带一路"、全球发展倡议、全球安全倡议、全球文明倡议等新理念,倡导全球治理观、正确义利观、安全观、发展观、合作观、生态观等重要理念,体现了鲜明的中国特色、中国风格、中国气派。

（四）兼收并蓄人类优秀文明成果

构建人类命运共同体理念,把人类历史长河中跨越时空、超越国度、富有永恒魅力、具有当代价值的优秀文化弘扬起来,凝聚不同民族、不同信仰、不同文化、不同地域人民的价值共识,汲取世界多元文明相融相通优秀成果,反映了全人类的普遍愿望和共同心声。

世界各国文明中都蕴含着构建人类命运共同体的历史智慧。古希腊哲学家以城邦为蓝本对人类共同体进行了早期探索,认为需要通过一致行动追求共同利益,主张人类必须互相保持和谐生活。印度古老典籍记载着"天下一家"的箴言。非洲传统价值理念乌班图精神,倡导"我们在故我在",强调人们彼此依存、密不可分。

构建人类命运共同体理念,反映了和平发展、团结共生、合作共赢等不同文明之间的互通之处。俄罗斯有谚语"风雨同舟就能无惧风雨";瑞士有作家提出"不应为战争和毁灭效劳,而应为和平与谅解服务";德国有谚语"一个人的努力是加法,一个团队的努力是乘法";非洲有谚语"一根原木盖不起一幢房屋";阿拉伯有谚语"独行快,众行远";墨西哥诗人有名句"唯有益天下,方可惠本国";印度尼西亚有谚语"甘蔗同穴生,香茅成丛长";蒙古国有谚语"邻里心灵相通,命运与共"等等。这些都体现了深厚的世界文化渊源和丰富的思想底蕴。

构建人类命运共同体理念,以公认的国际关系基本原则为遵循。近代以来,建立公正合理的国际秩序是人类孜孜以求的目标。从《威斯特伐利亚和约》确立的平等和主权原则,到日内瓦公约确立的国际人道主义精神;从联合国宪章明确的四大宗旨和七项原则,到万隆会议倡导的和平共处五项原则,这些国际关系演变积累的公认原则,成为构建人类命运共同体的重要基础。

四、既有目标方向，也有实现路径

构建人类命运共同体，是中国从世界和平与发展的大势出发处理当代国际关系的中国智慧，是完善全球治理的中国方案，是应对21世纪的各种挑战的中国主张。理念引领行动，方向决定出路，国际社会应当携手努力，把宏伟蓝图变成路线图，一步一个脚印把美好愿景变为现实。

（一）推动新型经济全球化

经济全球化是世界经济发展的必然趋势，契合各国人民要发展、要合作的时代潮流。历史上的经济全球化，促成了贸易大繁荣、投资大便利、人员大流动、技术大发展，为世界经济发展作出了重要贡献。

但是，经济全球化也积存了不少问题和弊端，出现"回头浪"。目前的经济全球化模式，难以反映广大发展中国家呼声、体现广大发展中国家利益；"弱肉强食"的丛林法则和"你输我赢""赢者通吃"的零和博弈，造成富者愈富、贫者愈贫，发达国家与发展中国家以及发达国家内部的贫富差距越拉越大；个别国家把内部治理问题归咎于经济全球化，归咎于其他国家，动辄采取单边主义、保护主义、霸凌主义，破坏全球产业链、价值链、供应链、消费链，导致现有国际贸易秩序紊乱甚至冲突。

推动新型经济全球化,是构建人类命运共同体的必然要求。各国应该坚持开放的政策取向,旗帜鲜明反对保护主义,反对"筑墙设垒",反对单边制裁、极限施压,推动各国经济联动融通,共同建设开放型世界经济。各国应该推动构建公正、合理、透明的国际经贸规则体系,推进贸易和投资自由化便利化,促进全球经济进一步开放、交流、融合,推动形成开放、包容、普惠、平衡、共赢的经济全球化,让各国人民共享经济全球化和世界经济增长成果。

开放应是双向奔赴,不能是单行道,不能一边要求别的国家开放,一边关闭自己的大门。一些国家总想对中国实行"脱钩断链",构筑"小院高墙",最终只会反噬自身。一些人炒作要"降依赖""去风险",这样的做法实质是制造新的风险。防风险和合作不是对立的,不合作才是最大的风险,不发展才是最大的不安全。如果以"去风险""降依赖"之名行"去中国化"之实,就是在去机遇、去合作、去稳定、去发展。

当前正在发生的以人工智能为标志的科技革命,将对新一轮经济全球化和人类社会发展产生难以估量的深刻影响。要探索建立相关规则和标准,既有利于科学技术的创新发展,又坚守人类安全底线,还要平衡照顾各国特别是发展中国家利益,确保技术创新在法治轨道和公认的国际准则基础上运行,由人类主导、为人类服务、符合人类价值观。

（二）走和平发展道路

历史告诉我们，一个国家要发展繁荣，必须把握和顺应世界发展大势，反之必然会被历史抛弃。当今世界的潮流是和平、发展、合作、共赢，殖民主义、霸权主义的老路不仅走不通，而且一定会碰得头破血流，和平发展道路才是人间正道。

和平、和睦、和谐的追求深深植根于中华民族的精神世界之中，深深溶化在中国人民的血脉之中。中国历史上曾经长期是世界上最强大的国家之一，但没有留下殖民和侵略他国的记录。中国坚持走和平发展道路，是对几千年来中华民族热爱和平的文化传统的继承和发扬。

中国始终坚持独立自主的和平外交政策，始终强调中国外交政策的宗旨是维护世界和平、促进共同发展。中国反对各种形式的霸权主义和强权政治，不干涉别国内政，永远不称霸，永远不搞扩张。中国在政策上是这样规定的、制度上是这样设计的，在实践中更是一直这样做的。

世界需要和平，就像人需要空气一样，就像万物生长需要阳光一样。和平发展道路对中国有利、对世界有利，我们想不出有任何理由不坚持这条道路。中国坚持走和平发展道路，也希望其他国家共同走和平发展道路。各国只有共谋和平、共护和平、共享和平，才能实现自己的发展目标，为世界作出更大贡献。只有大家都走和平发展道路,国与国才能和平相处,构建人类命运共同体才有希望。

（三）构建新型国际关系

新型国际关系之所以新,在于走出了一条国与国交往的新道路,开辟了不同文明、不同制度国家和平共处、共同发展的世界历史新篇章,为构建人类命运共同体创造了条件。

构建新型国际关系,应秉持相互尊重、公平正义、合作共赢原则。相互尊重,就是坚持以诚待人,平等相待,反对强权政治和霸凌主义。公平正义,就是各国应摒弃单纯的物质主义取向和竞争至上法则,确保不同的国家都能获得平等的发展权利和机会。合作共赢,就是各国应摒弃一味谋求自身更大利益的理念,在追求本国利益时兼顾各国合理关切,在谋求本国发展时促进各国共同发展。

构建新型国际关系的基础在于深化拓展平等、开放、合作的全球伙伴关系。中国坚持在和平共处五项原则基础上同各国发展友好合作。促进大国协调和良性互动,推动构建和平共处、总体稳定、均衡发展的大国关系格局。坚持亲诚惠容和与邻为善、以邻为伴周边外交方针,深化同周边国家友好互信和利益融合。秉持真实亲诚理念和正确义利观加强同发展中国家团结合作,维护发展中国家共同利益。

大国是构建新型国际关系的关键因素。大国之大,不在于体量大、块头大、拳头大,而在于胸襟大、格局大、担当大。大国要以人类前途命运为要,对世界和平与发展担负更大责任,而不是依仗实力对地区和国际事务谋求垄断。大国要加强协调和合作,尊重彼此核心利益和重大关切,坚持换位思考和相互理解,对小国要平等相待。通过构建人类命运共同体,新兴大国和守成大国才能避免跌入"修昔底德陷阱",找到相互尊重、和平共处、合作共赢的正确相处之道,实现不同文明、不同社会制度国家求同存异、共同发展。

（四）践行真正的多边主义

构建人类命运共同体必须践行真正的多边主义。"小圈子的多边主义"是集团政治,"本国优先的多边主义"是单边思维,"有选择的多边主义"是双重标准。世界要公道,不要霸道。中国反对一切形式的单边主义,反对搞针对特定国家的阵营化和排他性"小圈子",反对打着所谓"规则"旗号破坏国际秩序、制造"新冷战"和意识形态对抗的行径。

中国始终坚定维护联合国宪章宗旨和原则,坚定维护联合国权威和地位。当今世界发生的各种对抗和不公,不是因为联合国宪章宗旨和原则过时了,而恰恰是由于这些宗旨和原则未能得到有效履行。中国坚持世界只有一个体系,就是以联合国为核心的国际体系;只有一个秩序,就是以国际法为基础的国际秩序;只有一套规则,就是以联合国宪章宗旨和原则为基础的国际关系基本准则。

中国积极参与引领全球治理体系变革。坚持共商共建共享的全球治理观,就是全球事务要由大家一起商量,治理体系要由大家一起建设,治理成果要由大家一起分享,让各国成为世界和平与发展的参与者、贡献者、受益者。

(五) 弘扬全人类共同价值

中国提出和平、发展、公平、正义、民主、自由的全人类共同价值,以宽广胸怀理解不同文明对价值内涵的认识,尊重不同国家人民对自身发展道路的探索,弘扬中华文明蕴含的全人类共同价值,超越所谓"普世价值"的狭隘历史局限,体现了人类命运共同体的价值追求。

和平发展是共同事业。贫瘠的土地上长不成和平的大树,连天的烽火中结不出发展的硕果。要解决好各种全球性挑战,根本出路在于谋求和平、实现发展。公平正义是共同理想。任何国家都不能在世界上我行我素,搞霸权霸道霸凌。民主自由是共同追求。不存在定于一尊的民主,更不存在高人一等的民主。民主不是可口可乐,一国生产原浆,全世界一个味道;民主不是装饰品,而是要用来解决实际问题的。试图垄断民主"专利"、强行划定民主"标准",炮制"民主对抗威权"的伪命题,挑动政治制度与意识形态之争,是假借民主之名的伪民主。弘扬全人类共同价值,不是要把哪一家的价值观奉为一尊,而是倡导求同存异、和而不同,充分尊重文明的多样性,尊重各国自主选择社会制度和发展道路的权利。

人类社会越发展,越要加强文明交流互鉴。各国应相互尊重、平等相待,摒弃傲慢与偏见,加深对自身文明和其他文明差异性的认知,推动不同文明交流对话、和谐共生;应各美其美、美人之美、美美与共,既让本国文明生机盎然,也为他国文明发展创造条件,让世界文明百花园群芳竞艳;应开放包容、互学互鉴,努力打破文化交往的壁垒,积极汲取其他文明的养分,相互借鉴,取长补短,共同进步;应与时俱进、创新发展,不断吸纳时代精华,用创新为文明发展提供不竭动力。

五、中国既是倡导者也是行动派

千里之行,始于足下。10年来,中国用笃定的信念和扎实的行动,为构建人类命运共同体贡献中国力量。

(一) 推动高质量共建"一带一路"

共建"一带一路"倡议是构建人类命运共同体的生动实践,是中国为世界提供的广受欢迎的国际公共产品和国际合作平台。共建"一带一路"倡议提出10年来,坚持共商共建共享原则,秉持开放、绿色、廉洁理念,以高标准、可持续、惠民生为目标,沿着高质量发展方向不断前进,从夯基垒台、立柱架梁到落地生根、持久发展,奏响"硬联通""软联通""心联通"的交响乐,搭建了各方广泛参与、汇聚国际共识、凝聚各方力量的重要实践平台。

专栏1　希腊比雷埃夫斯港获得新生

希腊最大港口比雷埃夫斯港,公元前400多年建港以来,一直是重要港口,守望着欧洲"南大门"。十多年前,比雷埃夫斯港一度深陷危机,遭受巨额亏损。2010年,中国远洋海运集团正式参与比雷埃夫斯港运营,给港口注入蓬勃生机。目前比雷埃夫斯港年吞吐能力达720万标准箱,世界排名从2010年第93位提升至2022年第33位,为当地直接创造就业岗位3000多个,间接创造就业岗位1万多个,累计为当地带来直接贡献超过14亿欧元。

政策沟通不断深化，截至 2023 年 7 月，全球超过四分之三的国家和 30 多个国际组织签署合作文件。中国分别于 2017 年、2019 年成功举办首届和第二届"一带一路"国际合作高峰论坛，今年将举办第三届"一带一路"国际合作高峰论坛，凝聚起携手推动高质量共建"一带一路"的最大合力。设施联通不断加强，"六廊六路多国多港"的互联互通架构基本形成，以新亚欧大陆桥等经济走廊为引领，以中欧班列、陆海新通道等大通道和信息高速路为骨架，以铁路、港口、管网等为依托的陆、海、天、网"四位一体"互联互通布局不断完善。贸易畅通不断提升，世界银行发布的《"一带一路"经济学》报告认为，"一带一路"倡议的全面实施将使参与国间的贸易往来增加 4.1%。到 2030 年，"一带一路"倡议每年将为全球产生 1.6 万亿美元收益。资金融通不断扩大，亚洲基础设施投资银行、丝路基金等相继成立，已为数百个项目提供投融资支持。民心相通不断促进，一条条"幸福路"、一座座"连心桥"、一片片"发展带"在共建国家不断涌现，菌草、水井、杂交水稻等"小而美、见效快、惠民生"项目扎实推进，不断增进共建国家民众的获得感、幸福感。

专栏 2 "中国菌草是我们的'幸福草'"
菌草技术通过"以草代木"栽培食用菌，解决了"食用菌生产必须靠砍伐树木"的世界难题。20 多年来，中国先后举办了 270 期菌草技术国际培训班，为 106 个国家培训 1 万多名学员，在 16 个国家建立了菌草技术实验示范中心或基地，创造了数十万个绿色就业机会。在斐济，菌草技术被誉为"岛国农业的新希望"；在莱索托，因短时间就有收获，农民称菌草为"致富草"；在卢旺达，有 3800 多户贫困户因为参与菌草生产，现在每户每年收入增加了 1 至 3 倍。

共建"一带一路"倡议源于中国,机会和成果属于世界。中巴经济走廊启动 10 年来为巴基斯坦经济社会发展注入强劲动能,中老铁路实现了老挝人民"变陆锁国为陆联国"的夙愿,雅万高铁成为东南亚国家首条实现 350 公里时速的铁路,蒙内铁路拉动了当地经济增长超过 2 个百分点,马拉维 600 眼水井成为润泽当地 15 万民众的"幸福井",中欧班列"钢铁驼队"助力中国与欧洲双向奔赴,"鲁班工坊"帮助塔吉克斯坦等国家年轻人掌握了职业技能,健康、绿色、数字、创新等领域合作蓬勃发展。

专栏 3　　中老铁路和雅万高铁
中老铁路全长 1035 公里,历时 11 年艰苦建设,挖通 167 座隧道,架设 301 座桥梁,于 2021 年 12 月 3 日开通运营。开建以来,带动当地就业超过 11 万人次,帮助沿线村民修建道路、水渠接近 2000 公里,为当地百姓带来了大量看得见、摸得着的利益。截至 2023 年 1 月 31 日,中老铁路累计开行旅客列车 20000 列,发送旅客 1030 万人次。 　　雅万高铁是东南亚第一条高速铁路,最高设计时速 350 公里,建成通车后雅加达至万隆之间的旅行时间由 3 个多小时缩短至 40 分钟。

这一倡议是经济合作倡议,不是搞地缘政治联盟或军事同盟,不针对谁也不排除谁;是开放包容进程,不是要关起门来搞"小圈子"或者"中国俱乐部";是中国同世界共享机遇、共谋发展的"百花园",不是要营造自己的后花园;是各方携手前进的阳光大道,不是某一方的私家小路,所有感兴趣的国家都可以加入进来,共同参与、共同合作、共同受益。

　　乌兹别克斯坦"安格连—帕普"铁路卡姆奇克隧道是乌兹别克斯坦有史以来第一条铁路隧道,也是共建"一带一路"倡议框架下中乌最重要的合作项目之一。2013 年 9 月 5 日正式开工,2016 年 2 月 25 日全隧贯通,中国建设者用时 900 天,造就了火车 900 秒穿行大山的奇迹。当地人感慨说:"项目全球招标时,欧美竞标公司给出施工期 5 年,中国公司仅用了 900 天,你们究竟怎么做到的?"

　　国际社会高度评价这一倡议,认为"一带一路"不是简单的一条路或一条经济带,而是让全人类共同进步的倡议,为各国共同发展开辟了新道路。"一带一路"倡议助推发展中国家现代化的进程,促进跨大洲协力合作进入新时代。

（二）落实"三大全球倡议"

　　人们普遍认识到,和平稳定、物质丰富、精神富有是人类社会发展的基本追求。发展是安全和文明的物质基础,安全是发展和文明的根本前提,文明是发展和安全的精神支撑。中国提出全球发展倡议、全球安全倡议、全球文明倡议,从发展、安全、文明三个维度指明人类社会前进方向,彼此呼应、相得益彰,成为推动构建人类命运共同体的重要依托,是解答事关人类和平与发展重大问题的中国方案。

　　——中国提出全球发展倡议,发出了聚焦发展、重振合作的时代强音,为破解发展难题、推进全球发展事业贡献中国力量。全球发展倡议,最根本的目标是加快落实联合国 2030 年可持续发展议程,最核心的要求是坚持以人民为中心,最重要的理念是倡导共建团结、平等、均衡、普惠的全球发展伙伴关系,最关键的举措在于坚持行动导向,推动实现更加强劲、绿色、健康的全球发展,共建全球发展共同体。

中国主持召开全球发展高层对话会,提出落实倡议的 32 项重要举措,包括创设"全球发展和南南合作基金",总额为 40 亿美元;启动中国—联合国粮农组织第三期南南合作信托基金,并将加大对中国—联合国和平与发展基金投入。两年来,全球发展倡议得到国际社会广泛响应,落实机制不断健全,务实合作逐步落地,共同应对粮食安全、减贫、能源安全等突出问题。全球发展促进中心顺利运转,全球发展倡议项目库不断扩大,200 多个合作项目开花结果。同时,中方发布《全球发展报告》,推动建立全球发展知识网络,为破解发展难题贡献了中国智慧。目前已有 100 多个国家和国际组织支持全球发展倡议,70 多个国家参与在联合国成立的"全球发展倡议之友小组"。

中国坚持以自身发展促进世界发展。深入贯彻新发展理念,着力推进高质量发展,推动构建新发展格局。14 亿多中国人整体迈进现代化社会,意味着几乎再造一个相当于现有发达国家规模总和的市场,为各国各方共享中国大市场提供更多机遇。中国开创性举办中国国际进口博览会,办好中国国际服务贸易交易会、中国进出口商品交易会、中国国际消费品博览会等重大展会。推动各国各方共享中国制度型开放机遇，稳步扩大规则、规制、管理、标准等制度型开放。实施外商投资法及相关配套法规、新版《鼓励外商投资产业目录》等，持续缩减外资准入负面清单，高质量建设自由贸易试验区，加快建设海南自由贸易港。

中国坚持合作共赢、共同发展。作为世界上最大的发展中国家和"全球南方"的一员，中国力所能及地为其他发展中国家提供援助，帮助受援国提高发展能力。积极开展国际交流合作，同世界粮食计划署、联合国开发计划署、儿童基金会、难民署、世界卫生组织、红十字国际委员会等近20个国际组织开展合作，在埃塞俄比亚、巴基斯坦、尼日利亚等近60个国家实施了130多个项目，聚焦"小而美、惠民生"，涵盖减贫、粮食安全、抗疫、气候变化等领域，受益人数超过3000万人。积极推动并全面落实二十国集团缓债倡议，在二十国集团缓债倡议中贡献最大，同19个非洲国家签署缓债协议或达成缓债共识，帮助非洲减缓债务压力。

中国坚定推动建设开放型世界经济。中国已经成为140多个国家和地区的主要贸易伙伴，同28个国家和地区签署了21个自贸协定。高质量实施《区域全面经济伙伴关系协定》，积极推进加入《全面与进步跨太平洋伙伴关系协定》和《数字经济伙伴关系协定》，扩大面向全球的高标准自由贸易区网络。推动人民币国际化，提升金融标准和国际化水平，更好实现中国和其他国家利益融合。

——坚持发展优先。将发展置于全球宏观政策框架的突出位置,加强主要经济体政策协调,保持连续性、稳定性、可持续性,构建更加平等均衡的全球发展伙伴关系,推动多边发展合作进程协同增效,加快落实联合国2030年可持续发展议程。

——坚持以人民为中心。在发展中保障和改善民生,保护和促进人权,做到发展为了人民、发展依靠人民、发展成果由人民共享,不断增强民众的幸福感、获得感、安全感,实现人的全面发展。

——坚持普惠包容。关注发展中国家特殊需求,通过缓债、发展援助等方式支持发展中国家尤其是困难特别大的脆弱国家,着力解决国家间和各国内部发展不平衡、不充分问题。

——坚持创新驱动。抓住新一轮科技革命和产业变革的历史性机遇,加速科技成果向现实生产力转化,打造开放、公平、公正、非歧视的科技发展环境,挖掘疫后经济增长新动能,携手实现跨越发展。

——坚持人与自然和谐共生。完善全球环境治理,积极应对气候变化,构建人与自然生命共同体。加快绿色低碳转型,实现绿色复苏发展。

——坚持行动导向。加大发展资源投入,重点推进减贫、粮食安全、抗疫和疫苗、发展筹资、气候变化和绿色发展、工业化、数字经济、互联互通等领域合作,构建全球发展共同体。

——中国提出全球安全倡议,目的是同国际社会一道,弘扬联合国宪章精神,倡导以团结精神适应深刻调整的国际格局,以共赢思维应对各种传统安全和非传统安全风险挑战,走出一条对话而不对抗、结伴而不结盟、共赢而非零和的新型安全之路。

2023年2月,中国正式发布《全球安全倡议概念文件》,进一步阐释了倡议核心理念与原则,明确了倡议重点合作方向,并就倡议合作平台和机制提出建议设想,展现了中国对维护世界和平的责任担当、对守护全球安全的坚定决心。全球安全倡议是国际公共产品,服务的是全世界人民的利益,维护的是全世界人民的安宁。

专栏6　全球安全倡议的六项主张
——坚持共同、综合、合作、可持续的安全观,共同维护世界和平和安全;
——坚持尊重各国主权、领土完整,不干涉别国内政,尊重各国人民自主选择的发展道路和社会制度;
——坚持遵守联合国宪章宗旨和原则,摒弃冷战思维,反对单边主义,不搞集团政治和阵营对抗;
——坚持重视各国合理安全关切,秉持安全不可分割原则,构建均衡、有效、可持续的安全架构,反对把本国安全建立在他国不安全的基础之上;
——坚持通过对话协商以和平方式解决国家间的分歧和争端,支持一切有利于和平解决危机的努力,不能搞双重标准,反对滥用单边制裁和"长臂管辖";
——坚持统筹维护传统领域和非传统领域安全,共同应对地区争端和恐怖主义、气候变化、网络安全、生物安全等全球性问题。

中国是维护世界和平的中流砥柱。坚持通过谈判协商方式处理同有关国家的领土主权和海洋权益争端,以谈判协商方式同14个陆上邻国中的12个国家和平解决陆地边界问题,并完成中越北部湾海域划界。忠实履行安理会常任理事国职责和使命,是联合国第二大会费国、联合国第二大维和摊款国和安理会常任理事国中第一大维和行动出兵国。30多年来,中国已派出维和人员5万余人次,赴20多个国家和地区参加联合国维和行动,成为联合国维和的关键力量。中方累计派出45批100余艘次舰艇在亚丁湾—索马里海域为7000余艘中外船只护航。

面对此起彼伏的热点问题,中国始终致力于发挥负责任大国作用,推动朝鲜半岛、巴勒斯坦、伊朗核、叙利亚、阿富汗等国际地区问题解决。在乌克兰问题上，中方积极劝和促谈，先后提出"四个应该""四个共同""三点思考"的主张，发布《关于政治解决乌克兰危机的中国立场》文件。派出中国政府欧亚事务特别代表，就政治解决乌克兰危机同有关各方广泛接触和交流。在中国斡旋下，沙特和伊朗实现历史性和解，为地区国家通过对话协商化解矛盾分歧、实现睦邻友好树立了典范，有力引领了中东地区"和解潮"。

中国积极致力于同各方开展反恐、生物安全、粮食安全等非传统安全领域合作，在二十国集团框架下提出国际粮食安全合作倡议，推动通过《金砖国家粮食安全合作战略》。正式启用中国—太平洋岛国防灾减灾合作中心，是中国在倡议框架下帮助发展中国家应对非传统安全挑战的又一有力行动。

专栏7　中方为政治解决乌克兰危机提出的重要主张

"四个应该"：各国主权、领土完整都应该得到尊重，联合国宪章宗旨和原则都应该得到遵守，各国合理安全关切都应该得到重视，一切有利于和平解决危机的努力都应该得到支持。

"四个共同"：国际社会应该共同支持一切致力于和平解决乌克兰危机的努力，呼吁有关各方保持理性和克制，尽快开展直接接触，为重启谈判创造条件；共同反对使用或威胁使用核武器，倡导核武器用不得、核战争打不得，防止亚欧大陆出现核危机；共同努力确保全球产业链供应链稳定，防止国际能源、粮食、金融等合作受到干扰，损害全球经济复苏特别是发展中国家经济财政稳定；共同为危机地区的平民过冬纾困，改善人道主义状况，防止出现更大规模人道主义危机。

"三点思考"：冲突战争没有赢家，复杂问题没有简单解决办法，大国对抗必须避免。

——中国提出全球文明倡议,共同倡导尊重世界文明多样性,共同倡导弘扬全人类共同价值,共同倡导重视文明传承和创新,共同倡导加强国际人文交流合作。全球文明倡议向全世界发出增进文明交流对话、在包容互鉴中促进人类文明进步的真挚呼吁,为推动构建人类命运共同体注入了精神动力。

中国召开中国共产党与世界政党高层对话会、中国共产党与世界政党领导人峰会、亚洲文明对话大会等,广泛开展双多边政党交流合作活动,推进形式多样的民间外交、城市外交、公共外交。持续深化与联合国教科文组织、联合国世界旅游组织合作,中国列入联合国教科文组织非物质文化遗产名录、名册项目达 43 个。

中国举办中国意大利文化和旅游年、中国希腊文化和旅游年、中国西班牙文化和旅游年等 30 余个大型文化和旅游年(节),推动金砖国家文化部长会议等 16 个多边交流合作机制和 25 个双边合作机制不断发展,持续举办"阿拉伯艺术节"、"相约北京"国际艺术节等主场文化活动,"欢乐春节"连续举办二十余年,2017 年在 130 余个国家举办约 2000 场活动,在全球举办"茶和天下"·雅集等品牌活动。推动"一带一路"文化和旅游交流,实施"文化丝路"计划,建立丝绸之路国际剧院、博物馆、艺术节、图书馆、美术馆联盟。同各国建立了约 3000 对友好城市(省州)关系。开展"你好! 中国"入境游推广工作。

　　——共同倡导尊重世界文明多样性,坚持文明平等、互鉴、对话、包容,以文明交流超越文明隔阂、文明互鉴超越文明冲突、文明包容超越文明优越。

　　——共同倡导弘扬全人类共同价值,和平、发展、公平、正义、民主、自由是各国人民的共同追求,要以宽广胸怀理解不同文明对价值内涵的认识,不将自己的价值观和模式强加于人,不搞意识形态对抗。

　　——共同倡导重视文明传承和创新,充分挖掘各国历史文化的时代价值,推动各国优秀传统文化在现代化进程中实现创造性转化、创新性发展。

　　——共同倡导加强国际人文交流合作,探讨构建全球文明对话合作网络,丰富交流内容,拓展合作渠道,促进各国人民相知相亲,共同推动人类文明发展进步。

　　国际社会积极评价"三大全球倡议",认为这体现了中国的全球视野和与日俱增的国际影响力,为当前人类面临的难题提供了综合性解决方案。全球发展倡议同联合国 2030 年可持续发展议程高度契合,尤其呼应了广大发展中国家追求发展的心声;全球安全倡议秉持共同安全理念,重视综合施策,坚持合作之道,寻求可持续安全,为应对国际安全挑战贡献智慧;全球文明倡议倡导所有国家尊重世界文明多样性,有助于促进不同文明交流互鉴。

(三) 与越来越多的国家和地区共同行动

　　中国提出一系列构建地区和双边层面命运共同体倡议,与有关各方共同努力,凝聚共识,拓展合作,为地区和平发展发挥建设性作用。

　　中非命运共同体是最早提出的区域命运共同体,坚持真诚友好、平等相待、义利相兼、以义为先，发展为民、务实高效，开放包容、兼收并蓄，成为中国与地区国家构建命运共同体的典范。中阿、中拉、中国—太平洋岛国等命运共同体建设蹄疾步稳，成为发展中国家团结合作、携手共进的生动写照。

周边命运共同体不断落地生根，中国—东盟命运共同体建设持续推进，中国—东盟合作在东亚区域合作中最富成果、最具活力、最有实质内容，双方政治互信不断提高，高层往来频密，建立了近50个领域和机构的对话合作机制。澜沧江—湄公河国家命运共同体建设不断取得新进展。上海合作组织命运共同体成果丰硕，中国—中亚命运共同体建设迈出坚实步伐，成功召开首届中国—中亚峰会、成立中国—中亚元首会晤机制，为地区和世界持久和平、共同繁荣作出积极贡献。

在双边层面，中国正在同越来越多的友好伙伴构建不同形式的命运共同体。中国同老挝、柬埔寨、缅甸、印度尼西亚、泰国、马来西亚、巴基斯坦、蒙古国、古巴、南非等国家就构建双边命运共同体发表行动计划、联合声明或达成重要共识，同中亚五国双边层面践行人类命运共同体全覆盖，理念更加深入人心，实践成果喷涌而出，实实在在地推动了当地发展建设，促进了民生福祉。

人类命运共同体是一个生机勃勃、开放包容的体系。不同地理区域、历史文化、社会制度、经济体量、发展阶段的国家，只要认同人类命运共同体的核心理念，就可以求同存异、和而不同、加强合作、谋求共赢。中国将同越来越多的地区和国家携手努力推动构建人类命运共同体,为推动各国发展事业和人类文明进步作出应有贡献。

（四）为各领域国际合作注入强劲动力

人类命运共同体理念直指当今世界面临的和平赤字、发展赤字、安全赤字、治理赤字,在卫生健康、气候变化、网络安全等领域提出丰富主张,转化为具体行动,为解决世界性难题作出了中国的独特贡献。

面对肆虐的新冠疫情,中国提出构建人类卫生健康共同体。中国站在国际抗疫合作"第一方阵",开展全球紧急人道主义救援,向150多个国家和国际组织提供力所能及的援助和支持。秉持疫苗公共产品"第一属性",最早承诺将新冠疫苗作为全球公共产品,最早支持疫苗研发知识产权豁免,最早同发展中国家开展疫苗合作生产。担当疫苗公平分配"第一梯队",以自己的坚定承诺和实际行动为人类健康事业贡献中国力量。

面对混乱失序的网络空间治理,中国提出构建网络空间命运共同体。积极参与联合国网络安全进程,支持联合国在网络空间全球治理中发挥核心作用。举办世界互联网大会,成立世界互联网大会国际组织,为全球互联网共享共治搭建平台。发起《全球数据安全倡议》,分别同阿拉伯国家联盟、中亚五国发表《中阿数据安全合作倡议》及《"中国+中亚五国"数据安全合作倡议》,推动全球数字治理规则制定。推动完善深海、极地、外空等新疆域的治理规则,确保各国权利共享、责任共担。在制定新疆域治理新规则时，充分反映新兴市场国家和发展中国家的利益和诉求。

面对核安全全球治理的根本性问题，中国提出打造核安全命运共同体，坚定维护国际核不扩散体系，促进和平利用核能，秉持理性、协调、并进的核安全观。为应对不断上升的核冲突风险，中国推动五核国领导人共同发表联合声明，重申"核战争打不赢，也打不得"。积极倡导全面禁止和彻底销毁核武器，是唯一公开承诺不首先使用核武器、不对无核武器国家和无核武器区使用或威胁使用核武器的核国家。

面对日益复杂的海上问题，中国提出构建海洋命运共同体，始终致力于通过对话协商和平解决领土主权和海洋权益争端。同东盟国家签署和全面有效落实《南海各方行为宣言》，持续推进"南海行为准则"磋商。提出共建蓝色经济伙伴关系，加强海上互联互通建设。坚持走搁置争议、共同开发的合作之路，同海上邻国积极探讨资源共同开发。

面对日益严峻的全球气候挑战，中国先后提出构建人与自然生命共同体、地球生命共同体等重要理念。中国积极推动经济发展转型，承诺力争 2030 年前实现碳达峰、努力争取 2060 年前实现碳中和，构建完成碳达峰碳中和"1+N"政策体系。中国建成了世界最大的清洁发电网络，贡献了本世纪以来全球 25% 的新增绿化面积，以年均 3% 的能源消费增速支撑了年均超过 6% 的经济增长，成为全球水电、风电、太阳能发电装机容量最多的国家。积极参与全球环境治理,倡导国际社会全面有效落实《联合国气候变化框架公约》及其《巴黎协定》,坚持"共同但有区别的责任"原则。尽己所能帮助发展中国家提高应对气候变化能力,大力支持发展中国家能源绿色低碳发展,与39个发展中国家签署46份应对气候变化南南合作谅解备忘录,为120多个发展中国家培训约2300名气候变化领域的官员和技术人员。作为《生物多样性公约》第十五次缔约方大会(COP15)主席国,全力推动会议成功举行,率先出资成立昆明生物多样性基金,推动达成"昆明—蒙特利尔全球生物多样性框架"。

专栏9　一路"象"北

2020年3月,栖息在云南省西双版纳国家级自然保护区的野生亚洲象"旅行团"一路"象"北,途经云南省多地,游历约一年半后,在当地政府、民众的关爱和精心看护下平安南返家园。这场亚洲象的集体迁移不仅在国内屡屡登上热搜,也吸引了全世界网民的目光,引起了国内外关于构建人与自然和谐共生的地球家园的热烈讨论。

无论是应对眼下的危机,还是共创美好的未来,各国都需要同舟共济、团结合作。面对深刻而宏阔的百年大变局,中国提出构建人类命运共同体,呼吁各国秉持命运与共理念,充分沟通协商,共担治理责任,形成应对全球性问题的广泛共识和一致行动,为人类迈向光明未来注入信心和动力。

结　束　语

凡益之道，与时偕行。人类命运共同体理念的提出和实践，已经在国际上凝聚起团结合作的广泛共识，汇聚起应对挑战的强大合力。展望未来，这一理念必将焕发出愈发鲜明的真理力量、更为彰显的引领作用和超越时空的思想伟力，为人类社会开辟共同发展、长治久安、持续繁荣的美好愿景。人类的前途是光明的，但光明的前途不会自动到来。构建人类命运共同体既是一个美好愿景，也是一个历史过程，需要一代又一代人接力跑才能实现。

实现这个美好愿景，信心和决心是首要。和平、发展、合作、共赢的时代潮流不可阻挡，构建人类命运共同体是世界各国人民前途所在。同时，构建人类命运共同体不可能一蹴而就，也不可能一帆风顺，需要付出长期艰苦努力，需要锲而不舍、驰而不息相向而行。不能因现实复杂而放弃梦想，也不能因理想遥远而放弃追求。

实现这个美好愿景，格局与胸怀是基础。大时代需要大格局，大格局呼唤大胸怀。面对共同挑战，任何人、任何国家都无法独善其身，人类只有和衷共济、和合共生这一条出路。各国只有加强协调和合作，把本国人民利益同世界各国人民利益统一起来，才能共同朝着构建人类命运共同体的方向前行。

实现这个美好愿景，担当与行动是关键。大道至简，实干为要。

构建人类命运共同体有赖于各国共同行动。各国应有以天下为己任的担当精神,积极做行动派、不做观望者,加强对话、凝聚共识、促进和平、推动发展、完善治理,开展全球行动、全球应对、全球合作。

道阻且长,行则将至;行而不辍,未来可期。前方的路纵然曲折,但也充满希望。只要世界各国团结起来,共行天下大道,向着构建人类命运共同体的正确方向,一起来规划,一起来实践,一点一滴坚持努力,日积月累不懈奋斗,就一定能够建设一个持久和平、普遍安全、共同繁荣、开放包容、清洁美丽的世界,共同创造人类更加美好的未来!

共建"一带一路"：构建人类命运共同体的重大实践

（2023 年 10 月）

中华人民共和国
国务院新闻办公室

前　言

两千多年前,我们的先辈怀着友好交往的朴素愿望,穿越草原沙漠,开辟出联通亚欧非的陆上丝绸之路,开辟了人类文明史上的大交流时代。一千多年前,我们的先辈扬帆远航,穿越惊涛骇浪,闯荡出连接东西方的海上丝绸之路,开启了人类文明交融新时期。

古丝绸之路绵亘万里,延续千年,不仅是一条通商易货之路,也是一条文明交流之路,为人类社会发展进步作出了重大贡献。上世纪 80 年代以来,联合国和一些国家先后提出欧亚大陆桥设想、丝绸之路复兴计划等,反映了各国人民沟通对话、交流合作的共同愿望。

2013 年 3 月,习近平主席提出构建人类命运共同体理念;9 月和 10 月,先后提出共建“丝绸之路经济带”和“21 世纪海上丝绸之路”。共建“一带一路”倡议,创造性地传承弘扬古丝绸之路这一人类历史文明发展成果,并赋予其新的时代精神和人文内涵,为构建人类命运共同体提供了实践平台。

10 年来,在各方的共同努力下,共建“一带一路”从中国倡议走向国际实践,从理念转化为行动,从愿景转变为现实,从谋篇布局的“大写意”到精耕细作的“工笔画”,取得实打实、沉甸甸的成就,成为深受欢迎的国际公共产品和国际合作平台。

10年来,共建"一带一路"不仅给相关国家带来实实在在的利益,也为推进经济全球化健康发展、破解全球发展难题和完善全球治理体系作出积极贡献,开辟了人类共同实现现代化的新路径,推动构建人类命运共同体落地生根。

　　为介绍共建"一带一路"10年来取得的成果,进一步增进国际社会的认识理解,推进共建"一带一路"高质量发展,让"一带一路"惠及更多国家和人民,特发布此白皮书。

一、源自中国属于世界

当今世界正处于百年未有之大变局,人类文明发展面临越来越多的问题和挑战。中国着眼人类前途命运和整体利益,因应全球发展及各国期待,继承和弘扬丝路精神这一人类文明的宝贵遗产,提出共建"一带一路"倡议。这一倡议,连接着历史、现实与未来,源自中国、面向世界、惠及全人类。

(一) 根植历史,弘扬丝路精神

公元前140年左右的中国汉代,张骞从长安出发,打通了东方通往西方的道路,完成了"凿空之旅"。中国唐宋元时期,陆上和海上丝绸之路共同发展,成为连接东西方的重要商道。15世纪初的明代,郑和七次远洋航海,促进了海上丝绸之路商贸往来。千百年来,古丝绸之路犹如川流不息的"大动脉",跨越尼罗河流域、底格里斯河和幼发拉底河流域、印度河和恒河流域、黄河和长江流域,跨越埃及文明、巴比伦文明、印度文明、中华文明的发祥地,跨越佛教、基督教、伊斯兰教信众的汇集地,跨越不同国度和肤色人民的聚集地,促进了亚欧大陆各国互联互通,推动了东西方文明交流互鉴,创造了地区大发展大繁荣,积淀了以和平合作、开放包容、互学互鉴、互利共赢为核心的丝路精神。

作为东西方交流合作的象征,千年古丝绸之路深刻昭示:只要坚持团结互信、平等互利、包容互鉴、合作共赢,不同民族、不同信仰、不同文化背景的国家完全可以共享和平、共同发展。丝路精神与中华民族历来秉持的天下大同、万国咸宁的美好理念相契合,与中国人一贯的协和万邦、亲仁善邻、立己达人的处世之道相符合,与当今时代和平、发展、合作、共赢的时代潮流相适应。

中国共产党是胸怀天下的大党,中国是坚持和平发展的大国。共建"一带一路"在新的时代背景下弘扬丝路精神,唤起人们对过往时代的美好记忆,激发各国实现互联互通的热情。共建"一带一路"既是向历史致敬,再现古丝绸之路陆上"使者相望于道,商旅不绝于途"的盛况、海上"舶交海中,不知其数"的繁华;更是向未来拓路,从古丝绸之路和丝路精神中汲取智慧和力量,沿着历史的方向继续前进,更好地融通中国梦和世界梦,实现各国人民对文明交流的渴望、对和平安宁的期盼、对共同发展的追求、对美好生活的向往。

(二) 因应现实,破解发展难题

发展是解决一切问题的总钥匙,经济全球化为世界经济发展提供了强大动力。500 多年前,在古丝绸之路中断半个多世纪后,大航海时代来临,根本改变了人类社会的发展格局。近代以来,随着科技革命和生产力的发展,经济全球化成为历史潮流。特别是 20 世纪 90

年代后,经济全球化快速发展,促进了贸易大繁荣、投资大便利、人员大流动、技术大发展,为人类社会发展进步作出重要贡献。但是,少数国家主导的经济全球化,并没有实现普遍普惠的发展,而是造成富者愈富、贫者愈贫,发达国家和发展中国家以及发达国家内部的贫富差距越来越大。很多发展中国家在经济全球化中获利甚微甚至丧失自主发展能力,难以进入现代化的轨道。个别国家大搞单边主义、保护主义、霸权主义,经济全球化进程遭遇逆流,世界经济面临衰退风险。全球经济增长动能不足、全球经济治理体系不完善、全球经济发展失衡等问题,迫切需要解决;世界经济发展由少数国家主导、经济规则由少数国家掌控、发展成果被少数国家独享的局面,必须得到改变。

共建"一带一路"既是为了中国的发展,也是为了世界的发展。经济全球化的历史大势不可逆转,各国不可能退回到彼此隔绝、闭关自守的时代。但是,经济全球化在形式和内容上面临新的调整,应该朝着更加开放、包容、普惠、平衡、共赢的方向发展。中国是经济全球化的受益者,也是贡献者。中国积极参与经济全球化进程,在与世界的良性互动中实现了经济快速发展,成功开辟和推进了中国式现代化,拓展了发展中国家走向现代化的路径选择。中国经济快速增长和改革开放持续推进,为全球经济稳定和增长、开放型世界经济发展提供了重要动力。中国是经济全球化的坚定支持者、维护者。共建"一带一路"在理念、举措、目标等方面与联合国2030年可持续发展议程高度契合,既是中国扩大开放的重大举措,旨在以更高水平开放促进更高质量发展,与世界分享中国发展机遇;也是破解全球发展难题的中国方案,旨在推动各国共同走向现代化,推进更有活力、更加包容、更可持续的经济全球化进程,让发展成果更多更公平地惠及各国人民。

（三） 开创未来,让世界更美好

随着世界多极化、经济全球化、社会信息化、文化多样化深入发展,各国相互联系和彼此依存比过去任何时候都更频繁、更紧密,人类越来越成为你中有我、我中有你的命运共同体。同时,全球和平赤字、发展赤字、安全赤字、治理赤字有增无减,地区冲突、军备竞赛、粮食安全、恐怖主义、网络安全、气候变化、能源危机、重大传染性疾病、人工智能等传统和非传统安全问题交叉叠加,人类共同生活的这颗美丽星球面临严重威胁。面对层出不穷的全球性问题和挑战,人类社会需要新的思想和理念,需要更加公正合理、更趋平衡、更具韧性、更为有效的全球治理体系。建设一个什么样的世界,人类社会如何走向光明的未来,攸关每个国家、每个人,必须回答好这一时代课题,作出正确的历史抉择。

作为负责任的发展中大国,中国从人类共同命运和整体利益出发,提出构建人类命运共同体,建设一个持久和平、普遍安全、共同繁荣、开放包容、清洁美丽的世界,为人类未来勾画了新的美好愿景。共建"一带一路"以构建人类命运共同体为最高目标,并为实现这一目标搭建了实践平台、提供了实现路径,推动美好愿景不断落实落地,是完善全球治理的重要公共产品。共建"一带一路"跨越不同地域、不同文明、不同发展阶段,超越意识形态分歧和社会制度差异,推动各国共享机遇、共谋发展、共同繁荣,打造政治互信、经济融合、文化包容的利益共同体、责任共同体和命运共同体,成为构建人类命运共同体的生动实践。共建"一带一路"塑造了人们对世界的新认知新想象,开创了国际交往的新理念新范式,推动全球治理体系朝着更加公正合理的方向发展,引领人类社会走向更加美好的未来。

二、铺就共同发展繁荣之路

共建"一带一路"秉持人类命运共同体理念,倡导并践行适应时代发展的全球观、发展观、安全观、开放观、合作观、文明观、治理观,为世界各国走向共同发展繁荣提供了理念指引和实践路径。

(一) 原则:共商、共建、共享

共建"一带一路"以共商共建共享为原则,积极倡导合作共赢理念与正确义利观,坚持各国都是平等的参与者、贡献者、受益者,推动实现经济大融合、发展大联动、成果大共享。

共建"一带一路"坚持共商原则,不是中国一家的独奏,而是各方的大合唱,倡导并践行真正的多边主义,坚持大家的事由大家商量着办,充分尊重各国发展水平、经济结构、法律制度和文化传统的差异,强调平等参与、沟通协商、集思广益,不附带任何政治或经济条件,以自愿为基础,最大程度凝聚共识。各国无论大小、强弱、贫富,都是平等参与,都可以在双多边合作中积极建言献策。各方加强双边或多边沟通和磋商,共同探索、开创性设立诸多合作机制,为不同发展阶段的经济体开展对话合作、参与全球治理提供共商合作平台。

共建"一带一路"坚持共建原则,不是中国的对外援助计划和地缘政治工具,而是联动发展的行动纲领;不是现有地区机制的替代,而是与其相互对接、优势互补。坚持各方共同参与,深度对接有关国家和区域发展战略,充分发掘和发挥各方发展潜力和比较优势,共同开创发展新机遇、谋求发展新动力、拓展发展新空间,实现各施所长、各尽所能,优势互补、联动发展。通过双边合作、第三方市场合作、多边合作等多种形式,鼓励更多国家和企业深入参与,形成发展合力。遵循市场规律,通过市场化运作实现参与各方的利益诉求,企业是主体,政府主要发挥构建平台、创立机制、政策引导的作用。中国发挥经济体量和市场规模巨大,基础设施建设经验丰富,装备制造能力强、质量好、性价比高以及产业、资金、技术、人才、管理等方面的综合优势,在共建"一带一路"中发挥了引领作用。

共建"一带一路"坚持共享原则,秉持互利共赢的合作观,寻求各方利益交汇点和合作最大公约数,对接各方发展需求、回应人民现实诉求,实现各方共享发展机遇和成果,不让任何一个国家掉队。共建国家大多属于发展中国家,各方聚力解决发展中国家基础设施落后、产业发展滞后、工业化程度低、资金和技术缺乏、人才储备不足等短板问题,促进经济社会发展。中国坚持道义为先、义利并举,向共建国家提供力所能及的帮助,真心实意帮助发展中国家加快发展,同时,以共建"一带一路"推动形成陆海内外联动、东西双向互济的全面开放新格局,建设更高水平开放型经济新体制,加快构建以国内大循环为主体、国内国际双循环相互促进的新发展格局。

（二）理念：开放、绿色、廉洁

共建"一带一路"始终坚守开放的本色、绿色的底色、廉洁的亮色，坚持开放包容，推进绿色发展，以零容忍态度打击腐败，在高质量发展的道路上稳步前行。

共建"一带一路"是大家携手前行的阳光大道，不是某一方面的私家小路，不排除、也不针对任何一方，不打地缘博弈小算盘，不搞封闭排他"小圈子"，也不搞基于意识形态标准划界的小团体，更不搞军事同盟。从亚欧大陆到非洲、美洲、大洋洲，无论什么样的政治体制、历史文化、宗教信仰、意识形态、发展阶段，只要有共同发展的意愿都可以参与其中。各方以开放包容为导向，坚决反对保护主义、单边主义、霸权主义，共同推进全方位、立体化、网络状的大联通格局，探索开创共赢、共担、共治的合作新模式，构建全球互联互通伙伴关系，建设和谐共存的大家庭。

共建"一带一路"顺应国际绿色低碳发展趋势，倡导尊重自然、顺应自然、保护自然，尊重各方追求绿色发展的权利，响应各方可持续发展需求，形成共建绿色"一带一路"共识。各方积极开展"一带一路"绿色发展政策对话，分享和展示绿色发展理念和成效，增进绿色发展共识和行动，深化绿色基建、绿色能源、绿色交通、绿色金融等领域务实合作，努力建设资源节约、绿色低碳的丝绸之路，为保护生态环境、实现碳达峰和碳中和、应对气候变化作出重要贡献。中国充分发挥在可再生能源、节能环保、清洁生产等领域优势,运用中国技术、产品、经验等,推动绿色"一带一路"合作蓬勃发展。

共建"一带一路"将廉洁作为行稳致远的内在要求和必要条件,始终坚持一切合作在阳光下运行。各方一道完善反腐败法治体系建设和机制建设,深化反腐败法律法规对接,务实推进国际反腐合作,坚决反对各类腐败和其他国际犯罪活动,持续打击商业贿赂行为,让资金、项目在廉洁中高效运转,让各项合作更好地落地开展,让"一带一路"成为风清气正的廉洁之路。2019年4月,中国与有关国家、国际组织以及工商学术界代表共同发起了《廉洁丝绸之路北京倡议》,呼吁各方携手共商、共建、共享廉洁丝绸之路。中国"走出去"企业坚持合规守法经营,既遵守中国的法律,也遵守所在国当地法律和国际规则,提升海外廉洁风险防范能力,加强项目监督管理和风险防控,打造良心工程、干净工程、精品工程;中央企业出台重点领域合规指南868件,制定岗位合规职责清单5000多项,中央企业、中央金融企业及分支机构制定和完善境外管理制度1.5万余项。2020年11月,60余家深度参与"一带一路"建设的中方企业共同发起《"一带一路"参与企业廉洁合规倡议》。

(三)目标:高标准、可持续、惠民生

共建"一带一路"以高标准、可持续、惠民生为目标,努力实现更高合作水平、更高投入效益、更高供给质量、更高发展韧性,推动高质

量共建"一带一路"不断走深走实。

共建"一带一路"引入各方普遍支持的规则标准,推动企业在项目建设、运营、采购、招投标等环节执行普遍接受的国际规则标准,以高标准推动各领域合作和项目建设。倡导对接国际先进规则标准,打造高标准自由贸易区,实行更高水平的贸易投资自由化便利化政策,畅通人员、货物、资金、数据安全有序流动,实现更高水平互联互通和更深层次交流合作。坚持高标准、接地气,对标国际一流、追求高性价比,先试点、再推广,倡导参与各方采用适合自己的规则标准、走符合自身国情的发展道路。中国成立高规格的推进"一带一路"建设领导机构,发布一系列政策文件,推动共建"一带一路"顶层设计不断完善、务实举措不断落地。

共建"一带一路"对接联合国 2030 年可持续发展议程,走经济、社会、环境协调发展之路,努力消除制约发展的根源和障碍,增强共建国家自主发展的内生动力,推动各国实现持久、包容和可持续的经济增长,并将可持续发展理念融入项目选择、实施、管理等各个方面。遵循国际惯例和债务可持续原则,不断完善长期、稳定、可持续、风险可控的投融资体系,积极创新投融资模式、拓宽投融资渠道,形成了稳定、透明、高质量的资金保障体系,确保商业和财政上的可持续性。没有任何一个国家因为参与共建"一带一路"合作而陷入债务危机。

共建"一带一路"坚持以人民为中心,聚焦消除贫困、增加就业、改善民生,让合作成果更好惠及全体人民。各方深化公共卫生、减贫减灾、绿色发展、科技教育、文化艺术、卫生健康等领域合作,促进政党、社会组织、智库和青年、妇女及地方交流协同并进,着力打造接地气、聚人心的民生工程,不断增强民众的获得感和幸福感。中国积极推进对外援助和惠及民生的"小而美"项目建设,足迹从亚洲到非洲,从拉丁美洲到南太平洋,一条条公路铁路,一座座学校医院,一片片农田村舍,助力共建国家减贫脱贫、增进民生福祉。

(四) 愿景:造福世界的幸福路

作为一个发展的倡议、合作的倡议、开放的倡议,共建"一带一路"追求的是发展、崇尚的是共赢、传递的是希望,目的是增进理解信任、加强全方位交流,进而促进共同发展、实现共同繁荣。

和平之路。和平是发展的前提,发展是和平的基础。共建"一带一路"超越以实力抗衡为基础的丛林法则、霸权秩序,摒弃你输我赢、你死我活的零和逻辑,跳出意识形态对立、地缘政治博弈的冷战思维,走和平发展道路,致力于从根本上解决永久和平和普遍安全问题。各国尊重彼此主权、尊严、领土完整,尊重彼此发展道路和社会制度,尊重彼此核心利益和重大关切。中国作为发起方,积极推动构建相互尊重、公平正义、合作共赢的新型国际关系,打造对话不对抗、结伴不结盟的伙伴关系,推动各方树立共同、综合、合作、可持续的新安全观,营造共建共享的安全格局,构建和平稳定的发展环境。

繁荣之路。共建"一带一路"不走剥削掠夺的殖民主义老路,不做凌驾于人的强买强卖,不搞"中心—边缘"的依附体系,更不转嫁问题、以邻为壑、损人利己，目标是实现互利共赢、共同发展繁荣。各方紧紧抓住发展这个最大公约数，发挥各自资源和潜能优势，激发各自增长动力，增强自主发展能力，共同营造更多发展机遇和空间，推动形成世界经济增长新中心、新动能，带动世界经济实现新的普惠性增长，推动全球发展迈向平衡协调包容新阶段。

开放之路。共建"一带一路"超越国界阻隔、超越意识形态分歧、超越发展阶段区别、超越社会制度差异、超越地缘利益纷争，是开放包容的合作进程；不是另起炉灶、推倒重来，而是对现有国际机制的有益补充和完善。各方坚持多边贸易体制的核心价值和基本原则，共同打造开放型合作平台，维护和发展开放型世界经济，创造有利于开放发展的环境，构建公正、合理、透明的国际经贸投资规则体系，推进合作共赢、合作共担、合作共治的共同开放，促进生产要素有序流动、资源高效配置、市场深度融合，促进贸易和投资自由化便利化，维护全球产业链供应链稳定畅通，建设开放、包容、普惠、平衡、共赢的经济全球化。

创新之路。创新是推动发展的重要力量。共建"一带一路"坚持创新驱动发展，把握数字化、网络化、智能化发展机遇，探索新业态、新技术、新模式，探寻新的增长动能和发展路径，助力各方实现跨越式发展。各方共同加强数字基础设施互联互通，推进数字丝绸之路建设，加强科技前沿领域创新合作，促进科技同产业、科技同金融深度融合，优化创新环境，集聚创新资源，推动形成区域协同创新格局，缩小数字鸿沟，为共同发展注入强劲动力。

文明之路。共建"一带一路"坚持平等、互鉴、对话、包容的文明观,弘扬和平、发展、公平、正义、民主、自由的全人类共同价值,以文明交流超越文明隔阂,以文明互鉴超越文明冲突,以文明共存超越文明优越,推动文明间和而不同、求同存异、互学互鉴。各方积极建立多层次人文合作机制,搭建更多合作平台,开辟更多合作渠道,密切各领域往来,推动不同国家间相互理解、相互尊重、相互信任,更好地凝聚思想和价值共识,实现人类文明创新发展。

三、促进全方位多领域互联互通

共建"一带一路"围绕互联互通,以基础设施"硬联通"为重要方向,以规则标准"软联通"为重要支撑,以共建国家人民"心联通"为重要基础,不断深化政策沟通、设施联通、贸易畅通、资金融通、民心相通,不断拓展合作领域,成为当今世界范围最广、规模最大的国际合作平台。

(一)政策沟通广泛深入

政策沟通是共建"一带一路"的重要保障。中国与共建国家、国际组织积极构建多层次政策沟通交流机制,在发展战略规划、技术经济政策、管理规则和标准等方面发挥政策协同效应,共同制订推进区域合作的规划和措施,为深化务实合作注入了"润滑剂"和"催化剂",共建"一带一路"日益成为各国交流合作的重要框架。

战略对接和政策协调持续深化。在全球层面,2016年11月,在第71届联合国大会上,193个会员国一致赞同将"一带一路"倡议写入联大决议;2017年3月,联合国安理会通过第2344号决议,呼吁通过"一带一路"建设等加强区域经济合作;联合国开发计划署、世界卫生组织等先后与中国签署"一带一路"合作协议。在世界贸易组织,中国推动完成《投资便利化协定》文本谈判,将在超过 110 个国家和地区建立协调统一的投资管理体系,促进"一带一路"投资合作。在区域和多边层面,共建"一带一路"同联合国 2030 年可持续发展议程、《东盟互联互通总体规划 2025》、东盟印太展望、非盟《2063 年议程》、欧盟欧亚互联互通战略等有效对接,支持区域一体化进程和全球发展事业。在双边层面,共建"一带一路"与俄罗斯欧亚经济联盟建设、哈萨克斯坦"光明之路"新经济政策、土库曼斯坦"复兴丝绸之路"战略、蒙古国"草原之路"倡议、印度尼西亚"全球海洋支点"构想、菲律宾"多建好建"规划、越南"两廊一圈"、南非"经济重建和复苏计划"、埃及苏伊士运河走廊开发计划、沙特"2030 愿景"等多国战略实现对接。截至 2023 年 6 月底,中国与五大洲的 150 多个国家、30 多个国际组织签署了 200 多份共建"一带一路"合作文件,形成一大批标志性项目和惠民生的"小而美"项目。

政策沟通长效机制基本形成。以元首外交为引领,以政府间战略沟通为支撑,以地方和部门间政策协调为助力,以企业、社会组织等开展项目合作为载体,建立起多层次、多平台、多主体的常规性沟通渠道。中国成功举办两届"一带一路"国际合作高峰论坛,为各参与国家和国际组织深化交往、增进互信、密切来往提供了重要平台。2017 年的第一届"一带一路"国际合作高峰论坛,29 个国家的元首和政府首脑出席,140 多个国家和 80 多个国际组织的 1600 多名代表参会,形成了 5 大类、279 项务实成果。2019 年的第二届"一带一路"国际合作高峰论坛,38 个国家的元首和政府首脑及联合国秘书长、国际货币基金组织总裁等 40 位领导人出席圆桌峰会,超过 150 个国家、92 个国际组织的 6000 余名代表参会,形成了 6 大类、283 项务实成果。

多边合作不断推进。在共建"一带一路"框架下,中外合作伙伴发起成立了 20 余个专业领域多边对话合作机制,涵盖铁路、港口、能源、金融、税收、环保、减灾、智库、媒体等领域,参与成员数量持续提升。共建国家还依托中国—东盟(10+1)合作、中非合作论坛、中阿合作论坛、中拉论坛、中国—太平洋岛国经济发展合作论坛、中国—中东欧国家合作、世界经济论坛、博鳌亚洲论坛、中国共产党与世界政党领导人峰会等重大多边合作机制平台,不断深化务实合作。

规则标准对接扎实推进。标准化合作水平不断提升,截至 2023 年 6 月底,中国已与巴基斯坦、俄罗斯、希腊、埃塞俄比亚、哥斯达黎加等 65 个国家标准化机构以及国际和区域组织签署了 107 份标准化合作文件,促进了民用航空、气候变化、农业食品、建材、电动汽车、油气管道、物流、小水电、海洋和测绘等多领域标准国际合作。"一带一路"标准信息平台运行良好,标准化概况信息已覆盖 149 个共建国家,可提供 59 个国家、6 个国际和区域标准化组织的标准化题录信息精准检索服务,在共建国家间架起了标准互联互通的桥梁。中国标准外文版供给能力持续提升,发布国家标准外文版近 1400 项、行业标准外文版 1000 多项。2022 年 5 月,亚非法协在香港设立区域仲裁中心,积极为共建"一带一路"提供多元纠纷解决路径。中国持续加强与俄罗斯、马来西亚、新加坡等 22 个国家和地区的跨境会计审计监管合作,为拓展跨境投融资渠道提供制度保障。

（二） 设施联通初具规模

设施联通是共建"一带一路"的优先领域。共建"一带一路"以"六廊六路多国多港"为基本架构,加快推进多层次、复合型基础设施网络建设,基本形成"陆海天网"四位一体的互联互通格局,为促进经贸和产能合作、加强文化交流和人员往来奠定了坚实基础。

经济走廊和国际通道建设卓有成效。共建国家共同推进国际骨干通道建设,打造连接亚洲各次区域以及亚欧非之间的基础设施网络。中巴经济走廊方向,重点项目稳步推进,白沙瓦—卡拉奇高速公路(苏库尔至木尔坦段)、喀喇昆仑公路二期(赫韦利扬—塔科特段)、拉合尔轨道交通橙线项目竣工通车,萨希瓦尔、卡西姆港、塔尔、胡布等电站保持安全稳定运营,默拉直流输电项目投入商业运营,卡洛特水电站并网发电,拉沙卡伊特别经济区进入全面建设阶段。新亚欧大陆桥经济走廊方向,匈塞铁路塞尔维亚贝尔格莱德—诺维萨德段于2022年3月开通运营,匈牙利布达佩斯—克莱比奥段启动轨道铺设工作;克罗地亚佩列沙茨跨海大桥迎来通车一周年;双西公路全线贯通;黑山南北高速公路顺利建成并投入运营。中国—中南半岛经济走廊方向,中老铁路全线建成通车且运营成效良好,黄金运输通道作用日益彰显;作为中印尼共建"一带一路"的旗舰项目,时速350公里的雅万高铁开通运行;中泰铁路一期(曼谷—呵叻)签署线上工程合同,土建工程已开工11个标段(其中1个标段已完工)。中蒙俄经济走廊方向,中俄黑河公路桥、同江铁路桥通车运营,中俄东线天然气管道正式通气,中蒙俄中线铁路升级改造和发展可行性研究正式启动。中国—中亚—西亚经济走廊方向,中吉乌公路运输线路实现常态化运行,中国—中亚天然气管道运行稳定,哈萨克斯坦北哈州粮油专线与中欧班列并网运行。孟中印缅经济走廊方向,中缅原油和天然气管道建成投产,中缅铁路木姐—曼德勒铁路完成可行性研究,曼德勒—皎漂铁路启动可行性研究,中孟友谊大桥、多哈扎里至科克斯巴扎尔铁路等项目建设取得积极进展。在非洲,蒙内铁路、亚吉铁路等先后通车运营,成为拉动东非乃至整个非洲国家纵深发展的重要通道。

专栏1　蒙内铁路促进肯尼亚经济社会发展

肯尼亚蒙内铁路东起东非第一大港口蒙巴萨,经首都内罗毕,向西北延伸到苏苏瓦站,全长592公里,采用中国标准、技术、装备和运营管理,是中肯共建"一带一路"的重要成果之一,被誉为友谊之路、合作共赢之路、繁荣发展之路和生态环保之路。

蒙内铁路是肯尼亚独立以来最大的基础设施建设项目,自2017年开通运营以来,对肯尼亚经济社会发展和民生改善产生了积极影响,也大幅降低了东非内陆地区的产品经蒙巴萨港出口的物流成本。截至2023年8月31日,蒙内铁路日均开行6列旅客列车,累计发送旅客1100万人次,平均上座率保持在95%以上;日均开行17列货运列车,累计发送货物2800万吨。据肯尼亚政府估计,蒙内铁路对肯尼亚经济增长的贡献率达2%。

在蒙内铁路建设和运营过程中,中国企业注重技术转移,对当地员工进行培训。建设期间,对超过3万名肯尼亚员工进行了入职培训,每年选拔当地青年赴中国参加培训和学历教育。自开通运营以来,采取"因人因专业因岗位"的培训方式,已为肯尼亚培养专业技术成熟人员1152名。

海上互联互通水平不断提升。共建国家港口航运合作不断深化,货物运输效率大幅提升:希腊比雷埃夫斯港年货物吞吐量增至500万标箱以上,跃升为欧洲第四大集装箱港口、地中海领先集装箱大港;巴基斯坦瓜达尔港共建取得重大进展,正朝着物流枢纽和产业基地的目标稳步迈进;缅甸皎漂深水港项目正在开展地勘、环社评等前期工作;斯里兰卡汉班托塔港散杂货年吞吐量增至120.5万吨;意大利瓦多集装箱码头开港运营,成为意大利第一个半自动化码头;尼日利亚莱基深水港项目建成并投入运营,成为中西非地区重要的现代化深水港。"丝路海运"网络持续拓展,截至2023年6月底,"丝路海运"航线已通达全球43个国家的117个港口,300多家国内外知名航运公司、港口企业、智库等加入"丝路海运"联盟。"海上丝绸之路海洋环境预报保障系统"持续业务化运行,范围覆盖共建国家100多个城市。

"空中丝绸之路"建设成效显著。共建国家间航空航线网络加快拓展,空中联通水平稳步提升。中国已与104个共建国家签署双边航空运输协定,与57个共建国家实现空中直航,跨境运输便利化水平不断提高。中国企业积极参与巴基斯坦、尼泊尔、多哥等共建国家民航基础设施领域合作,助力当地民航事业发展。中国民航"一带一路"合作平台于2020年8月正式成立,共建国家民航交流合作机制和平台更加健全。新冠疫情期间,以河南郑州—卢森堡为代表的"空中丝绸之路"不停飞、不断航,运送大量抗疫物资,在中欧间发挥了"空中生命线"的作用,为维护国际产业链供应链稳定作出了积极贡献。

　　国际多式联运大通道持续拓展。中欧班列、中欧陆海快线、西部陆海新通道、连云港—霍尔果斯新亚欧陆海联运等国际多式联运稳步发展。中欧班列通达欧洲 25 个国家的 200 多个城市,86 条时速 120 公里的运行线路穿越亚欧腹地主要区域,物流配送网络覆盖欧亚大陆;截至 2023 年 6 月底,中欧班列累计开行 7.4 万列,运输近 700 万标箱,货物品类达 5 万多种,涉及汽车整车、机械设备、电子产品等 53 大门类,合计货值超 3000 亿美元。中欧陆海快线从无到有,成为继传统海运航线、陆上中欧班列之外中欧间的第三条贸易通道,2022 年全通道运输总箱量超过 18 万标箱,火车开行 2600 余列。西部陆海新通道铁海联运班列覆盖中国中西部 18 个省(区、市),货物流向通达 100 多个国家的 300 多个港口。

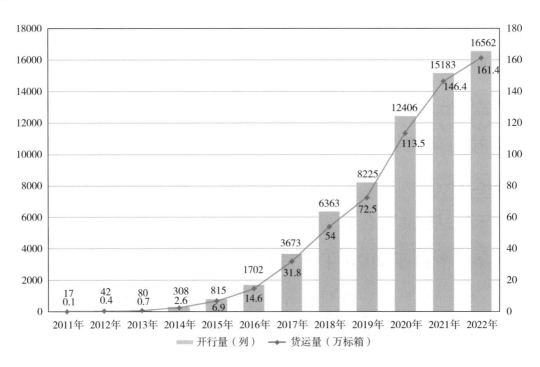

图 1　2011—2022 年中欧班列开行量及货运量

（三）贸易畅通便捷高效

贸易投资合作是共建"一带一路"的重要内容。共建国家着力解决贸易投资自由化便利化问题，大幅消除贸易投资壁垒，改善区域内和各国营商环境，建设自由贸易区，拓宽贸易领域、优化贸易结构，拓展相互投资和产业合作领域，推动建立更加均衡、平等和可持续的贸易体系，发展互利共赢的经贸关系，共同做大做好合作"蛋糕"。

贸易投资规模稳步扩大。2013—2022年，中国与共建国家进出口总额累计19.1万亿美元，年均增长6.4%；与共建国家双向投资累计超过3800亿美元，其中中国对外直接投资超过2400亿美元；中国在共建国家承包工程新签合同额、完成营业额累计分别达到2万亿美元、1.3万亿美元。2022年，中国与共建国家进出口总额近2.9万亿美元，占同期中国外贸总值的45.4%，较2013年提高了6.2个百分点；中国民营企业对共建国家进出口总额超过1.5万亿美元，占同期中国与共建国家进出口总额的53.7%。

贸易投资自由化便利化水平不断提升。共建国家共同维护多边主义和自由贸易，努力营造密切彼此间经贸关系的良好制度环境，在工作制度对接、技术标准协调、检验结果互认、电子证书联网等方面取得积极进展。截至2023年8月底，80多个国家和国际组织参与中国发起的《"一带一路"贸易畅通合作倡议》。中国与28个国家和地区签署21个自贸协定；《区域全面经济伙伴关系协定》（RCEP）于

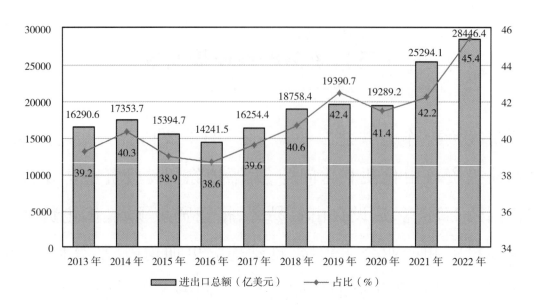

图 2　2013—2022 年中国与共建国家进出口总额及其占中国外贸总值比重

2022 年 1 月 1 日正式生效,是世界上人口规模和经贸规模最大的自贸区,与共建"一带一路"覆盖国家和地区、涵盖领域和内容等方面相互重叠、相互补充,在亚洲地区形成双轮驱动的经贸合作发展新格局。中国还积极推动加入《全面与进步跨太平洋伙伴关系协定》(CPTPP)和《数字经济伙伴关系协定》(DEPA)。中国与 135 个国家和地区签订了双边投资协定;与 112 个国家和地区签署了避免双重征税协定(含安排、协议);与 35 个共建国家实现"经认证的经营者"(AEO)互认;与 14 个国家签署第三方市场合作文件。中国与新加坡、巴基斯坦、蒙古国、伊朗等共建国家建立了"单一窗口"合作机制、签署了海关检验检疫合作文件,有效提升了口岸通关效率。

贸易投资平台作用更加凸显。中国国际进口博览会是全球首个以进口为主题的国家级展会,已连续成功举办五届,累计意向成交额近 3500 亿美元,约 2000 个首发首展商品亮相,参与国别与参与主体多元广泛,成为国际采购、投资促进、人文交流、开放合作、全球共享的国际公共平台。中国进出口商品交易会、中国国际服务贸易交易会、中国国际投资贸易洽谈会、中国国际消费品博览会、全球数字贸易博览会、中非经贸博览会、中国—阿拉伯国家博览会、中俄博览会、中国—中东欧国家博览会、中国—东盟博览会、中国—亚欧博览会等重点展会影响不断扩大,有力促进了共建国家之间的经贸投资合作。中国香港特别行政区成功举办了 8 届"一带一路"高峰论坛,中国澳门特别行政区成功举办了 14 届国际基础设施投资与建设高峰论坛,在助力共建"一带一路"经贸投资合作中发挥了重要作用。

产业合作深入推进。共建国家致力于打造协同发展、互利共赢的合作格局,有力促进了各国产业结构升级、产业链优化布局。共建国家共同推进国际产能合作,深化钢铁、有色金属、建材、汽车、工程机械、资源能源、农业等传统行业合作,探索数字经济、新能源汽车、核能与核技术、5G 等新兴产业合作,与有意愿的国家开展三方、多方市场合作,促进各方优势互补、互惠共赢。截至 2023 年 6 月底,中国已同 40 多个国家签署了产能合作文件,中国国际矿业大会、中国—东盟矿业合作论坛等成为共建国家开展矿业产能合作的重要平台。上海合作组织农业技术交流培训示范基地助力共建"一带一路"农业科技发展,促进国家间农业领域经贸合作。中国与巴基斯坦合作建设的卡拉奇核电站 K2、K3 两台"华龙一号"核电机组建成投运,中国与哈萨克斯坦合资的乌里宾核燃料元件组装厂成功投产,中国—

东盟和平利用核技术论坛为共建国家开展核技术产业合作、助力民生和经济发展建立了桥梁和纽带。中国企业与共建国家政府、企业合作共建的海外产业园超过 70 个,中马、中印尼"两国双园"及中白工业园、中阿(联酋)产能合作示范园、中埃(及)·泰达苏伊士经贸合作区等稳步推进。

(四) 资金融通日益多元

资金融通是共建"一带一路"的重要支撑。共建国家及有关机构积极开展多种形式的金融合作,创新投融资模式、拓宽投融资渠道、丰富投融资主体、完善投融资机制,大力推动政策性金融、开发性金融、商业性金融、合作性金融支持共建"一带一路",努力构建长期、稳定、可持续、风险可控的投融资体系。

金融合作机制日益健全。中国国家开发银行推动成立中国—中东欧银联体、中国—阿拉伯国家银联体、中国—东盟银联体、中日韩—东盟银联体、中非金融合作银联体、中拉开发性金融合作机制等多边金融合作机制,中国工商银行推动成立"一带一路"银行间常态化合作机制。截至 2023 年 6 月底,共有 13 家中资银行在 50 个共建国家设立 145 家一级机构,131 个共建国家的 1770 万家商户开通银联卡业务,74 个共建国家开通银联移动支付服务。"一带一路"创新发展中心、"一带一路"财经发展研究中心、中国—国际货币基金组织联合能力建设中心相继设立。中国已与 20 个共建国家签署双边本币互换协议,在 17 个共建国家建立人民币清算安排,人民币跨境支付系统的参与者数量、业务量、影响力逐步提升,有效促进了贸易投资便利化。金融监管合作和交流持续推进,中国银保监会(现国家金融监督管理总局)、证监会与境外多个国家的监管机构签署监管合作谅解备忘录,推动建立区域内监管协调机制,促进资金高效配置,强化风险管控,为各类金融机构及投资主体创造良好投资条件。

投融资渠道平台不断拓展。中国出资设立丝路基金,并与相关国家一道成立亚洲基础设施投资银行。丝路基金专门服务于"一带一路"建设,截至 2023 年 6 月底,丝路基金累计签约投资项目 75 个,承诺投资金额约 220.4 亿美元;亚洲基础设施投资银行已有 106 个成员,批准 227 个投资项目,共投资 436 亿美元,项目涉及交通、能源、公共卫生等领域,为共建国家基础设施互联互通和经济社会可持续发展提供投融资支持。中国积极参与现有各类融资安排机制,与世界银行、亚洲开发银行等国际金融机构签署合作备忘录,与国际金融机构联合筹建多边开发融资合作中心,与欧洲复兴开发银行加强第三方市场投融资合作,与国际金融公司、非洲开发银行等开展联合融资,有效撬动市场资金参与。中国发起设立中国—欧亚经济合作基金、中拉合作基金、中国—中东欧投资合作基金、中国—东盟投资合作基金、中拉产能合作投资基金、中非产能合作基金等国际经济合作基金,有效拓展了共建国家投融资渠道。中国国家开发银行、中国进出口银行分别设立"一带一路"专项贷款,集中资源加大对共建"一带一路"的融资支持。截至 2022 年底,中国国家开发银行已直接为 1300 多个"一带一路"项目提供了优质金融服务,有效发挥了开发性金融引领、汇聚境内外各类资金共同参与共建"一带一路"的融资先导作用;中国进出口银行"一带一路"贷款余额达 2.2 万亿元,覆盖超过 130 个共建国家,贷款项目累计拉动投资 4000 多亿美元,带动贸易超过 2 万亿美元。中国信保充分发挥出口信用保险政策性职能,积极为共建"一带一路"提供综合保障。

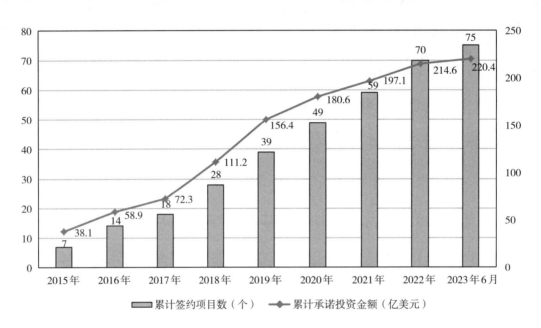

图 3 2015 年以来丝路基金历年累计签约项目数和承诺投资金额

投融资方式持续创新。基金、债券等多种创新模式不断发展,共建"一带一路"金融合作水平持续提升。中国证券行业设立多个"一带一路"主题基金,建立"一带一路"主题指数。2015 年 12 月,中国证监会正式启动境外机构在交易所市场发行人民币债券("熊猫债")试点,截至 2023 年 6 月底,交易所债券市场已累计发行"熊猫债"99 只,累计发行规模 1525.4 亿元;累计发行"一带一路"债券 46 只,累计发行规模 527.2 亿元。绿色金融稳步发展。2019 年 5 月,中国工商银行发行同时符合国际绿色债券准则和中国绿色债券准则的首只"一带一路"银行间常态化合作机制（BRBR）绿色债券；截至2022年底，已有40多家全球大型机构签署了《"一带一路"绿色投资原则》；2023年6月，中国进出口银行发行推进共建"一带一路"国际合作和支持共建"一带一路"基础设施建设主题金融债。中国境内证券期货交易所与共建国家交易所稳步推进股权、产品、技术等方面务实合作，积极支持哈萨克斯坦阿斯塔纳国际交易所、巴基斯坦证券交易所、孟加拉国达卡证券交易所等共建或参股交易所市场发展。

债务可持续性不断增强。按照平等参与、利益共享、风险共担的原则，中国与28个国家共同核准《"一带一路"融资指导原则》，推动共建国家政府、金融机构和企业重视债务可持续性，提升债务管理能力。中国借鉴国际货币基金组织和世界银行低收入国家债务可持续性分析框架，结合共建国家实际情况制定债务可持续性分析工具，发布《"一带一路"债务可持续性分析框架》，鼓励各方在自愿基础上使用。中国坚持以经济和社会效益为导向，根据项目所在国需求及实际情况为项目建设提供贷款，避免给所在国造成债务风险和财政负担；投资重点领域是互联互通基础设施项目以及共建国家急需的民生项目，为共建国家带来了有效投资，增加了优质资产，增强了发展动力。许多智库专家和国际机构研究指出，几乎所有"一带一路"项目都是由东道国出于本国经济发展和民生改善而发起的，其遵循的是经济学逻辑，而非地缘政治逻辑。

（五）民心相通基础稳固

民心相通是共建"一带一路"的社会根基。共建国家传承和弘扬丝绸之路友好合作精神，广泛开展文化旅游合作、教育交流、媒体和智库合作、民间交往等，推动文明互学互鉴和文化融合创新，形成了多元互动、百花齐放的人文交流格局，夯实了共建"一带一路"的民意基础。

文化旅游合作丰富多彩。截至 2023 年 6 月底，中国已与 144 个共建国家签署文化和旅游领域合作文件。中国与共建国家共同创建合作平台，成立了丝绸之路国际剧院联盟、博物馆联盟、艺术节联盟、图书馆联盟和美术馆联盟，成员单位达 562 家，其中包括 72 个共建国家的 326 个文化机构。中国不断深化对外文化交流，启动实施"文化丝路"计划，广泛开展"欢乐春节""你好！中国""艺汇丝路"等重点品牌活动。中国与文莱、柬埔寨、希腊、意大利、马来西亚、俄罗斯及东盟等共同举办文化年、旅游年，与共建国家互办文物展、电影节、艺术节、图书展、音乐节等活动及图书广播影视精品创作和互译互播，实施"一带一路"主题舞台艺术作品创作推广项目、"一带一路"国际美术工程和文化睦邻工程，扎实推进亚洲文化遗产保护行动。中国在 44 个国家设立 46 家海外中国文化中心，其中共建国家 32 家；在 18 个国家设立 20 家旅游办事处，其中共建国家 8 家。

教育交流合作广泛深入。中国发布《推进共建"一带一路"教育行动》,推进教育领域国际交流与合作。截至2023年6月底,中国已与45个共建国家和地区签署高等教育学历学位互认协议。中国设立"丝绸之路"中国政府奖学金,中国地方省份、中国香港特别行政区、中国澳门特别行政区和高校、科研机构也面向共建国家设立了奖学金。中国院校在132个共建国家办有313所孔子学院、315所孔子课堂;"汉语桥"夏令营项目累计邀请100余个共建国家近5万名青少年来华访学,支持143个共建国家10万名中文爱好者线上学习中文、体验中国文化。中国院校与亚非欧三大洲的20多个共建国家院校合作建设一批鲁班工坊。中国与联合国教科文组织连续7年举办"一带一路"青年创意与遗产论坛及相关活动;合作设立丝绸之路青年学者资助计划,已资助24个青年学者研究项目。中国政府原子能奖学金项目已为26个共建国家培养了近200名和平利用核能相关专业的硕博士研究生。共建国家还充分发挥"一带一路"高校战略联盟、"一带一路"国际科学组织联盟等示范带动作用,深化人才培养和科学研究国际交流合作。

媒体和智库合作成果丰硕。媒体国际交流合作稳步推进,共建国家连续成功举办6届"一带一路"媒体合作论坛,建设"丝路电视国际合作共同体"。中国—阿拉伯国家广播电视合作论坛、中非媒体合作论坛、中国—柬埔寨广播电视定期合作会议、中国—东盟媒体合作论坛、澜湄视听周等双多边合作机制化开展,亚洲—太平洋广播联盟、阿拉伯国家广播联盟等国际组织活动有声有色,成为凝聚共建国家共识的重要平台。中国与共建国家媒体共同成立"一带一路"

新闻合作联盟,积极推进国际传播"丝路奖"评选活动,截至 2023 年 6 月底,联盟成员单位已增至 107 个国家的 233 家媒体。智库交流更加频繁,"一带一路"国际合作高峰论坛咨询委员会于 2018 年成立,"一带一路"智库合作联盟已发展亚洲、非洲、欧洲、拉丁美洲合作伙伴合计 122 家,16 家中外智库共同发起成立"一带一路"国际智库合作委员会。

民间交往不断深入。民间组织以惠民众、利民生、通民心为行动目标,不断织密合作网。在第二届"一带一路"国际合作高峰论坛民心相通分论坛上,中国民间组织国际交流促进会等中外民间组织共同发起"丝路一家亲"行动,推动中外民间组织建立近 600 对合作伙伴关系,开展 300 余个民生合作项目,"深系澜湄""国际爱心包裹""光明行"等品牌项目产生广泛影响。60 余个共建国家的城市同中国多个城市结成 1000 余对友好城市。72 个国家和地区的 352 家民间组织结成丝绸之路沿线民间组织合作网络,开展民生项目和各类活动 500 余项,成为共建国家民间组织开展交流合作的重要平台。

(六)新领域合作稳步推进

共建国家发挥各自优势,不断拓展合作领域、创新合作模式,推动健康、绿色、创新、数字丝绸之路建设取得积极进展,国际合作空间更加广阔。

卫生健康合作成效显著。共建国家积极推进"健康丝绸之路"

建设,推动构建人类卫生健康共同体,建立紧密的卫生合作伙伴关系。截至 2023 年 6 月底,中国已与世界卫生组织签署《关于"一带一路"卫生领域合作的谅解备忘录》,与 160 多个国家和国际组织签署卫生合作协议,发起和参与中国—非洲国家、中国—阿拉伯国家、中国—东盟卫生合作等 9 个国际和区域卫生合作机制。中国依托"一带一路"医学人才培养联盟、医院合作联盟、卫生政策研究网络、中国—东盟健康丝绸之路人才培养计划(2020—2022)等,为共建国家培养数万名卫生管理、公共卫生、医学科研等专业人才,向 58 个国家派出中国医疗队,赴 30 多个国家开展"光明行",免费治疗白内障患者近万名,多次赴南太岛国开展"送医上岛"活动,与湄公河流域的国家、中亚国家、蒙古国等周边国家开展跨境医疗合作。新冠疫情暴发以后,中国向 120 多个共建国家提供抗疫援助,向 34 个国家派出38 批抗疫专家组,同 31 个国家发起"一带一路"疫苗合作伙伴关系倡议,向共建国家提供 20 余亿剂疫苗,与 20 余个国家开展疫苗生产合作,提高了疫苗在发展中国家的可及性和可负担性。中国与 14 个共建国家签订传统医药合作文件,8 个共建国家在本国法律法规体系内对中医药发展予以支持,30 个中医药海外中心投入建设,百余种中成药在共建国家以药品身份注册上市。

绿色低碳发展取得积极进展。中国与共建国家、国际组织积极建立绿色低碳发展合作机制,携手推动绿色发展、共同应对气候变化。中国先后发布《关于推进绿色"一带一路"建设的指导意见》《关于推进共建"一带一路"绿色发展的意见》等,提出 2030 年共建"一带一路"绿色发展格局基本形成的宏伟目标。中国与联合国环境规划署签署《关于建设绿色"一带一路"的谅解备忘录（2017—2022）》，与 30 多个国家及国际组织签署环保合作协议，与 31 个国家共同发起"一带一路"绿色发展伙伴关系倡议，与超过 40 个国家的 150 多个合作伙伴建立"一带一路"绿色发展国际联盟，与 32 个国家建立"一带一路"能源合作伙伴关系。中国承诺不再新建境外煤电项目，积极构建绿色金融发展平台和国际合作机制，与共建国家开展生物多样性保护合作研究，共同维护海上丝绸之路生态安全，建设"一带一路"生态环保大数据服务平台和"一带一路"环境技术交流与转移中心，实施绿色丝路使者计划。中国实施"一带一路"应对气候变化南南合作计划，与 39 个共建国家签署 47 份气候变化南南合作谅解备忘录，与老挝、柬埔寨、塞舌尔合作建设低碳示范区，与 30 多个发展中国家开展 70 余个减缓和适应气候变化项目，培训了 120 多个国家3000 多人次的环境管理人员和专家学者。2023 年 5 月，中国进出口银行联合国家开发银行、中国信保等 10 余家金融机构发布《绿色金融支持"一带一路"能源转型倡议》，呼吁有关各方持续加大对共建国家能源绿色低碳转型领域支持力度。

科技创新合作加快推进。共建国家加强创新合作，加快技术转移和知识分享，不断优化创新环境、集聚创新资源，积极开展重大科技合作和共同培养科技创新人才，推动科技创新能力提升。2016 年10 月，中国发布《推进"一带一路"建设科技创新合作专项规划》；2017 年 5 月，"一带一路"科技创新行动计划正式启动实施，通过联合研究、技术转移、科技人文交流和科技园区合作等务实举措，提升共建国家的创新能力。截至 2023 年 6 月底，中国与 80 多个共建国家签署《政府间科技合作协定》，"一带一路"国际科学组织联盟（ANSO）成员单位达 58 家。2013 年以来，中国支持逾万名共建国家青年科学家来华开展短期科研工作和交流，累计培训共建国家技术和管理人员 1.6 万余人次，面向东盟、南亚、阿拉伯国家、非洲、拉美等区域建设了 9 个跨国技术转移平台，累计帮助 50 多个非洲国家建成 20 多个农业技术示范中心，在农业、新能源、卫生健康等领域启动建设 50 余家"一带一路"联合实验室。中国与世界知识产权组织签署《加强"一带一路"知识产权合作协议》及修订与延期补充协议，共同主办两届"一带一路"知识产权高级别会议，并发布加强知识产权合作的《共同倡议》和《联合声明》；与 50 余个共建国家和国际组织建立知识产权合作关系，共同营造尊重知识价值的创新和营商环境。

"数字丝绸之路"建设亮点纷呈。共建国家加强数字领域的规则标准联通，推动区域性数字政策协调，携手打造开放、公平、公正、非歧视的数字发展环境。截至 2022 年底，中国已与 17 个国家签署"数字丝绸之路"合作谅解备忘录，与 30 个国家签署电子商务合作谅解备忘录，与 18 个国家和地区签署《关于加强数字经济领域投资合作的谅解备忘录》，提出并推动达成《全球数据安全倡议》《"一带一路"数字经济国际合作倡议》《中国—东盟关于建立数字经济合作伙伴关系的倡议》《中阿数据安全合作倡议》《"中国+中亚五国"数据安全合作倡议》《金砖国家数字经济伙伴关系框架》等合作倡议，牵头制定《跨境电商标准框架》。积极推进数字基础设施互联互通，加快建设数字交通走廊，多条国际海底光缆建设取得积极进展，构建起130套跨境陆缆系统，广泛建设5G基站、数据中心、云计算中心、智慧城市等，对传统基础设施如港口、铁路、道路、能源、水利等进行数字化升级改造，"中国—东盟信息港"、"数字化中欧班列"、中阿网上丝绸之路等重点项目全面推进，"数字丝路地球大数据平台"实现多语言数据共享。空间信息走廊建设成效显著，中国已建成连接南亚、非洲、欧洲和美洲的卫星电信港，中巴（西）地球资源系列遥感卫星数据广泛应用于多个国家和领域，北斗三号全球卫星导航系统为中欧班列、船舶海运等领域提供全面服务；中国与多个共建国家和地区共同研制和发射通信或遥感卫星、建设卫星地面接收站等空间基础设施，依托联合国空间科技教育亚太区域中心（中国）为共建国家培养大量航天人才，积极共建中海联合月球和深空探测中心、中阿空间碎片联合观测中心、澜湄对地观测数据合作中心、中国东盟卫星应用信息中心、中非卫星遥感应用合作中心，利用高分卫星16米数据共享服务平台、"一带一路"典型气象灾害分析及预警平台、自然资源卫星遥感云服务平台等服务于更多共建国家。

专栏2　"丝路电商"拓展经贸合作新渠道

以跨境电商、海外仓为代表的国际贸易新业态和新模式蓬勃发展，为全球消费者提供更为便利的服务和更加多元的选择，正在有力推动全球贸易创新。"丝路电商"是中国充分发挥电子商务技术应用、模式创新和市场规模等优势，与共建国家拓展经贸合作领域、共享数字发展机遇的重要举措。截至2023年9月底，中国已与五大洲

30个国家建立双边电子商务合作机制,在中国—中东欧国家、中国—中亚机制等框架下建立了电子商务多边合作机制。"双品网购节丝路电商专场""非洲好物网购节"等特色活动成效显著,线上国家馆促进伙伴国优质特色产品对接中国市场。"云上大讲堂"已为80多个国家开展线上直播培训,成为共建国家共同提升数字素养的创新实践。"丝路电商"不断丰富合作内涵,提升合作水平,已经成为多双边经贸合作的新平台、高质量共建"一带一路"的新亮点。

四、为世界和平与发展注入正能量

10年来,共建"一带一路"取得显著成效,开辟了世界经济增长的新空间,搭建了国际贸易和投资的新平台,提升了有关国家的发展能力和民生福祉,为完善全球治理体系拓展了新实践,为变乱交织的世界带来更多确定性和稳定性。共建"一带一路",既发展了中国,也造福了世界。

(一)为共建国家带来实实在在的好处

发展是人类社会的永恒主题。共建"一带一路"聚焦发展这个根本性问题,着力解决制约发展的短板和瓶颈,为共建国家打造新的经济发展引擎,创建新的发展环境和空间,增强了共建国家的发展能力,提振了共建国家的发展信心,改善了共建国家的民生福祉,为解决全球发展失衡问题、推动各国共同走向现代化作出贡献。

激活共建国家发展动力。10年来,共建"一带一路"着力解决制约大多数发展中国家互联互通和经济发展的主要瓶颈,实施一大批基础设施建设项目,推动共建国家在铁路、公路、航运、管道、能源、通信及基本公共服务基础设施建设方面取得长足进展,改善了当地的生产生活条件和发展环境,增强了经济发展造血功能。一些建设周期长、服务长远发展的工程项目,就像播下的种子,综合效益正在逐步展现出来。基础设施的联通,有效降低了共建国家参与国际贸易的成本,提高了接入世界经济的能力和水平,激发了更大发展潜力、更强发展动力。亚洲开发银行的研究表明,内陆国家基础设施贸易成本每降低10%,其出口将增加20%。产业产能合作促进了共建国家产业结构升级,提高了工业化、数字化、信息化水平,促进形成具有竞争力的产业体系,增强了参与国际分工合作的广度和深度,带来了更多发展机遇、更大发展空间。中国积极开展应急管理领域国际合作,先后派出救援队赴尼泊尔、莫桑比克、土耳其等国家开展地震、洪灾等人道主义救援救助行动,向汤加、马达加斯加等国家提供紧急人道主义物资援助和专家技术指导。

增强共建国家减贫能力。发展中国家仍面临粮食问题。中国积极参与全球粮农治理,与相关国家发布《共同推进"一带一路"建设农业合作的愿景与行动》,与近90个共建国家和国际组织签署了100余份农渔业合作文件,与共建国家农产品贸易额达1394亿美元,向70多个国家和地区派出2000多名农业专家和技术人员,向多个国家推广示范菌草、杂交水稻等1500多项农业技术,帮助亚洲、非洲、南太平洋、拉美和加勒比等地区推进乡村减贫,促进共建国家现代农业发展和农民增收。促进就业是减贫的重要途径。在共建"一带一路"过程中,中国与相关国家积极推进产业园区建设,引导企业通过开展高水平产业合作为当地居民创造就业岗位,实现了"一人就业,全家脱贫"。麦肯锡公司的研究报告显示,中国企业在非洲雇员本地化率达 89%,有效带动了本地人口就业。世界银行预测,到 2030 年,共建"一带一路"相关投资有望使共建国家 760 万人摆脱极端贫困、3200 万人摆脱中度贫困。

专栏 3　菌草扶贫得到世界普遍赞誉

中国的菌草技术实现了光、热、水三大农业资源综合高效利用,植物、动物、菌物三物循环生产,经济、社会、环境三大效益结合,有利于生态、粮食、能源安全。

2001 年,菌草技术作为官方援助项目首次在巴布亚新几内亚落地。20 多年来,中国已举办 270 多期菌草技术国际培训班,为 106 个国家培训 1 万多名学员,在亚非拉和南太平洋地区的 13 个国家建立了菌草技术试验示范中心或基地。如今,菌草技术已经在 100 多个国家落地生根,给当地青年和妇女创造了数十万个绿色就业机会。巴新前内阁部长给女儿起名"菌草"。莱索托人民创作歌颂菌草的民歌,至今仍在传唱。2017 年,菌草技术项目被列为"中国—联合国和平与发展基金"重点项目,为国际减贫事业贡献更多中国智慧和中国方案。

民生项目成效显著。维修维护桥梁,解决居民出行难题;打出水井,满足村民饮水需求;安装路灯,照亮行人夜归之路……一个个"小而美""惠而实"的民生工程、民心工程,帮助当地民众解决了燃眉之急、改善了生活条件,增进了共建国家的民生福祉,为各国人民带来实实在在的获得感、幸福感、安全感。10 年来,中国企业先后在共建国家实施了 300 多个"爱心助困""康复助医""幸福家园"项目,援建非洲疾病预防控制中心总部、巴基斯坦瓜达尔博爱医疗急救中心,帮助喀麦隆、埃塞俄比亚、吉布提等国解决民众饮水难问题,等等。"丝路一家亲"行动民生合作项目涵盖扶贫救灾、人道救援、环境保护、妇女交流合作等 20 多个领域,产生了广泛影响。

　　2020 年 1 月起,中国通过实施"澜湄甘泉行动计划——澜湄国家农村供水安全保障技术示范"项目,在柬埔寨、老挝和缅甸等国典型区域开展农村安全供水示范工程,显著提升当地农村供水工程建设水平和供水安全保障能力,在推动澜湄国家实现联合国 2030 年可持续发展目标中的"水与卫生"指标、促进民生改善等方面发挥了积极作用。截至 2022 年 12 月,在澜湄国家共计建成农村供水安全保障技术示范点 62 处,为 7000 多名居民提供饮水安全保障,累计为澜湄国家农村供水相关管理部门和工程运行管理人员提供 400 余人次培训交流机会。

（二）为经济全球化增添活力

　　在逆全球化思潮不断涌动的背景下,共建"一带一路"致力于实现世界的互联互通和联动发展,进一步打通经济全球化的大动脉,畅通信息流、资金流、技术流、产品流、产业流、人员流,推动更大范围、更高水平的国际合作,既做大又分好经济全球化的"蛋糕",努力构建普惠平衡、协调包容、合作共赢、共同繁荣的全球发展格局。

　　增强全球发展动能。共建"一带一路"将活跃的东亚经济圈、发达的欧洲经济圈、中间广大腹地经济发展潜力巨大的国家联系起来,进一步拉紧同非洲、拉美大陆的经济合作网络,推动形成一个欧亚大陆与太平洋、印度洋和大西洋完全连接、陆海一体的全球发展新格局,在更广阔的经济地理空间中拓展国际分工的范围和覆盖面,扩大世界市场,最终促进世界经济新的增长。同时,共建"一带一路"通过基础设施互联互通带来了国际投资的催化剂效果,激发了全球对基础设施投资的兴趣和热情,既有利于共建国家经济成长和增益发展,又有效解决国际公共产品供给不足问题,为世界经济增长提供持续动力。

深化区域经济合作。共建"一带一路"依托基础设施互联互通,推动各国全方位多领域联通,由点到线再到面,逐步放大发展辐射效应,推动各国经济政策协调、制度机制对接,创新合作模式,开展更大范围、更高水平、更深层次的区域合作,共同打造开放、包容、均衡、普惠的区域经济合作框架,促进经济要素有序自由流动、资源高效配置和市场深度融合,提升国家和地区间经济贸易关联性、活跃度和共建国家在全球产业链供应链价值链中的整体位置。各国充分运用自身要素禀赋,增强彼此之间产业链的融合性、互动性、协调性,推动产业优势互补,提升分工效率,共同推动产业链升级;打破贸易壁垒和市场垄断,释放消费潜力,推动跨境消费,共同扩大市场规模,形成区域大市场;通过产业合作中的技术转移与合作,建立技术互动和彼此依存关系,共同提高创新能力,推动跨越式发展。

促进全球贸易发展。共建"一带一路"有计划、有步骤地推进交通、信息等基础设施建设和贸易投资自由化便利化,消除了共建国家内部、跨国和区域间的交通运输瓶颈及贸易投资合作障碍,极大提升了对外贸易、跨境物流的便捷度和国内国际合作效率,构建起全方位、多层次、复合型的贸易畅通网络,推动建立全球贸易新格局,对全球贸易发展发挥了重要促进作用。同时,共建"一带一路"增强了参与国家和地区对全球优质资本的吸引力,提升了其在全球跨境直接投资中的地位。其中,2022 年东南亚跨境直接投资流入额占全球比重达到 17.2%,较 2013 年上升了 9 个百分点;流入哈萨克斯坦的外商直接投资规模同比增速高达 83%,为历史最高水平。世界银行《"一带一路"经济学:交通走廊的机遇与风险》研究报告显示,共建"一带一路"倡议提出之前,六大经济走廊的贸易低于其潜力的30%,外国直接投资低于其潜力的 70%;共建"一带一路"实施以来,仅通过基础设施建设,就可使全球贸易成本降低 1.8%,使中国—中亚—西亚经济走廊上的贸易成本降低 10%,为全球贸易便利化和经济增长作出重要贡献;将使参与国贸易增长 2.8%—9.7%、全球贸易增长 1.7%—6.2%、全球收入增加 0.7%—2.9%。

专栏 5　中老铁路助力老挝"陆锁国"变"陆联国"

　　中老铁路是连接中国昆明市和老挝万象市的电气化铁路,是共建"一带一路"倡议提出后第一个以中方为主投资建设、共同运营并与中国铁路网直接联通的跨国铁路,全长 1035 公里,于 2021 年 12 月 3 日正式开通运营。2023 年 4 月 13 日,中老铁路开行国际旅客列车,昆明至万象间动车直达。

　　作为泛亚铁路中线重要组成部分,中老铁路改变了老挝交通运输格局,实现了老挝从"陆锁国"到"陆联国"的夙愿,推动了交通、投资、物流、旅游等多方面的发展,为老挝及沿线地区经济发展注入新动力。截至 2023 年 8 月 31 日,中老铁路累计发送旅客 2079 万人次、货物 2522 万吨,成为联通内外、辐射周边、双向互济、安全高效的国际黄金大通道。

　　中老铁路是民心工程,也是廉洁示范工程。中老两党两国领导人就"将中老铁路建成廉洁之路"达成重要共识,两国纪检监察部门建立政府层面的监督协调机制,参建企业始终把廉洁建设与工程建设同谋划、同部署、同实施、同检查,加强制度机制建设和过程管控,创新反腐败合作方式,共同推进中老铁路廉洁建设,将中老铁路建设成为友谊之路、廉洁之路、幸福之路。

世界银行《从内陆到陆联：释放中老铁路联通潜力》研究报告称，从长期看，中老铁路将使老挝总收入提升21%；到2030年，每年沿中老铁路途经老挝的过境贸易将达到390万吨，包括从海运转向铁路的150万吨。

维护全球供应链稳定。共建"一带一路"致力于建设高效互联的国际大通道，对维护全球供应链稳定畅通具有重要作用。新冠疫情期间，港口和物流公司纷纷取消或减少船舶和货运的服务，以海运为主的全球供应链受到严重冲击。中欧班列作为共建"一带一路"的拳头产品，有效提升了亚欧大陆铁路联通水平和海铁、公铁、空铁等多式联运发展水平，开辟了亚欧大陆供应链的新通道，叠加"关铁通"、铁路快通等项目合作及通关模式创新，为保障全球经济稳定运行作出重要贡献。多个国际知名物流协会公开表示，中欧班列为世界提供了一种能够有效缓解全球供应链紧张难题、增强国际物流保障能力的可靠物流方案。

（三）为完善全球治理提供新方案

治理赤字是全球面临的严峻挑战。共建"一带一路"坚持真正的多边主义，践行共商共建共享的全球治理观，坚持对话而不对抗、拆墙而不筑墙、融合而不脱钩、包容而不排他，为国家间交往提供了新的范式，推动全球治理体系朝着更加公正合理的方向发展。

全球治理理念得到更多认同。共商共建共享等共建"一带一路"的核心理念被写入联合国、中非合作论坛等国际组织及机制的重要文件。人类命运共同体理念深入人心,中老命运共同体、中巴命运共同体等双边命运共同体越来越多,中非命运共同体、中阿命运共同体、中拉命运共同体、中国—东盟命运共同体、中国—中亚命运共同体、中国—太平洋岛国命运共同体等多边命运共同体建设稳步推进,网络空间命运共同体、海洋命运共同体、人类卫生健康共同体等不断落地生根。当代中国与世界研究院2020年发布的《中国国家形象全球调查报告》显示,共建"一带一路"倡议是海外认知度最高的中国理念和主张,超七成海外受访者认可共建"一带一路"倡议对个人、国家和全球治理带来的积极意义。欧洲智库机构布鲁盖尔研究所2023年4月发布《"一带一路"倡议的全球认知趋势》报告指出,世界各国对共建"一带一路"整体上持正面评价,特别是中亚到撒哈拉以南非洲等地区的广大发展中国家对共建"一带一路"的感情非常深厚。

多边治理机制更加完善。共建"一带一路"恪守相互尊重、平等相待原则,坚持开放包容、互利共赢,坚持维护国际公平正义,坚持保障发展中国家发展权益,是多边主义的生动实践。共建"一带一路"坚决维护联合国权威和地位,着力巩固和加强世界贸易组织等全球多边治理平台的地位和有效性,为完善现有多边治理机制注入强劲动力。共建"一带一路"积极推进亚洲基础设施投资银行等新型多边治理机制建设,加快与合作方共同推进深海、极地、外空、网络、人工智能等新兴领域的治理机制建设,丰富拓展了多边主义的内涵和实践。共建"一带一路"增强了发展中国家和新兴经济体在世界市场体系中的地位和作用,提升了其在区域乃至全球经济治理中的话语权,更多发展中国家的关切和诉求被纳入全球议程,对改革完善全球治理意义重大。

全球治理规则创新优化。共建"一带一路"充分考虑到合作方在经济发展水平、要素禀赋状况、文化宗教传统等方面的差异,不预设规则标准,不以意识形态划线,而是基于各方的合作诉求和实际情况,通过充分协商和深入交流,在实践中针对新问题共同研究创设规则。共建国家实现战略对接、规划对接、机制对接、项目及规则标准对接与互认,不仅让共建"一带一路"合作规则得到优化,促进了商品要素流动型开放向规则制度型开放转变,更形成了一些具有较强普适性的规则标准,有效地填补了全球治理体系在这些领域的空白。

(四)为人类社会进步汇聚文明力量

文明交流互鉴是推动人类文明进步和世界和平发展的重要动力。在个别国家固守"非此即彼""非黑即白"思维、炮制"文明冲突论""文明优越论"等论调、大搞意识形态对抗的背景下,共建"一带一路"坚持平等、互鉴、对话、包容的文明观,坚持弘扬全人类共同价值,共建各美其美、美美与共的文明交流互鉴之路,推动形成世界各国人文交流、文化交融、民心相通新局面。

人文交流机制日益完善。人文交流领域广泛,内容丰富,涉及政党、文化、艺术、体育、教育等多个方面。中国共产党与世界政党领导人峰会、中国共产党与世界政党高层对话会等各种多双边政党交流机制的世界影响力不断提升，党际高层交往的引领作用得到充分发挥，为增进民心相通汇聚了共识和力量。"一带一路"智库合作联盟、"一带一路"税收征管能力促进联盟、"一带一路"国际科学组织联盟、"一带一路"医学人才培养联盟、丝绸之路国际剧院联盟、丝绸之路博物馆联盟等各类合作机制集中涌现，形成了多元互动、百花齐放的人文交流格局，有力促进了各国民众间相互理解、相互尊重、相互欣赏。中国与吉尔吉斯斯坦、伊朗等中亚西亚国家共同发起成立亚洲文化遗产保护联盟，搭建了亚洲文化遗产领域首个国际合作机制，共同保护文化遗产这一文明的有形载体，所实施的希瓦古城修复项目等文化遗产保护项目得到联合国教科文组织高度评价。

共同打造一批优质品牌项目和活动。丝绸之路（敦煌）国际文化博览会、"一带一路"·长城国际民间文化艺术节、丝绸之路国际艺术节、海上丝绸之路国际艺术节、"一带一路"青年故事会、"万里茶道"文化旅游博览会等已经成为深受欢迎的活动品牌，吸引了大量民众的积极参与。"丝路一家亲""健康爱心包""鲁班工坊""幸福泉""光明行""爱心包裹""薪火同行国际助学计划""中医药风采行""孔子课堂"等人文交流项目赢得广泛赞誉。不断涌现的精彩活动、优质品牌和标志性工程，已经成为各方共同推进民心相通的重要载体，增强了各国民众对共建"一带一路"的亲切感和认同感。

　　鲁班是中国古代一位杰出的工匠和发明家。以鲁班命名的职业教育国际交流平台——鲁班工坊已成为中国职业教育"走出去"的一张"国家名片"。鲁班工坊重点面向东盟、上合组织、非洲国家,采取学历教育和职业培训相结合的方式,分享中国职业教育教学模式、教育技术、教育标准,建设培训中心,提供先进教学设备,组织中国教师和技术人员为合作国培养技术技能人才。自2016年在泰国共建第一个鲁班工坊以来,中国院校已在亚非欧三大洲的20多个共建国家合作建设一批鲁班工坊,开设了工业机器人、新能源、物联网等70多个专业,为相关国家培养了数以万计的技术技能人才,帮助更多年轻人实现就业。小小工坊,承载着各国人民对美好生活的憧憬向往,为共同发展之梦插上了翅膀。

　　青春力量广泛凝聚。共建"一带一路"的未来属于青年。10年来,共建国家青年以实际行动广泛开展人文交流和民生合作,为促进民心相通、实现共同发展汇聚了磅礴的青春力量。"中国青年全球伙伴行动"得到全球广泛响应,100多个国家青年组织和国际组织同中国建立交流合作关系。"一带一路"青年故事会活动连续举办16场,1500多名各国青年代表踊跃参加,围绕脱贫减贫、气候变化、抗疫合作等主题,分享各自在促进社会发展和自身成长进步方面的故事和经历,生动诠释了如何以欣赏、互鉴、共享的视角看待世界。"丝路孵化器"青年创业计划、中国—中东欧国家青年创客国际论坛等活动顺利开展,成为共建国家青年深化友好交流合作的重要平台。

五、推进高质量共建"一带一路"
　　行稳致远

　　10年来的实践充分证明,共建"一带一路"顺潮流、得民心、惠民生、利天下,是各国共同走向现代化之路,也是人类通向美好未来的希望之路,具有强劲的韧性、旺盛的生命力和广阔的发展前景。

　　当前,世界进入新的动荡变革期,大国博弈竞争加速升级,地缘政治局势持续紧张,全球经济复苏道阻且长,冷战思维、零和思维沉渣泛起,单边主义、保护主义、霸权主义甚嚣尘上,民粹主义抬头趋势明显,新一轮科技革命和产业变革带来的竞争空前激烈,和平赤字、发展赤字、安全赤字、治理赤字持续加重,全球可以预见和难以预见的风险显著增加,人类面临前所未有的挑战。个别国家泛化"国家安全"概念,以"去风险"为名行"脱钩断链"之实,破坏国际经贸秩序和市场规则,危害国际产业链供应链安全稳定,阻塞国际人文、科技交流合作,给人类长远发展制造障碍。在不确定、不稳定的世界中,各国迫切需要以对话弥合分歧、以团结反对分裂、以合作促进发展,共建"一带一路"的意义愈发彰显、前景更加值得期待。

　　从长远来看,世界多极化的趋势没有变,经济全球化的大方向没有变,和平、发展、合作、共赢的时代潮流没有变,各国人民追求美好生活的愿望没有变,广大发展中国家整体崛起的势头没有变,中国作为最大发展中国家的地位和责任没有变。尽管共建"一带一路"面临一些困难和挑战,但只要各国都能从自身长远利益出发、从人类整体利益出发,共同管控风险、应对挑战、推进合作,共建"一带一路"的未来就充满希望。

作为负责任的发展中大国,中国将继续把共建"一带一路"作为对外开放和对外合作的管总规划,作为中国与世界实现开放共赢路径的顶层设计,实施更大范围、更宽领域、更深层次的对外开放,稳步扩大规则、规制、管理、标准等制度型开放,建设更高水平开放型经济新体制,在开放中实现高质量发展,以中国新发展为世界提供新机遇。中国愿加大对全球发展合作的资源投入,尽己所能支持和帮助发展中国家加快发展,提升新兴市场国家和发展中国家在全球治理中的话语权,为促进世界各国共同发展作出积极贡献。中国真诚欢迎更多国家和国际组织加入共建"一带一路"大家庭,乐见一切真正帮助发展中国家建设基础设施、促进共同发展的倡议,共同促进世界互联互通和全球可持续发展。

在高质量共建"一带一路"的道路上,每一个共建国家都是平等的参与者、贡献者、受益者。中国愿与各方一道,坚定信心、保持定力,继续本着共商、共建、共享的原则,推进共建"一带一路"国际合作,巩固合作基础,拓展合作领域,做优合作项目,共创发展新机遇、共谋发展新动能、共拓发展新空间、共享发展新成果,建设更加紧密的卫生合作伙伴关系、互联互通伙伴关系、绿色发展伙伴关系、开放包容伙伴关系、创新合作伙伴关系、廉洁共建伙伴关系,推动共建"一带一路"高质量发展,为构建人类命运共同体注入新的强大动力。

结 束 语

一个理念,激活了两千多年的文明记忆;一个倡议,激发了150多个国家实现梦想的热情。

共建"一带一路"走过10年,给世界带来引人注目的深刻变化,成为人类社会发展史上具有里程碑意义的重大事件。

作为长周期、跨国界、系统性的世界工程、世纪工程,共建"一带一路"的第一个10年只是序章。从新的历史起点再出发,共建"一带一路"将会更具创新与活力,更加开放和包容,为中国和世界打开新的机遇之窗。

面向未来,共建"一带一路"仍会面临一些困难,但只要各方携手同心、行而不辍,就能不断战胜各种风险和挑战,实现更高质量的共商、共建、共享,让共建"一带一路"越来越繁荣、越走越宽广。

中国愿与各国一道,坚定不移推动高质量共建"一带一路",落实全球发展倡议、全球安全倡议、全球文明倡议,建设一个持久和平、普遍安全、共同繁荣、开放包容、清洁美丽的世界,让和平的薪火代代相传,让发展的动力源源不断,让文明的光芒熠熠生辉,共同绘制人类命运共同体的美好画卷!

中国的远洋渔业发展

（2023 年 10 月）

中华人民共和国
国务院新闻办公室

前　言

海洋的可持续开发利用与人类的生存发展息息相关。中国是世界上最早开发和利用海洋的国家之一，早在 4000 多年前，中国沿海地区人民就向海而生、以渔为业，与世界各国人民一道，开启了海洋探索开发利用之路。

中国远洋渔业自 1985 年起步以来，根据相关双边渔业合作协议或安排，与有关国家发展互利共赢的务实渔业合作；根据《联合国海洋法公约》等相关国际法，深入参与联合国框架下的多边渔业治理和区域渔业管理，积极行使开发利用公海渔业资源的权利，全面履行相关资源养护和管理义务。

中共十八大以来，在习近平新时代中国特色社会主义思想指引下，中国深入践行人类命运共同体和海洋命运共同体理念，持续加强海洋生态文明建设，始终坚持走远洋渔业绿色可持续发展道路，坚持优化产业结构，推进转型升级，提高质量效益，严控发展规模，强化规范管理，打击非法捕捞，致力于科学养护和可持续利用渔业资源，努力实现远洋渔业高质量发展。

为全面介绍中国远洋渔业的发展理念、原则立场、政策主张和履约成效，分享中国远洋渔业管理经验，促进远洋渔业国际合作与交流，特发布本白皮书。

一、中国远洋渔业高质量发展

远洋渔业是中国渔业的重要组成部分。中国始终秉承合作共赢、安全稳定、绿色可持续的发展理念,深化远洋渔业对外交流,多渠道、多形式开展互利共赢合作,坚持走远洋渔业高质量发展道路,努力为世界远洋渔业发展和水产品供给作出积极贡献。

(一)国际水产品生产和贸易稳步发展

水产品是全球公认的健康食物,在全球粮食和营养安全中发挥关键作用。可持续水产养殖发展和有效渔业管理对保障国际市场水产品供给至关重要。

近年来,水产品国际贸易增长显著。根据联合国粮农组织统计数据,从进口额看,欧盟为最大的单一进口市场,2020年在全球水产品进口总额中占比为16%(不包括欧盟内部贸易);美国为最大的进口国家,2020年进口额占全球水产品进口总额的15%。从出口额看,前三位出口国家为中国、挪威、越南,三国出口额合计占全球水产品出口总额的25%。据中国海关总署统计,2020年中国出口水产品374.74万吨,出口额占全球水产品出口总额的12%,主要出口目的地包括欧盟、东盟、日本、美国等国家和地区。中国作为世界最大的水产品出口国,为世界水产品的供给和消费作出了重要贡献。

根据联合国粮农组织《世界渔业和水产养殖状况 2022》公布的统计数据,2020 年全球渔业和水产养殖总产量达 2.14 亿吨,达历史最高水平,其中水产养殖产量达 1.226 亿吨,在全球渔业和水产养殖总产量中的比重达 57.29%。中国是世界最大的水产品生产国,2020年水产品总产量 6549 万吨,其中水产养殖产量 5224 万吨,约占水产品总产量的 80%。中国也是世界水产养殖产量最高的国家,全球的水产养殖产品约 40% 来自中国。中国渔业特别是水产养殖业的发展,为满足中国乃至世界水产品消费需求、减少对天然海洋渔业资源的利用和依赖、促进全球渔业资源科学养护和可持续利用作出了重要贡献。

(二)中国为世界远洋渔业发展作出积极贡献

世界远洋渔业有很长的发展历史,有较详细渔业统计数据的可追溯到 20 世纪 50 年代,不同历史时期均有不同的国家或地区参与。这些远洋渔业国家或地区与沿海国一道,为开发利用全球海洋渔业资源、促进海洋食物和营养供给、保障沿海社区生计和发展发挥了积极作用。

中国远洋渔业从 1985 年起步。虽然起步较晚,但经过 30 多年的艰苦奋斗,中国的远洋渔业取得了显著的发展成就。多年来,中国与亚洲、非洲、南美洲、大洋洲的有关国家(地区)签署互惠合作协议,根据协议安排和合作国法律规定,有序开展务实渔业合作,累计合作国家(地区)40多个。依据《联合国海洋法公约》等国际法,中国先后加入大西洋金枪鱼养护国际委员会、印度洋金枪鱼委员会、中西太平洋渔业委员会、南极海洋生物资源养护委员会、美洲间热带金枪鱼委员会、南太平洋区域渔业管理组织、北太平洋渔业委员会、南印度洋渔业协定等组织,核准《预防中北冰洋不管制公海渔业协定》。中国高度重视远洋渔业国际履约,积极履行多边渔业条约和区域渔业管理组织框架下的成员国义务,对尚无区域渔业管理组织管理的公海渔业履行船旗国①应尽的勤勉义务,并积极推动成立相关区域渔业管理组织,持续加强远洋渔业监管,促进全球渔业资源的科学养护和可持续利用。

2022年,中国拥有经批准的远洋渔业企业177家,远洋作业渔船2551艘(其中公海作业渔船1498艘),作业区域分布于太平洋、印度洋、大西洋公海和南极海域,以及相关合作国家管辖海域,年产量232.8万吨。

(三)推动中国远洋渔业更好发展

作为发展中国家,中国远洋渔业在渔船和捕捞装备水平、渔业资源探测能力、科技对产业发展的贡献率上,与发达国家相比仍有一定差距。为适应和履行国际渔业治理新要求,在结合自身发展需求基

---

① 船旗国是指为船舶登记注册并授权悬挂其船旗的国家。

础上,中国陆续发布了《"十四五"全国渔业发展规划》《关于促进"十四五"远洋渔业高质量发展的意见》《远洋渔业"监管提升年"行动方案》《远洋渔业人才建设三年行动方案》等政策文件,对远洋渔业发展作出规划。

"十四五"期间及今后一段时期,中国将继续以推动远洋渔业全产业链集聚发展,健全远洋渔业发展支撑体系,提升远洋渔业综合治理能力,加大远洋渔业发展保障力度为重点任务,通过优化产业结构,强化科技支撑,提升监管能力,深入参与国际渔业治理,完善政策体系,努力实现远洋渔业高质量发展。到 2025 年,中国远洋渔业总产量和远洋渔船规模保持稳定,行业整体素质和生产效益显著提升,违规事件和安全事故明显下降,区域与产业布局进一步优化,监督管理和国际履约成效显著提升。

二、统筹推进资源养护和
可持续利用

中国坚持在发展中保护、在保护中发展,实施公海自主休渔等重要举措,不断强化渔业资源养护,加强生态系统管理,重点关注气候变化与生物多样性养护,推进渔业资源长期可持续利用取得显著成效。

(一)坚持资源长期可持续利用原则

渔业资源作为一种可再生资源,在科学评估的基础上制定可捕量,是可持续利用资源的基础。中国坚持走绿色可持续发展道路,正确处理渔业资源养护与开发利用的关系,一贯主张在科学评估的基础上进行合理养护和长期可持续利用。支持中西太平洋渔业委员会、印度洋金枪鱼委员会等相关区域渔业管理组织制定捕捞策略,科学管理渔业资源,控制总捕捞能力。严格遵守大西洋金枪鱼养护国际委员会等区域渔业管理组织通过的捕捞限额制度和资源恢复计划,有关鱼种捕捞量长期控制在限额之内,支持配额及相关捕捞能力的合理转让。

休渔是国际上渔业管理和资源养护的重要措施,除按照区域渔业管理组织规定实施休渔(如中西太平洋金枪鱼围网季节性休渔)之外,中国从 2020 年起,对以鱿鱼为主捕对象的部分公海渔业实施自主休渔,这是中国进一步加强公海渔业资源科学养护和可持续利用的重要举措。

专栏 1　公海自主休渔

　　为促进公海渔业资源的养护和长期可持续利用,2020 年中国在西南大西洋和东太平洋公海相关海域试行为期三个月的自主休渔,并于 2021 年开始正式实施。休渔时间和海域为:7 月 1 日至 9 月 30 日,南纬 32 度至 44 度、西经 48 度至 60 度之间的西南大西洋公海海域;9 月 1 日至 11 月 30 日,北纬 5 度至南纬 5 度、西经 95 度至110 度之间的东太平洋公海海域。休渔期间,所有中国籍鱿钓渔船、拖网渔船停止捕捞作业。

　　2022 年中国进一步将印度洋北部公海纳入自主休渔范围,休渔时间和海域为:7月 1 日至 9 月 30 日,赤道至北纬 22 度、东经 55 度至 70 度之间的印度洋北部公海海域(不含南印度洋渔业协定管辖海域),休渔期间,中国籍鱿钓渔船、灯光围网渔船停止捕捞作业。自此,中国远洋渔业参与作业的尚无区域渔业管理组织管辖的公海海域(或鱼种)均已纳入自主休渔范围。

　　中国政府对自主休渔措施的实施情况进行严格监管,有关远洋渔船均严格遵守和执行了休渔措施。根据资源监测数据,西南大西洋和东南太平洋相关鱿鱼种类的相对资源丰度等指标有所改善。公海自主休渔作为中国积极养护公海渔业资源的创新举措,取得了显著效果。有关休渔时间和区域将根据实际情况和资源状况,经专家论证和公开征求意见后动态调整。

(二)加强兼捕物种保护和管理

　　中国高度关注与目标物种相关的兼捕物种资源可持续问题,注重评估和监测兼捕物种资源状况,鼓励并参与信息采集和科学研究,切实保护鲨鱼、蝠鲼、海龟、海鸟以及相关海洋哺乳动物。中国积极推动落实联合国粮农组织《鲨鱼养护和管理国际行动计划》,严格遵守区域渔业管理组织关于鲨鱼等物种的养护管理措施。中国制定实施《海龟保护行动计划(2019—2033年)》,在全国范围内对海龟保护管理工作进行统一部署。中国进一步加强海洋哺乳动物保护管理,要求远洋渔船严格遵守区域渔业管理组织的养护管理措施,深入做好对海洋哺乳动物等兼捕物种的有效释放、数据收集、信息报送、科学研究和监督管理。中国禁止公海大型流网作业,不批准新造双拖网、单船大型有囊灯光围网等破坏性作业渔船,积极开展生态和环境友好型渔船、渔具和捕捞技术的研发和应用,优化渔具选择性,推广鱿钓渔业节能型集鱼灯、金枪鱼延绳钓生态型渔具渔法,研制防缠绕和可生物降解的金枪鱼围网人工集鱼装置,开展南极磷虾渔业中降低海鸟损伤、有效释放误捕海洋哺乳动物等试验,切实推动兼捕物种和珍稀濒危物种保护。

(三)重视应对气候变化与生物多样性养护

中国高度重视应对气候变化和生物多样性养护问题,积极开展气候变化对鱼类等海洋生物的分布、洄游和种群再生能力的影响研究,以及气候变化与渔业资源及其生态系统相互影响的研究和相关管理工作。2019年支持中西太平洋渔业委员会通过气候变化研究提案,2022年支持印度洋金枪鱼委员会通过在金枪鱼渔业管理中关注气候变化的提案。海洋生物多样性与海洋生态系统保护和海洋可持续发展息息相关。中国作为主席国分两个阶段成功主持召开《生物多样性公约》第十五次缔约方大会，领导达成"昆明—蒙特利尔全球生物多样性框架"，积极参与国家管辖范围以外区域海洋生物多样性养护和可持续利用协定谈判工作，为推动全球生物多样性养护进程作出应有的贡献。

（四）加大资源养护和国际履约支持力度

中国以推动渔业高质量发展为目标，构建与渔业资源养护和产业结构调整相协调的新时代渔业发展支持政策体系，推动渔业高质量发展，提高渔业现代化水平，构建渔业发展新格局。从"十四五"开始，取消对远洋渔船的燃油补贴，支持建设渔业基础公共设施、渔业绿色循环发展、渔业资源调查养护和国际履约能力提升等方面，履行国际公约养护国际渔业资源，开展渔业资源调查监测评估等活动，促进渔业资源的长期可持续利用，构建绿色可持续的远洋渔业发展新格局。

远洋渔业企业和渔船是履行国际公约、合法合规从事渔业生产的主体。2022 年中国正式实施远洋渔业企业履约评估制度，将企业履约成绩与行政审批、政策支持等挂钩，通过正向激励、反向倒逼的方式，引导企业不断完善管理制度，严格执行管理措施，避免发生违规行为，切实提高履约能力。这一制度有力促进了远洋渔业企业规范管理和国际履约,得到了各方关注和广泛认可。

专栏 2　远洋渔业企业履约评估制度
为进一步提高远洋渔业企业国际履约能力和水平,持续推进远洋渔业高质量发展,促进全球渔业资源养护和长期可持续利用,中国自 2019 年起试行远洋渔业企业履约评估制度,并于 2022 年全面实施,就企业的管理制度建设、执行措施遵守、资源养护、科技创新、社会责任、违法违规等方面设定量化指标进行评分(包括 3 项一级指标、10 项二级指标、60 项三级指标)。通过企业自评、地方主管部门初审、国家渔业主管部门审定等程序确定企业年度履约得分。 　　2022 年,远洋渔业企业总体履约情况良好。通过开展履约评估,企业履约意识和能力明显提升,主要体现在:更积极地使用绿色、环保、生态型渔具渔法,更主动地参与实施电子渔捞日志、电子监控、国家观察员等工作,更有效地完善各类作业安全保障、环境保护等工作。

三、全面履行船旗国义务

作为负责任的渔业国家,中国严格执行《联合国海洋法公约》以及加入的多边渔业协定,从总量控制、限制船数、数据收集报送和国家观察员制度等方面全面履行船旗国义务[①],取得积极成效。

(一)不断强化远洋渔业许可制度

建立全面的远洋渔业许可制度和措施。根据《中华人民共和国渔业法》和《远洋渔业管理规定》,所有中国远洋渔船均应办理登记、检验手续,经批准后方可作业;根据区域渔业管理组织要求,对在相关海域作业的远洋渔船,按规定履行注册程序。多部门联合强化远洋渔船审批、登记、捕捞许可和报废监管,统一发布《中华人民共和国渔业捕捞许可证(公海)》等渔业船舶证书证件标准化格式。

(二)严格实施投入和产出控制制度

严格遵守区域渔业管理组织关于捕捞渔船数量和吨位限额制

---

① 指船旗国必须对给予悬挂该国国旗的船舶承担一定的义务,这些义务主要包括:对船舶技术条件的控制、对船员特别是船长和高级船员的适任管理、对船舶给予本国法律约束和保护、遵守相关国际公约等。

度、分鱼种捕捞配额制度。"十三五"期间,远洋渔业规模保持稳定;"十四五"期间继续严格控制远洋渔业规模,坚持远洋渔船数量控制在 3000 艘以内、远洋渔业总产量控制在 230 万吨左右的目标。2021年,明确不再新增公海鱿钓渔船、不再扩大鱿钓渔船规模,制定实施秋刀鱼单船捕捞配额分配管理方案,有效规范生产秩序。严格执行各区域渔业管理组织有关禁渔区、禁渔期的养护管理措施,主动实施公海自主休渔措施。

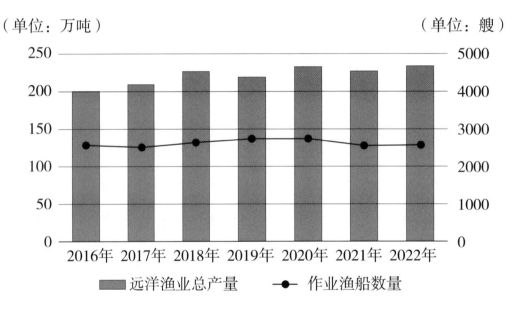

图 1 "十三五"以来中国远洋渔业总产量及作业渔船数量
(数据来源:中国远洋渔业数据中心)

(三)逐步完善数据收集和报送体系

不断完善远洋渔业基本生产统计数据的收集报送,提高数据质量,推进数据共享和集成管理。建立了涵盖远洋渔业企业信息、远洋渔船信息、船位监测、渔捞日志、渔获转载、国家观察员、港口采样、科学调查和生产性探捕等全方位的远洋渔业数据采集体系,并按照有关区域渔业管理组织的规定,及时报送各类渔业数据。中国主张充分合理的数据共享和研究,使科学数据在管理决策中尽可能发挥最大作用,同时切实保障数据安全,为各区域渔业资源养护和长期可持续利用作出应有的贡献。

(四)稳步施行电子渔捞日志制度

中国对公海海域金枪鱼、鱿鱼、竹笺鱼和秋刀鱼等渔业全面实施渔捞日志制度,渔捞日志回收率达 100%,填报质量逐年提高;对在有关合作国家海域开展的渔业活动,按合作国家要求填报渔捞日志。积极开展电子渔捞日志的研发、测试和推广应用工作,逐步实现公海渔船电子渔捞日志的全覆盖,积极参与区域渔业管理组织的电子渔捞日志计划,提高数据获取的实时性和准确性。2022 年 7 月,中国发布公海渔船电子渔捞日志有关管理措施,明确经中国政府批准的所有公海渔船,自 2024 年 1 月起全面实施电子渔捞日志管理。

(五)推进实施国家观察员制度

中国积极实施国家观察员制度,持续推进国家观察员派遣工作规范化、制度化。中西部太平洋、南太平洋区域的观察员项目均通过相关区域渔业管理组织的审查或认证。在满足区域渔业管理组织有关观察员覆盖率（5%）的规定要求基础上，积极推动电子观察员应用。2021年起启动实施公海转载观察员制度，对未纳入区域渔业管理组织管理的转载活动，进行监管。不断加强职业观察员队伍建设，将渔业观察员纳入《中华人民共和国职业分类大典（2022年版）》职业工种范围，为观察员制度的实施提供了制度保障。

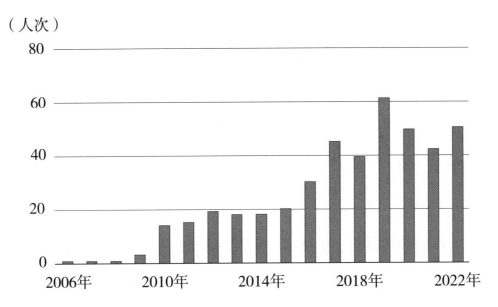

图2　2006—2022年中国远洋渔业国家观察员派遣人次
（数据来源：中国远洋渔业数据中心）

（六）巩固提升公海渔船管理水平

中国严格落实区域渔业管理组织养护管理措施，对北太平洋、南太平洋等区域以及金枪鱼、鱿鱼等重要品种的生产活动制定和实施专门管理措施，切实加强公海渔业监督管理和国际履约。对中国远洋渔船作业较为集中的部分公海海域,2021 年首次实施远洋鱿钓渔船总量控制管理制度,重点加强无区域渔业管理组织管理的远洋鱿钓渔船管理,合理优化作业渔船布局,规范渔船生产作业秩序,积极履行船旗国勤勉义务。

四、严格实施远洋渔业监管

中国对远洋渔船实施全球最严的船位监测管控措施,坚持"零容忍"打击非法捕捞。通过强化监管、完善机制、提升能力等措施,推进渔船监控等难点问题得到有效治理,船员管理等重点环节明显改善,重点海域监管切实加强,推动远洋渔业综合监管能力显著提升,保障远洋渔业生产秩序总体稳定。

(一)积极实施公海转载监管

在有效实施区域渔业管理组织有关公海转载措施的基础上,中国于 2020 年开始全面实施远洋渔业公海转载自主监管,建立远洋渔业海上转载管理平台,将所有远洋渔业运输船纳入平台监控,落实所有公海转载活动提前申报和事后报告程序,为运输船逐步配备观察员或安装视频监控系统。2021 年 4 月,首次派遣公海转载观察员登临远洋渔业运输船,代表中国政府执行公海转载监督任务。2022 年 5 月,积极参与联合国粮农组织公海转载自愿准则技术磋商,为顺利完成磋商通过准则作出有益贡献。

（二）加强远洋水产品进出口监管

中国严格实施水产品进出口监管，积极履行市场国义务。根据相关区域渔业管理组织养护管理措施的要求，对包括中国远洋渔船捕捞产品在内的大目金枪鱼、剑鱼、蓝鳍金枪鱼以及南极犬牙鱼实施进出口合法性认证。根据韩国、智利、欧盟等进口国（地区）以及俄罗斯等出口国要求，对相关进出口产品进行合法性认证，并按照相关国家核查要求进行调查反馈，确保进出口渔获物来源合法合规。对列入《濒危野生动植物种国际贸易公约》管制的物种，按照要求实施海上引进。

（三）严厉打击非法渔业活动

中国对远洋渔业实施严格监管，坚持对违规行为"零容忍"，积极采取立法、行政等措施打击违规远洋渔船和远洋渔业企业。对相关国家和国际组织等提供的有关中国渔船涉嫌违规线索，认真予以调查，对调查核实的违规远洋渔业企业和远洋渔船进行严厉处罚，并通过适当形式通报。2016年以来，先后取消6家、暂停22家远洋渔业企业从业资格，根据违规情节轻重对相关企业所属渔船及船长给予取消项目、暂停项目、不予申报新项目、罚款等不同程度的处罚，处罚金额达10多亿元。

坚决支持并积极配合国际社会打击各种非法渔业活动。2020年起,中国每年派遣执法船赴北太平洋公海开展渔业执法巡航,查处违规作业行为。2016年,配合南极海洋生物资源养护委员会成功扣押处置了一艘外籍渔船非法转载南极犬牙鱼案件。2018年起,将中国加入的相关区域渔业管理组织公布的非法、不报告和不管制渔船名单通报国内各港口,拒绝此类渔船进港以及卸货、补给、加油等活动。

专栏 3　成功处置外籍 IUU 渔船"安德烈"号

中国积极研究加入联合国粮农组织《关于预防、制止和消除非法、不报告和不管制捕捞的港口国措施协定》,参照该协定和相关措施要求开展港口检查,打击非法捕捞,并取得积极成效。2016年5月,根据南极海洋生物资源养护委员会通报,中国有关部门对进入中国山东港口的涉嫌违规转载渔获的冷藏运输船"安德烈"号进行检查,经查证确认该船非法转载南极犬牙鱼。经南极海洋生物资源养护委员会研究,确认将该外籍运输船列入非法、不报告和不管制渔船名单,并请中国政府对该批非法渔获予以处置。农业农村部会同外交部、地方主管部门等有关方面,组织对该批非法转载的110吨南极犬牙鱼进行拍卖,并将拍卖所得在扣除必要支出后,全部捐献给南极海洋生物资源养护委员会,以支持打击南极海域的非法渔业活动,养护南极海洋生物资源。此次成功处置外籍船舶非法转载南极犬牙鱼的事件,彰显了中国政府开展港口检查、打击非法捕捞的坚定决心。

（四）支持开展公海登临检查

中国支持在有关区域渔业管理组织框架内开展以打击非法渔业活动、有效实施养护管理措施为目的的公海登临检查,严格要求中国籍渔船接受并积极配合按照相关区域渔业管理组织公海登临检查措施规定开展的公海登临检查。

2020年，中国开始在北太平洋渔业委员会注册执法船，正式启动北太平洋公海登临检查工作，切实履行成员国义务。2021年起，中国海警舰艇编队在北太平洋实施公海登临检查，逐步推进按程序向其他区域渔业管理组织管辖区域派遣执法船，为国际社会共同打击公海非法渔业活动作出积极贡献。

五、强化远洋渔业科技支撑

中国通过开展公海渔业资源科学调查、参与区域渔业管理组织相关研究、改善升级渔船和捕捞装备等举措,不断加强科技创新,促进渔业提质增效、转型升级和高质量发展。《"十四五"全国渔业发展规划》提出,渔业科技进步贡献率努力从 2020 年的 63% 提高到 2025 年的 67%。

(一)完善科技支撑体制机制

中国远洋渔业管理坚持以科学为基础,建立并完善由主管部门、行业协会、科研单位通力合作的管理和履约科技支撑体系,共同制定渔业管理策略、实施管理措施并对实施效果进行评价。充分发挥行业协会在组织协调渔业生产、规范企业行为、组织从业人员培训、加强行业自律、推广示范应用等方面的作用,成立远洋渔业履约研究中心、远洋渔业数据中心,完善履约工作机制,加强相关科研机构和智库建设,逐步提高履约能力和成效。

中国高度重视远洋渔业企业履约能力建设和培训,每年由各级主管部门、行业协会、科研单位组织多种形式、针对各类履约事项的培训活动,部分远洋渔业企业自发开展管理措施和履约培训工作。其中,最为突出的举措是针对远洋渔业企业主要管理人员的培训。自2014年起,中国严控远洋渔业从业人员资格和条件,实行远洋渔业从业人员准入机制,要求远洋渔业企业负责人(企业法人或总经理)、具体项目负责人(项目经理)等中高层管理人员,必须参加农业农村部远洋渔业培训中心开展的从业人员资格培训,完成规定课程并通过考核,取得相应资格证书。截至2022年底,通过各种形式,培训中高层管理人员共计4000多人次。

通过远洋渔业企业从业人员资格培训等各类培训工作,有效提升了远洋渔业企业管理人员在国际渔业法规和管理制度、中国远洋渔业政策和管理制度、涉外渔业问题处理等方面的知识水平,提高了远洋渔业企业依法依规生产和执行管理措施的能力。中国将进一步加强远洋渔业从业人员培训,并将企业负责人、远洋渔船船长和职务船员作为培训重点。

(二)推动远洋渔业信息化发展

中国积极推进远洋渔船机械化、自动化和信息化,加强物联网、人工智能等技术在远洋渔业领域的研发和应用,开展远洋渔业北斗智能监控应用系统研发。推进远洋渔船视频监控系统研究和测试工作,参与制定远洋渔船视频监控设备安装标准规范,逐步开展重点鱼种或区域作业渔船推广试验。积极参与区域渔业管理组织的电子监控(电子观察员)标准制定,分享试验经验。2023年5月,中国支持印度洋金枪鱼委员会通过关于电子监控标准的决议,该决议成为金枪鱼区域渔业管理组织中首个关于电子监控的管理措施。目前,中国安装使用电子监控系统的金枪鱼渔船已达 100 多艘,约占全部金枪鱼渔船的 20%。

(三)加强远洋渔业资源调查与监测

渔业资源评估和管理建议的提出依赖科学数据,资源调查监测是国际上普遍采用的获取第一手科学数据的重要途径。从"十四五"开始,中国系统规划远洋渔业资源调查与监测,为科学养护渔业资源、可持续发展渔业提供科学和数据支撑。依托专业科学调查船,开展西北太平洋、中西太平洋公海渔业资源综合科学调查,鼓励科研机构与远洋渔业企业合作开展渔业资源生产性调查。基于调查数据,向中西太平洋渔业委员会提交科学调查进展,后续将继续提交调查研究成果,为资源评估和管理措施制定提供科学依据。积极与有关国家联合开展渔业资源科学调查,促进合作国家海域的渔业资源养护与长期可持续利用。实施全球重要鱼种资源监测评估项目,对重要经济鱼种、兼捕鱼种和保护物种的种群状态进行研究监测,建立数据库系统,为生产管理和资源养护提供科学参考。

(四)创新研究制定自主养护管理措施

结合国内外研究成果和中国远洋渔业发展实际情况,通过政产学研结合,积极创新研究制定自主养护管理措施。2020 年 6 月,中国出台加强公海鱿鱼资源养护、促进远洋渔业可持续发展有关管理规定,提出鱿鱼资源调查和评估、实行公海鱿鱼渔业自主休渔、加强鱿鱼全产业链管理制度研究等措施。为增强资源认知能力,规范引导行业可持续发展,中国积极探索编制远洋渔业指数。2020年开始,以鱿鱼为试点,研究发布中国远洋鱿鱼指数,包含鱿鱼资源丰度指数、鱿鱼价格指数、产业景气指数三大指标,以详实、动态的数据信息,监测鱿鱼产品与远洋鱿鱼渔业的总体发展。下一步,将研究发布金枪鱼渔业发展指数。

(五)及时研究转化国际养护管理措施

中国坚持以资源评估和最佳科学证据作为提出养护管理建议、制定管理措施的重要依据,积极参与区域渔业管理组织科学管理建议的研究,支持科研人员参加各类科学会议并担任相关科学职务,以资源评估为重点,开展鱼类种群生物学、生态系统管理、休渔效果评价等研究工作,参与有关研究计划,提交各类研究报告。深入研究各区域渔业管理组织通过的养护和管理措施,先后就有关金枪鱼渔业组织、北太平洋渔业组织和南太平洋渔业组织通过的养护管理措施印发文件,及时推动转化为国内相关管理规定,部署加强渔业管理和国际履约工作。

六、加强远洋渔业安全保障

中国持续提升远洋渔业基础设施现代化水平，着眼于安全、环保、可持续和劳工保护等目标，在控制远洋渔船规模的同时，不断改善渔船安全和船员生活环境。

（一）提升远洋渔船安全环保水平

鼓励支持远洋渔船更新改造，提升安全性和环境友好水平。严格限制过度扩大远洋渔船吨位，最大化降低捕捞活动对海洋环境及生态系统的影响。根据国际海事组织《国际防止船舶造成污染公约》等相关防止污染、海上安全国际公约的要求以及国家有关规定，2021 年修订远洋渔船标准化船型参数，完善远洋渔船检验规则，规范远洋渔船报废程序，强化新建远洋渔船的稳定性、安全设备及防污染装备的配置。

（二）推进远洋渔船船位监测监控

高度重视远洋渔船船位监测，不断升级远洋渔业服务平台和船位监测系统，全面覆盖所有远洋渔船，提高报位频率，不断完善船位监测数据采集及统计、重点区域监控、越界提醒等功能,推进渔捞日志、监测监控电子化,努力提高监测能力和服务水平;加强远洋渔业数据中心系统建设,开发渔业数据质量巡检控制功能,提高生产统计报告、渔捞日志数据、观察员数据等科学管理水平。

专栏 5　远洋渔船船位监测

为加强远洋渔业监管和履约,中国自 2006 年开始运行远洋渔船船位监测系统。经过 10 多年的发展,此项工作已成为中国远洋渔业管理的重点环节,覆盖所有中国远洋渔船,即所有中国远洋渔船的日常活动范围和位置均在主管部门的监控之下,船位报送频率为每小时一次,高于国际行业标准。

2021 年起,中国进一步实行远洋渔船船位监测统计日报制度,即每日由专门技术支撑单位统计汇报所有远洋渔船 24 小时内的船位活动情况,若出现不按要求报送船位、位置异常等情况,第一时间通知主管部门对企业进行跟踪核查,及时做出整改。远洋渔船船位监测系统功能也不断完善,除常规的船位监测外,兼具越界预警、航行安全提醒等功能。远洋渔船船位监测系统在保障远洋渔船航行作业安全、实施远洋渔船活动监管、履行船旗国义务和遵守国际渔业管理措施中发挥了重要作用。

(三)维护远洋渔业船员合法权益

中国是国际劳工组织创始成员国之一,高度重视劳工权益保护,截至 2023 年 4 月已批准 28 项国际劳工公约,包括《1930 年强迫劳动公约》和《1957 年废除强迫劳动公约》等 7 项核心公约。中国高度重视远洋渔业船员权益维护,持续规范远洋渔业船员的使用和管理,压实远洋渔业企业主体责任,加强行业自律,强化用工监督,依法保障包括外籍船员在内的船员工作条件和待遇。要求企业按时支付船员薪酬,不得无故拖欠工资;合理安排船员工作与休息,提供良好的生活工作条件;妥善处理船员合理诉求,理解、尊重、包容船员的风俗习惯、宗教信仰和文化差异,不得歧视、虐待、打骂船员。对船员加强安全生产技能培训,提升安全生产意识;确保渔船配备必要的劳动保护用品和设施,保障船员安全生产条件及环境;配备基本药品,及时为生病船员提供必要的医疗救治和心理帮助,对超出渔船处理能力的伤病船员应及时报告、组织救治。

（四）加强海上安全生产和救助

高度重视远洋渔业安全生产,加强安全检查和隐患排查,保障渔业船舶航行和渔民作业安全。建立行业协会24小时应急救助服务机制,加强海上互救保障机制建设。探索建立远洋渔业突发事件应急处理机制。严格海洋渔业船员违法违规管理,对船员违反安全航行作业等行为实行计分处理,推动维护渔业安全生产秩序。加强与有关国家和组织合作,积极参与全球海上救助。

专栏6　坚持生命至上理念开展海上救助
中国远洋渔船近年多次成功搜救秘鲁、毛里求斯、所罗门群岛、基里巴斯等国渔船渔民,积极履行生命优先的国际义务。2018年3月,"中水702"船在太平洋岛国所罗门群岛海域救起在海上漂泊20多天的3名当地渔民。仅2021—2022年期间,中国远洋渔船对他国船舶或船员进行海上救助的海域就涉及冈比亚、塞内加尔、所罗门群岛、马绍尔群岛、巴布亚新几内亚、库克群岛、瓦努阿图、基里巴斯海域和相关公海海域。

积极开展海上医疗站建设,解决远洋船员突发疾病无法得到及时治疗的难题。2017年开始,安排随船医务人员到东南太平洋公海渔场,为远洋渔船船员提供医疗服务。2021年建成的"浙普远98"远洋渔业综合保障船,配备专业医疗设备和医生,定期在东南太平洋公海巡航,为在该海域捕捞作业的远洋渔船船员开展医疗服务。

七、深化国际渔业合作

当前,渔业资源的持续利用面临气候和环境变化等威胁,渔业资源的跨区域分布、流动性和洄游性也呈现出新的特点,决定了渔业管理必须进一步加强国际合作。中国深入践行海洋命运共同体理念,深化远洋渔业对外交流,多渠道、多形式开展互利共赢合作,不断巩固多双边政府间渔业合作机制,助力合作国家和地区渔业发展。

(一)积极参与全球渔业治理

中国积极参与联合国框架下的多边渔业治理,推动构建更加公平合理的全球渔业治理体系。积极研究加入联合国粮农组织《关于预防、制止和消除非法、不报告和不管制捕捞的港口国措施协定》,开展国际海事组织国际渔船安全公约《2012年开普敦协定》等涉渔公约研究。将公海作业渔船列入联合国粮农组织全球渔船记录,加强与国际海事组织合作,要求远洋渔船申请注册国际海事组织编号。

近年来,国际社会高度关注渔业补贴,中国坚定支持多边贸易体制,顺应世界贸易组织渔业补贴谈判总体趋势。长期积极参与世界贸易组织渔业补贴谈判,秉承"促谈、促和、促成"原则,尽可能照顾各参与方的利益和发展中成员的诉求,努力弥合成员分歧,提出案文修订建议,积极响应其他成员的意见,充分显示灵活性,为最终达成《渔业补贴协定》作出了积极贡献。中国已于 2023 年 6 月 27 日向世界贸易组织递交《渔业补贴协定》议定书的接受书,今后将全面落实协定规定,并积极参与协定后续谈判。

重视与世界自然基金会、绿色和平组织等非政府组织就可持续渔业管理、打击非法捕捞等开展交流,在公海自主休渔、鱿鱼资源养护措施制定中吸收其合理化建议。

(二)深入参与区域渔业管理

中国致力于扩大和加强区域渔业合作,全面履行区域渔业管理组织成员国义务。通过及时足额缴纳会费、自愿捐赠等方式,支持各区域渔业管理组织开展相关职能活动。积极组织主管部门、科研单位、行业协会和企业代表参加区域渔业管理组织各项工作,参与研究制定养护管理措施、渔业资源调查评估与科学研究等活动,积极贡献中国智慧与力量。加强与相关区域渔业管理组织及各成员的交流合作,共同促进和提升区域渔业治理水平。

(三)开展双边渔业合作交流

中国致力于加强双边合作与对话交流,逐步建立双边合作机制,促进互利共赢,共同打击非法渔业活动。与俄罗斯、韩国、日本、越南、美国、阿根廷、新西兰、欧盟等国家(地区)建立了双边渔业会谈或对话机制,并与印度尼西亚、巴拿马、秘鲁、厄瓜多尔等国家(地区)进行沟通交流,议题涵盖双边渔业合作、区域渔业治理、打击非法捕捞、兼捕物种保护、加拉帕戈斯群岛等重点海域生态环境保护等方面。与亚洲、非洲、南美洲、大洋洲的 40 多个国家(地区)在互利互惠前提下开展渔业合作,鼓励支持合作企业在相关国家投资兴业,积极促进当地就业和经济发展。

专栏 7 加强渔业对外合作交流

中国高度重视渔业对外合作,坚持创新、协调、绿色、开放、共享的发展理念,积极推进渔业对外合作,促进合作共赢。

加强多边渔业合作。积极参加国家管辖范围以外区域海洋生物多样性协定、预防中北冰洋不管制公海渔业协定、联合国大会可持续渔业决议、世界贸易组织渔业补贴谈判等谈判磋商,推动形成公平合理、可持续的国际渔业治理机制。参加国际海事组织渔船安全及非法、不报告和不受管制捕捞部长级会议,签署《托雷莫利诺斯声明》。中国已加入 8 个区域渔业管理组织,基本覆盖全球重要公约水域,参与了联合国、联合国粮农组织、世界贸易组织、濒危野生动植物物种国际贸易公约、亚太经合组织以及有关区域渔业管理组织等 30 多个涉渔国际组织活动。2021 年 9 月,中国与联合国粮农组织、亚太水产养殖中心网共同主办第四届全球水产养殖大会,希望与世界各国深化务实合作,携手推动全球水产养殖业的可持续发展,为保障世界粮食安全作出贡献。

促进双边渔业合作。中国与美国、欧盟、挪威、加拿大、澳大利亚、新西兰等重要渔业国家(地区)建立高级别对话机制,并与亚洲、非洲、拉美等区域的多个国家开展双边渔业合作。2021 年 12 月和 2023 年 5 月,两次举办中国—太平洋岛国渔业合作发展论坛,进一步支持岛国渔业及相关产业的发展。

（四）推动发展中国家渔业发展

中国秉承海洋命运共同体理念,积极践行共建"一带一路"倡议,促进"南南合作",一贯支持发展中国家,特别是发展中小岛国和最不发达国家发展渔业及社区经济,在技术、人才等方面,力所能及地给予帮助。推动发展中国家开展渔业基础设施建设、资源调查、技术培训、手工渔民和小规模渔业发展,帮助发展养殖、加工、贸易等产业。同时,中国积极支持发展中国家在多边领域的合理主张,维护其发展权益。

（五）推动全球渔业可持续发展

渔业对全球粮食和营养安全以及沿海地区人民生计具有重要作用,国际社会对此有高度共识。中国高度重视全球渔业可持续发展,倡导通过发展水产养殖,增加食物供给,特别是保障发展中国家的粮食安全,减少对野生渔业资源的依赖。中国水产养殖产量连续32年稳居世界第一,成为全球最大的水产品加工和出口国,为保障世界粮食安全作出积极贡献。

中国主张在平等互利基础上,完善多边磋商机制,深化科技交流,扩大经贸合作,打击非法捕捞,促进全球渔业资源科学养护和长期可持续利用,为保障全球粮食安全、造福沿海地区人民发挥积极作用;坚决反对单边主义和保护主义,反对强权政治和霸凌行径,反对没有国际法依据的单边制裁和"长臂管辖",维护公正合理的国际海洋秩序。

结　束　语

走向深蓝,是人类探索海洋、利用海洋、保护海洋的必由之路。中国将坚持创新、协调、绿色、开放、共享的理念,积极实践全球发展倡议,根据相关国际法和双边合作协议,加强多双边渔业合作和对话,努力促进远洋渔业高质量发展,不断提升国际渔业公约和养护管理措施的履行能力,积极承担与自身发展相适应的国际义务。

当前,全球海洋治理面临新形势新挑战。站在新的历史起点上,中国愿继续同国际社会一道,在平等、互利、相互尊重的基础上,加强海洋及海洋资源养护和可持续利用,保护海洋生物多样性,为实现《联合国2030年可持续发展议程》目标,推动构建海洋命运共同体,助力全球海洋的绿色可持续发展不断书写新的篇章。

新时代党的治藏方略的实践及其历史性成就

（2023 年 11 月）

中 华 人 民 共 和 国
国务院新闻办公室

前　言

党的十八大以来,以习近平同志为核心的党中央坚持以人民为中心的发展思想,站在实现中华民族伟大复兴的战略高度,着眼于西藏同全国一道实现全面小康和现代化,高度重视西藏发展,亲切关怀西藏人民。党中央先后召开第六次、第七次西藏工作座谈会,明确提出做好西藏工作的指导思想、总体要求和重点任务,为推进西藏长治久安和高质量发展、实现西藏各族人民对美好生活的向往、建设社会主义现代化新西藏指明了方向。

中央第七次西藏工作座谈会确立了新时代党的治藏方略,并将其概括为"十个必须":必须坚持中国共产党领导、坚持中国特色社会主义制度、坚持民族区域自治制度,必须坚持治国必治边、治边先稳藏的战略思想,必须把维护祖国统一、加强民族团结作为西藏工作的着眼点和着力点,必须坚持依法治藏、富民兴藏、长期建藏、凝聚人心、夯实基础的重要原则,必须统筹国内国际两个大局,必须把改善民生、凝聚人心作为经济社会发展的出发点和落脚点,必须促进各民族交往交流交融,必须坚持我国宗教中国化方向、依法管理宗教事务,必须坚持生态保护第一,必须加强党的建设特别是政治建设。

新时代党的治藏方略,立足中国特色社会主义实践和西藏工作实际,深刻揭示了西藏工作的内在规律,科学回答了一系列方向性、全局性、战略性问题,是中国共产党领导人民治藏稳藏兴藏成功经验的总结提炼和创新发展,是习近平新时代中国特色社会主义思想关于西藏工作的集中体现,为做好西藏工作提供了根本遵循。

在新时代党的治藏方略引领下,在全国人民大力支持下,西藏各族干部群众团结奋斗,各项事业取得全方位进步、历史性成就。西藏社会大局持续稳定向好、经济建设全面快速发展、人民生活水平不断提高、民族和睦宗教和顺、文化事业繁荣进步、生态安全屏障日益坚实、边疆巩固边境安全、党的建设全面加强,与全国人民一道迎来了从站起来、富起来到强起来的伟大飞跃,踏上了全面建设社会主义现代化国家新征程。

一、新发展理念全面贯彻

人民对美好生活的向往，就是中国共产党矢志不渝的奋斗目标。西藏认真践行以人民为中心的发展思想，全面贯彻创新、协调、绿色、开放、共享的新发展理念，聚焦发展不平衡不充分的问题，优化产业结构布局，培育内生动力，彻底摆脱了束缚千百年的绝对贫困问题，"十三五"发展目标如期完成，经济总量不断迈上新台阶。

——经济持续健康快速发展

经济发展态势良好。西藏紧紧围绕使市场在资源配置中起决定性作用和更好发挥政府作用，深化经济体制改革，统筹做好稳增长、促改革、调结构、惠民生、防风险、保稳定各项工作，经济活跃度不断提升。2022年全区地区生产总值达到2132.64亿元，按不变价计算，比2012年增长1.28倍，年均增长8.6%，经济增速位居全国前列。产业结构日趋合理，自我发展能力显著增强。

特色农业优质发展。重点发展青稞产业、优质畜牧业、设施农业，告别靠天吃饭、靠天养畜的老路。一大批优质青稞粮油生产、无公害蔬菜种植、标准化奶牛规模养殖、牦牛藏羊养殖等农牧业特色产业基地建成。2022年，农畜产品加工业总产值达到60亿元。

工业发展富有成效。第二产业发展势头强劲,建立起富有当地特色的现代工业体系。2012年至2022年,工业增加值增长1.77倍,产业链深度和广度不断延伸。2022年,规模以上工业企业数量比上年增长1.1%,高新技术企业达15家。

　　第三产业活力增强。在中央支持下着力推动重要世界旅游目的地建设,拉萨雪顿节、日喀则珠峰文化旅游节、山南雅砻文化旅游节、林芝桃花节、那曲羌塘恰青赛马艺术节等成为重要的旅游品牌。2012年至2022年,接待旅游人数从1058.39万人次增加到3002.76万人次,旅游收入从126.48亿元增加到407.07亿元,增长2.2倍。山南市乃东区昌珠镇扎西曲登社区将雪巴藏戏与民宿旅游结合起来,走出致富新路。藏戏传承人尼玛次仁说:"旧社会,我们跳藏戏是为了让农奴主高兴,而今天表演,是为了让我们自己和更多人过上美好日子。"

　　改革创新纵深推进。深化农村土地制度改革,重点健全承包土地合同管理、经营权流转管理、权属登记管理等制度。2014年,曲水县白堆村农牧民群众领取到不动产权证书(土地承包经营权),这是西藏历史上首次为农户农村土地颁证。实施新型农业经营主体培育工程,家庭农场、农牧民专业合作社等逐步发挥其在农村改革中的示范引领作用。持续推进国企国资改革,做强做优做大国有资本,2022年,全区国有企业资产总额较2012年增长13.05倍。优化税收营商环境,推进"证照分离"改革,深化"减证便民",压缩企业开办时间。西藏各类市场主体从2012年的12.44万户发展到

2022 年的 43.76 万户。创新驱动发展,数字经济增加值增长 10% 以上。

投资金融进一步惠及民生。2012 年至 2022 年,中央财政补贴累计达 1.73 万亿元。在国家财政支持下,全社会固定资产投资从 2012 年到 2022 年增长 2.33 倍。投资重点放在增强西藏经济发展基础和自我发展能力的基础设施、公共服务等领域,在不同时期相继安排一大批关系西藏长远发展和人民生活的重大工程项目,极大改善了人民生产生活条件。招商引资累计到位资金 4650 亿元,民间投资活力增强。金融机构组织体系持续改善,逐步形成银行、证券、保险等多层次、多元化、多功能的金融组织体系,金融支持经济社会发展作用明显增强。

区域交流合作持续深化。加强与周边省区交流合作,积极融入成渝地区双城经济圈、大香格里拉经济圈、陕甘宁青经济圈、长江经济带等周边经济圈,努力打造面向南亚开放的重要通道。启动通关一体化改革,南亚标准化(拉萨)研究中心挂牌成立。吉隆边境经济合作区获国务院批准设立,拉萨综合保税区通过国家验收。吉隆口岸扩大开放为国际性公路口岸,实现中尼双边开放。2022 年,西藏外贸进出口总值 46.01 亿元,贸易伙伴遍及 95 个国家和地区。中国西藏发展论坛、西藏智库国际论坛、中国西藏旅游文化国际博览会、跨喜马拉雅国际自行车极限赛等,已成为推动西藏与世界各地交流互鉴、合作发展的重要平台。

援藏工作成效显著。坚持不懈执行对口援藏政策,从 1994 年至

2022年,先后有 10 批共 11900 名援藏干部人才奋战在高原各地。不断加强同各对口援藏省市的协调,探索与援藏省市和中央企业协同发展、产业合作以及援藏工作管理新模式,统筹融合经济援藏、产业援藏、科技援藏、就业援藏、扶贫援藏等,以及医疗、教育人才"组团式"援藏,实现从给资金、建项目的"输血式"帮扶,逐步向产业培育、技术支持、人才培养等的"造血式"帮扶转变。仅"十三五"期间,17 个省市规划安排援藏项目就达 1260 个,完成总投资200 亿元。

——基础设施建设全面加强

交通设施建设超常规发展。以公路为基础,铁路、航空、管道运输协调发展的综合交通运输体系日益完善。2022 年初,公路通车总里程突破 12.14 万公里,其中,高等级公路通车里程达到 1105 公里,形成了以 20 条国道为主骨架,以 36 条省道、边防公路、农村公路为基础,基本辐射全区的公路网络。铁路营业里程从 2012 年的 701 公里增加到 2022 年的 1359 公里,青藏铁路格拉段完成扩能改造,川藏铁路雅安至林芝段全线开工、拉萨至林芝段通车运行,"复兴号"开进西藏、开到拉萨。2022 年,管道运输量 0.31 亿吨公里。西藏航空顺利开航运营。国际国内航线达到 154 条,通航城市 70 个,民航西藏区局 2022 年旅客吞吐量达到 334.6 万人次。

电网工程建设取得重大突破。西藏电力实现从紧缺限电到富余输出的历史性转变。先后建成青藏、川藏、藏中、阿里4条"电力天路"和"三区三州"电网建设等重点项目,在世界屋脊织起一张安全可靠的"光明网""民生网"和"幸福网",形成覆盖所有县区和主要乡镇的西藏统一电网,累计外送清洁电量130亿千瓦时以上。通动力电的行政村比重达到96.5%,用电量从2012年的28.84亿千瓦时增长到2022年的119.8亿千瓦时,增幅连续多年保持全国前列。阿里与藏中电网联网工程全线贯通,区内电网联为一体,结束了阿里电网长期孤网运行的历史。

水利设施建设取得崭新进展。"十三五"期间全口径投资较"十二五"期间增长52%,建成一批标志性重大水利项目。拉洛工程入选全国有影响力十大水利工程,旁多、拉洛水利枢纽并网发电、灌区通水,湘河水利枢纽及配套灌区工程开工建设。水利惠及更多民生,防洪减灾成效明显,河湖生态持续改善,农村饮水安全问题得到有效解决,城乡供水保障能力显著提升。

数字基础设施建设取得长足发展。自治区电子政务网、自治区统一基础云平台、自治区大数据控制中心基本建成,积极融入"东数西算"布局,西藏首个云计算中心建成,并获评国家绿色数据中心。累计建成5G基站8099座、光缆线路近31.26万公里。5G网络实现县区及重点乡镇覆盖,移动信号覆盖3A级以上景区,光纤宽带、4G信号、广播电视信号基本实现行政村全覆盖。现代通信"云网融合",实现寻常百姓与世界联通。

——绝对贫困得到历史性消除

脱贫攻坚全面胜利。西藏始终坚持精准扶贫、精准脱贫基本方略。落实"五个一批"脱贫措施,2019年底,累计实现62.8万建档立卡贫困人口脱贫,74个贫困县(区)全部摘帽,彻底摆脱了束缚西藏千百年的绝对贫困问题。2022年脱贫人口人均收入达到1.38万元,年均增长率高于农村居民人均可支配收入增长水平。脱贫群众享有稳定的吃、穿、住、学、医等保障,享有更加和谐的安居乐业环境、更加均衡的基础设施条件和基本公共服务、更加完善的社会保障体系。

乡村振兴加快实施。2021年以来,累计实施建设美丽宜居村300个,创建认定美丽宜居示范村505个;建设高标准农田,实施农机深松整地作业,建设国家级畜禽养殖标准化示范创建场,农牧综合服务中心覆盖所有乡镇;新型农村集体经济组织达6172个,带动农业生产组织化和规模化水平提升;着力发展高原特色产业和绿色有机产业,创建优势特色产业集群4个、国家现代农业产业园7个、农业产业强镇18个;脱贫攻坚成果巩固拓展,脱贫人口外出务工稳定在20万人以上,建设非遗工坊173个,带动脱贫群众实现居家就业、就近就业,谱写了新时代乡村全面振兴的西藏篇章。

——共同富裕程度显著提升

收入水平高速增长。2022年,城镇居民人均可支配收入由2012年的18363元提高到48753元,增长1.7倍;农村居民人均可支配收入由2012年的5698元提高到18209元,增长2.2倍;城乡居民收入比由2012年的3.22降低至2.67,收入差距持续缩小;全体居民人均可支配收入由2012年的8568元提高到26675元。自2015年起,全体居民人均可支配收入增速连续8年居全国首位。

消费市场更加繁荣。2022年,社会消费品零售总额726.52亿元,比2012年的318.39亿元增长1.3倍。2022年,货运周转量达130.88亿吨公里,推动产地和消费地之间的有效衔接;全区邮政行业业务收入(不包括邮政储蓄银行直接营业收入)完成7.44亿元,邮政行业寄递业务量完成17882.59万件,其中,快递业务量完成1219.31万件。19家大型全国性电商和物流快递企业陆续落户,冷链仓储面积达11.3万平方米。市县乡村四级电商服务全面推开,2022年,网上零售额达91.4亿元。

二、精神文明建设成效明显

全面贯彻新时代党的治藏方略,需要各族人民坚定信心,团结奋斗,振奋精气神,汇聚正能量。西藏大力弘扬社会主义主流价值,积极传承和保护民族优秀传统文化,大力推进公共文化服务体系建设,繁荣文化事业,发展文化产业,使社会主义核心价值观真正深入人心,更好满足各族群众精神文化生活新期盼。

——社会主流价值广为弘扬

核心价值观引领绵绵用力。西藏坚持用中国特色社会主义共同理想凝聚力量,印发《关于贯彻〈关于培育和践行社会主义核心价值观的意见〉实施意见》,把坚持社会主义核心价值体系与学习贯彻习近平总书记系列重要讲话精神结合起来、与贯彻落实中央重大方针政策和决策部署结合起来、与推进西藏改革发展稳定的实践结合起来、与各项重大主题宣传教育活动结合起来,加强党史、新中国史、改革开放史、社会主义发展史、西藏地方与祖国关系史教育,帮助各族干部群众树立正确的国家观、历史观、民族观、文化观、宗教观,为建设社会主义新西藏注入强大精神动力。

红色文化教育发扬光大。2021年,西藏百万农奴解放纪念馆新馆建成。全国援藏展览馆、西藏自治区"两路"精神纪念馆、布达拉宫雪城系列展陈馆、江孜抗英遗址、拉萨市林周农场红色遗址、尼木县革命烈士陵园、波密县扎木中心县委红楼、昌都市革命历史博物馆、江达县岗托十八军军营旧址、改则县进藏先遣连纪念馆等,命名为西藏自治区爱国主义教育基地,为社会主义核心价值观的培育提供了更加丰富的站点基石。

——优秀传统文化焕发活力

历史文化遗产得到有效保护。西藏现有中国历史文化名城 3 座,中国历史文化名镇 5 个,中国历史文化名村 4 个。80 个村落列入中国传统村落名录,29 个村寨获评中国少数民族特色村寨。现已调查登记各类文物点 4468 处,各级文物保护单位 2373 处,其中全国重点文物保护单位 70 处。布达拉宫历史建筑群(含布达拉宫、罗布林卡、大昭寺)被列入《世界遗产名录》。编制布达拉宫、罗布林卡、大昭寺、帕拉庄园等一批全国重点文物保护单位保护规划,完成布达拉宫、罗布林卡等重大文物保护工程,实施文物保护专项监测。完成萨迦寺、桑耶寺等重大文物保护工程,对平措林寺、托林寺、科迦寺等文物建筑和壁画持续开展保护修复,开展同卡寺、查杰玛大殿、色拉寺等珍贵文物预防性保护项目。2013 年起,10 万余件各类珍贵文物在数字化建档中得到更加科学的保护。在阿里噶尔县故如甲木墓地进行的考古挖掘,出土"王侯文鸟兽纹锦"和茶叶,充分证明早在 1800

多年前西藏西部就已通过丝绸之路与祖国其他地区建立了密切联系。札达县桑达隆果墓地考古发掘获 2020 年度全国十大考古新发现。日益丰富的考古发现展现了中华文明的博大灿烂。

藏医药得到传承和创新发展。2019 年,国家投资 10 亿元用于西藏藏医药大学新校区建设,该校累计培养了 7000 余名藏医药专业人才。截至 2022 年初,西藏公立藏医医疗机构达 49 所,乡镇卫生院和村卫生室藏医药服务覆盖率分别达到 94.4% 和 42.4%。藏医药产业体系基本形成,实现藏药生产标准化、规范化、规模化。先后整理出版 300 多部藏医药古籍文献,收集珍贵古籍文本 600 多卷。藏医药学巨著《四部医典》入选世界记忆亚太地区名录。

藏文古籍文献和非遗得到保护利用。2013 年,国家组织实施《中华大典·藏文卷》重点文化工程,计划用 15 年时间,出版从吐蕃时期至西藏和平解放前的藏文文献典籍,这是我国保护和弘扬藏族优秀传统文化的又一个标志性工程。2012 年至 2022 年,国家和自治区投入非物质文化遗产保护资金 3.25 亿余元,用于西藏非物质文化遗产代表性项目保护、国家级非遗代表性传承人记录工作、开展传习活动以及保护利用设施建设等。现有国家级非遗代表性项目 106 项、国家级非遗代表性传承人 96 名,自治区级非遗代表性项目 460 项、自治区级非遗代表性传承人 522 名。《格萨(斯)尔》、藏戏、藏医药浴法等已列入人类非物质文化遗产代表作名录。

藏语言文字学习使用得到依法保障。藏语言文字在卫生、邮政、通讯、交通、金融、科技等领域都得到广泛使用。公共场所设施、招牌和广告都可见国家通用语言文字和藏文标识,随时可以收听收看国家通用语言文字和藏语文的节目。中小学校均开设国家通用语言文字课程和藏语文课程。截至 2022 年底,西藏公开发行藏文期刊 17 种、藏文报纸 11 种,累计出版藏文图书 7959 种、4501.3 万册。2015 年,国家标准《信息技术　藏文词汇》正式发布。全国藏语术语标准化工作委员会于 2018 年发布《党的十八大以来审定的藏语新词术语》,包含藏语新词术语近 1500 条;2022 年发布《党的十九大以来藏语新词术语(汉藏对照)》,包含藏语新词术语 2200 条。

——公共文化事业蓬勃发展

公共文化服务体系日趋完善。基本建成自治区、市(地)、县(区)、乡(镇)、村(居)五级公共文化设施网络,实现市(地)有图书馆、群众艺术馆、博物馆,县(区)有综合文化活动中心,乡(镇)有综合文化活动站,村(居)有文化活动室。西藏现有 10 个专业文艺院团、76 个县区艺术团、153 个民间藏戏队、395 个乡镇文艺演出队和 5492 个建制村文艺演出队,专兼职文艺演出人员超过 10 万人。西藏农村电影放映全面实现数字化,全区 478 套数字电影放映设备,每年放映 6.3 万余场电影。建成 6263 个县乡村三级新时代文明实践中心(站、所)。开展中华优秀传统文化进基层活动,提升基层文化设施服务功能,建强 100 个村级群众性文化示范阵地。

文化艺术创作繁荣发展。推出歌舞晚会《共产党来了苦变甜》

《祖国·扎西德勒》《西藏儿女心向党》,话剧《共同家园》《八廓街北院》,藏戏《次仁拉姆》《藏香情》,歌舞剧《天边格桑花》等一大批坚守中华文化立场、彰显时代精神、体现西藏特色、群众喜闻乐见的优秀文艺作品。话剧《不准出生的人》、歌舞晚会《西藏儿女心向党》、舞蹈《欢腾的高原》、广场舞《奋进新时代》、少儿藏戏《喜迎新春》先后在全国获奖。

体育事业快速发展。各类群众性体育赛事活动丰富多彩,民族传统体育得到传承发展,山地户外运动广泛开展。竞技体育水平逐步提高,"十三五"期间获得国际国内赛事奖牌231枚。2018年雅加达亚运会,运动员多布杰夺得男子马拉松赛铜牌,创造了我国男子马拉松亚运会最好成绩。2020年洛桑冬青奥会,索朗曲珍在滑雪登山女子个人越野赛和短距离赛两个项目上创造了我国历史最好成绩。2021年第十四届全国运动会,西藏代表团共取得3金1银2铜的好成绩。2022年北京冬奥会,西藏两名运动员取得参赛资格,实现了西藏竞技体育新突破。

广播影视出版事业发展壮大。广播、电视综合人口覆盖率分别达到99.41%、99.56%。创作电影《布德之路》《我的喜马拉雅》《七十七天》《宁都啦》,电视剧《呀啦索　幸福家园》,纪录片《你好！新西藏》《西藏　我们的故事》《党的光辉照边疆》等优秀影视作品。截至2022年底,共有数字影院74家,银幕191块,2022年电影票房达3722.87万元,观影人次87.97万。建好用好市地、县区融媒体中心,建设推广使用自治区级融媒体平台"珠峰云"。积极创作播出中华优秀文化纪录片,制作译制民族语言广播节目时长超 15000 小时,每年制作译制民族语言电影 80 部以上,制作译制民族语言电视节目时长达 7300 小时。现有各类印刷企业 40 家,各类出版发行单位 219 家,出版期刊 231.73 万册、图书 270.7 万册,出版物销售总额 12.93 亿元,建成 5400 多个农家书屋和 1700 多个寺庙书屋,有力推动新闻出版繁荣发展,不断丰富农牧民群众的科学文化知识。

——文化产业发展势头良好

文化市场活跃兴盛。制定实施《西藏自治区人民政府办公厅关于大力推进文化和旅游深度融合加快发展特色文化产业的意见》,出台招商引资优惠政策,对在藏注册的各类文化企业在金融税收等各方面提供支撑政策,各类奖励资金、扶持资金持续发力。截至 2022 年底,各类文化企业达 8000 余家,从业人员超 7 万人,文化及相关产业增加值达 63.29 亿元,拥有四级文化产业示范园区(基地)344 家。7 家关联企业上榜"2021 西藏自治区百强民营企业",4 家关联企业上榜"2021 西藏自治区民营企业就业 20 强",1 家民营文化企业 4 次荣获"全国文化企业 30 强"提名企业。

重点文化产业项目推进顺利。"十三五"期间,91 个文化产业重点项目顺利实施,总投资近 500 亿元。"西藏宝贝"文化电商平台、西藏文化旅游创意园区、西藏出版文化产业园、中国西藏珠峰文化旅游创意产业园区等平台相继建成。藏文化大型史诗剧《文成公主》

及舞台剧《金城公主》等一大批特色文化项目走向市场。植根于西藏文化沃土、具有浓郁民族特色和时代气息的动漫、影视、唐卡等文化产品市场反响良好。

三、民族宗教工作扎实推进

铸牢中华民族共同体意识,是新时代党的民族工作的主线,也是西藏工作的战略性任务。西藏坚持铸牢中华民族共同体意识,推动民族工作高质量发展,平等团结互助和谐的社会主义民族关系日益巩固。西藏依法管理宗教事务,宗教信仰自由得到充分保障,宗教领域持续和谐稳定,宗教与社会主义社会更相适应。

——中华民族共同体意识不断铸牢

中华民族共有精神家园加快构筑。西藏编写出版铸牢中华民族共同体意识系列读本等民族团结进步教材和读本,打造"互联网+民族团结"交流平台,开展"中华民族一家亲、同心共筑中国梦"主题宣传教育,引导各族人民牢固树立休戚与共、荣辱与共、生死与共、命运与共的共同体理念。围绕"西藏百万农奴解放纪念日""西藏和平解放纪念日""民族团结进步宣传活动月"等时间节点,在各级党政机关、学校、企事业单位、城乡社区等广泛开展民族团结进步知识竞赛、文艺表演等群众喜闻乐见的活动。深化中华民族视觉形象塑造,建成中华文化主题公园,让中华文化始终成为西藏各民族人心凝聚、团结奋进的强大精神纽带。

各民族交往交流交融更加紧密。因地制宜构建互嵌式社区,各族群众共居共学、共建共享、共事共乐的格局已然形成,涌现出拉萨市河坝林社区等一批汉族、藏族、回族、蒙古族等多民族和谐街道(社区、家庭)典型。日喀则市仁布县切娃乡普纳村 59 户村民来自不同地区不同民族,村民们自发将民族团结写入村规民约,约定每年召开民族团结座谈会,凝心聚力共谋发展。促进各族学生共同学习、共同进步。在 17 个援藏省市建立西藏高校毕业生区外就业服务联络站,支持帮助毕业生就业创业,毕业生就业率连续多年保持在 95% 以上。鼓励支持区外种养大户、致富能手和涉农企业到西藏创业兴业。西藏处处呈现出各民族共同团结奋斗、共同繁荣发展的生动局面。

——民族团结进步持续巩固

民族团结进步创建工作切实开展。广泛开展民族团结进步模范区创建,大力推进各民族交往交流交融,推进民族团结市县行活动。2020 年,颁布《西藏自治区民族团结进步模范区创建条例》;2021 年,出台《西藏自治区民族团结进步模范区创建规划(2021—2025 年)》。西藏先后有 140 个集体、189 名个人受到国务院表彰,荣获全国民族团结进步模范集体(个人)称号。拉萨等 7 地(市)均成功创建成为全国民族团结进步示范市。"民族团结杰出贡献者"国家荣誉称号获得者热地的事迹广为传颂,全社会掀起向"时代楷模"卓嘎、央宗姐妹学习的热潮,争当民族团结进步模范。

反渗透反颠覆反分裂斗争不断深入。西藏根据维护国家安全的总要求和自身实际,坚持依法治藏原则,紧紧依靠各族群众,牢牢把握反分裂斗争主动权,深入揭批达赖集团的反动本质,坚决抵制、严厉打击各种分裂破坏活动。"团结稳定是福,分裂动乱是祸"的观念深入人心,各族群众维护祖国统一、维护国家主权、维护民族团结的态度日益坚决。

——宗教信仰自由充分保障

宗教活动有序开展。西藏现有藏传佛教宗教活动场所1700多处,僧尼约4.6万人;清真寺4座,世居穆斯林群众约1.2万人;天主教堂1座,信徒700余人。雪顿节、燃灯节、萨嘎达瓦、转山转湖等1700多项宗教民俗活动既保存历史的仪礼传统和庄严,也加入现代的文化体验和活力。活佛转世传承方式得到国家和西藏各级政府的承认和尊重。2007年,国家颁布《藏传佛教活佛转世管理办法》,就藏传佛教活佛转世应坚持的原则、应具备的条件、应履行的申请报批程序等作出详细规定,也明确了包括达赖、班禅等大活佛转世必须遵循的国内寻访、金瓶掣签、中央政府批准原则,保障依法有序开展活佛转世事宜。2016年,"藏传佛教活佛查询系统"上线。截至2022年底,已有93位新转世活佛得到批准认定。

寺庙公共服务有效保障。从2015年开始,积极推进寺庙卫生室建设、僧医培养工作,完善寺庙僧尼社会保障体系,逐年提高寺庙僧尼社会保障待遇,积极提供社会公共服务。政府每年补贴2600多万元,实现在编僧尼医保、养老保险、低保、意外伤害险和健康体检的全覆盖。大力改善寺庙基础设施,绝大部分寺庙实现通路、通讯、通电、通水、通广播电视,广大僧尼的学习生活条件越来越现代化。

——藏传佛教活动健康有序

依法管理宗教事务稳步推进。西藏全面贯彻党的宗教工作基本方针,积极引导藏传佛教与社会主义社会相适应,加快推进宗教事务管理法治化、规范化、制度化建设。先后颁布实施《西藏自治区实施〈宗教事务条例〉办法》《西藏自治区大型宗教活动管理办法》《西藏自治区〈藏传佛教活佛转世管理办法〉实施细则》等规范性文件,依法保障宗教界合法权益,维护宗教领域正常秩序,妥善处理涉及宗教的各类矛盾和纠纷,依法加强和改进寺庙管理,促进宗教和谐。

藏传佛教研究与人才培养不断加强。支持宗教团体结合西藏实际,引导宗教界人士增强依法依规开展宗教活动的自觉性,推动藏传佛教界内部管理规范化、制度化、现代化。按照传统教育与现代教育相契合、传统学位与现代学衔相衔接,规范"三级学衔"制度,培养爱国爱教、学问精深的现代僧才。截至2022年底,已有164名学经僧人获得格西"拉让巴"学位,273名僧人获得藏传佛教最高学衔"拓然巴"学位。2016年至2022年,中国佛教协会西藏分会每年举办藏传佛教讲经阐释交流会,中国藏学研究中心每年举办藏传佛教教义阐释工作研讨会,出版《藏传佛教教义阐释(试讲本)》《藏传佛教教义阐释研究文集》等 11 部成果著作,教规教义研究日益精深。

四、社会大局持续安定向好

新时代党的治藏方略要求，要准确把握西藏工作的阶段性特征，提高社会治理水平，确保国家安全、社会稳定、人民幸福。西藏坚持把维护祖国统一、加强民族团结作为西藏工作的着眼点和着力点，不断完善工作机制、提高治理水平，谋长久之策，行固本之举，社会大局持续稳定向好，群众的获得感、幸福感、安全感不断增强。

——社会事业全面进步

教育事业高质量发展。涵盖学前教育、基础教育、职业教育、高等教育、继续教育、特殊教育的比较完整的现代教育体系已经形成。自 2012 年秋季学期开始，辍学问题得到历史性解决，建立起全学段学生资助体系，资助范围覆盖所有家庭经济困难学生。2012 年至 2022 年，国家累计投入西藏的教育经费达 2515.06 亿元，现有各级各类学校 3409 所，在校学生 94.4 万多人，学前教育毛入学率达 89.52%，义务教育巩固率达 97.73%，高中阶段毛入学率达 91.07%。第七次全国人口普查数据显示，西藏每 10 万人中拥有大学文化程度的由 2010 年的 5507 人上升到 2020 年的 11019 人，新增劳动力人均受教育年限提高至 13.1 年。

住房保障更加完善。深入实施城镇保障性安居工程建设和易地搬迁,全力推进老旧小区、棚户区及农村危房改造,加大公租房供给,实施城镇供暖工程,重点推进5个高寒高海拔县城和边境县城集中供暖工作。2016年以来,累计安排中央财政补助资金17.06亿元,完成农牧区建档立卡贫困户等4类重点对象4.36万户危房改造,接续实施动态新增农村低收入群体等重点对象危房改造和农房抗震改造。2022年,城镇居民和农牧民人均住房建筑面积分别达到44.82平方米和40.18平方米,居住条件显著改善。

公共卫生事业持续壮大。涵盖基本医疗服务和妇幼保健、疾病防控、藏医药等公共卫生服务体系全面建立。医疗人才"组团式"支援取得长足发展,援藏省市助力受援地成功创建6家三级甲等医院,帮带1165个医疗团队、3192名本地医疗人员,填补2219项技术空白。实现400多种"大病"不出自治区,2400多种"中病"不出市地,常见"小病"在县级医院就能得到及时治疗。孕产妇、婴幼儿死亡率分别由20世纪50年代初的5000/10万、430‰,下降到2022年的45.8/10万、7‰,人均预期寿命提高到72.19岁。包虫病、大骨节病等地方病和先天性心脏病、白内障等常见病得到有效控制和消除。近年来,采取病区改良水质、换粮、易地搬迁等综合防治措施,大骨节病高发流行态势得到有效遏制,54个病区县全部达到国家消除标准,2018年至今无儿童新发案例。2012年以来,开展先天性心脏病患儿医疗救治工作,已筛查366万多人次,对6246名患者在区内外医院实施介入或手术治疗,绝大多数患儿病情得到根治,重获健康。

多层次社会保障体系基本建成。不断推进城乡社会保障体系一体化,加快健全覆盖全民、统筹城乡、公平统一、可持续的分类分层社会保障体系。城镇调查失业率低于全国平均水平,零就业家庭持续动态清零。城乡居民基本养老保险待遇确定和基础养老金正常调整机制逐步建立,居民基本养老保险待遇水平与经济发展同步提高,基本医疗保险参保人数达 342.88 万人,参保率持续稳定在 95%以上,城乡居民住院产生的合规医疗费用最高报销比例达到 90%以上。持续推进藏药纳入国家基本药物目录(民族药)工作,大病专项救治病种扩大到 38 种,实现医保报销一次性和跨省异地直接结算。

——平安西藏建设卓有成效

高水平平安建设切实推进。强化社会面管理,平安县、平安乡镇、平安小区、平安单位、平安寺庙、平安学校等基层平安创建活动持续推进,向更高水平综合治理迈进。坚持预防与化解相统一,积极推动解决合理诉求和实际困难,法理情并用推动"事心双解",培育打造"朗扎"调解室、"雪莲花"调解室、"乡贤帮帮忙"等模式,依靠群众、发动群众,为人民群众安居乐业构筑社会根基。拉萨市 7 次登上中国最具幸福感城市榜单,西藏各族群众安全感满意度指数连续多年保持在 99%以上。

——治理现代化水平明显提升

社会治理体系不断健全。西藏创新社会治理机制,制定出台全区市域社会治理现代化试点工作联系点工作方案、健全完善矛盾纠纷多元化解机制的实施意见、乡村治理领域专项整治实施方案等,立体化、智能化治安防控体系建设不断推进,综治中心和"智慧城市""智慧边防"建设加快推进。在城乡村居、社区广泛开展"双联户"服务管理和"创先争优强基础惠民生"活动,引导群众广泛参与社会治理,形成党委领导、政府负责、民主协商、社会协同、公众参与、法治保障、科技支撑的社会治理全覆盖新格局,打造人人有责、人人尽责、人人享有的社会治理共同体。

——固边兴边工作稳步推进

兴边富民建设有力推动。西藏着力创建国家固边兴边富边行动示范区,坚持固边和兴边并重,出台村镇建设规划,制定村镇建设实施方案,坚持把小康村建设与乡村振兴战略有机结合,推进完善边境地区基础设施和公共服务设施,实现农牧民群众就地就近就业,不断铸牢中华民族共同体意识,基本建成设施完善、产业兴旺、生态良好、宜居宜业的富裕文明村镇。边境地区群众生活大幅改善,自觉争做神圣国土的守护者、幸福家园的建设者,像格桑花一样扎根在雪域边陲。

五、生态安全屏障日益坚实

西藏是国家重要的生态安全屏障。保护好西藏生态环境,利在千秋、泽被天下。西藏坚持生态保护第一,处理好保护与发展的关系,走绿色可持续发展之路,着力打造全国乃至国际生态文明高地,美丽西藏建设不断释放生态红利。

——生态环境持续保持良好

生态功能区建设有序推进。积极推动羌塘、珠穆朗玛峰、冈仁波齐、高黎贡山、雅鲁藏布大峡谷等典型区域纳入《国家公园空间布局方案》,西藏自然保护地体系建设进入新阶段。现有各级各类自然保护区47个,总面积41.22万平方公里。第三次全国国土调查数据显示,林地、草地、湿地、水域等生态功能较强的地类增加到108.11万平方公里。设立三江源国家公园(唐北区域),加强了长江源区、澜沧江源区等中国江河源头的保护与修复。

高原生物多样性逐渐提升。2016年至2022年,完成营造林832万亩,实现森林覆盖率和草原综合植被盖度双增长。西藏有陆生野生脊椎动物1072种,其中雪豹、野牦牛、藏羚羊、黑颈鹤、滇金丝猴等国家一级保护野生动物65种,国家二级保护野生动物152种,大中型野生动物种群数量居全国之首;已记录维管束植物 7504 种,其中巨柏、喜马拉雅红豆杉等国家一级重点保护野生植物 9 种,国家二级重点保护野生植物 148 种。根据全国第二次陆生野生动植物资源调查,藏羚羊种群数量由 20 世纪 90 年代的 7 万余只增长到 30 余万只,野牦牛种群数量由 20 世纪不足 1 万头增长到 2 万余头,黑颈鹤数量由 20 世纪不足 3000 只增长到 1 万余只。曾被国际社会认为已绝种的西藏马鹿"失而复得",由发现时的 200 余头增长到 800 余头。发现白颊猕猴等野生动物新物种 5 种、中国新记录物种 5 种,发现野生植物新物种——吉隆毛鳞菊。

人居环境状况持续改善。"十三五"以来,环境空气质量优良天数比例达 99% 以上,主要城镇环境空气质量整体保持优良,7 个市地 6 项污染物浓度均达到国家二级及以上标准。珠穆朗玛峰区域环境空气质量持续保持在优良状态,达到一级标准。2022 年,拉萨市在全国 168 个重点城市空气质量排名中位列第一,林芝市、昌都市环境空气质量优良天数达到 100%。主要江河、湖泊水质整体保持优良。金沙江、雅鲁藏布江、澜沧江、怒江干流水质达到 II 类标准,拉萨河、年楚河、尼洋河等流经重要城镇的河流水质达到 II 类及以上标准,发源于珠穆朗玛峰的绒布河水质达 I 类标准。班公错、羊卓雍错和纳木错水质均为 III 类标准。地级城市集中式饮用水水源地水质达标率 100%。全面实施土壤污染防治行动,西藏土壤环境质量状况处于安全水平,总体维持自然本底状态。

——生态保护与经济建设相适宜

绿色低碳产业发展壮大。加快建设国家清洁能源基地,电力装机容量中清洁能源比重占到近90%,为国家碳达峰、碳中和贡献西藏力量。大力发展高原绿色农牧业,"三品一标"产品总数达到1014个。帕里牦牛和亚东黑木耳被评为中国百强农产品。加查县安绕镇核桃、隆子县热荣乡黑青稞、芒康县纳西民族乡葡萄获批"三品一标"产品,品牌效应开始凸显。

生态保育工作成效显现。推进《西藏生态安全屏障保护与建设规划(2008—2030年)》落地,实施"两江四河"(雅鲁藏布江、怒江、拉萨河、年楚河、雅砻河、狮泉河)流域绿化、乡村"四旁"(宅旁、路旁、田旁、水旁)植树等项目。加强建设项目的生态修复和绿色施工。雅鲁藏布江上的藏木水电站建设过程中,通过修建2.6公里长的鱼类洄游通道和每年大规模的增殖放流等方式,有力保护了高原珍稀鱼类的生存和繁殖。拉日铁路建设过程中,选植优良树种,确保边坡植草及乔木成活率和固沙防沙,在主要地段为野生动物迁徙留出高架通道。拉林铁路建设过程中,有效保护黑颈鹤的最大越冬栖息地。

——生态文明高地加快建设

生态环境治理体系日益完善。落实《青藏高原生态环境保护和可持续发展方案》,施行《中华人民共和国青藏高原生态保护法》,颁布实施《西藏自治区国家生态文明高地建设条例》等政策法规。统筹山水林田湖草沙冰一体化保护和系统治理,全面推进河湖林草保护责任到人。2017年,西藏全面推行河湖长制,实现河流、湖泊全覆盖。实行最严格水资源管理制度,建立"河湖长+检察长+警长"协作机制,强化水域岸线管控,维护河湖生命健康,实现河湖功能永续利用。全面推行林长制,初步构建起党委领导、党政同责、属地负责、部门协同、源头治理、全域覆盖的林草资源保护发展长效机制。不断加强与周边地区的合作,2020年,与青海、云南签订《跨省流域上下游突发水污染事件联防联控机制合作协议》;2021年,与四川、云南、青海、甘肃、新疆和新疆生产建设兵团联合制定实施《关于建立青藏高原及周边区域生态检察司法保护跨省际区划协作机制的意见》,实现青藏高原协同保护。不断完善监测监察考核体系,深化领导干部自然资源资产责任审计,在11个国家级自然保护区设立35个公益诉讼检察联络室,提升生态环境领域公益诉讼执法能力。

科学考察和技术攻关取得突破性进展。国家启动第二次青藏高原综合科学考察研究,聚焦水、生态、人类活动,深入分析青藏高原环境变化与机理,在国际地球科学和生命科学前沿领域产出一批原创性理论成果,对青藏高原的科学认识达到新的高度。加强青藏高原科学研究基地平台建设,建成国家青藏高原科学数据中心西藏分中心,科考成果为保护青藏高原生态环境、应对气候变化、防控自然灾害、促进绿色发展等提供科学支撑。2012年以来,持续在气候变化影响、生物多样性等领域开展技术攻关和应用示范研究,产生了一批创新成果。高原典型退化生态系统修复技术研究突破退化草地植被恢复关键技术,获得 10 项新技术新方法新工艺。建成拉萨地球系统多维网生态保护修复治理示范工程,提出生态保护修复治理的系统方案。推动山水林田湖草沙冰系统治理,查明青藏高原生态系统变化和碳汇功能,服务国家生态安全屏障体系优化和碳中和国家目标。建成西藏首家种质资源库,累计入库保存种质资源 2047 种 8458 份,为生物多样性保护提供基础支撑。研究形成高原固废生物质低碳化能量利用技术体系,有效降低固废处理成本约 15%,环境污染减排大于 75%,相关成果已推广至青海等地,实现经济效益近 3 亿元。

——美丽西藏建设释放生态红利

生态保护机制持续发力。2018 年以来,累计落实山水林田湖草沙冰一体化保护修复资金 49.33 亿元。建立覆盖森林、湿地、草原、水生态等领域的生态保护补偿机制。各类生态保护补偿资金从 2012 年的 37 亿元,快速增加到 2022 年的 161 亿元。

生态扶贫向生态富民转变。2016 年至 2022 年,年均为群众提供生态保护岗位 53.77 万个,累计兑现生态补偿资金 126.37 亿元。大力发展生态产业和碳汇经济,带动群众绿色就业创业。截至 2022 年底,家庭民宿(旅馆)数量达 2377 家,乡村旅游接待游客 1274 万人次,实现收入 15.87 亿元,农牧民直接和间接参与乡村旅游就业 6.4

万人次,人均增收 4500 余元。

　　生态环保生活方式蔚然成风。人与自然和谐共生、追求可持续发展的高原生态文化得到进一步激发。林芝市成功创建国家森林城市。林芝市波密、山南市琼结、昌都市江达等 11 个市县区成为国家生态文明建设示范区。林芝市巴宜区、山南市隆子县、拉萨市柳梧新区达东村入选"绿水青山就是金山银山"实践创新基地。2016 年起,"那曲地区城镇植树关键技术研发与绿化模式示范项目"在那曲示范推广植树 200 余亩,选育出班公柳、高山柳、云杉、江孜沙棘等多种高抗树种,结束了那曲种不活一棵树的历史。许多农牧民从曾经的砍树人变成种树人、护树人,丰富的生态资源成为当地群众看得见守得住的"幸福不动产"。

六、民主法治建设不断加强

做好西藏工作,必须厉行法治,加强社会主义民主建设。西藏始终坚持党的领导、人民当家作主和依法治藏有机统一;保证人民代表大会制度、中国共产党领导的多党合作和政治协商制度、民族区域自治制度、基层群众自治制度在西藏贯彻落实。西藏政治建设迈出新步伐,有效保障各族人民享有当家作主的权利,极大推动各项事业发展进步。

——社会主义民主建设深入推进

人民代表大会制度优越性充分体现。党的十八大以来,西藏自治区进行的两次换届选举中,90%以上的选民参加了县、乡直接选举,有些地方参选率达到100%。人大代表履职尽责的体制机制更加完善,自治区人大建立落实了人大常委会组成人员直接联系基层人大代表、基层人大代表联系人民群众的"双联系"制度。米林市南伊珞巴民族乡人大代表达娃秉承"群众选我当代表,我为群众办实事"理念,与有关部门沟通,为昌都三岩搬迁群众修建温室大棚、解决群众入冬吃菜难的问题。截至目前,西藏共创建772个"人大代表之家",覆盖所有市(地)、县(区)、乡(镇、街道),部分行政村建有"代表小组"活动室,人大闭会期间代表履职活动更加经常化、规范化、制度化。

社会主义协商民主独特优势更加彰显。西藏把协商民主深深嵌入社会主义民主政治全过程,充分发挥人民政协作为协商民主重要渠道和专门协商机构的作用,围绕经济社会发展中的重大问题和涉及群众切身利益的实际问题建真言献良策。人民政协吸收民族宗教、党外知识分子、新的社会阶层等各界、各族人士参加。政协第十二届西藏自治区委员会共有委员 440 人,其中非中共党员占比59.3%。74 个县(区)政协组织全覆盖,全区政协委员超过 8000 名,85.7%是少数民族。2013 年至 2022 年,政协西藏自治区委员会共收到提案 4356 件,已全部办复。政协推动委员认真履行政治协商、民主监督、参政议政职责。

基层民主实践广泛真实生动。西藏社会主义基层民主实践形式不断丰富,农村建立村民代表会议制度,城市社区全部建立社区居民代表大会、社区居委会等社区组织,为社区居民自治提供了充分的组织保障。2019 年,《西藏自治区村务公开办法》颁布实施,90%以上的行政村设立村务公开栏,保障群众的知情权、参与权、决策权、监督权。2015 年,出台《西藏自治区职工代表大会工作规范(试行)》。迄今全区有基层工会组织 8821 个,工会会员 60.7 万人。企事业单位职工通过职工代表大会等民主管理制度,在重大决策和涉及职工切身利益等重大事项中充分行使民主权利。

——民族区域自治制度全面实施

民族区域自治制度进一步贯彻落实。民族区域自治制度赋予自治区在政治、经济、社会、文化等方面的发展权利;自治区人大及其常委会还制定多项全国性法律的实施办法,成为国家立法的重要补充。贯彻"收入全留、补助递增、专项扶持"财政补贴优惠政策,把中央关心、全国支援与自力更生、艰苦奋斗有机结合起来,合理安排使用地方财政收入。民族区域自治制度在西藏的实践不断深化,具体举措和实现形式与时俱进。

宪法和法律赋予的权利得到充分行使。西藏自治区人民代表大会常务委员会主任或副主任由藏族公民担任,自治区主席由藏族公民担任。全区 42153 名四级人大代表中,藏族和其他少数民族占89.2%。第十四届全国人民代表大会的西藏代表共有 24 名,其中藏族和其他少数民族代表 16 名,占 66.7%,门巴族、珞巴族等人口较少民族也有自己的代表。29 名住藏全国政协委员中,少数民族委员占比 86.2%。妇女在各级人大代表、政协委员中的比例较以往明显提高。少数民族干部培养使用工作不断加强,为西藏的全面繁荣稳定和发展进步作出重要贡献。

——依法治藏工作取得重大进展

法规体系建设长足发展。党的十八大以来,西藏践行"治国必治边、治边先稳藏"的战略思想,制定实施一批地方性法规、政府规章和规范性文件,建立科学完备的法规体系,加强法治政府和法治社会一体化建设,实现对自治区各项事务治理的制度化、规范化、程序化。截至 2022 年底,自治区人大及其常委会先后制定实施 160 件地方性法规和具有法规性质的决议、决定,确保稳定、发展、生态、强边四件大事及涉及社会管理、民生福祉等各类事项都能在法治轨道上运行。自治区人大及其常委会从地方实际出发,突出地方特色,立足重要的国家安全屏障和生态安全屏障,先后制定并颁布实施《西藏自治区民族团结进步模范区创建条例》《西藏自治区国家生态文明高地建设条例》。从 2021 年开始,西藏所有设区的市都拥有地方立法权。地方立法主体的扩大和地方立法体制的完善,为西藏社会的稳定繁荣提供了法治保障。

法治政府建设迈出新步伐。持续优化营商环境,制定出台《西藏自治区优化政务环境工作方案》《西藏自治区推进西南五省政务服务"跨省通办"工作实施方案》。强化权力制约监督,出台《西藏自治区行政执法监督条例》《西藏自治区规范行政执法裁量权规定》《西藏自治区重大行政决策程序暂行规定》等地方性法规、政府规章和规范性文件。依法公开政务信息,"互联网+政务服务"扎实推进,政务服务事项网上可办率显著提升,进一步优化政务服务,方便群众办事。

法治社会建设实现新突破。中共中央办公厅、国务院办公厅出台《关于加快推进公共法律服务体系建设的意见》,公共法律服务体系向纵深推进,县级以上司法行政机关全部挂牌运行公共法律服务实体平台,逐步向社区基层面延伸。仅2021年,西藏法律援助机构共组织提供法律咨询2.73万余人次,办理法律援助案件7626件,为受援人挽回经济损失9847万元。出台《西藏自治区法治宣传教育条例》,深入开展以宪法为核心的中国特色社会主义法律体系宣传教育,切实加强乡村法治文化阵地、校园法治文化阵地及宗教活动场所法治文化阵地建设,分区分类营造浓厚的法治氛围。大力实施乡村"法律明白人"培养工程,建立村居法律服务微信群,实现村居法律顾问全覆盖。坚持送法下乡,深入开展以案释法和全国民主法治示范村(社区)创建等工作,引导带动更多群众尊法学法守法用法。

结　束　语

伟岸的喜马拉雅山,见证西藏和平解放以来的沧桑巨变;奔腾的雅鲁藏布江,奏响新时代西藏发展进步的恢弘乐章。党的十八大以来,西藏步入发展最好、变化最大、群众得实惠最多的历史时期。西藏经济社会的发展进步是中国建设发展辉煌成就的一个典型缩影,是中国式现代化在世界屋脊创造的人类发展奇迹。

实践充分证明,只有全面深入贯彻落实新时代党的治藏方略,坚持所有发展都要赋予民族团结进步的意义,都要赋予维护统一、反对分裂的意义,都要赋予改善民生、凝聚人心的意义,都要有利于提升各族群众获得感、幸福感、安全感,抓好稳定、发展、生态、强边四件大事,才能确保西藏长治久安和高质量发展。

党的二十大报告提出,中国共产党的中心任务就是团结带领全国各族人民全面建成社会主义现代化强国、实现第二个百年奋斗目标,以中国式现代化全面推进中华民族伟大复兴。这为新时代西藏工作树立了新航标,将鼓舞激励西藏各族人民以铸牢中华民族共同体意识为主线,坚定不移走中国特色解决民族问题的正确道路,贯彻落实新时代党的治藏方略,完整准确全面贯彻新发展理念,全面推进民族团结进步事业,继续谱写西藏长治久安和高质量发展的绚烂华章。

第二部分　英文版

China's Green Development in the New Era

The State Council Information Office of
the People's Republic of China

January 2023

Preface

Green is the color of nature and the symbol of life. A sound eco-environment is the basic foundation for a better life, and the common aspiration of the people. Green development is development that follows the laws of nature to promote harmonious coexistence between humanity and nature, development that obtains the maximum social and economic benefits at minimum cost in resources and environmental impact, and sustainable and high-quality development that protects the eco-environment. It has become the goal of all countries.

Respecting and protecting nature has made an important contribution to the survival and prosperity of the Chinese nation over thousands of years. The concept of "harmony between humanity and nature" is a distinct characteristic of Chinese civilization. To vigorously promote the building of a socialist eco-civilization, China has established a fundamental national policy of conserving resources and protecting the environment, and a national strategy of sustainable development since the launch of reform and opening up.

Since the 18th CPC National Congress in 2012, under the guidance of Xi Jinping Thought on Socialism with Chinese Characteristics for a New Era, China has firmly upheld the belief that lucid waters and lush mountains are invaluable assets. It has prioritized eco-environmental conservation and green development, promoted the comprehensive green transformation of economic and social development, and achieved modernization based on harmony between humanity and nature. Wonders have been accomplished in eco-environmental protection and green development, and great strides have been made in building a beautiful China. Green is the defining feature of China in the new era and green development features the Chinese path to modernization. With more blue skies, green mountains, and lucid waters, the Chinese people could enjoy more accessible and sustainable green benefits. China's green development has helped to expand the greening areas of its own land and the earth, benefitting both China and the world at large.

As the world's largest developing country, China is committed to the idea of a global community of shared future. It has offered unwavering support to multilateralism, proposed the Global Development Initiative and the Global Security Initiative, expanded practical cooperation, and actively participated in global environment and climate governance. It has contributed Chinese wisdom and strength to implementing the UN 2030 Agenda for Sustainable Development, creating a community of life for humanity and nature, and building a clean, beautiful and prosperous world of sustainable development.

The Chinese government is publishing this white paper to present a full picture of China's ideas, actions, and achievements in green development in the new era, and to share with the world its experience in this regard.

I. Staying Firmly Committed to Green Development

To meet the people's desire for a better life, China has treated lucid waters and lush mountains as invaluable assets and worked to maintain harmony between humanity and nature in its development. China favors high-quality economic growth, high-level environmental protection, and a path of sound development based on higher economic output and living standards, and healthy ecosystems.

1. Applying a people-centered development philosophy

The people-centered philosophy is a governing principle of the Communist Party of China (CPC), and a sound eco-environment is the fairest public product and the most inclusive public benefit. As China's modernization advances and living standards improve, the popular demand for a beautiful environment is growing. In the people's happiness index, the weight of environment has increased. To meet the growing demand for a beautiful environment, China has strengthened eco-environmental conservation and protection and vigorously promoted eco-friendly ways of work and life. It has focused on solving the major environmental problems that seriously endanger people's health, improved the quality of the environment and ecosystems, and provided more quality eco-environmental goods, so as to help people feel happier, more satisfied, and more secure in a beautiful environment.

2. Focusing on sustainable development in China

Society will prosper when the environment improves, and lose vigor as the environment degrades. Nature provides the basic conditions for human survival and development. Respecting, accommodating, and protecting nature is essential for sustainable development. Bearing in mind that its environmental capacity is limited and its ecosystem is fragile, China has not only pursued development for the present generation, but also mapped out plans for generations to come. It regards eco-environmental conservation as fundamental to sustainable development in China. It values both the environment and economic development, works to translate eco-environmental strengths into development strengths, and always looks to realize the economic and social value that lucid waters and lush mountains have, which will bring about financial returns, eco-environmental benefits, social benefits, and harmony between humanity and nature.

3. Applying systems thinking and a coordinated approach

Green development is an all-round revolutionary change in our values, and in how we work, live, and think. China has applied systems thinking to the whole process of economic and social development and eco-environmental conservation and protection. It has taken a sound approach to the relationships between development and protection, between overall and local interests, and between the present and the future. It has taken a scientific, moderate, and orderly approach to the use of territorial space, and promoted a sound economic structure that facilitates green, low-carbon, and circular development. It has fostered an institutional system that combines both constraints and incentives to coordinate industrial restructuring, pollution control, eco-environmental conservation, and climate response. China has endeavored to cut carbon emissions, reduce pollution, expand green development, and pursue economic growth. It has prioritized eco-environmental protection, conserves resources and uses them efficiently for green and low-carbon development. It has developed spatial configurations, industrial structures, and ways of work and life that help conserve resources and protect the environment, and promoted greener economic and social development in all respects.

4. Working together for global sustainable development

Protecting the environment and countering climate change are the common responsibilities of all countries. Only when all countries unite and work together to promote green and sustainable development can we maintain the overall balance in the earth's ecology and protect humanity's one and only home. China has shouldered its responsibilities, actively participated in global environmental governance, and pledged to reach

---

Panel 1 Policies and Actions on Carbon Emissions Peaking and Carbon Neutrality

The "1+N" policy framework for carbon emissions peaking and carbon neutrality:

The "1+N" policy framework comprises of two top-level design documents, i.e., the Working Guidance for Carbon Dioxide Peaking and Carbon Neutrality in Full and Faithful Implementation of the New Development Philosophy, the Action Plan for Carbon Dioxide Peaking Before 2030, and the action plans to achieve carbon emissions peak in key areas and sectors such as energy, industry, transport, urban and rural construction, iron & steel, non-ferrous metals, and cement, plus the support measures in technology, finance, standards, and talent development.

Ten major actions for carbon emissions peaking:

In accordance with the Action Plan for Carbon Dioxide Peaking Before 2030, China will take 10 actions:
- for green and low-carbon energy transition;
- for energy saving, carbon emissions reduction, and efficiency improvement;
- for carbon emissions peaking in industry;
- for carbon emissions peaking in urban and rural development;
- for promoting green and low-carbon transport;
- for facilitating carbon emissions reduction through the circular economy;
- for encouraging innovation in green and low-carbon technology;
- for consolidating and improving carbon sink capacity;
- for advocating a green and low-carbon lifestyle nationwide;
- for reaching carbon emissions peak by different regions in a structured and orderly manner.

---

carbon emissions peak by 2030 and carbon neutrality by 2060. It will advance the green transition with these goals as the lead, play a more active part in bilateral and multilateral international cooperation on green development, promote a fair and equitable system of global environmental governance, and contribute its wisdom and strength to global sustainable development.

II. A Basic Green Territorial Configuration Is in Place

China is making efforts to optimize its governing system of territorial space. The country has strengthened the overall planning and coordinated management and control of territorial space for working and living and for the environment. It has intensified efforts to protect and restore ecosystems, effectively expanded the capacity of the eco-environment, and promoted the rapid accumulation of natural wealth and eco-environmental wealth, leading to historic, transformative, and comprehensive changes in eco-environmental protection and providing strong support for the sustainable and healthy development of the economy and society.

1. Optimizing the development and protection of territorial space

A country's territorial space is the carrier for green development. China has implemented a functional zoning strategy and established a unified territorial space planning system that is science-based, efficient and built upon clearly defined powers and responsibilities. Taking into consideration factors such as population distribution, regional economic structures, land use, and eco-environmental protection, it has planned for the development and protection of territorial space with a holistic approach, so as to achieve higher-quality and more sustainable development of its territorial space.

China has integrated different plans into a single master plan for territorial space development. It has integrated functional zoning, land use, urban and rural planning, and other spatial planning into a unified territorial space plan. A comprehensive system integrating planning approval, implementation supervision, regulations, policies and technical standards is taking shape. The role of territorial space planning has been strengthened in guiding and constraining various specific plans. It has sped up the drafting of various plans for territorial space at all levels. As a result, an overall master plan will eventually be drawn up for the development and protection of territorial space.

Concerted efforts have been made to optimize the use of territorial space. Based on the results of national land resource surveys, China has carried out an evaluation of the carrying capacity of resources and the environment, and suitability of land development. It has scientifically designated agricultural, ecological, urban and other functional zones, and improved the territorial space layout that consists of three major zones – main agricultural production zones, key ecosystem service zones and urbanized zones. To strengthen national and regional eco-environmental security, China has designated permanent basic cropland, drawn red lines for eco-environmental protection, delineated boundaries for urban development, and set protection lines for all types of sea areas, in a coordinated manner. It has established centralized control over the use of territorial space and ensured that these lines are not crossed.

China has strengthened the management of key ecosystem service zones and endeavored to prevent and control eco-environmental risks. County-level administrative units that perform important ecological functions such as water conservation, soil and water conservation, inhibiting winds, fixing sand, and protecting biodiversity are designated as key ecosystem service zones, which should focus on protecting the environment and providing eco-environmental products and be restricted from large-scale industrialization and urbanization. As a result, China's natural ecosystems are generally stable or improving, eco-environmental services have improved, and the supply of eco-environmental products has continued to increase.

2. Strengthening eco-environmental conservation and restoration
Mountains, rivers, forests, farmland, lakes, grasslands and deserts

are communities of life. China has stepped up systematic, comprehensive, and law-based environment governance, tackling problems at their sources. Prioritizing protection and focusing on natural restoration, it has vigorously pressed forward with the protection and restoration of ecosystems, so as to build a solid national eco-environmental security barrier and strengthen the foundations for the sustainable development of the Chinese nation.

A new type of protected area (PA) system has been set up. PAs are major platforms for eco-environmental conservation. China is developing a PA system with national parks as the mainstay, supported by nature reserves and supplemented by nature parks. It has created its first batch of five national parks – the Three-River-Source National Park, the Giant Panda National Park, the Northeast China Tiger and Leopard National Park, the Hainan Tropical Rainforest National Park, and the Wuyishan National Park. It is making steady progress in building national parks in environmentally important regions. As of the end of 2021, nearly 10,000 PAs of various types and levels had been established, covering more than 17 percent of China's land area, bringing under effective protection 90 percent of its natural terrestrial ecosystem types and 74 percent of key state-protected wildlife species.

Setting up scientific eco-environmental conservation red lines (ECRLs). ECRLs are the lifeline of national eco-environmental security. China has brought functional areas of vital importance, exceedingly fragile areas, and areas of potentially vital eco-environmental value within the scope of the ECRL framework. More than 30 percent of China's land area – including integrated and optimized PAs – is now under the protection of ECRLs. Through drawing ECRLs and drafting ecological protection and restoration plans, the country has consolidated an overall eco-environmental conservation configuration composed of Three Eco-zones and Four Shelterbelts – the Qinghai-Tibet Plateau Eco-zone, the Yellow River Eco-zone (including the Loess Plateau Ecological Barrier), the Yangtze River Eco-zone (including the Sichuan-Yunnan Ecological Barrier), and

Panel 2   Protected Area (PA) System

PAs are terrestrial or marine areas legally defined or confirmed by governments at various levels, assigned to carry out long-term conservation of important ecosystems, natural relics, and natural landscapes as well as their natural resources, ecological services and cultural values. In accordance with management goals and efficacy, and profiting from international experience, China has classified PAs into national parks, nature reserves and nature parks according to their environmental value and protection sensitivity.

National parks are specific areas of land or sea set aside with the main goal of protecting China's unique ecosystems to achieve scientific conservation and rational utilization of natural resources. They are the most important of the country's natural ecosystems – those with the most distinctive natural landscapes, the finest natural relics, and the richest biodiversity.

Nature reserves are areas with particular ecosystems, natural and concentrated distributions of rare or endangered wildlife species, and natural relics of special significance. Nature reserves are set up to guarantee the safety of the subjects under protection, and maintain and restore populations of rare or endangered wild flora and fauna species and the habitats on which they depend for survival.

Nature parks are areas containing important ecosystems, natural relics, and natural landscapes of ecological, sightseeing, cultural or scientific value that can be used sustainably. Their role is to ensure the effective protection of scarce natural resources such as forests, oceans, wetlands, rivers, glaciers, grasslands and wildlife, as well as the views, geological landforms, and cultural diversity they contain. Nature parks include forest parks, geological parks, marine parks, wetland parks, desert parks and grassland parks.

the Northeast, North, South, and Coastal Shelterbelts.

Carrying out major projects for the conservation and restoration of key national ecosystems. With a focus on major national eco-environmental functional areas, ECRLs and PAs, China has launched projects for holistic conservation and restoration of mountains, rivers, forests, farmland, lakes, grasslands and deserts, taking comprehensive and systematic measures to deal with problems by addressing their root causes. It has carried out shelterbelt and natural forest protection and restoration programs such as the shelterbelt program in northeast China, north China and northwest China, programs returning marginal farmland to forests and grasslands, the program for ecological restoration of abandoned mines, the Blue Bay environment improvement initiative, the coastal belts protection and restoration program, the comprehensive management of the Bohai Sea water environment, the conservation and restoration of mangrove forests, and other restoration and rehabilitation projects of significant eco-environmental importance. China has carried out large-scale afforestation projects, steadily increased the area of forests, grasslands, wetlands, rivers and lakes, and effectively reversed the trend of desertification.

From 2012 to 2021, 64 million hectares of trees were planted. During this period, desertification prevention and control was carried out over 18.53 million hectares of land, and 40 million hectares of land were improved through sowing grass, and more than 800,000 hectares of wetland were added or restored. In 2021, the forest coverage ratio hit 24 percent, while the forest stock volume grew to 19.5 billion cubic meters. Both figures represented 30 consecutive years of growth, making China the country with the highest growth in forest resources and the largest area of man-made forest. China is also the first country to realize zero net land degradation – its desertified and sandified areas are both shrinking, and this is helping the world to reach the global goal of zero net land degradation in 2030. Since 2000, China has led the world in greening the planet, contributing around one fourth of the newly added green areas in the world.

3. Promoting the green development of key regions

China gives full play to the guiding role of major strategies for regional development and the implementation of these strategies, based on prioritizing eco-environmental conservation and promoting green

Panel 3　Saihanba – From Desert to Oasis

　　Saihanba is located in the north of Hebei Province, about 300 kilometers to the north of Beijing. In the 1950s it was a barren land ravaged by yellow sand without so much as a tree for a bird to perch on. Sand whipped up by wind encroached southward, threatening Beijing. To remedy this dire problem, shelter the capital city from sand, and conserve water sources for Beijing and Tianjin, China set up the Saihanba Mechanized Forest Farm in the early 1960s. An initial team of 369 started to reclaim the wasteland. Under sand-blotted sky and on this sand-locked land, several dedicated Saihanba generations have worked without respite, building the world's largest man-made forest and creating a "desert-to-oasis" miracle. They have created a green barrier safeguarding the Beijing-Tianjin-Hebei region, and setting an example for China and the world in terms of desertification control.

　　Today, the Saihanba Forest Farm covers an area of 76,733 hectares. It has a growing forest stock volume of 10.4 million cubic meters, and every year it conserves and cleans 284 million cubic meters of freshwater, effectively preventing soil erosion and laying a solid foundation for high-quality development in the Beijing-Tianjin-Hebei region. The forest farm has also boosted seedling bases and rural tourism, creating jobs for more than 4,000 locals and benefiting more than 40,000 people in the surrounding area. The forest farm has generated enormous eco-environmental and social benefits, and changed the work and lives of the local people for the better.

　　The green "Great Wall" built by the Saihanba Forest Farm has earned international honors. In 2017, the forest farm won the UN Champions of the Earth Award, and in 2021 it received the Land for Life Award from the UN.

development. It works to build the key regions into pioneers and models in green development to boost green social and economic development across the country.

　　Pushing for breakthroughs in environmental protection in the coordinated development of the Beijing-Tianjin-Hebei region. The strategy for the region's coordinated development has been implemented, spurring the integrated development of areas such as transport, environment, industry and public services, and strengthening joint prevention and control of environmental problems. With the region as a focus, comprehensive efforts have been made to address overexploitation of groundwater in north China, with the groundwater level going down continuously since the 1980s being reversed. In this region, Xiongan New Area is being built according to forward-looking plans and high standards, with a focus on developing it into a destination for entities relocated from Beijing as their functions are non-essential to Beijing's role as the capital. Xiongan will be built into an eco-friendly exemplar city of high-quality green development with a rational layout, a good balance of blue water, green areas, clean air, clear skies and urban facilities. In 2021, in 13 cities in the region, 74 percent of days had good air quality. This was an increase of 32 percentage points compared with 2013. Beijing has set an example in air quality control for the world.

Promoting well-coordinated environmental conservation and avoiding excessive development while developing the Yangtze River Economic Belt. The Yangtze River is the mother river of the Chinese nation, and a powerhouse for China's development. The restoration of the Yangtze River's eco-environment is a top priority. China is coordinating economic development and environmental protection and building an economic belt epitomizing green development and harmony between humanity and nature.

Taking advantage of the opportunities offered by industrial integration, the Yangtze River Economic Belt is building a green industrial system and accelerating its green economic transformation. A tough battle has been launched to protect and restore the eco-environment in the Yangtze River Basin: Intense efforts have been made to carry out the "4+1" project – the treatment of urban sewage and garbage, chemical pollution, agricultural non-point source pollution, ship pollution and tailing pond pollution; a comprehensive 10-year fishing ban in the Yangtze River Basin has been implemented; action has been taken to regulate banks development projects and remove illegal dykes. Since 2018, unauthorized structures along 162 kilometers of the river banks have been demolished, more than 12 square kilometers along the banks have been revegetated, and 4,533 hectares have been returned to water. The water quality at the state-monitored sections of the mainstream of the Yangtze River has reached Grade II level (the second best level) for the past two years.

The pioneering role of the Yangtze River Delta region in green development. The construction of the Yangtze River Delta Integrated Green Development Demonstration Zone will be accelerated, to explore ways to translate eco-environmental strengths into social and economic benefits, and ways for the region to transition from coordinated project execution to regional integrated institutional innovation. With picturesque scenery,

---

Panel 4　Ten-Year Fishing Ban in the Yangtze River Basin

At midnight on January 1, 2021, a 10-year fishing ban came into effect in key water areas including the mainstream and major tributaries of the Yangtze River and large lakes connected with it. During this period, fishing for commercial purpose is prohibited. The 111,000 fishing vessels and 231,000 fishermen have all ceased fishing. 222,000 fishermen eligible for social insurance have been covered by this insurance, and 165,000 who are willing and able to work have been transferred into other jobs.

The 10-year ban is an essential measure in protecting biodiversity, restoring the river's ecological functions, and safeguarding the country's environment. Since the ban took effect, the aquatic biological resources in areas along the river have increased remarkably, and the ecological functions of the waters are also gradually recovering. The Yangtze finless porpoise, known as the "smiling angel", is now seen more frequently in Poyang Lake, Dongting Lake, Yichang City of Hubei Province and in the lower reaches of the Yangtze River. Ochetobius elongates, after disappearing from the Yangtze River for 20 years, have reappeared in the middle reaches. Fishery resources in the Chishui River, a tributary of the upper reaches of the Yangtze River, have also rebounded in numbers, with the populations of its fish species having increased from 32 before the ban to 37. The volume of fishery resources has almost doubled since the ban.

a rich culture, specialty industries, and a cluster of innovation resources, the region will lay a solid foundation for green development, and develop into a hub for green and innovation-driven development.

Eco-environmental conservation and high-quality development in the Yellow River Basin. Protecting the Yellow River is a long-term strategy of fundamental importance to the Chinese nation. China has made coordinated plans and carried out ecological protection and improvement in the entire Yellow River Basin, including soil erosion and desertification control in its upper and middle reaches and comprehensive treatment of river courses and banks in the lower reaches. The sediment load of the Yellow River has steadily fallen, which helps to ensure its safety. Water availability has been a determining factor in urban and industrial development, agriculture, and population distribution. A path of intensive water-conservation has been followed so that water security has been effectively ensured, water resources are used efficiently, and the ecology has improved. Areas along the Yellow River are being protected in order to carry forward and disseminate the Yellow River culture, develop specialty industries and nurture new industries and business models. This has raised both the eco-environmental and economic value of the river, to the benefit of the people.

Building a beautiful Guangdong-Hong Kong-Macao Greater Bay Area. China has vigorously improved the quality of the eco-environment in the bay area, explored green and low-carbon urban construction and operation models, and promoted sustainable development, making its skies bluer, mountains greener, and water clearer. The area will enjoy a safe and beautiful eco-environment, a stable society, and cultural prosperity.

4. Building a beautiful home with a pleasant living environment

Urban and rural areas are the carriers of human settlements and activities. China integrates the philosophy of green development into urban and rural construction, and promotes beautiful cities and beautiful countryside initiatives. With priority given to environmental pollution control,

China strives to improve the living environment to build a beautiful home featuring lush mountains, green fields, singing birds, and blossoming flowers.

Building beautiful cities featuring harmony between humanity and nature. China has placed great emphasis on urban eco-environmental conservation and has adopted a people-centered approach to urbanization. It has made sound plans for spaces for working, living and eco-environmental conservation, and has worked to make cities livable, resilient and smart. The aim is to build cities into beautiful homes where humanity and nature coexist in harmony. In pursuing urbanization, China respects and accommodates the requirements of nature. It has made use of mountains, waters, and other unique landscapes to integrate cities into nature, so that urban dwellers can enjoy the view and are reminded of their rural origins. Efforts have been made to expand urban eco-environmental space through construction of national garden cities and forest cities, as well as parks and greenways in cities. With increased greenery coverage, the urban eco-environment has been effectively restored. From 2012 to 2021, green coverage of built-up urban areas increased from 39 percent to 42 percent, and the per capita area of park greenery has increased from 11.8 square

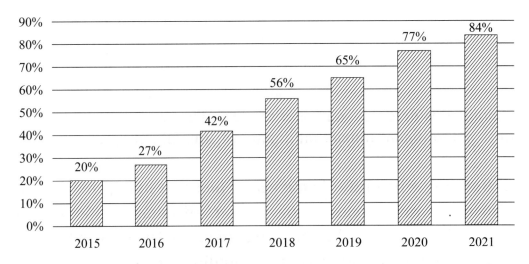

Figure 1 Yearly increased green building areas as a proportion of new urban building areas in China (2015-2021)

meters to 14.78 square meters. Great efforts have been made to construct green and low-carbon buildings, and renovation of existing ones has been promoted, contributing to increasingly higher energy efficiency.

Building a beautiful and harmonious countryside that is pleasant to live and work in. Green development is a new driver of rural revitalization, and China is exploring new paths for green development in rural areas. It is actively developing new industries and new forms of business such as eco-agriculture, rural e-commerce, leisure agriculture, rural tourism, health, and elderly care, while advancing projects to protect and restore ecosystems. These efforts allow China to approach its goal of having strong agriculture and a beautiful and revitalized countryside. China is continuing to redevelop the whole rural living environment and steadily advancing the construction of modern and livable homes with sanitary toilets in rural areas, strengthening the treatment and recycling of domestic waste and sewage. As a result, more and more rural areas have access to safe and clean water, paved roads, streetlights, and clean energy. With an improved environment, the vast rural areas have become more sustainable. Lush groves, orchards, and gardens of flowers and vegetables set each other off, and the splendid pastoral scene is a treat for the eyes. A beautiful countryside where the skies are blue, the lands are green, and the waters are clear brings people delight with its scenic view. Greater efforts have also been made to protect and utilize traditional villages and carry forward their fine traditions, which have increased their cultural charm.

Taking further steps to prevent and control pollution. The environment has a significant impact on quality of life. Green mountains display beauty, and blue skies bring happiness. China is curbing pollution in a law-based, scientific, and targeted way. Priority has been given to addressing the thorniest problems of air, water and soil contamination that are of greatest concern to the public. Effective measures have been taken to keep skies blue, waters clear, and land pollution-free. The mechanism of coordinated prevention and control across regions and approaches in

> **Panel 5   Improving Urban and Rural Environmental Infrastructure**
>
> China attaches great importance to the construction of environmental infrastructure and strives to address areas of weaknesses, optimize layouts, and improve quality. It has improved facilities for sewage collection, treatment, and recycling, and boosted the classification and treatment capacity of domestic waste. China has also worked to ensure the safe and effective disposal of solid waste, hazardous waste, and medical waste, promoted the integrated, intelligent, and green development of environmental infrastructure, and built a system of environmental infrastructure that integrates facilities and monitoring and supervising capabilities for the treatment and disposal of sewage, garbage, solid waste, hazardous waste, and medical waste. An environmental infrastructure network extending from cities to towns and villages has taken shape. By the end of 2021, the sewage treatment capacity of cities and counties has reached 247 million cubic meters per day, the incineration treatment capacity of urban domestic waste exceeded 770,000 tonnes per day, and the harmless treatment rate of urban domestic waste was close to 100 percent.

dealing with heavy air pollution have achieved remarkable results. The average PM2.5 density of China's cities at prefecture level and above dropped from 46 micrograms per cubic meter in 2015 to 30 micrograms per cubic meter in 2021. On 87.5 percent of the days in 2021, people enjoyed good air quality. China is making the fastest progress in air quality improvement. With an accelerated pace in curbing industrial, agricultural and domestic pollution sources, and in regulating water ecological systems, China has significantly reduced seriously polluted water bodies and sub-standard water bodies, and the safety of drinking water is ensured. In 2021, the proportion of surface water at or above Grade III in the country's five-tier water quality system reached 84.9 percent. China has banned the import of foreign waste, fulfilling its goal of "zero import" of solid waste while basically bringing the threat of soil contamination under control. Brilliant blue skies are dotted with white clouds during the day; when the sun sets, twinkling stars pattern the firmament. The shores are green and the waters are clean, with fish gliding under the clear water. People are breathing fresher air, drinking cleaner water, and eating safer food. Living in a beautiful environment, people can truly feel the happiness and beauty brought about by eco-environmental conservation.

III. Adjusting and Improving the Industrial Structure

China is committed to the philosophy of innovative, coordinated, green, open and shared development, and takes innovation-driven development as the driving force to create new momentum and build new strengths for economic development. China has placed rigid constraints on the exploitation of resources and the environment to promote comprehensive adjustment of the industrial structure, and strengthened regional cooperation to optimize the spatial configuration of industry. As a result, China's economy has registered a steady improvement in the quality of development while maintaining a reasonable pace of growth.

1. Vigorously developing strategic emerging industries

China implements the innovation-driven development strategy. It takes scientific and technological innovation as the driving force and guarantee for adjustment of industrial structure and green and low-carbon transition of the economy and society and regards strategic emerging industries as a key driver for economic development, reaping remarkable economic and social benefits as a result.

China has intensified investment in scientific and technological innovation. The nation's gross domestic research and development (R&D) spending grew from RMB1.03 trillion in 2012 to more than RMB2.8 trillion in 2021. Its R&D spending intensity, or the expenditure on R&D as a percentage of its GDP, rose from 1.91 percent in 2012 to 2.44 percent in 2021, approaching the average level of the Organization for Economic Cooperation and Development (OECD) countries. Chinese enterprises' investment in R&D has continued to increase, accounting for more than 76 percent of the country's total R&D investment. By the end of 2021, China's energy conservation and environmental protection industry owned 49,000 valid invention patents, and the new energy industry held 60,000, 1.6 and 1.7 times more than in 2017. From 2011 to 2020, the number of patent applications filed by China for environment-related technology inventions was close to 60 percent of the world total, making it the most active country in environmental technology innovation.

Emerging technologies have become the main props of China's economic development. Thanks to accelerated efforts to implement emerging technologies such as artificial intelligence (AI), big data, blockchain, and quantum communication, new products and business forms including intelligent terminals, telemedicine, and online education have been cultivated, and their role in boosting growth has continued to increase. China's digital economy ranks second in the world. During the 13th Five-year Plan period (2016-2020), the average annual growth rate of the added value of information transmission, software and information technology services reached 21 percent. The internet, big data, AI, 5G and other emerging technologies are deeply integrated with traditional industries, facilitating the integration of advanced manufacturing with modern services. The value-added output of high-tech and equipment manufacturing in 2021 accounted for 15.1 and 32.4 percent of that of industries above designated size, up 5.7 and 4.2 percentage points from 2012 respectively. China is on the way to realize the transformation and upgrading from "made in China" to "intelligent manufacturing in China".

China's green industries continue to grow. The renewable energy industry is growing rapidly, and China leads the world in the manufacture of clean energy generation facilities for wind and photovoltaic power. China produces more than 70 percent of the global total of polysilicon, wafers, cells and modules. The quality and efficiency of the energy-saving and environmental protection industries have continued to improve. China has developed a green technical equipment manufacturing system covering various sectors such as energy and water conservation, environmental protection, and renewable energy. The manufacturing and supply capacity of green technical equipment increases markedly while the cost keeps dropping. Technology in the fields of energy and water conservation equipment, pollution control, and environmental monitoring meets the highest international standards. New forms and models of business continue to grow, such as comprehensive energy services, contract-based energy and water management, third-party treatment of environmental pollution, and comprehensive carbon emissions management services. In 2021, the output value of China's energy conservation and environmental protection industries exceeded RMB8 trillion. Extensive pilot projects have been carried out at local level to explore methods and pathways to realize the value of eco-environmental products. New models of eco-friendly industry such as urban modern agriculture, leisure agriculture, eco-environmental tourism, forest healthcare, boutique homestays, and pastoral leisure complexes have witnessed rapid development.

2. Taking well-ordered steps to develop resource-based industries

China continues to expand supply-side structural reform and reverse the extensive development model that relies heavily on resource consumption at the cost of high pollution and emissions. With environmental capacity as a rigid constraint, it has exerted tight control over the production capacity of energy-intensive industries and industries with high emissions or water consumption, in order to optimize its industrial structure.

Easing overcapacity and closing down outdated production facilities. While protecting industrial and supply chains, China has taken active and well-ordered steps to ease overcapacity and close down outdated production facilities. Measures have been taken to curb industries that over-exploit resources and cause environmental damage, such as steel, cement and electrolytic aluminum. A swap system has been introduced that allows producers to open equal or lower amounts of new capacity in return for closures elsewhere. During the 13th Five-year Plan period (2016-

2020), China has removed more than 150 million tonnes of excess steel production capacity and 300 million tonnes of excess cement production capacity. Substandard steel products have been eliminated and almost all outdated production capacity in industries such as electrolytic aluminum and cement manufacturing has been removed.

China is resolved to stop the blind development of energy-intensive projects with high emissions and outdated production techniques. It has raised the entry threshold for some key industries in terms of land use, environmental protection, energy and water conservation, technology, and safety. A differentiated system has been introduced for energy-intensive industries, covering differentiated electricity pricing, tiered electricity pricing, and punitive electricity pricing. For energy-intensive projects with high emissions and outdated production techniques, China applies a list-based management approach involving classification and dynamic monitoring. It resolutely investigates and punishes all projects that violate laws or regulations. In areas with problems of water shortage or overconsumption, restrictions are imposed on various types of new development zones and projects requiring high water consumption.

3. Optimizing regional distribution of industries

Fully considering factors such as energy resources, environmental capacity, and market potential, China promotes the convergence of some industries in areas with more suitable conditions and greater potential for development. To expedite the formation of a modern and efficient industrial development configuration, it improves the distribution of productive forces and expands the division of industries and coordination across regions.

Working to bring about a rational distribution of raw material industries. China employs overall planning of resources such as coal and water and takes into consideration environmental capacity. Several modern coal chemical industry demonstration zones have been established in the central and western regions to pilot projects for technology upgrading in the coal chemical industry. A group of large-scale high-quality petrochemical industry bases has been constructed in coastal areas to promote the safe, green, intensive, and efficient development of the industry.

Expanding the division of industries and cooperation across regions. China is seeking to establish and improve a benefit-sharing mechanism by employing the comparative strengths of every region, each relying on its own resources and environmental advantages, and on the foundations of industrial development. Multi-type and multi-mechanism industrial division and coordination have been strengthened, along with cooperation between the east and the central and western regions, creating a framework of coordination, complementarity of strengths, and common development. Transferring industries and cooperation across regions are measures that help to break through the environmental and resource constraints that stifle industrial development. They also make room for the development of high-tech industries in the eastern region and propel the industrialization and urbanization process of underdeveloped areas in the central and western regions, improving the balance and strengthening the coordination of regional development.

IV. Extensive Application of Green Production Methods

China has accelerated the building of a green, circular, and low-carbon economy. It practices green production methods, promotes the energy revolution, the economical and intensive use of resources, and cleaner production, and pursues synergy in the reduction of pollution and carbon emissions. All these efforts have contributed to the coordinated development and balanced progress of the economy, society, and environmental protection.

1. Promoting the green transformation of traditional industries

In order to build a green, circular, and low-carbon production system, China has integrated the concept of green development into the entire life cycles of industry, agriculture and the service sector. To conserve energy, reduce emissions, raise efficiency, and facilitate the comprehensive green transformation of traditional industries, China has encouraged innovations in technology, models, and standards.

Promoting the green development of industry. China is committed to establishing a green manufacturing system, and creating green factories, green industrial parks, green supply chains, and green product evaluation standards. In order to accelerate the building of green industrial chains and supply chains, China provides guidance for enterprises to achieve innovations in the design of green products and adopt green, low-carbon and eco-friendly processes and equipment, and optimizes the spatial layout of enterprises, industries and infrastructure in industrial parks. Following the principles of "coupling of industries, extended responsibility of enterprises, and circular use of resources", it has promoted the transformation of industrial parks, circular combination of industries and circular production in enterprises. China has transformed its major industries to achieve clean production, and carried out comprehensive inspections of clean production. It has promoted digital transformation across the board. The digital control rate of key processes in key areas increased from 24.6 percent in 2012 to 55.3 percent in 2021, and the penetration rate of digital R&D and design tools increased from 48.8 percent to 74.7 percent in the same period. By the end of 2021, China hosted a total of 2,783 green factories, 223 green industrial parks, and 296 green supply chain management enterprises. The manufacturing sector has been significantly upgraded for green production.

Transforming the production methods of agriculture. China has created new systems and mechanisms for the green development of agriculture, expanded the functions of agriculture, explored the diversified rural values, and strengthened the protection and efficient use of agricultural resources. It has gradually improved the farmland protection system and the system of fallowing and crop rotation, put permanent basic cropland under special protection, and thereby made initial progress in containing the decline in the size of farmland. It has steadily advanced the conservation of chernozem soil. The quality of farmland has been upgraded steadily throughout the country. Measures have been taken to save water for agricultural irrigation and reduce the volume of chemical fertilizers and pesticides used by targeting higher efficiency. In 2021, the irrigation efficiency was raised to 0.568. China has developed a circular agricultural economy by promoting circular agricultural production modes – integrating planting and breeding with processing, farming and animal husbandry with fishing, and production and processing with marketing. It has increased the utilization of agricultural waste as a resource. It has taken a coordinated approach to promoting green and organic agricultural products, products with quality certifications and those with geographical indications, cultivating new breeds, improving product quality, fostering agricultural brands and standardizing agricultural production. China has implemented programs to protect agricultural products with geographical indications. There are now 60,000 types of green food and organic agricultural products across the country. The quality and safety standards of agricultural products have been steadily upgraded. The supply of high-quality agricultural products has increased significantly, which has effectively contributed to the upgrading of the whole industry, and generated higher incomes for farmers.

Advancing the green transformation of the service sector. China has actively cultivated green firms of business circulation, and launched a campaign to create green shopping malls. Nationwide, a total of 592 green shopping malls had been built by the end of 2021. China has continued to improve the energy efficiency of the information service industry, with some world-leading green data centers. To accelerate the reduction, standardization and recycling of express delivery packages, it has upgraded and improved the express delivery packaging standard system. To promote the green development of e-commerce enterprises, it has given guidance for producers and consumers to use renewable and degradable express delivery packages. By the end of 2021, 80.5 percent of e-commerce parcels were free of secondary packaging, all express delivery packages were sealed with thinner (45mm) tape, and all transit bags used in the sector were renewable.

China has promoted the green development of the convention and exhibition industry by formulating green standards and facilitating the repeated use of facilities. China has significantly reduced paper usage by introducing electronic railway tickets nationwide and encouraging electronic invoicing. In the catering industry, disposable tableware is being phased out. Guest houses and hotels have been encouraged not to offer disposable items as part of their services.

2. Promoting green and low-carbon energy

China applies the principle of building the new before discarding the old in a well-planned way. With growing capacity to ensure energy supply, it has moved faster to build a new energy system. The proportion of clean energy sources has increased significantly. Success has been achieved in the green and low-carbon transformation of the country's energy mix.

Vigorously developing non-fossil energy. China has made rapid progress in building large-scale wind and photovoltaic power stations on infertile and rocky terrain and in deserts. It has steadily developed offshore wind farms, actively promoted rooftop photovoltaic power generation in urban and rural areas, and encouraged distributed wind power generation in rural areas. China has built a structured matrix of large hydropower stations in the basins of major rivers, especially those in the southwest. In accordance with local conditions, it has developed solar, biomass, geothermal and ocean energy, and power generation through urban solid waste incineration. It has developed nuclear power in a safe and orderly manner. Committed to innovation-driven development, China has worked on developing hydrogen energy. It has accelerated the construction of a new power system to adapt to the steady increase in the proportion of new energy. To promote the efficient use of renewable energy, it has carried out appraisals of relevant parties' performance in meeting the set goals for consumption of power generated from renewable energy. The proportion of clean energy sources in total energy consumption increased from 14.5 percent in 2012 to 25.5 percent by the end of 2021, and the proportion of coal decreased from 68.5 percent to 56 percent over the same period. The installed capacity of renewable energy was more than one billion kilowatts, accounting for 44.8 percent of China's overall installed capacity. The installed capacity of hydropower, wind power, and photovoltaic power each exceeded 300 million kilowatts, all ranking the highest in the world.

Advancing the clean and efficient use of fossil energy. To promote the clean and low-carbon development of coal-fired power, China has upgraded coal-fired power plants to conserve resources, reduce carbon emissions and make their operation more flexible, and transformed heating

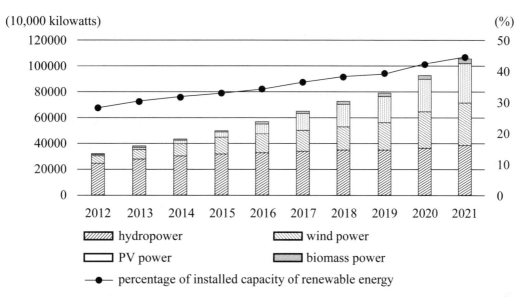

(10,000 kilowatts)

(%)

hydropower

wind power

PV power

biomass power

—●— percentage of installed capacity of renewable energy

Figure 2 China's installed capacity of renewable energy and percentage in the country's overall installed capacity (2012-2021)

facilities. It has implemented stricter energy-saving standards for newly-installed coal-fired generating units. The efficiency and pollutant control levels of these units are on par with the most advanced international standards. China has promoted clean end-use energy by replacing coal with natural gas, electricity, and renewable energy. It has actively supported clean heating in winter in northern China. It has made the use of natural gas more efficient in urban areas, as well as in industrial fuel, power generation, and transport, and promoted natural gas combined cooling, heating, and power (CCHP). It has launched a campaign to upgrade the quality of refined oil products. In less than 10 years China achieved the upgrading that took developed countries 30-plus years, and its refined oil products are now of the best quality by international standards. As a result, vehicle pollutant discharge has been effectively reduced.

3. Building a green transport network

The transport sector is one that consumes a large amount of energy and generates significant pollutant and greenhouse gas emissions. This

Panel 6　Green Electricity for the 2022 Beijing Winter Olympics

　　The Beijing Winter Olympic Games opened on February 4, 2022. These games were different from their predecessors in that green electricity was used in all the 26 venues in the three competition zones – the first time in the history of the Olympic Games that all the venues had been powered by green electricity. Green electricity served all the purposes of the Beijing Winter Olympic Games – venue lighting, ice surface maintenance, production of artificial snow, TV broadcasting, timekeeping, security and logistical support. China put into action the concept of sustainable development it advocated when bidding for the Games. To supply the Games with green electricity, China built a large number of wind and PV power projects in Beijing, Zhangjiakou and other regions, and launched the Zhangjiakou-Beijing flexible HVDC pilot project, to transmit clean electricity to the Games venues. This not only met the demand of the Games for lighting, operations, transport and other purposes, but also raised by a substantial margin the share of clean energy consumption in Beijing and surrounding areas. Seizing the opportunities presented by hosting the green Winter Olympic Games, China has realized the large-scale transmission, grid-connection, and uptake of clean energy, accumulating valuable practical experience for the further development of clean energy, and demonstrating its confidence and determination in achieving the goals of carbon emissions peaking and carbon neutrality.

is an area that deserves more attention in the pursuit of green development. By upgrading the energy efficiency of transport equipment, China has accelerated the building of a green transport network, with optimizing the structure of energy consumption and improving the efficiency of organization as its priorities, so that transport will be more eco-friendly, and travel will be more low-carbon.

Optimizing the structure of transport. China has accelerated the construction of special railway lines, promoted the shift of freight transport from road to railway and waterway, and encouraged intermodal transport. In 2021, the railway and waterway freight volume accounted for 24.56 percent of the total in China, an increase of 3.85 percentage points over

2012. China has also emphasized the strategy of giving priority to urban public transport. By the end of 2021, there were 275 urban rail transit lines in operation in 51 cities, with a total track length of more than 8,700 kilometers. The length of exclusive bus lanes increased from 5,256 kilometers in 2012 to 18,264 kilometers in 2021.

Promoting the green transformation of transport vehicles. China has vigorously promoted the use of new-energy vehicles in public transport, taxi service, environmental sanitation, logistics, distribution, civil aviation, airports, and Party and government institutions. By the end of 2021, the number of China's registered new energy vehicles had reached 7.84 million, accounting for about half of the global figure. There were 508,900 new energy buses, accounting for 71.7 percent of the total number of buses in China. There were 207,800 new energy taxis. China has continued the green transformation of mobile railway equipment. The proportion of internal combustion locomotives decreased from 51 percent in 2012 to 36 percent in 2021. China has also updated the pollutant discharge standards for motor vehicles, promoted the use of liquefied natural

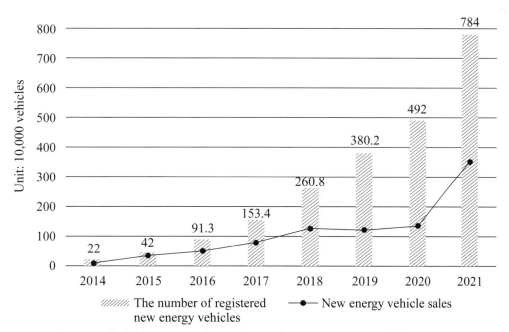

**Figure 3 China's total number of new energy vehicles and
such vehicle sales (2014-2021)**

gas (LNG) powered boats and transformation of shore power facilities, and accelerated the transformation or elimination of obsolete vehicles and boats. Since 2012, more than 30 million yellow-label vehicles with high emissions have been eliminated, and 47,100 obsolete inland river boats have been re-engineered or mothballed.

Upgrading transport infrastructure for green development. China has initiated a special program for the construction of green highways, and the recycling of waste road surface materials. By the end of 2021, more than 95 percent of the waste materials from expressways and 80 percent of the waste materials from national and provincial highways had been recycled. China has steadily improved afforestation along its roads. Green belts have been built along 570,000 kilometers of its trunk roads, about 200,000 kilometers more than in 2012. China has continued the electrification of its railways, with the proportion of electric railways increasing from 52.3 percent in 2012 to 73.3 percent in 2021. It has also built more green port and road transport support facilities. By the end of 2021, five types of shore power facilities had been built in 75 percent of the specialized berths of major ports, and 13,374 charging piles had been built in expressway service areas – the highest number in the world.

4. Promoting the economical and intensive use of resources

As a country with a great demand for resources, China has accelerated the fundamental change in the way resources are utilized. To make a major contribution to the sustainable development of global resources and the environment, and to ensure a happy life for the people today as well as sufficient resources to meet the needs of future generations, China tries to obtain the maximum social and economic benefits at a minimum cost in resources and the environment.

Improving the efficiency of energy use. China is exercising better control over the amount and intensity of energy consumption, particularly the consumption of fossil fuels. It has vigorously promoted technical, managerial, and structural energy conservation, to constantly improve the efficiency of energy use. It has initiated campaigns for all industrial enterprises, especially the big consumers of energy, to save energy, reduce carbon emissions, and improve the efficiency of energy use. The "forerunners" have been encouraged to play an exemplary role for other enterprises. China has organized the transformation of energy-intensive industries such as steel, power generation, and chemicals, to help them save energy and reduce carbon emissions. It has also strengthened the energy-saving management of key energy consumers, to enable large and medium-sized enterprises in key industries to reach advanced international levels in energy efficiency. Since 2012, China's average annual economic growth of 6.6 percent has been supported by an average annual growth of 3 percent in energy consumption, and the energy consumption per RMB10,000 of GDP in 2021 was 26.4 percent lower than in 2012.

Improving the efficiency of water utilization. China has imposed increasingly rigid constraints on water use. Industrial and urban configurations are determined scientifically in accordance with water availability. China has launched nationwide water-saving campaigns to control the total amount and intensity of water consumption. It has upgraded water-saving technologies for industries with high water consumption, and promoted highly water-efficient irrigation for agriculture. It has advocated the building of water-saving cities, established a water efficiency labeling system, introduced certification standards for water conservation products, and promoted the use of water-saving products and appliances. The comprehensive per capita water consumption in cities is falling steadily. China has also incorporated unconventional water sources, such as reclaimed water, desalinated seawater, collected rainwater, brackish water, and mine water, into the unified allocation of water resources, which has effectively eased the strain on demand in areas with a shortage of water. Water consumption per RMB10,000 of GDP in 2021 was 45 percent lower than in 2012.

Strengthening the economical and intensive use of land. China has improved the standards for urban and rural land use. The designation, standards and approval of land use for all kinds of construction projects are strictly controlled, and the economical and intensive use of land in the construction of transport, energy, and water infrastructure is encouraged. China has strengthened the management of rural land, and promoted the economical and intensive use of rural land for collective construction projects. It has also established mechanisms for coordinating the use of existing land resources and made the arrangements for additional resources, and for recovering idle land, in order to put all existing land resources to good use. From 2012 to 2021, the area of land designated for construction projects per unit of GDP decreased by 40.85 percent.

Making scientific use of marine resources. China has strictly controlled land reclamation from the sea. It has prohibited all coastal reclamation activities except those for major national projects, and dealt with problems left over from history in this regard with different approaches. It has established a control system to retain natural shorelines, and carried out classified protection and economical utilization of them. It has strictly protected uninhabited islands at sea and minimized their development and utilization.

Ensuring the comprehensive use of resources. China has advocated the construction of green mines, promoted green exploration and exploitation, and worked to increase the recovery rate, processing recovery rate, and multipurpose utilization rate of major mineral resources. A total of 1,101 state-level green mines have been built. China has selected a total of 100 pilot projects and 100 backbone enterprises to promote the comprehensive use of resources and started the construction of national demonstration bases for recovering mineral resources from city waste. It has also updated the waste material collection network, coordinated the recycling of waste resources, and improved the processing and utilization of renewable resources. In 2021, 385 million tonnes of nine renewable resources – waste iron and steel, copper, aluminum, lead, zinc, paper, plastic, rubber, and glass – were recycled for new purposes.

V. Eco-Friendly Living Becomes
the Prevailing Ethos

Green development requires everyone's efforts, and each of us can promote and practice green living. China actively promotes the values and ideas of eco-environmental conservation, raises public awareness to conserve resources and protect the eco-environment, and advocates the practice of a simpler, greener, and low-carbon lifestyle, creating a conducive social atmosphere for jointly promoting green development.

1. Continuing progress towards raising conservation awareness

China places particular emphasis on cultivating its citizens' conservation awareness. It organizes systematic publicity and other awareness-raising activities in this regard, and advocates a social environment and lifestyle of diligence and frugality. Publicity activities themed on National Energy-Saving Publicity Week, China's Water Week, National Urban Water-Saving Week, National Low-Carbon Day, National Tree-Planting Day, World Environment Day, the International Day for Biological Diversity, and Earth Day, are organized on a regular basis to encourage and persuade the whole of society to engage in green development activities. The idea of eco-friendly living has become widely accepted in families, communities, factories, and rural areas. Material on green development has been incorporated into China's national education system through compiling textbooks on eco-environmental conservation and carrying out education in primary and secondary schools on the condition of national resources including forests, grasslands, rivers and lakes, land, water and grain. Respect for and love of nature have been advocated. Environmental

Code of Conduct for Citizens (for Trial Implementation) was published to guide the public to follow a green lifestyle. As a result, a culture of ecological and environmental protection has joined the mainstream and been cherished by all.

2. Widespread initiatives to promote eco-friendly lifestyles

China has launched initiatives to promote the building of resource-conserving Party and government offices, and develop eco-friendly families, schools, communities, transport services, shopping malls, and buildings, popularizing eco-friendly habits in all areas including clothing, food, housing, transport, and tourism. To date, 70 percent of Party and government offices at and above county level are now committed to resource conservation, almost 100 colleges and universities have realized smart monitoring of water and electricity consumption, 109 cities have participated in green transport and commutes initiatives. Household waste sorting has been widely promoted in cities at or above prefecture level. Much progress is being made as residents gradually adopt the habit of sorting their waste. The Law of the People's Republic of China on Food Waste has been enacted, and initiatives launched to promote food saving and curb food waste including a "clean plate" campaign on a large scale, which have yielded remarkable results as more people are saving food.

3. Growing market of green products

China has actively promoted energy-saving and low-carbon products such as new-energy vehicles and energy-efficient household appliances. It has provided tax reductions or exemptions and government subsidies for new-energy vehicles and continued to improve charging infrastructure. As a result, the sales of new-energy vehicles have rapidly risen from 13,000 in 2012 to 3.52 million in 2021. For the seven years since 2015, China has ranked first in the world in the production and sales of new-energy vehicles. In addition, China has steadily improved the certification and promotion system for green products and the green government procurement system, implemented an energy efficiency and water efficiency labeling system to encourage the consumption of green products. It has promoted the construction of green infrastructure in the circulation sector such as green shopping malls, and supported new business models such as the sharing economy and second-hand transactions. There is a richer variety of green products and a growing number of people who spend on green products.

VI. Improving the Institutions and Mechanisms for Green Development

Sound institutions and mechanisms are essential to green development. With this understanding, China has stepped up efforts to create an eco-environmental conservation system based on clear orientation, sound decision-making, effective implementation, and strong incentives, and continued to improve government performance in promoting green development. This provides a solid guarantee for the realization of the country's green development goals.

1. Strengthening the rule of law

China is committed to the rule of law in pursuing progress in eco-environmental conservation. It has written into its Constitution eco-environmental improvement and conservation, and promulgated and/or revised laws such as the Yangtze River Protection Law, the Yellow River Protection Law, the Land Administration Law, the Forest Law, the Grassland Law, the Wetland Protection Law, the Environmental Protection Law, the Law on Environmental Protection Tax, the Law on the Prevention and Control of Atmospheric Pollution, the Law on the Prevention and Control of Water Pollution, the Law on the Prevention and Control of Soil Pollution, and the Nuclear Safety Law. A legal system for eco-environmental conservation that covers all key areas, all types of resources, and all environmental factors has taken shape. China has also made consistent efforts to refine green development standards for key areas – more than 3,000 such standards have been formulated or amended.

To better investigate and strictly punish violations of laws and regulations concerning natural resources and the eco-environment, China has reformed the system that places the monitoring, supervision, and law enforcement activities of environmental protection bodies below the provincial level under the leadership of the same type of bodies at the immediate higher level. To strengthen coordination between the criminal justice system and law enforcement by government departments, China has established a system for procuratorates, courts, public security organs, and government departments responsible for coordinated law enforcement for environmental protection, enabling them to share relevant information, issue case briefings, and transfer cases among them. This has built a strong synergy for the investigation and punishment of environmental crimes, and provided powerful legal safeguards for green development.

2. Tightening supervision and management

China has improved the performance evaluation system for green development, and taken strict measures to ensure that enterprises fulfill their principal responsibilities and that the government performs the duty of supervision in pursuing green development. GDP growth is no longer the sole criterion for the assessment of the development of regions or the performance of officials. Instead, binding targets concerning resources and the environment are set for economic and social development, and a more balanced assessment system for economic and social development is in progress – one that measures the use of resources, energy consumption, environmental damage, and the eco-environmental impact. This allows assessment to play its full guiding role in promoting green development.

China has put in place an accountability system for leading officials, and formulated and/or revised a number of CPC regulations, including the Measures for Holding Leading Officials of the Party and the Government Accountable for Environmental Damage (for Trial Implementation), the Regulations on Central Environmental Inspections, and the Regulations on the Auditing of Natural Resource Assets for Leading Officials at the End of Their Tenures (for Trial Implementation). These are designed to ensure that Party committees and governments assume equal responsibilities for environmental protection, that leading officials perform their environmental protection responsibilities with diligence, in addition to their other prescribed duties, and that they are held accountable when they fail to do so. China mandates end-of-tenure auditing of natural resource assets for leading officials, and imposes lifelong accountability for environmental damage. By implementing the central environmental inspection system, China has ensured that all parties concerned truly fulfill their responsibilities for environmental protection, and has solved many environmental issues of pressing public concern.

3. Improving market-based mechanisms

China is creating institutions and mechanisms for green development through which the government provides strong guidance, enterprises are fully engaged, and the market plays an effective role, thereby generating society-wide enthusiasm and participation. It has introduced new measures to improve the pricing mechanisms in key areas such as water and energy saving, sewage and waste treatment, and air pollution control, adopted more than 50 preferential policies to cut taxes and fees, encouraged better resource allocation, and supported conservation and efficient use of resources to advance green development. China has enforced a unified registration system for ownership of natural resources and an eco-environmental conservation compensation system that covers forests, grasslands, wetlands, deserts, water bodies and farmland. It is working on mechanisms for realizing the market value of ecosystem goods and services. China also encourages and supports private investment in environmental conservation and rehabilitation.

On the base of a reasonable ceiling for total consumption, China has established initial allocation and trading systems for water, energy, pollution, and carbon permits. With the opening of the national carbon emissions trading market and trials in green electricity trading, progress is being made in allowing the market to play a fundamental role in the

Panel 7   Compensation System for Eco-Environmental Conservation

China has taken active steps to improve its compensation system for eco-environmental conservation, and continued to increase fiscal support for this compensation in key areas. Interregional cooperation has been steadily expanded, and new progress has been made in establishing market-based compensation mechanisms.

China has improved the mechanism for fiscal compensation from higher-level to lower-level governments. Governments are required to play the leading role in ensuring that all parties concerned fulfill their responsibilities for environmental protection. A compensation mechanism has been established for the conservation of key ecological systems including forests and grasslands. More support is provided to main players in eco-environmental conservation. The mechanism for compensation and transfer payments to key functional zones now covers more than 800 counties across the country.

China has strengthened interregional cooperation in compensation for eco-environmental conservation. Policies have been introduced to support transregional compensation mechanisms in the Yangtze River and Yellow River basins. Guidelines were formulated on compensation in the Dongting Lake, Poyang Lake and Taihu Lake basins. To encourage closer ties between the regions which carry out eco-environmental conservation and those regions which benefit from these endeavors, and between the regions located in the upper reaches of a river and those in the lower reaches, China has initiated a compensatory relationship for pollution control and cooperation on industrial projects. As of the end of 2021, 14 cross-provincial compensation mechanisms had been established for eco-environmental conservation across river basins.

China has adopted creative measures to develop market-based compensation mechanisms. By leveraging the roles of both the government and the market, China encourages and guides all stake-holders to participate in compensation systems, so as to open up more financing channels. It has continuously improved its systems for carbon emissions, pollutant discharge, and water use permits, and refined its policies concerning green finance, green labelling, and green buildings in support of green industries.

allocation of eco-environmental resources.

In order to boost green finance, China has developed a multi-level market and a portfolio of green financial products, such as green credit, green bonds, green insurance, green funds, and green trust. At the end of 2021 China's green loan balance in RMB and foreign currencies stood at RMB15.9 trillion, and its outstanding green bonds at RMB1.1 trillion, both ranking among the largest in the world.

VII. Building the Earth into a Beautiful Home

Green development and eco-environmental progress are the responsibility of all humanity. China has always been a major participant, contributor, and torchbearer in the global movement for building an eco-civilization. It firmly safeguards multilateralism, and is actively forging an international eco-environmental governance pattern in which countries align their interests and share their rights and responsibilities. This is how China does its part in pursuing the sustainable development of humanity.

1. Participating in global climate governance

Following the principles of equity, common but differentiated responsibilities and respective capabilities, China has acted in accordance with the United Nations Framework Convention on Climate Change, actively participated in global climate negotiations in a constructive manner, and made historic contributions to the conclusion and implementation of the Paris Agreement. In doing so, it helps to build a fair, rational, and mutually beneficial global climate governance system.

China has reinforced the effort to achieve its Nationally Determined Contributions (NDCs). It will make the steepest cuts in the world to the intensity of its carbon emissions, and complete the process from carbon emissions peaking to carbon neutrality in the shortest span of time. This fully demonstrates its strong sense of responsibility as a major country.

China is also an active participant in South-South cooperation on climate change. Since 2016, working in other developing countries, it has launched 10 low-carbon demonstration zones, 100 projects for climate change mitigation and adaption, training sessions on climate change response for 1,000 people, and more than 200 foreign assistance programs on climate change.

International cooperation on climate change may encounter difficulties and setbacks, but China will remain committed to improving global climate governance and taking solid actions. As always, it will work with firm resolve towards the goals of carbon emissions peaking and carbon neutrality, actively participate in international cooperation on climate change, engage in international negotiations on climate change in a constructive manner, and do everything in its power to support and assist other developing countries in this realm. In doing so, China will continue to contribute to global efforts to tackle the grave challenge of climate change.

2. Building a green Belt and Road

China is committed to working with other countries on promoting green development under the Belt and Road Initiative (BRI), making it a green initiative. In order to establish a cooperation mechanism for green and low-carbon development under the BRI, China has signed an MoU with the United Nations Environment Programme on building a green Belt and Road, and reached more than 50 cooperation agreements on eco-environmental conservation with relevant countries and international organizations. It has also launched the Initiative for Belt and Road Partnership on Green Development with 31 countries, established the Belt and Road Energy Partnership (BREP) with 32 countries, led the creation of the Belt and Road Initiative International Green Development Coalition (BRIGC), founded the BRI Green Development Institute, and launched the BRI Environmental Big Data Platform.

China has helped other participants in the BRI to build up their environmental governance capacity and improve their people's well-being. It also helps these countries in training personnel for green development, having trained 3,000 people from more than 120 countries under the Green Silk Road Envoys Program. China formulated the Green Investment Principles for the Belt and Road to encourage such investments in related regions. Concurrently, Chinese enterprises have funded renewable energy projects in other BRI countries, and helped them build a number of major clean energy facilities. All these efforts have boosted green development in these countries.

3. Carrying out extensive bilateral and multilateral cooperation

China has taken active steps to advance practical cooperation on saving resources and protecting the eco-environment. It successfully hosted the first part of the 15th meeting of the Conference of the Parties to the

---

Panel 8   Forging Green, Inclusive BREP

During the second Belt and Road Forum for International Cooperation in April 2019, China and 29 other countries initiated the Belt and Road Energy Partnership to promote common development and prosperity in the energy sector under the BRI. With the subsequent accession of Cuba, Morocco and Thailand, membership of this partnership has expanded to 33.

BREP is the first international cooperation platform in the energy sector initiated by China. Through this platform, China has hosted two sessions of the Belt and Road Energy Ministerial Conference and two sessions of the Belt and Road Energy Partnership Forum. These have set the stage for cooperation on bilateral and multilateral projects and on technological exchanges among participating countries, and facilitated practical cooperation on a number of issues. Partnership countries have released multiple key documents, including the Cooperation Principles and Concrete Actions of the Belt and Road Energy Partnership and the Belt and Road Green Energy Cooperation Qingdao Initiative, which have reinforced consensus and pooled the strengths of all parties concerned.

Partnership countries have also issued the Best Practice Cases of Belt and Road Energy Cooperation to highlight green energy projects that are low in pollution and high in efficiency and quality. To advance practical cooperation on green energy, they have founded a cooperation network consisting of government agencies, energy businesses, university think tanks and financial institutions, and they have organized partnership capacity building activities to share experience and advances in green energy development among developing countries.

Convention on Biological Diversity (COP15) and the 14th meeting of the Conference of the Contracting Parties to the Ramsar Convention on Wetlands. China is an active participant in cooperation on energy transition and energy efficiency under the frameworks of G20, China-ASEAN partnership, ASEAN Plus Three, East Asia Summit, Forum on China-Africa Cooperation, BRICS, Shanghai Cooperation Organization, and Asia-Pacific Economic Cooperation (APEC). It took the lead in formulating the G20 Energy Efficiency Leading Programme, a key outcome of the G20 Hangzhou Summit. It has put into action the Global Development Initiative, and worked for the establishment of the Global Clean Energy Cooperation Partnership.

China has also carried out cooperation with other countries and regions – including India, Brazil, South Africa, the United States, Japan, Germany, France, and ASEAN countries – in the fields of energy conservation, environmental protection, clean energy, response to climate change, biodiversity protection, prevention and control of desertification, and conservation of marine and forest resources.

China also supports international organizations, including the UN agencies, Asian Development Bank, Asian Infrastructure Investment Bank, New Development Bank, Global Environment Facility, Green Climate Fund, International Energy Agency, and International Renewable Energy Agency, in carrying out technological assistance, capacity building and trial programs for green and low-carbon development in key sectors such as industry, agriculture, energy, transport, and urban-rural development. Through these efforts China has made a significant contribution to advancing sustainable development worldwide.

Conclusion

China has embarked on a new journey to build itself into a modern socialist country in all respects and advance the rejuvenation of the Chinese nation. Harmony between humanity and nature is an important feature of China's modernization.

The just-concluded 20th CPC National Congress has made strategic plans for China's future development which will help to create a better environment with greener mountains, cleaner water, and clearer air. China will keep to the path of green development, continue to build an eco-civilization, and strive to realize development with a higher level of quality, efficiency, equity, sustainability and security. We will make "green" a defining feature of a beautiful China and allow the people to share the beauty of nature and life in a healthy environment.

The earth is our one and only home, and humanity and nature form a community of life. It is the common responsibility of all countries to protect the environment and promote sustainable development. China stands ready to work with the international community to advance eco-environmental conservation, promote green development, protect the green earth, and build a cleaner and more beautiful world.

China's Law-Based Cyberspace Governance in the New Era

The State Council Information Office of
the People's Republic of China

March 2023

Preface

The internet is one of humanity's great achievements. Although it facilitates economic and social development, at the same time it poses severe challenges in terms of administration and governance. The development and governance of the internet is a goal shared by all countries for the benefit of humanity, and the rule of law has proved to be essential to internet governance. It has become a global consensus to apply law-based thinking and approaches based on an understanding of the rule of law.

Since China was fully connected to the internet in 1994, it has committed itself to law-based cyberspace governance, ensuring that the internet develops within the confines of the law. In the new era, guided by Xi Jinping Thought on Socialism with Chinese Characteristics for a New Era, China has made law-based cyberspace governance an essential part of the overall strategy of the rule of law and the drive to build up its strength in cyberspace.

Marked improvements have been made in ensuring law-based cyberspace governance. China has boosted cyberspace governance by developing a complete system of laws and regulations, a highly efficient enforcement system, a stringent supervision system, and an effective supporting system. With participation of the government, businesses, social organizations and netizens, cyber legislation, law enforcement, and judiciary work have advanced alongside programs to spread legal knowledge via the internet, publicize cyber laws and cultivate the public's awareness in laws. This is a pioneering approach to cyberspace governance in line with international best practices. With stronger domestic capacity in law-based internet governance, China has contributed ideas and solutions to global internet governance.

The Chinese government is publishing this white paper to introduce China's progress and experience in law-based cyberspace governance.

I. Upholding the Rule of Law in Cyberspace

Adapting to the developing trends of global information technology, China set out from its own realities to integrate law-based cyberspace governance into the overall national strategy of the rule of law, gaining knowledge and experience in the process. It has pioneered a distinctive Chinese approach to law-based cyberspace governance.

– People-centered development. In China, the people contribute ideas and solutions and play a principal role. Their rights, interests, aspirations and wellbeing are the focus in every aspect of cyber legislation, law enforcement, judiciary work, public education, and all other areas of law-based cyberspace governance. China protects people's legitimate rights and interests in cyberspace, and fully respects netizens' right to express ideas and exchange views. It has strengthened law-based cyberspace governance, taking resolute action against cybercrimes to keep order in this virtual world, and striving to create a safe, fair, healthy, clean and sound cyber environment.

– Further development of the internet. The purpose of law-based cyberspace governance is to guarantee the healthy and orderly development of the internet, not to hold it back. Under law-based cyberspace governance, China has guided and regulated efforts to build a high-quality digital China – improving the governance system for the digital economy, the legal framework of digital government, and the digital society initiative. Placing equal emphasis on development and security, China has consolidated its lines of defense so that the internet grows in a secure environment and further boosts cybersecurity. Cyberspace has thus been turned into a powerful engine for socioeconomic growth, rather than an area of uncertainty.

– Proceeding from realities. China is the world's largest developing country and has the largest number of internet users. It boasts a large number of business platforms that offer all types of products and services. As a result, there are diverse legal subjects, relationships and situations where different laws apply. With all this in mind, China handles the relationships between development and security, freedom and order, openness and autonomy, and administration and service in an appropriate manner. It has conducted in-depth research on frontier areas of overbearing importance, employing law-based thinking and approaches to break through bottlenecks in internet development and find solutions for healthy internet growth.

– Innovation-driven cyberspace governance. The internet is a result of innovation and has flourished because of it. Law-based cyberspace governance cannot be achieved without innovation. With a keen understanding of the unprecedented difficulties and complications in cyberspace governance, China has been forward-looking in responding to the risks and challenges brought by new internet technologies, applications, and business forms and models, and promoted innovation in the concept, content, approach and methods of law-based cyberspace governance. By creating and improving rules on algorisms, blockchain technology, and other new technologies and domains, it has filled gaps in key areas where legislation once lagged behind. A system for comprehensive cyberspace governance is now in place, and new models of cyber judiciary work have been created. Driven by innovation, China has raised its capacity for internet governance in all areas.

– Openness and cooperation. Upholding cyber sovereignty, China has drawn from the experience of other countries in cyberspace governance, planning internet development in a global context and pioneering a distinctively Chinese model of internet governance in line with international best practice. It has played an active part in working with other countries to formulate rules for cyberspace governance, and engaged in international exchanges and cooperation in law-based cyberspace governance. It is committed to building a multilateral, democratic and transparent global internet governance system together with other countries.

In the new era, China set out from its realities and learned from advanced foreign experience to explore its own approach to cyberspace regulation and governance, maintaining the right orientation while pursuing innovation. Significant achievements have been made in a range of areas, building up China's strength in cyberspace and adding momentum to law-based governance of the country, as well as contributing to national governance by the CPC in the information age.

— A guarantee of the transformation from scale to strength. China is building up its strength in cyberspace through these goals: universally available network infrastructure, significantly greater capacity of independent innovation, comprehensive development of the digital economy, guarantee of cybersecurity, and balanced ability of cyber attacks and defense. Major progress has been made in China towards these goals, as evidenced by the world's largest number of netizens, the largest and most advanced fiber-optic broadband and mobile telecommunication networks, and world-leading 5G technology, industry and applications. China's Internet of Things (IoT) now connects more cellular terminals than mobile phone users.

China's digital economy has been growing with a strong momentum. In 2021, its value reached RMB45.5 trillion, ranking second in the world. New internet technologies are widely used in areas such as education, employment, social security, medical and health care, sports, housing, transport, support for persons with disabilities, and elderly care. Internet Plus services are running on a track of healthy development in accordance with the law. China has created the world's largest active digital society.

— Law-based national governance fully implemented in cyberspace. In China, the principle of law-based governance of the country applies equally in cyberspace. The Law-based Governance of China Initiative has been implemented, and progress has been made in law-based cyberspace governance by ensuring sound lawmaking, strict enforcement, impartial administration of justice, and the observance of the law by all. Under socialist rule of law with Chinese characteristics in cyberspace, the groundwork for cyber legislation has been laid, contributing to and improving China's socialist legal system. Cyber law enforcement has continued to strengthen. By taking tough action against illegal behaviors in cyberspace, China has fostered a sound cyber environment and maintained online order, which contributes to peace and harmony in the society as a whole. Rules of cyber adjudication have improved, more online cases have been handled, and justice is served in cyberspace as elsewhere. Knowledge of cyber laws has been further spread, and netizens have acted accordingly – respecting, learning, abiding by, and using the law. The Chinese people's awareness of and literacy in the law has increased.

– Contributing ideas, experience and solutions to global internet governance. Cyberspace is a shared space for human activities; it must be developed and managed by all countries. China has formed its own approach to law-based cyberspace governance by advancing legislation, law enforcement, judiciary work, and programs to spread knowledge about cyber laws, and has shared its experience with the world. It has taken an active part in global internet governance, promoting the G20 Digital Economy Development and Cooperation Initiative and the Global Data Security Initiative, and other proposals and declarations. It raised the principle of cyber sovereignty, and advocates that the principle of sovereign equality established by the UN Charter be applied to cyberspace, thereby contributing ideas and solutions to cyberspace governance.

II. Consolidating the Legal System for Cyberspace Governance

The law is a powerful tool for governing a country, and sound laws are the prerequisite for good governance. Following the trend of internet development, China has advanced the legal system for cyberspace governance through legislation that is enacted in a well-conceived and democratic way and in accordance with the law. Cyber legislation is becoming systematic, holistic, coordinated, and time-efficient.

Cyber legislation in China has undergone a long, gradual process that can be roughly divided into three stages. The first stage ran from 1994 to 1999, a period when China became connected to the internet. Internet users and devices grew steadily in number. Legislation during this stage focused on network infrastructure security, specifically computer systems security and network security. The second stage lasted from 2000 to 2011, when personal computers (PC) served as the main terminal for internet connection. As PCs and internet users grew rapidly in numbers, internet connection services became more affordable and web-based information services boomed. Legislation during this stage shifted to internet services and content management. The third stage, which began in 2012, is dominated by mobile internet. Legislation now is gradually focusing on comprehensive cyberspace governance by covering areas such as network information services, information technology development, and cybersecurity.

Over the years, China has promulgated more than 140 laws on cyberspace, forming a cyber legislation framework with the Constitution as the foundation, supported by laws, administrative regulations, departmental

Panel 1   Cyber Legislation in China

Type	Examples
Law	• Electronic Commerce Law • Electronic Signature Law • Cybersecurity Law • Data Security Law • Personal Information Protection Law • Law on Combating Telecom and Online Fraud
Administrative Regulation	• Regulations on the Security and Protection of Computer Information Systems • Regulations on Computer Software Protection • Administrative Measures on Internet Information Services • Telecommunications Regulations • Regulations on the Administration of Foreign Investment in Chinese Telecommunications Businesses • Regulations on the Protection of the Right of Communication Through Information Networks • Regulations on the Security and Protection of Critical Information Infrastructure
Departmental Rule	• Regulations on the Protection of Children's Online Personal Information • China Internet Domain Name Regulations • Measures on the Supervision and Administration of Online Transactions • Provisions on the Administration of Internet News and Information Services • Regulations on the Governance of Online Information and Content • Regulations on the Management of Algorithmic Recommendations for Internet Information Services
Local Regulation	• Guangdong Provincial Digital Economy Promotion Act • Zhejiang Provincial Digital Economy Promotion Act • Hebei Provincial Regulations on Information Technology Development • Guizhou Provincial Regulations on Government Data Sharing • Shanghai Municipal Data Regulations
Local Administrative Rule	• Measures of Guangdong Province on Public Data Management • Measures of Anhui Province on the Management of Data and Resources for Government Affairs • Measures of Jiangxi Province on the Protection of Computer Information System Security • Interim Measures of Hangzhou City on the Administration of Online Transactions
Total Number	Exceeding 140

rules, local regulations and local administrative rules, endorsed by traditional legislation, and underpinned by specialized cyber laws governing online content and management, cybersecurity, information technology, and other elements. This system of laws on cyberspace governance provides a strong institutional guarantee for building up China's strength in cyberspace.

1. Establishing a System of Laws for Protecting People's Rights and Interests in Cyberspace

China has established a sound system of laws to protect people's rights and interests in cyberspace, laying the legal groundwork for protecting both online and offline rights.

– Protecting the freedom and confidentiality of correspondence. This is a prerequisite for citizens to air views and needs in cyberspace of their own volition. China enacted the Measures on Ensuring Security of Internationally Connected Computer Information Networks in 1997, to provide legal protection of the freedom and confidentiality of correspondence as enshrined in the Constitution. It formulated the Telecommunications Regulations in 2000, stipulating that citizens' freedom to use telecom services and their confidentiality of correspondence are protected by law. It revised the Regulations on Radio Administration in 2016, further strengthening the protection of the confidentiality of correspondence via radio service. Thus, this basic right enjoys full protection in cyberspace.

– Protecting personal information rights and interests. China has built a line of defense in law for protecting personal information rights and interests. In 2020, the Civil Code was adopted at the Third Session of the 13th National People's Congress, which makes systemic provisions on protecting personal information in civil cases based on previous legal stipulations. In 2009 and 2015, amendment (VII) and (IX) to the Criminal Law added provisions on the crime of infringing upon citizens' personal information, thus strengthening the protection of personal information in the Criminal Law. In terms of cyber legislation, the Standing Committee of the National

People's Congress issued the Decision on Strengthening Online Information Protection in 2012, announcing clearly to protect electronic information that may reveal citizen's identity and privacy. The Cybersecurity Law enacted in 2016 further refined rules on personal information protection.

The Personal Information Protection Law, promulgated in 2021, represented an overall upgrading of personal information protection. It defined and refined principles on protecting personal information and rules on processing personal information, and specified how state agencies should process personal information in accordance with the law. It empowered the subjects of personal information with a range of rights, emphasized the obligations of personal information processors, improved the mechanism for protecting personal information, and set clear and strict legal liabilities.

— Safeguarding citizen's property. China has strengthened legislation to curb infringements upon citizens' property by way of the internet. In 2018, the Electronic Commerce Law was promulgated, stipulating that products or services from e-commerce suppliers should not undermine personal safety or the security of property. The Civil Code has clear provisions on the legal liability of those who infringe upon others' property rights and interests by way of the internet. In 2022, China enacted the Law on Combating Telecom and Online Fraud, providing strong legal support for fighting crime and safeguarding people's property rights and interests.

— Protecting the digital rights of special groups. Through multilevel and multifaceted legislation, China has invested a real effort to close the digital divide for minors, elderly people, and persons with disabilities, so that everybody can join in the digital society on an equal basis and enjoy the benefits of the digital age as much as possible.

As stipulated in the Cybersecurity Law, the state supports research and development on internet products and services that are beneficial to minors' healthy growth, and punishes by law those who place their physical and mental health at risk via the internet. In 2019, China issued the

Regulations on the Protection of Children's Online Personal Information, prioritizing the protection of personal information for children. In 2020, the Law on the Protection of Minors was revised, to strengthen minors' education on internet literacy, online supervision and regulation of content for minors, protection of minors' personal information online, and prevention and control of internet addiction, all to safeguard minors' legitimate rights and interests in cyberspace. The Data Security Law, promulgated in 2021, stipulates that providers of smart public services should take into full consideration the needs of elderly people and persons with disabilities, and make sure they do not create obstacles to their daily life.

2. Improving Law-Based Governance of the Digital Economy

To transform from high-speed growth to high-quality growth, China has continued to improve institutions fundamental to data development, maintain order in the digital market, and regulate new business forms and models of the digital economy, laying a sound framework of rules for the healthy growth of the digital economy.

– Creating institutions fundamental to data development. Data is a fundamental resource and an engine for innovation. The Data Security Law contains provisions on implementing the big data strategy, supporting R&D on data-related technology and business innovation, advancing data-related standards, and developing data trading markets. These provisions aim to improve data development and utilization, and promote the growth of the digital economy in which data serves as a key factor.

– Regulating the operation of the digital market. China regulates and develops the digital market in accordance with the law, stands firmly against monopolies and unfair competition, and improves digital rules to ensure a market environment for fair competition.

The Electronic Commerce Law provides a full set of regulations on e-commerce operation, with clear provisions on the responsibilities of e-commerce platform operators and business owners on these platforms. It stipulates that e-commerce operators with a dominant share of the market should not abuse their position to eliminate or limit competition, so that fair competition is maintained. The Law on the Protection of Consumer Rights and Interests (2013 Revision) established a seven-day unconditional return policy for online shopping, to reinforce the primary responsibility of online business operators in consumer rights protection. The Law Against Unfair Competition (2017 Revision) has separate provisions regarding the internet, to ban unfair competition that takes advantage of technology. The Measures on the Supervision and Administration of Online Transactions, enacted in 2021, contain detailed provisions on the relevant regulations in the Electronic Commerce Law, to strengthen online trading supervision. In 2021, the Anti-monopoly Commission under the State Council issued the Anti-monopoly Guidelines for Platform Economy, to strengthen and improve anti-monopoly supervision based on the status, characteristics, and development of the platform economy. In 2022, the Anti-monopoly Law was amended to improve the anti-monopoly framework for the platform economy, banning operators from abuse of a monopoly position by leveraging their strengths in data and algorithms, technology, capital, and platform rules.

– Regulating new business forms and models of the digital economy. The rapid rise of new business forms and models in the digital economy created social and economic impetus and potential, and also posed new challenges for social governance and industrial growth. Focusing on problems unique to the new forms and models in certain areas, China has advanced legislation in both the comprehensive and special laws to prevent and defuse risks.

The Civil Code improved the rules on the conclusion and execution of electronic contracts, and brought data and virtual assets under legal protection, giving a boost to the digital economy. To expand the legal framework for governing Internet Plus services, China has introduced an array of regulations, including the Interim Measures on the Administration of Online Taxi Booking Services, Regulations on the Administration of Algorithmic Recommendations for Internet Information Services,

Regulations on the Administration of Blockchain Information Services, Interim Measures on the Administration of Business Activities of Intermediary Agencies for Online Lending, and Interim Regulations on the Administration of Online Tourist Services.

3. Safeguarding Cybersecurity by Law

Cybersecurity is a new component of national security, and an issue of paramount importance. By formulating the National Security Law, Cybersecurity Law, and Data Security Law, China has defined the legal institutional framework for cybersecurity, to boost its defenses against cyber threats and effectively respond to cybersecurity risks.

– Setting rules for cybersecurity. The Regulations on the Security and Protection of Computer Information Systems was released in 1994, designed to safeguard and supervise computer information system security. In 2000, the Standing Committee of the National People's Congress issued the Decision on Ensuring Internet Security, detailing security requirements in operation and information, and establishing a framework of responsibilities for cybersecurity composed of civil, administrative and criminal liabilities.

The Cybersecurity Law specifies the systems for ensuring security of network operation, online products and services, data, and information. Some of its provisions are further elaborated in the Measures on Cybersecurity Review and the Regulations on the Management of Security Loopholes of Online Products. After years of effort, China now has a complete set of legal rules on cybersecurity, and greater capacity for ensuring cybersecurity through institutional development.

– Ensuring security for critical information infrastructure. Critical information infrastructure is the nerve center of socioeconomic operation, and the top concern for cybersecurity. Its security is central to maintaining cyber sovereignty and national security, guaranteeing sound socioeconomic development, and protecting the public interest and the legitimate rights and interests of individual citizens.

In 2021, China released the Regulations on the Security and Protection of Critical Information Infrastructure, with provisions defining what constitutes critical information infrastructure and the principles and goals of protection. The procedures for identifying critical information infrastructure were improved, and the operators' responsibility for cybersecurity was clarified. There were also provisions on improving the mechanisms for network security and protection, setting up special security management agencies, conducting safety monitoring and risk assessment, and regulating the purchase of online products and services. The Regulations provide the legal ground for upgrading the country's capacity for safeguarding critical information infrastructure.

– Developing the legal framework for data security management. Proceeding from reality and focusing on the outstanding problems in data security, China has strengthened its capacity for data security through legislation. The Data Security Law has clear provisions on establishing mechanisms for categorized and classified data protection, risk monitoring and early warning, emergency response, and data security review; it also contains measures to facilitate data security and development and provisions for the security and openness of government data.

4. Improving Regulation for a Sound Cyber Environment

Cyberspace is a public space for internet users. A clean and sound cyber environment is in accord with the people's expectations. Out of a strong sense of responsibility towards society and the people, China has introduced laws and regulations for comprehensive cyberspace governance, to clean up the cyber environment with a focus on online information and content.

– Regulating the orderly dissemination of online information. To strengthen online information governance, a global challenge, China formulated the Civil Code, Cybersecurity Law, and Administrative Measures on Internet Information Services, to define the rules for the dissemination of online information and the liabilities of relevant subjects. These laid the legal groundwork for tackling illegal information that threatens national security, harms the public interest, and infringes upon the legitimate rights and interests of individuals.

– Sharpening the legal weapons against cyberterrorism. China stands firm against the threat of cyberterrorism. The Criminal Law, Criminal Procedure Law, and Anti-Money Laundering Law contain provisions on criminal liability for terrorist activities and judicial proceedings in the investigation of terrorist crimes, as well as on monitoring the money for funding terrorist activities. The Counterterrorism Law promulgated in 2015 has separate provisions on the targets, measures and mechanisms for combating terrorism in cyberspace.

III. Keeping Order in a Rule-Based Cyberspace

Strict law enforcement is a critical link in law-based cyberspace governance. China has taken rigorous measures to ensure fair and rule-based law enforcement in cyberspace, strengthening enforcement in key areas of immediate concern to the people, and protecting the legitimate rights and interests of the individual as well as the general public. A sound, rule-based order has been created in a clean cyber environment.

1. Protecting Personal Information

With a thriving digital economy come a growing number of crimes, such as the illegal collection, buying and selling, use and leakage of personal information, which threaten people's personal and property security and disrupt social and economic order. Personal information protection concerns people's legitimate rights and interests, as well as public security governance and the future of the digital economy.

Targeting covert, high-frequency personal information infringements with high-tech means, China has adopted new thinking and methods of supervision, taking tougher action against illegal activities. For example, it carries out regular actions against mobile applications that illegally collect and use personal data. Since 2019, the authorities in China have inspected 3.22 million mobile applications, issuing notice of criticism to or removing about 3,000 applications that violated laws and regulations. Through these targeted actions, violations of personal information rights have been effectively curbed, as many more applications are now conforming to relevant regulations and the public has also built a strong awareness of personal data protection. Respecting and protecting personal information is recognized as essential by all.

2. Protecting Online Intellectual Property Rights

Strengthening online intellectual property rights (IPR) protection is central to innovation in internet technology. As new technologies and applications flourish, IPR infringements online have become cheaper and more diversified and covert, posing a severe challenge to law enforcement in terms of tracing, evidence collection, and enforcement.

Over the years, China has developed a keen understanding of online IPR creation, protection and application, and taken strong actions for online IPR protection. These include: establishing and improving supervision mechanisms, creating a new dynamic of IPR protection by all members of society, launching cross-platform cooperation for IPR protection, and punishing online infringement and piracy. Integrated online-offline law enforcement has been strengthened to enable firm action against online trademark infringements and counterfeiting of patented products. Regular targeted actions have been taken against all types of infringements and piracy, including online copyright infringement, pirated film copies and illegal dissemination, and copyright infringement in key markets and areas. During the Beijing Winter Olympics and Paralympics, more than 110,000 unauthorized links containing content about the Games were deleted from internet platforms. Through years of effort, China has achieved a marked improvement in online IPR protection.

3. Maintaining Order in the Online Market

The rapid rise of the online market has played a major role in stabilizing the economy, spurring consumption, securing employment, and serving the people's wellbeing. China has tried out new models of law enforcement adapted to the online market, a new business form, and supported its sound and sustainable growth by regulating the market for fair competition and taking resolute action against all forms of illegal transactions.

– Ensuring fair competition in the online market. As online platforms expand in size and grow in strength, they have increasingly hampered fair competition by acquiring the best-performing startups in their sectors, deliberately blocking URL links of other platforms, compelling platform users to choose one platform over another, engaging in big data-enabled price discrimination against existing customers, and hijacking traffic.

In response to public appeal, China has taken a range of measures to address disorderly competition among online platforms, support their innovation-driven growth, and regulate and guide capital growth by law. Acts of unfair competition by major online platforms such as price cheating and dumping, monopoly abuse, and other acts of unfair competition have been redressed through regulatory means including administrative admonition, administrative guidance, and guidance on rules. Cases relating to concentration of platform operators in key areas such as finance, high-tech, media that affect people's wellbeing have been reviewed and handled in accordance with the law. Mergers and acquisitions that might adversely affect market competition and innovation have been prevented, and online platform businesses are advised to increase their awareness of rules and regulate their operations.

All this has contributed to an improved market environment for the platform economy, a sound business environment of fair competition, and broader space for small and medium-sized enterprises (SMEs) to grow. A

Panel 2   Cases of Unfair Competition and Monopoly Involving Online Platforms

In 2020-21, China investigated two typical cases of compelling platform users to choose one platform over another, in e-business and online food delivery services, and imposed total fines of RMB21.67 billion. In 2021, 1,998 cases of unfair competition online were investigated, resulting in fines of RMB119 million. From 2020 to the first half of 2022, 56 cases of concentration of platform operators with prior notification were reviewed, and 159 cases of illegal concentration of platform operators that failed to file a prior notification were investigated in accordance with the law.

unified, open, fair, competitive, and orderly online business environment is taking shape.

– Regulating online trading and transactions. Rule-based online trading and transactions are essential to creating a sound online market environment and protecting the rights of those engaged in these activities.

China has launched Operation Wangjian to fight online sales of pirated, counterfeit, and sub-standard products, and illegal trading of wildlife and products. It has made sure that online platforms assume their due responsibilities, and strengthened supervision over internet advertisement. In response to new online trading forms such as livestreaming e-commerce and mini online stores, China has exercised strict regulation over customer soliciting by online channels, and investigated a number of websites and platform users suspected of wrongdoing. Targeted actions have been taken against online pyramid selling, particularly under the disguise of e-commerce, investment and money management, and online business startups. Online trading and transactions by main market players in key areas have thus been effectively regulated.

Panel 3   Operation Wangjian

Since 2018, China has launched Operation Wangjian (meaning "web sword") to fight online sales of pirated, counterfeit and sub-standard products, illegal trading of wildlife and products, and illegal advertising. About 1.83 million items of illegal product information have been deleted from online trading platforms, 23,900 websites have been closed, 105,000 website and platform services have been served with cessation orders, and 119,700 internet-related cases have been handled. The operation has safeguarded the legitimate rights and interests of consumers and ensured a sound online trading order for fair competition.

---

4. Safeguarding National Cybersecurity

A strong line of defense against cyber threats is the precondition and basis for the healthy development of the internet. China has continued to carry out law enforcement in securing core internet resources, key network systems, and internet data, effectively preventing and defusing risks to cybersecurity, and creating a safe online environment in the internet age.

In the area of core internet resources, it has strengthened the management of websites, domains and IP addresses, and improved early warning systems through more sophisticated technical means to guarantee security. In the area of key network systems, it has further strengthened protection for network security and monitored cybersecurity threats, effectively guarding against large-scale denial-of-service attacks and other major security incidents. In the area of internet data, through monitoring systems and category-specific management at all levels, it has increased the ability to protect and oversee data security, and strengthened law enforcement on data security involving the Industrial Internet, Internet of Vehicles, and 5G application.

5. Creating a Clean Cyberspace

In response to public demand and expectations, China has acted to regulate online information dissemination and rectify disorder in cyberspace. It has launched Operation Clean Net, Operation Qinglang and other special campaigns to address outstanding problems of strong public concern on the internet, such as pornography, fake information, cyberbullying, and abuse of algorithms. Websites and platforms spreading information that violates laws and regulations have received administrative admonition, rectification orders and warnings, and punishments such as fines and temporary bans on issuing new content. In addition, websites and platforms have been urged to assume their principal responsibility, and manage the information released by their users in accordance with the law and their user agreements. A complaint and reporting system for online information security is now in place to form synergy for cyber governance. With continued improvements to the online environment, the internet has become much cleaner and netizens more civil and better-behaved.

China prioritizes special protection for minors, creating a sound, friendly online environment for them. It has cleaned up the internet through Operation Child Protector and other special programs to maintain a safe online environment for minors, with a focus on illegal and harmful information, online gaming addiction, and unhealthy online socializing. It has strengthened the education on online safety among minors, and punished online crimes that harm the physical and mental health of minors, creating a sound and safe online environment for minors supported by joint efforts from families, schools, and society.

Panel 4   Operation Child Protector

Since 2011, China has regularly launched Operation Child Protector for the protection of minors. Offline, law enforcement teams have conducted regular inspections of markets near campuses, removing publications for children that contain content involving porn, violence or drug-abuse, or promote cult organizations and superstitions. Online, luring yet harmful content has been cleaned up through concerted efforts. Online platforms are urged to introduce youth-friendly versions that work, and key internet businesses are encouraged to assign offices and staff for Operation Child Protector. The Operation has expanded into a franchise of programs, to provide public education and communication, build education bases, and help schools and families strictly supervise teenagers' use of mobile phones and other smart terminal devices.

IV. Defending Fairness and Justice in Cyberspace

An impartial judiciary is the last line of defense for social fairness and justice. China has stayed committed to the principle of maintaining judicial justice and administrating justice for the people. Actively responding to the needs of justice in the age of the internet, China has employed internet and information technology to empower the traditional judiciary, improved rules of cyber justice, and reformed models of cyber justice. This has allowed it to settle new types of cyber disputes in accordance with the law, combat cybercrime, safeguard the rights and interests of cyberspace players, and deliver judicial services that are more fair, just, open, transparent, efficient, accessible, inclusive, and equitable.

1. Defining New Rules of Cyber Justice

As new internet technologies, applications and business forms develop quickly, legal relationships in cyberspace are becoming more diverse, posing new challenges to the administration of justice in cyberspace. This calls for better-defined rules of cyber justice.

For this purpose, China has produced timely judicial interpretations of civil and criminal issues such as intellectual property rights, the right to dignity, online transactions, and unfair competition on the internet, as well as telecom and online fraud. It has handled a good number of unprecedented, complicated cases that are closely related to the internet, such as those involving internet infrastructure security, algorithms, data rights and trading, protection of personal information, and management of online platforms. In the process, it has refined the criteria for the application of the law and made the standards for adjudication consistent. This has led to increasing clarity on the rules, code of conduct, and boundaries of rights, obligations and responsibilities in cyberspace. China has formulated rules for online litigation, mediation and operation of the people's courts, refined rules on taking electronic data as evidence, and standardized the procedures for handling cybercrime cases. As a result, a system of rules and procedures for cyber justice is taking shape. This systematic development of relevant rules provides regulatory guidance and institutional safeguards for cyber justice, which is therefore becoming more rule-based.

2. Exploring New Models of Cyber Justice

China has been active in exploring new channels, domains and models for further integrating internet technology with judicial activities, for the purpose of speedier delivery of justice. In order to build a cyber justice model with Chinese characteristics, it has piloted measures in applying the latest technologies such as big data, cloud computing, artificial intelligence and blockchain in judicial proceedings, judgment enforcement, judicial administration, and other fields.

Local courts are encouraged to explore new mechanisms with regional features for internet-empowered adjudication, on the basis of the development of local internet industry and the characteristics of local cyber disputes. Internet courts have been established in Hangzhou, Beijing and Guangzhou, in an attempt to realize adjudication of internet-related cases via the internet. In the process of digitalizing procuratorial work, China has used big data to empower legal oversight. It has systematically integrated a wide range of case information, worked on models and platforms for big data-based legal oversight, and implemented oversight of the prosecution of individual cases and of similar cases in order to address the common problems they raise. This has helped improve the quality and efficiency of legal oversight in the new era. The emergence of these new models signifies the further development of a socialist judicial system with Chinese characteristics in cyberspace, and is becoming a salient feature of China's judicial system.

Panel 5   Internet Courts

Internet courts represent a success in creating new judicial models. The Hangzhou Internet Court was established on August 18, 2017, followed by the opening of two more such courts in Beijing on September 9, 2018 and in Guangzhou on September 28. These internet courts focus on 11 types of internet-related dispute in the cities under their jurisdiction, including those involving online loan contracts, online infringement, and online copyright. They have helped advance technological innovation, rule-making, and cyberspace governance.

During the period between August 2017 and October 2019, these three courts handled a total of 118,764 internet-related cases, and concluded 88,401 of them. As many as 96.8 percent of these cases were filed online, and in 80,819 of these the entire process was handled via the internet. Online hearings took 45 minutes and case processing 38 days on average, which are in turn 40 percent and half of the time needed for conventional court trials. In 98 percent of the concluded cases, litigants accepted the ruling at first instance. All this indicates the good quality, efficiency and impact of internet courts.

---

3. Judicial Protection of Online Rights and Interests

China has carried out judicial activities to combat cybercrime, so that the people can see that justice is served in every judicial case.

Strengthening judicial protection of online civil rights and interests. To protect the online civil rights and interests of all parties concerned, China handles civil and commercial cases involving personal information, intellectual property rights, online transactions, and online infringement in accordance with the law. For protection of personal information, the focus is put on online platforms that process huge amounts of personal information. Civil public-interest litigations have been launched against online platforms suspected of abusing personal information. In adjudicating these cases, the courts have clarified the rules and limits for the commercial use of customers' personal information, and prompted companies running online platforms to collect and use data in accordance with laws and regulations. For protection of intellectual property rights in internet-related cases of high technological complexity such as those involving patents, integrated circuit designs, technological secrets, and computer software, the courts have introduced a technology investigator system. Step by step, safeguards are being set up in cyberspace to protect citizens' legitimate rights and interests there.

Intensifying punishment for cybercrime. As internet technology evolves swiftly, conventional crimes are transforming rapidly into internet-enabled, no-contact forms, leading to a rise in illicit acts such as telecom and online fraud, online gambling, and online pornography. China handles new types of cybercrime in accordance with the law. In recent years China has carried out a systematic "internet clean-up" campaign, combating cyber hacking, invasion of individual privacy, and many other criminal acts that cause strong concern to the public. It has launched a number of campaigns against telecom and online fraud, including those to hunt fugitives via cloud services and platforms, freeze the SIM cards and bank accounts used by suspects, intercept domestic recruitment by criminal groups operating from abroad, and pursue the heads and key members of criminal groups. It combats all types of predatory lending including trap loans, the student loan, reverse mortgage, and elder investment scams. It punishes in accordance with the law the shadowy businesses that provide services such as internet connection, domain registration, server hosting, mobile application development, online payment, and promotion to criminal groups behind telecom and online fraud.

China has also updated its national anti-fraud big data platform and anti-fraud app, built a national fraud database, and improved the mechanisms for quick freezing of payments and retrieval of swindled money. It takes resolute action against online gambling and delivers harsh punishments for online pornography. Through these efforts, remarkable progress has been made in combating cybercrime, giving the people a stronger sense of security and reinforcing social harmony and stability.

Panel 6   Going after Cybercrime

Telecom and online fraud harms citizens' immediate interests and property safety, and undermines social harmony and stability. It is therefore deeply loathed by the people. To address this global scourge, China targets all elements with in-depth measures, which have achieved good results. Between 2019 and 2021 China prosecuted 129,000 people on charges of telecom and online fraud. Between 2017 and 2021 it concluded 103,000 lawsuits of such fraud in the first instance, and convicted 223,000 criminals.

Exploring new avenues for judicial protection of minors in cyberspace. While focusing on forestalling and punishing cybercrime, China takes targeted measures against online criminal activities such as virtual sexual harassment, and has increased punishments for those preying on minors. Through law-based punishment and individualized assistance and education, the state does its utmost to rehabilitate underage people involved in cybercrime. China has strengthened the protection of minors in cyberspace, making breakthroughs in typical cases such as those concerning circulation of audio and video about narcotics, violation of minors' personal information rights and interests, and excessive livestream rewards from minor viewers. By taking action in the form of public-interest litigation, written suggestions from prosecutorial organizations, support for prosecutions, and briefings on relevant information, China is working to pool the strength of online platforms, the public, and the government to foster a healthy cyber environment for young people.

V. Promoting Public Awareness and Competence in Law-Based Cyberspace Governance

Public participation is necessary for spreading knowledge of the rule of law in cyberspace. China makes every effort to break new ground in the content, form and means of spreading legal knowledge via the internet. The Chinese netizens' awareness and understanding of the rule of law have generally increased, and online platforms have assumed their primary responsibility for legal compliance and the industry has embraced self-discipline. Respecting, learning, abiding by, and using the law is a shared understanding and basic principle, and the spirit of the socialist rule of law is fully manifested in cyberspace.

1. Internet Plus Public Legal Education

The internet has become a new space where people study, work and live; it provides a new platform for them to obtain information and access public services, which makes it a new avenue and means to spread knowledge of the law. The internet has changed the structure of legal literacy from unidirectional communication to interactive, service-based and immersive communication, and interpreted technical terms in plain everyday language. The participants have become increasingly active with better experiences and more gain.

Employing the internet to spread knowledge of the law. Government websites and WeChat official accounts set up special columns and features to spread legal knowledge regarding eco-environmental progress, food and drug safety, protecting personal information, and other matters of public concern, with a focus on the Constitution, Civil Code, National Security Law, Cybersecurity Law, and other important laws and regulations. China makes full use of the legal publicity website (legalinfo.moj. gov.cn), its weibo account, WeChat account and app and builds a smart legal publicity platform to spread knowledge and experience of the rule of law in China, so as to inculcate the idea in the public that rights and duties are integral to each other, as are personal freedom and social responsibility, to raise legal consciousness that laws should be applied to regulate behaviors and solve problems and conflicts, and to guide the people to advocate, abide by and defend the socialist rule of law.

Strengthening legal literacy through online media. With their strengths in content, channels, and resources, internet media have created a large number of graphics, cartoons, comics, short videos, livestream, and online music products on internet forums, blogs, microblogs, WeChat official accounts, instant messaging tools, livestreaming, search engines, Q&A communities and through many other channels that are tailored to meet the different needs of various groups in spreading legal awareness and explaining laws and regulations. These give the people direct access to the government's public legal education information that has deeply penetrated businesses, communities, campuses, and villages. Legal literacy has improved significantly among all the people.

Extending real-world legal literacy efforts into the virtual world. With the widespread integration of the internet with the economy and social life, those lectures, legal literacy initiatives in communities, legal consulting services, and artistic performances on the rule of law that used to be conducted in the real world are now expanding their influence and coverage through the internet. Online legal literacy training courses, micro-video contests, and quiz games are integrating with and complementing those face-to-face activities, attracting wider participation, and benefiting a larger population.

2. Publicizing Cyber Laws and Regulations
Cyber laws and regulations are the main content of public legal

education in cyberspace. They are becoming increasingly familiar to the public, providing the foundation for a sound and law-based cyberspace with high ethical standards.

Cyber laws and regulations are publicized during the whole legislative process. When drafting cyber laws and regulations such as the Cybersecurity Law, Data Security Law, and Personal Information Protection Law, the opinions of citizens, legal persons and other organizations are heard and can be adopted through public solicitation, deliberation, and appraisal via both online and offline channels. When these laws and regulations were promulgated, questions were explained through press conferences, answers to media questions, and expert interpretation. The public have been encouraged to learn more about cyber laws and regulations, and abide by them, which lays a solid public foundation for the law-based governance of cyberspace.

Legal literacy efforts are also being made in law enforcement and judicial activities when appropriate. To explain cyber laws, China releases information on typical cases of public concern, including online dissemination of illegal and harmful information, infringement of rights and interests relating to personal information, telecom and online fraud, and protection of minors in cyberspace. All cases relating to cyberspace are accessible to the public through four websites – adjudication procedure information (splcgk.court.gov.cn), court trial information (tingshen.court.gov.cn), judgment information (wenshu.court.gov.cn), and enforcement information (zxgk.court.gov.cn). The general public can access this information in a more direct and vivid way, and have evolved from onlookers to participants, supporters and advocates.

3. Raising Legal Awareness of Key Groups

The authority of the law comes from the people's firm belief and sincere support. China focuses its legal literacy efforts on key groups like teenagers and internet company employees. Teenagers are guided to adhere to laws, conduct themselves with civility, and follow cybersecurity protocols when surfing the internet. Internet companies are under supervision for their compliance with laws and regulations, and they are also required to guard against legal risks.

Improving education on cyber laws among teenagers. Teenagers are the future of the country and the hope of our nation. They are a growing demographic in China's netizen population. As the pioneers of the internet, they are the most active participants in online classes, communication, and life, but their legitimate rights and interests are also vulnerable to infringement on the internet. To protect their rights and interests and promote their healthy growth and well-rounded development, China makes every effort to improve their understanding of the rule of law in cyberspace, especially on critical concerns such as internet addiction, cyberbullying, and online pornography. Varied and vivid forms are adapted to their physical and mental development and their realities, such as story books, micro variety shows, plays for kids, radio stories, online classes, quiz games, and law classes taught in primary and secondary schools by police officers, prosecutors and judges who serve as part-time vice principals. A public legal education framework integrating government, society, schools and families has taken shape, which promotes the all-round legal awareness of juvenile netizens and builds their cybersecurity competence.

Panel 7　A Website for Promoting Legal Literacy Among Teenagers – qspfw.moe.gov.cn

China launched the teenagers' legal literacy website (qspfw.moe.gov.cn) in 2012, which features columns such as animated films/TV programs, real-life stories, and laws taught through pictures. More than 190,000 schools have now registered with the website, involving over 150 million users. In 2021 alone, there were 8.3 billion views on the website to learn about the Constitution.

Strengthening internet companies' compliance with the law. Internet companies are the main market players in the digital economy, and should promote its healthy development. Honesty and observing the law must be their cardinal principles. China is intensifying its efforts to promote legal literacy among internet companies, and requiring them to incorporate cyber laws into their induction and routine training. This applies especially to laws with a direct bearing on corporate operations and industry development, such as the Electronic Commerce Law, Cybersecurity Law, Data Security Law, Personal Information Protection Law, Anti-Monopoly Law, and Anti-Unfair Competition Law. Industry associations are encouraged to provide legal education in various forms for internet companies and their employees, and to ensure that the companies place equal emphasis on economic returns and social benefit. They are also required to guide – through improving industry norms, formulating industry standards, and issuing business integrity initiatives – the companies to fulfill their legal and social responsibilities. With such measures, consumers' legitimate rights and interests are fully protected, and fair competition in the market is ensured.

4. Strengthening Research and Education on Law-Based Cyberspace Governance

Education and professional practitioners of law-based cyberspace governance underpin a cyber power and drive innovation. Facing major theoretical problems in law-based cyberspace governance and a demand for talented people, China has established a preliminary system for cultivating professionals and conducting research that combines theory and practice, adapts to the development of cyberspace, and provides intellectual support and sufficient talented people for the country's law-based cyberspace governance.

Improving comprehensive research capabilities on law-based cyberspace governance. Universities and scientific research institutes have set up new-type think tanks to conduct relevant research and established a number of comprehensive research centers. By June 2022, China had more than 90 research institutes in this field. Serving as a bank of brain trusters, ideas, and talented people, these think tanks have conducted research in many frontier areas like data, algorithms, and platform management, and produced remarkable academic results. Experts and academics are fully engaged in relevant activities and offer constructive advice on China's major plans, legislation and reforms in law-based cyberspace governance.

Strengthening the training of personnel for law-based cyberspace governance. China integrates conventional legal studies with internet-related disciplines. Cybersecurity studies has been categorized as a primary discipline, and some universities have set up secondary disciplines like internet and information law studies, digital law studies, and artificial intelligence law studies. In line with specified regulations and procedures, institutions of higher learning, on their own initiative, have run undergraduate courses on the rule of law in cyberspace such as cybersecurity and law enforcement. Teams of research and teaching in cyber law have been organized to teach interdisciplinary courses that integrate legal knowledge with computer science and statistics, such as network and information security, laws and artificial intelligence, cyber law studies, blockchain and digital evidence, and legal analytics. A group of practical textbooks covering frontier research have been compiled for students in relevant majors, including cyber law, computational jurisprudence, data law, and personal information protection law. A large number of personnel with professional knowledge of both law and technology have been trained, providing a solid foundation for building up China's strength in cyberspace.

VI. Increasing International Exchanges and Cooperation in Law-Based Cyberspace Governance

Cyberspace is a shared activity space for all of humanity. All countries around the globe share the same desire to develop the digital economy; all face the same challenges posed by cybersecurity threats and have the same need for strengthening cyberspace governance.

China is fully engaged in international exchanges and cooperation in the field of law-based governance of cyberspace. Upholding independence, equality, and mutual respect, it joins with other countries to reform the global cyberspace governance system, to ensure that all countries share the opportunities and fruits brought by the development of the internet, and to jointly build a community with a shared future in cyberspace.

1. Playing an Active Role in Rule Making

China is committed to international fairness and justice. It resolutely safeguards the international system with the United Nations at its core, and the international order with international law as its foundation, and upholds the basic norms of international relations based on the purposes and principles of the UN Charter. It supports the participation of all countries in global cyberspace governance on an equal footing, and in laying down international cyberspace rules that are universally accepted.

China supports the UN's role as the main channel in international cyberspace governance. It supports the UN effort to formulate a global-level cybercrime convention, has pushed for the General Assembly to adopt a resolution to establish an open-ended ad hoc intergovernmental committee of experts, and has played a constructive role in the negotiations on a convention. It calls on the international community to reach agreement on an authoritative and universal convention at the earliest possible time to lay a legal foundation for the battle against cybercrime. China values the UN's key role in responding to international information security threats, and together with other Shanghai Cooperation Organization member states it submitted the original International Code of Conduct for Information Security to the UN General Assembly, and an updated version in 2015. It launched the Global Data Security Initiative, and issued the China-League of Arab States Cooperation Initiative on Data Security together with the League of Arab States in March 2021, and the Data Security Cooperation Initiative of China+Central Asia together with five Central Asian countries (Kazakhstan, Kyrgyzstan, Tajikistan, Turkmenistan and Uzbekistan) in June 2022, which provide a blueprint for developing global data security rules. China encouraged the UN to draw up a framework for responsible state behavior in cyberspace, making clear that the principles of international law – such as equal sovereignty, peaceful settlement of disputes, non-use of force, non-interference in other countries' domestic affairs – are also applicable in cyberspace, and that impartial global security standards for the supply chain of information technology products should be formulated. It has expanded its cyberspace cooperation with the UN's special organizations, taken an active part in formulating UNESCO's Recommendation on the Ethics of Artificial Intelligence, and conducted extensive cooperation with the World Intellectual Property Organization in formulating domain name rules and settling disputes in this field.

Taking an active part in the formulation of regional cyberspace governance rules. China signed the Regional Comprehensive Economic Partnership agreement, under which the 15 member states including China laid down regional rules regarding electronic signature and electronic authentication, online consumer protection, online personal information protection, cybersecurity, cross-border transfer of information by electronic means, and intellectual property right protection. Its e-commerce chapter is by some margin the world's most extensive and most used set of e-commerce rules. China has also taken vigorous steps to join the Comprehensive and Progressive Agreement for Trans-Pacific Partnership and the Digital Economy Partnership Agreement, in order to participate in the formulation of high-standard rules in the digital economy.

2. Conducting Extensive Exchanges and Cooperation

As a longstanding supporter of international exchanges and cooperation in the rule of law in cyberspace, China takes part in dialogues, negotiations, exchanges, and mutual learning with other countries. It continues to expand and strengthen the network of global partnerships based on equality, openness, and cooperation, and to promote international cyberspace governance that is driven by common progress and designed for shared benefit.

Engaging in bilateral and multilateral dialogues and exchanges in law-based cyberspace governance. China has established the Sino-Russian Information Security Consultation Mechanism, China-EU Taskforce, China-ASEAN Cyber Dialogue Mechanism, and China-Japan-ROK Trilateral Cyber Consultation Mechanism, and co-hosted the 2019 China-Germany Dialogue on the Internet Economy, China-UK Internet Roundtable, China-ROK Internet Roundtable, China-Cuba Internet Development Forum, and China-Brazil Internet Governance Seminar. Through these pragmatic exchanges, it has worked with other countries on cyber policies, laws, regulations, and governance experience. It has responded promptly to the concerns of various parties, and settled disputes through negotiation on an equal footing. It has signed cybersecurity cooperation memorandums with countries including Thailand and Indonesia to strengthen exchanges and sharing in cybersecurity policies, laws and regulations, and to jointly build capacity in cybersecurity.

Increasing international law enforcement and judicial cooperation on cybersecurity. China has reached agreements on cybersecurity with many other countries and carried out in-depth and pragmatic cooperation in fighting cyberterrorism and telecom and online fraud. To combat cyber-terrorism, China has increased cooperation with other countries through joint counterterrorism maneuvers, joint border defense operations, and police and judicial cooperation to meet threats and challenges and safe-guard world peace and regional stability. In fighting telecom and online fraud, China has strengthened law enforcement and judicial cooperation with other countries, investigated major cross-border cases, and achieved substantial results. Between March and June 2022, 76 countries including China took part in an operation codenamed First Light 2022 initiated by the International Criminal Police Organization, with some 2,000 suspects arrested and some US$50 million worth of illicit funds intercepted, which effectively curbed transnational social engineering scams.

Jointly protecting the rights and interests of minors in cyberspace. China cooperates with the United Nations Children's Fund, the International Association of Internet Hotlines, and other international organizations, and relevant departments of the United Kingdom, Germany, the United Arab Emirates and other countries to fight online child pornography. As a member of WeProtect Global Alliance, China works with other member governments, companies and civil society organizations – totaling more than 200 – to combat child sexual exploitation and abuse online and create a safer cyber environment for children.

3. Creating Platforms for Dialogue

As a responsible major country, China has made great efforts to build a global platform promoting connectivity between China and the rest of the world, and a Chinese platform for the global internet to be shared and governed by all. It has played an active role in promoting connections, understanding, and mutual trust in the rule of law in cyberspace between different countries.

Hosting the world internet conferences for exchanging ideas on the rule of law in cyberspace. Every year since 2014, China has hosted the

World Internet Conference, attended by representatives from governments, international organizations, internet companies, think tanks, industry associations, and technology communities. The organizing committee of the conference released a concept document named Jointly Build a Community with a Shared Future in Cyberspace, which calls for "respecting sovereignty in cyberspace" and points out that "the principle of sovereign equality enshrined in the Charter of the United Nations is a basic norm governing contemporary international relations. It covers all aspects of state-to-state relations, and should likewise apply to cyberspace." The organizing committee also launched the Initiative on Jointly Building a Community with a Shared Future in Cyberspace, proposing that "international exchanges and cooperation should be advanced in the fields of data security, personal information protection and relevant rules and standards, and efforts should be made to promote mutual recognition among countries on rules and standards on personal information protection in line with the purposes of the UN Charter." China has shared experience in legislation on the protection of minors, combated cybercrimes and cyberbullying targeted at minors, and further improved mechanisms for combating cybercrimes and cyberterrorism. It has supported and taken an active part in negotiations under the framework of the United Nations on the global convention against cybercrimes, and coordinated work on legislation and practices in different countries in a joint effort to tackle the threats of cybercrimes and cyberterrorism.

Panel 8 The International Organization of the World Internet Conference

China initiated the international organization of the World Internet Conference in 2022, with the goal of building a global internet platform featuring extensive consultation, joint contribution, and sharing of benefits. By promoting sharing of benefits through practical cooperation, it aims to identify strong points and contribute ideas to global internet governance. Institutes, organizations, enterprises, and individuals engaging in the internet from nearly 20 countries in six continents have now joined the organization as founding members.

Building multi-form, multi-channel and multi-tiered international platforms to exchange views, experience and practices on law-based cyberspace governance including legislation, law enforcement, judicial work, and public legal education. China organizes this through many multilateral platforms like the BRICS cooperation mechanism, Shanghai Cooperation Organization, Asian-African Legal Consultative Organization, and ASEAN Regional Forum. It hosted the World Forum on Rule of Law in Internet, and released the Wuzhen Declaration at the event, building a bridge for sharing experience, increasing understanding, and learning from each other in cyberspace justice. China supports industry associations of the internet to build international exchange platforms such as the China Internet Governance Forum, discussing such issues as digital inclusion and data governance. These platforms have promoted common understanding among Chinese and foreign internet communities, and facilitated joint solutions to the problems obstructing the development of the internet. China encourages Chinese experts and academics to attend academic forums and symposiums, conduct intellectual exchanges, and share research fruits with their foreign counterparts in frontier research on the digital economy, data security, governance of artificial intelligence, and other related matters.

Conclusion

Based on its own realities, and learning from other countries' experience, China has created a cyberspace governance model with distinct Chinese characteristics. On the new journey towards a modern socialist country, China will always be committed to all-round law-based governance of the country and of cyberspace. It will promote the lawful, orderly and healthy development of the internet in China, safeguard the high-quality development of a digital China under the rule of law, and provide a solid legal guarantee for building up China's strength in cyberspace.

The internet benefits the whole world. China champions the interests of the peoples of all countries in promoting the development and prosperity of cyberspace in accordance with the law. The rule of law in cyberspace is an important tool of digital governance, and a marker of digital progress. Facing the opportunities and challenges brought about by digitalization, China will follow the global governance principle of achieving shared growth through consultation and collaboration, and work together with the international community to ensure global cyberspace governance is law-based, and that digital progress will deliver greater benefit to the people. China stands ready to partner with all other countries to build a community with a shared future in cyberspace and create a better world.

A Global Community of Shared Future: China's Proposals and Actions

The State Council Information Office of
the People's Republic of China

September 2023

Preface

In the universe there is only one Earth, the shared home of humanity. Unfortunately, this planet on which we rely for our subsistence is facing immense and unprecedented crises, both known and unknown, both foreseeable and unforeseeable. Whether human civilization can survive these has become an existential issue that must be squarely faced. More and more people have come to the realization that rather than amassing material wealth, the most pressing task is to find a guiding beacon for the sustainable development of human civilization, because we all care about our future.

Ten years ago President Xi Jinping propounded the idea of building a global community of shared future, answering a question raised by the world, by history, and by the times: "Where is humanity headed?" His proposal lights the path forward as the world fumbles for solutions, and represents China's contribution to global efforts to protect our shared home and create a better future of prosperity for all.

To build a global community of shared future, all peoples, all countries, and all individuals – our destinies being interconnected – must stand together in adversity and through thick and thin, navigating towards greater harmony on this planet that we call home. We should endeavor to build an open, inclusive, clean and beautiful world that enjoys lasting peace, universal security, and common prosperity, turning people's longing for a better life into reality.

The vision of a global community of shared future bears in mind the wellbeing of all humanity. It is based on both observation of the present and visionary planning for the future. It lays out goals, charts the path, and offers action plans to achieve them. It concerns the future of humanity and the destiny of every human being.

President Xi Jinping first raised the vision of a global community of shared future when addressing the Moscow State Institute of International Relations in 2013. Over the past decade it has been steadily enriched. He fleshed it out with a five-point proposal[1] in his speech at the General Debate of the 70th Session of the UN General Assembly in 2015. He further proposed five goals for the world[2] in his speech at the United Nations Office in Geneva in 2017. This represents the steady increase in the depth and scope of the vision.

The past decade has seen steady progress in implementing the vision. From bilateral to multilateral and from regional to global dimensions, ground-breaking results have been achieved on every front. The Belt and Road Initiative, the Global Development Initiative, the Global Security Initiative, and the Global Civilization Initiative have taken root and borne fruits, bringing prosperity and stability to the world and creating substantive benefits for the people.

Over the past decade, the vision of a global community of shared future has gained broader support. More countries and people have come to the understanding that this vision serves the common interests of humanity, represents popular calls for peace, justice and progress, and can

---

[1] The five points are: We should build partnerships in which countries treat each other as equals, engage in extensive consultation, and enhance mutual understanding. We should create a security environment featuring fairness, justice, joint efforts, and shared interests. We should promote open, innovative and inclusive development that benefits all. We should increase inter-civilization exchanges to promote harmony, inclusiveness, and respect for differences. We should build an ecosystem that puts Mother Nature and green development first.

[2] The five goals are: We should build a world of lasting peace through dialogue and consultation. We should build a world of common security for all through joint efforts. We should build a world of common prosperity through win-win cooperation. We should build an open and inclusive world through exchanges and mutual learning. We should make our world clean and beautiful by pursuing green and low-carbon development.

create the greatest synergy among all nations for building a better world. It is now widely recognized in the international community that the vision has nothing to do with self-interest and protectionism. Instead, by presenting China's vision of the course of human development, it confronts the hegemonic thinking of certain countries that seek supremacy. It is therefore of great significance to promote solidarity and cooperation among all countries and create a better future for humanity.

The Chinese government is publishing this white paper to introduce the theoretical base, practice and development of a global community of shared future. We hope it will improve understanding and expand consensus in the international community, and reinforce the global effort to realize this vision.

I. Humanity at a Crossroads

This is an era of promise, and an era of challenges. At yet another crossroads in history, we have to choose between unity and division, between opening up and closing off, between cooperation and confrontation. With the overall interests of humanity at stake, this choice tests the wisdom of all countries.

1. Interdependence is the prevailing trend throughout history

In its history, humanity has progressed from primitive society to the Agricultural Revolution, the Industrial Revolution, and now the Information Revolution. While this process has seen a steep increase in productivity, one fundamental reality has remained unchanged: The Earth is our one and only home. All countries bear responsibility for the safety of this planet and the future of humanity. If the pursuit of power and profit escalates to vicious competition or even armed conflict, self-destruction will be the certain outcome.

Throughout history, peace and development have been the primary aspirations of humanity. Having experienced the ravages of wars and conflicts, especially the two world wars, people around the globe have built a keener awareness of cherishing peace, expanding cooperation, and seeking common development. The idea that "we are all one human family" is gaining traction, and the desire for a global community grows stronger than ever.

Globalization has improved the allocation of production factors worldwide, including capital, information, technology, labor and management. As if connecting scattered lakes and creeks into an uninterrupted expanse of water, it draws nations out of isolation and away from the obsolete model of self-reliance, merging their individual markets into a global one and combining their respective experiences into world history.

As information technology advances with every passing day, most prominently in the fields of Internet, big data, quantum computing, and artificial intelligence, human exchanges have become deeper, broader, and more extensive than ever before, and countries are more interconnected and interdependent than at any point in the past. Globalization is not an option; it is the reality and the way of life. The global village is getting smaller – the longest distance between two places on earth has been reduced to a flight of no greater than 24 hours, and our planet is becoming flat – one tap on a mobile phone connects us to the other side of the world in a split second. This is an integrated world. Those who turn their back on it will have no place in it.

Living on the same planet, all countries, adjacent or distant, large or small, developed or developing, are members of an emerging community of shared interests, responsibility, and destiny, whose wellbeing and security are interrelated. Only when appropriate attention is paid to the collective future of humanity is it possible that the wishes of every country, people and individual come true. Whatever we may encounter on our journey ahead, the only right choice is to work together for the benefit of all.

2. Global challenges call for global response

Our world is undergoing change on a scale unseen in a century. Various problems old and new and complex issues are converging with and compounding each other, posing unprecedented challenges for human society. Instability, uncertainty, and unpredictability are now the norm.

The peace deficit is growing. Though human society has largely maintained peace since the end of World War II, threats to world peace continue to amass. War has returned to the Eurasian continent, tensions are rising, and a series of flashpoints are emerging. The shadow of the arms race lingers on, and the threat of nuclear war – the Sword of Damocles that hangs over humanity – remains. Our world is at risk of plunging into confrontation and even war.

The development deficit is ballooning. The global economic recovery is sluggish, and unilateralism and protectionism are rampant. Some countries are turning to a "small yard, high fence" approach to wall themselves off; they are pushing for decoupling, severing and "derisking" supply chains. All this has caused setbacks to globalization. At the same time the Covid-19 pandemic has reversed global development, exacerbating the North-South gap, development fault lines, and the technology divide. The Human Development Index has declined for the first time in 30 years. The world's poor population has increased by more than 100 million, and nearly 800 million people live in hunger.

The security deficit is glaring. Due to more intense global strategic competition and a lack of mutual trust between major countries, the Cold War mindset has re-emerged, and calls for ideological confrontation have resurfaced. Some countries' hegemonic, abusive, and aggressive actions against others, in the form of swindling, plundering, oppression, and the zero-sum game, are causing great harm. Non-traditional security challenges are on the rise, including terrorism, cyber-attacks, transnational crime, and biological threats.

The governance deficit is more severe. The world is facing multiple governance crises. The energy crisis, food crisis, and debt crisis are intensifying. Global climate governance is urgently needed, and the transition to green, low-carbon development requires dedicated efforts over an extended period of time. The digital divide continues to expand, and sound governance of artificial intelligence is lacking. The Covid-19 pandemic is a mirror through which we have observed that the global governance system is falling further behind the times and keeps breaking down on issues requiring resolution. It has to be reformed and improved.

In the face of global crises, the 190-plus countries in the world are all in the same big boat. Only big boats can withstand battering winds and crashing waves. No country, however strong it may be, can do everything on its own. We must engage in global cooperation. Only when all countries work together, only when we align individual interests with the interests of all, and only when we truly build a global community of shared future, can humanity tide through the crises confronting us and sail towards a better future.

3. The new era calls for new ideas

This is an era when the world is undergoing rapid changes almost every day. We can no longer interpret the reality we are living in or find satisfactory solutions to the conundrums we are facing by means of traditional approaches to international relations. It is increasingly obvious that the idea that "all strong countries will seek hegemony", the obsession with superior strength, and the zero-sum mentality are in conflict with the needs of our times. Humanity is in great need of new ideas that generate positive developments and conform to positive historical trends.

There is no iron law that dictates that a rising power will inevitably seek hegemony. This assumption represents typical hegemonic thinking and is grounded in memories of catastrophic wars between hegemonic powers in the past. China has never accepted that once a country becomes strong enough, it will invariably seek hegemony. China understands the lesson of history – that hegemony preludes decline. We pursue development and revitalization through our own efforts, rather than invasion or expansion. And everything we do is for the purpose of providing a better life for our people, all the while creating more development opportunities for the entire world, not in order to supersede or subjugate others.

The strong preying on the weak is not a way for humans to coexist. If the law of the jungle is imposed on human society, and the idea that "might makes right" prevails, the principle of sovereign equality will be fundamentally undermined, and world peace and stability will be severely endangered. In the age of globalization, all countries are interdependent and interconnected. Therefore the law of the jungle and the winner-takes-all mindset will lead nowhere – inclusive development for the benefit of all is the right path forward. China has consistently championed equity and justice, and remains committed to friendly cooperation with other countries, on the basis of the Five Principles of Peaceful Coexistence, in order to advance democracy in international relations.

The zero-sum game in which one wins by causing others to lose is doomed to fail. Nevertheless, certain countries still cling to this mindset, blindly pursuing absolute security and monopolistic advantages. This will do nothing for their development over the long run; it will simply create a major threat to world peace and prosperity. No country should hope for others to fail. Instead, it should work together with other countries for the success of all. China consistently aligns its development with global development, and aligns the interests of the Chinese people with the common interests of all peoples around the world. When the world thrives, China thrives, and vice versa.

II. An Answer to the Call of the Times and a Blueprint for the Future

Standing at a crossroads, humanity is faced with two opposing options. One is to revert to the Cold War mentality that deepens division and antagonism and stokes confrontation between blocs. The other is to act for the common wellbeing of humanity, strengthen solidarity and cooperation, advocate openness and win-win results, and promote equality and respect. The tug of war between these two options will shape the future of humanity and our planet in a profound way.

To build a global community of shared future is to pursue openness, inclusiveness, mutual benefit, equity and justice. The goal is not to replace one system or civilization with another. Instead, it is about countries with different social systems, ideologies, histories, cultures and levels of development coming together to promote shared interests, shared rights, and shared responsibilities in global affairs. The vision of a global community of shared future stands on the right side of history and on the side of human progress. It introduces a new approach for international relations, provides new ideas for global governance, opens up new prospects for international exchanges, and draws a new blueprint for a better world.

1. Introducing a new approach to international relations

The current international order is facing a myriad of challenges. Some countries, holding to the notion of might makes right, willfully engage in bullying, plundering and zero-sum competition. The development gap is widening and the deficit in security is growing. The isolationist and exclusive practice of alliance-based confrontation runs counter to the trend towards multipolarity and the evolution of international relations in the post-Cold War era. Especially with the rise of a large number of emerging market and developing countries, the current international order is increasingly out of step with the changing times. "What kind of world we need and how to build such a world" has become a vital question with the future of humanity at stake.

China's answer to this question of the times is to build a global community of shared future. It means that with their futures closely interlocked, all nations and countries should stick together, share weal and woe, live together in harmony, and engage in mutually beneficial cooperation. The idea is based on a reasonable design for state-to-state relations. It reflects the general consensus and common expectations of the international community, and demonstrates China's sense of duty as a responsible major country.

In this global village, all human beings are one big family. With their interests intertwined and futures interlocked, countries are turning into a community of shared future. Such a vision rises above the exclusive rules of bloc politics, the notion of might makes right, and the "universal values" defined by a handful of Western countries. It conforms to the trend of the times, echoes the call for global cooperation, and contributes to a more just and equitable international order.

2. Highlighting the new features of global governance

The concept of a global community of shared future holds that all countries share a common future, and envisions a world characterized by openness and inclusiveness, equity and justice, harmonious coexistence, diversity and mutual learning, and unity and cooperation.

– Openness and inclusiveness. Countries should not draw lines based on ideology, target specific countries, or gang up to form exclusive blocs. The ocean is vast because it admits all rivers. To build a global community of shared future, countries should advance democracy in international relations to make sure that the future of the world is determined by all, that international rules are written by all, that global affairs are governed by all, and that the fruits of development are shared by all.

– Equity and justice. The world needs justice, not hegemonism. No country has the right to dominate global affairs, dictate the future of others, or monopolize development advantages. Countries should safeguard the international order based on international law, uphold the authority of the international rule of law, and ensure equal and unified application of international law. The practice of double standards or selective application of law should be rejected.

– Harmonious coexistence. Countries should strive to achieve peaceful coexistence and common development by seeking common ground while reserving differences. Planet Earth is not an arena for wrestling between countries, but a stage for human coexistence. Despite their differences and diverse features, countries can develop together in harmony and unity, and it is precisely such diversity that gives strength to global development.

– Diversity and mutual learning. Different histories, national conditions, ethnic groups, and customs have given birth to diverse civilizations. Diversity of human civilizations is a basic feature of our world. Mutual learning among civilizations provides important impetus to human progress. Countries should respect one another and jointly pursue common development through exchanges and mutual learning.

– Unity and cooperation. Countries should act for the greater good. Pursuing development behind closed doors can only result in poverty. Viewed from a "country-first" perspective, the world is small and crowded, and locked in "fierce competition"; viewed from the perspective of a shared future, the world is vast, and full of opportunities for cooperation. No country can overcome global development challenges on its own. Cooperation among all countries is the only viable option.

3. Opening up new prospects for international exchanges

China has made a five-point proposal for building a global community of shared future in the areas of partnerships, security environment, development, inter-civilization exchanges, and ecosystem. This has opened up new prospects for international exchanges.

We should build partnerships in which countries treat each other as equals, engage in extensive consultation, and enhance mutual understanding. The principle of sovereign equality runs through the UN Charter. All countries are equals. The big, the mighty and the wealthy should not bully the small, the weak and the poor. We should uphold multilateralism and reject unilateralism. We should replace the outdated mindset of winner takes all with a new vision of seeking win-win outcomes for all. We should forge global partnerships at both international and regional levels, and embrace a new approach to state-to-state relations, one founded on dialogue rather than confrontation and that seeks partnership rather than alliance. In handling their relations, major countries should follow the principles of no conflict, no confrontation, mutual respect, and win-win cooperation. Big countries should treat small countries as equals and take the right approach to friendship and interests, pursuing both friendship and interests and putting friendship first.

We should create a security environment featuring fairness, justice, joint efforts, and shared interests. In the age of economic globalization, the security of all countries is interlinked, and each has an impact on the others. No country can maintain absolute security on its own, and no country can achieve stability by destabilizing others. The law of the jungle leaves the weak at the mercy of the strong; it is not the way for countries to conduct their relations. Those who choose to oppress will invite harm to themselves, like lifting a rock only to drop it on their own feet. We should reject Cold War mentality in all its manifestation, and foster a new vision of common, comprehensive, cooperative and sustainable security.

We should promote open, innovative and inclusive development

that benefits all. Development is meaningful only when it is inclusive and sustainable. To achieve such development requires openness, mutual assistance and mutually beneficial relations. Long-term global development cannot be founded on one group of countries becoming increasingly prosperous while another group of countries remain chronically poor and backward. Development should be placed high on the international agenda, and efforts should be made to reduce inequality and imbalance in global development, leaving no country or individual behind.

We should increase inter-civilization exchanges to promote harmony, inclusiveness, and respect for differences. There are more than 200 countries and regions, over 2,500 ethnic groups and a vast number of religions in our world. Such cultural diversity is what makes the world colorful. Diversity breeds exchanges, exchanges lead to integration, and integration brings progress. Only by upholding the equality, mutual learning, dialogue and inclusiveness of civilizations, and working for mutual respect, experience sharing, and harmonious coexistence while preserving diversity, can the world maintain its diversity and thrive. We should respect all civilizations, treat each other as equals, and draw inspiration from each other to boost the creative development of human civilization.

We should build an ecosystem that puts Mother Nature and green development first. Humanity may have the ability to utilize nature and even transform it, but it is still a part of nature. We should care for nature and not place ourselves above it. We should reconcile industrial development with nature, and pursue harmony between humanity and nature to achieve sustainable global development and all-round human development. We should respect nature, follow its ways, and protect it. We should firmly pursue green, low-carbon, circular and sustainable development.

4. Outlining a new vision for building a better world

China proposes to build an open, inclusive, clean and beautiful world that enjoys lasting peace, common security, and common prosperity. From "the five-point proposal" to "the five goals", the concept of a global community of shared future has gained a broader historical perspective and deeper meaning, and set a clearer goal and drawn a clearer blueprint for the future of humanity.

We should build a world of lasting peace through dialogue and consultation. It means beating the swords of war into the plowshares of peace. The stone wall at the entrance to the UNESCO headquarters carries the inscription of one single message: "Since wars begin in the minds of men, it is in the minds of men that the defenses of peace must be constructed." Throughout human history, obsession with power and hegemony has led to frequent wars and loss of lives. The lessons are painful and profound, and we need to remove the fuses of war from our minds. Big countries should treat the smaller ones as equals instead of seeking unilateral dominance or imposing their will on others. No country should open Pandora's box by willfully provoking turmoil and armed conflict or undermining the international rule of law. Countries should respect each other's sovereignty and territorial integrity, respect each other's core interests and major concerns, and respect the development path and social system chosen by other peoples.

We should build a world of common security for all through joint efforts. It means turning absolute security for one into common security for all. There is no place in the world that enjoys absolute security, and a country cannot build its security on the turmoil of others. Threats to other countries can turn into a challenge to one's own country. When neighbors are in trouble, instead of reinforcing one's own fences, one should extend a helping hand. As challenges often take on global dimensions, it is all the more important for countries to cooperate in addressing them, turning pressure into motivation and crises into opportunities. Unilateral action or blind belief in the use of force cannot address the complex international security threats. The only solution lies in cooperative and common security. It is normal for countries to have differences, and they should be properly addressed through dialogue and consultation. As long as we show sincerity, goodwill and political wisdom, no conflict is too big to resolve and no ice is too thick to break.

We should build a world of common prosperity through win-win cooperation. It means bidding farewell to the winner-takes-all mindset and sharing development achievements. In this day and age, the international community has evolved into a sophisticated and integrated apparatus, as the removal of any single part will cause serious problems to its overall operation. We must keep to the correct direction of economic globalization, and oppose any attempt to set up technological blockades, cause technological divides, or seek development decoupling. While we should make the pie of the global economy bigger, it is even more important to divide it well, so that development achievements can benefit people of all countries more equitably, and bring about true cooperation and win-win results.

We should build an open and inclusive world through exchanges and mutual learning. It means bidding farewell to the mindset that one civilization is superior to another and starting to appreciate the strengths of other civilizations. Our world can fully accommodate the common growth and progress of all countries, and success for one country does not mean failure for another. There is no universally applicable development path. A development path that continuously benefits the people is the most viable one. Countries and nations should respect their differences and seek harmony without uniformity, and civilizations should draw strength from each other and make progress together. Exchanges and mutual learning between civilizations should be a driving force for human progress and a strong underpinning for world peace.

We should make our world clean and beautiful by pursuing green and low-carbon development. It means bidding farewell to the destructive exploitation of resources and preserving and enjoying the lush mountains and lucid waters. Humanity coexists with nature. Any harm we inflict on nature will eventually come back to haunt us. We often take natural resources such as air, water, soil and blue sky for granted. But we could not survive without them. Industrialization has created a level of material wealth never seen before, but it has also inflicted irreparable damage on the environment. We must not exhaust all the resources passed on to us by previous generations and leave nothing to our children, or pursue development in a destructive way. Lush mountains and lucid waters are invaluable assets. We must follow the philosophy of harmony between humanity and nature and observance of the laws of nature and pursue a path of sustainable development, so that everyone is able to enjoy a starry sky, lush mountains and fragrant flowers.

Building a global community of shared future is China's proposed strategy for reforming and improving the international governance system. This does not mean that the international system should be dismantled or started afresh. Rather, it means promoting greater democracy in international relations and making global governance more just and equitable. This important vision reflects the broadest common aspiration of the peoples of all countries in pursuit of peace, development, and stability, and the broadest consensus among countries with different cultural backgrounds and at different stages of development. It transcends outdated mindsets such as zero-sum game, power politics, and Cold War confrontations. It has become the overall goal of China's major-country diplomacy in the new era, and a great banner that leads the trend of the times and the direction of human progress.

III. Deep Roots in History and Cultural Traditions

The concept of a global community of shared future has deep roots in China's profound cultural heritage and its unique experience of modernization. It carries forward the diplomatic traditions of the People's Republic of China and draws on the outstanding achievements of all other civilizations. It manifests China's time-honored historical traditions, distinct characteristics of the times, and a wealth of humanistic values.

1. Inheriting the best of traditional Chinese culture

China's fine traditional culture epitomizes the essence of the Chinese civilization. It provides inspiring insights to help understand and shape the world and address current challenges, and contains elements of the vision of building a global community of shared future.

Harmony is the core concept of Chinese culture, which values the primacy of harmony and harmony within diversity, pursues the ideal of harmony and solidarity towards common progress, and embraces cultural diversity and global harmony.

The Chinese nation believes all nations together are one community, advocates fraternity among all peoples and peace for all countries, follows the principle of interstate relations that the strong do not bully the weak and the rich do not insult the poor, and pursues a world of fairness and justice for the common good.

The Chinese nation champions universal benevolence, holding that the virtuous are never left to stand alone, endorsing good neighborliness with good faith and good will, and pursuing both friendship and interests while putting friendship first.

The Chinese nation observes the rule that "to establish oneself, one must help others to establish themselves first; to succeed, one must help others to succeed first", believing that helping others is helping oneself. It also upholds the principle that "do not do to others what you do not want done to yourself", and never imposes its will upon other nations.

The Chinese nation acts on the belief that humans are part of nature and follows the old adage: "Fish with a line but not with a net; when fowling, do not aim at a roosting bird." It reveres the laws of the universe, loves nature, and pursues harmony between humanity and nature.

2. Showcasing the global vision of the Communist Party of China

Always championing a global vision is part of the valuable experience accumulated by the Communist Party of China (CPC) in its century-long history. Over the past one hundred years and more, the CPC has always sought happiness for the Chinese people and rejuvenation for the Chinese nation while pursuing progress for all of humanity and the common good of the world. It succeeded in leading the Chinese people onto a distinctively Chinese path to modernization and developing a new form of human advancement. These successes have laid a solid foundation for building a global community of shared future, charting the course and opening up broad prospects for this great endeavor.

The CPC is committed to seeking progress for China while benefiting the wider world, bringing a good life to the Chinese people and also helping other peoples to prosper, and contributing more to humanity. The report to the 20th CPC National Congress in 2022 drew a great blueprint for rejuvenating the Chinese nation on all fronts by pioneering a uniquely Chinese path to modernization, and pointed out that striving to build a global community of shared future is one of the intrinsic requirements of Chinese modernization, affirming the close bond between the future of China and the future of all humanity.

The CPC leads the Chinese people in blazing and expanding China's path to modernization based on both China's distinctive conditions and other countries' common approaches. Chinese modernization is the modernization of common prosperity for a huge population, coordinated material and cultural-ethical advancement, harmony between humanity and nature, and peaceful development. All these features have provided useful experience for other developing countries and a more robust and sustainable option for jointly building a global community of shared future.

3. Promoting the fine diplomatic traditions of New China

Over the past 70 years and more, China has made notable progress, established fine traditions, and forged a tenacious character and unique strengths in developing foreign relations. The initiative of building a global community of shared future builds on the PRC's diplomatic philosophies, strategic thinking and traditions, and opens up new horizons for major-country diplomacy with Chinese characteristics.

After the PRC was founded in 1949, China committed itself to an independent foreign policy of peace and put forward the Five Principles of Peaceful Coexistence, the Three Worlds theory and other principles, policies and ideas. This allowed China to find its place, win respect, and expand its reach in the international community. After the launch of reform and opening up in 1978, China asserted that peace and development are the underlying trends of the times. It advocated multipolarity and greater democracy in international relations, promoted a harmonious world, and achieved significant progress in China's diplomacy around the world.

In the new era, championing peace, development, and win-win cooperation, China has advanced its major-country diplomacy on all fronts and formed a multifaceted, multilevel, and all-dimensional diplomatic strategy. China has initiated a range of visionary initiatives, including a global community of shared future, a new type of international relations, the common values of humanity, the Belt and Road Initiative, the Global Development Initiative, the Global Security Initiative, and the Global

Civilization Initiative, and promoted a set of approaches to global governance, to friendship and interests, to security, to development, to cooperation, and to the eco-environment. All these carry distinctively Chinese features, style and ethos.

4. Incorporating the outstanding achievements of other civilizations

The concept of a global community of shared future incorporates the best of the cultures of enduring appeal and impact that have transcended time, space, and national borders in human history. It crystallizes the shared values of people from different regions, cultures, ethnic backgrounds and with different religious beliefs. It draws on the outstanding achievements of cultural integration between diverse civilizations. It embodies the common aspiration of all humanity.

All civilizations around the world have manifestations of the concept of a global community of shared future. Ancient Greek philosophers conducted primary research on this concept based on city-states, believing that humanity as one community should act in concert to pursue common interests and thus must live in harmony. Ancient Indian literature records the motto of "Under Heaven – one family". The African philosophy of Ubuntu holds that "I am because we are," emphasizing interdependence of humanity.

The concept of a global community of shared future reflects the common interests of all civilizations – peace, development, unity, coexistence, and win-win cooperation. A Russian proverb holds, "Together we can weather the storm." The Swiss-German writer Hermann Hesse proposed, "Serve not war and destruction, but peace and reconciliation." A German proverb reads, "An individual's effort is addition; a team's effort is multiplication." An African proverb states, "One single pillar is not sufficient to build a house." An Arabian proverb asserts, "If you want to walk fast, walk alone; if you want to walk far, walk together." Mexican poet Alfonso Reyes wrote, "The only way to be profitably national is to be generously universal." An Indonesian proverb says, "Sugarcane and lemongrass grow in dense clumps." A Mongolian proverb concludes, "Neighbors are connected at heart and share a common destiny." All the above narratives manifest the profound cultural and intellectual essence of the world.

In building a global community of shared future, all countries should observe the widely acknowledged norms of international relations. Since the advent of modern times, a fair and equitable international order has been the long-standing goal of all humanity. From the principle of equity and sovereignty established by the Peace of Westphalia in 1648, to international humanitarianism established by the Geneva Conventions in 1864, then to the four purposes and seven principles established by the Charter of the United Nations in 1945, and later to the Five Principles of Peaceful Coexistence proposed at the Bandung Conference in 1955, these norms of international relations have evolved into widely recognized principles and become the essential foundations of a global community of shared future.

IV. Direction and Path

The vision of a global community of shared future is the outcome of China's wisdom in handling contemporary international relations from the perspective of world peace and development – a Chinese plan for improving global governance, and a Chinese proposal to address various challenges in the 21st century. Vision guides action and direction determines the future. The international community should work together to turn the grand blueprint into a roadmap, and a beautiful vision into reality step by step.

1. Pressing ahead with a new type of economic globalization

Economic globalization is an irreversible trend of global economic development, and is in line with the desire for development and cooperation held by people of all countries. Economic globalization has greatly facilitated trade, investment, flows of people, and technological advances, making an important contribution to global economic development.

However, problems and drawbacks also accumulated in the process, and there are attempts at retreating from it. The current model of economic globalization fails to reflect the demands or represent the interests of developing countries. The law of the jungle, zero-sum game, and the "win-or-lose", "winner-takes-all" mindset have exacerbated the divide between the rich and poor, as evidenced by the widening gap between developed and developing countries, and that within developed countries. Some countries blame their problems in domestic governance on economic globalization or other countries, and resort to unilateral, protectionist, and bullying actions. This has damaged global industrial, value, supply and consumption chains, and caused turbulence and even conflict in the current international trade order.

Promoting a new type of economic globalization is essential for building a global community of shared future. Countries need to pursue a policy of openness and explicitly oppose protectionism, the erection of fences and barriers, unilateral sanctions, and maximum-pressure tactics, so as to connect economies and jointly build an open world economy. Countries should strive to build a system of fair, reasonable, and transparent international economic and trade rules, press ahead with trade and investment liberalization and facilitation, and promote further global economic openness, exchange, and integration in order to form an economic globalization that is open, inclusive, balanced and beneficial for all, so that people of all countries can share the fruits of economic globalization and world economic growth.

Opening up should be a two-way journey, not a one-way street; one cannot demand the opening of other countries while closing its own doors. Some countries are seeking to decouple from and break chains with China, enclosing themselves in "small yards, high fences", which will ultimately only backfire on themselves. Some people overstate the need to "reduce dependence" and "derisk", which is essentially creating new risks. Risk prevention and cooperation are not mutually contradictory, whereas non-cooperation is the biggest risk and non-development is the biggest threat to security. Pursuing de-sinicization in the name of derisking and reducing dependence undermines opportunities, cooperation, stability, and development.

The current revolution in science and technology marked by artificial intelligence will have a profound impact on the new round of economic globalization and social development. Relevant rules and standards should be established to support scientific and technological innovation and guard the red line of human security. The interests of all countries, especially developing ones, should be taken into account in a balanced manner, to ensure that technological innovation is placed under the rule of law and internationally recognized norms, and ensure that innovation is steered by and works for humanity, and is consistent with human values.

2. Following a peaceful development path

History tells us that for a country to develop and prosper, it must understand and follow the trend of global development; otherwise it will be abandoned by history. The trend now is the pursuit of peace, development, cooperation, and win-win results. The old path of colonialism and hegemonism leads to a dead end and those who follow it will pay a heavy price, whereas the path of peaceful development is the right one for the world to follow.

The pursuit of peace, amity and harmony is deeply rooted in the cultural realm of the Chinese nation and runs in the blood of the Chinese people. For a long time in the past, China was one of the most powerful countries in the world, but it does not have any record of colonization or aggression against other countries. China's adherence to the path of peaceful development is an extension of the millennia-old cultural tradition of the peace-loving Chinese nation.

China always adheres to an independent foreign policy of peace and has always emphasized that the goal of China's foreign policy is to maintain world peace and promote common development. China opposes all forms of hegemonism and power politics, and does not interfere in the internal affairs of other countries. It will never seek hegemony or engage in expansion. These principles are stated in China's policies, incorporated in its systemic designs, and always adhered to in its practices.

The world needs peace, just like a human being needs air and living things need sunshine. The path of peaceful development is beneficial to China and the world, and we cannot think of any reason not to stay on this path. China follows the path of peaceful development, and hopes that other countries will take this path as well. Only by working together to pursue peace, safeguard peace, and share peace can countries achieve their development goals and make greater contributions to the world. Only when everyone follows the path of peaceful development can countries coexist peacefully, and can there be hope for building a global community of shared future.

3. Fostering a new type of international relations

The new type of international relations is different in that it has created a new path for interactions between countries, opened up a new chapter of world history where different civilizations and countries with different systems coexist in peace and seek common development, and paved the way for building a global community of shared future.

A new type of international relations should be built on the principles of mutual respect, equity and justice, and mutually beneficial cooperation. Mutual respect means treating people with sincerity and equality, and opposing power politics and bullying practices. In upholding equity and justice, countries must discard extreme materialism and overemphasis on competition, and ensure that all countries have equal rights and opportunities for development. Mutually beneficial cooperation means that countries should reject the maximization of self-interest, address the legitimate concerns of other countries while pursuing their own interests, and promote common development of all countries alongside their own development.

The foundations for building a new type of international relations lie in broader and deeper global partnerships based on equality, openness, and cooperation. China adheres to the Five Principles of Peaceful Co-existence in pursuing friendship and cooperation with other countries. It works to reinforce coordination and positive interaction with other major countries in order to build major-country relations featuring peaceful co-existence, overall stability, and balanced development. Acting on the principles of amity, sincerity, mutual benefit, and inclusiveness, and the policy of forging friendships and partnerships with its neighbors, China strives to increase friendly ties, mutual trust, and converging interests with its neighboring countries. Guided by the principles of sincerity, real results, amity, and good faith and with a commitment to the right approach to friendship and interests, China endeavors to strengthen solidarity and cooperation with other developing countries and safeguard the common interests of the developing world.

Major countries are key actors in building a new type of international relations. The international status of a country is measured by its openness of mind, breadth of vision, and sense of responsibility rather than its size, strength or power. Major countries should direct their primary efforts to the future of humanity and assume greater responsibility for world peace and development, rather than wielding their power to seek monopoly over international and regional affairs. Major countries should strengthen coordination and cooperation, respect each other's core interests and major concerns, consider the perspectives of other parties and value mutual understanding, and treat smaller countries as equals. By building a global community of shared future, emerging countries and established powers can avoid falling into the Thucydides trap, find the right way to get along in mutual respect, peaceful coexistence and win-win cooperation, and build common ground and achieve common development for different civilizations and countries with different social systems.

4. Practicing true multilateralism

Building a global community of shared future requires practicing true multilateralism. Building cliques in the name of multilateralism is no more than bloc politics. Seeking supremacy in the name of multilateralism is still unilateral thinking. "Selective multilateralism" is practicing double standard. The world should be fair and free from domineering practices. China opposes all forms of unilateralism and the formation of camps and exclusive cliques targeting specific countries, and opposes actions that undermine the international order, create a new Cold War or stoke ideological confrontation in the name of the so-called rules-based order.

China firmly upholds the purposes and principles of the UN Charter, as well as the authority and status of the United Nations. The various confrontations and injustices in today's world do not arise because the purposes and principles of the UN Charter are outdated, but rather because these purposes and principles are not effectively followed. China maintains that for the world, there is only one system, which is the international system with the United Nations at its core, that there is only one order, which is the international order based on international law, and that there is only one set of rules, which is the basic norms governing international relations based on the purposes and principles of the UN Charter.

China actively participates in and leads the reform of the global governance system. It follows the vision of global governance featuring extensive consultation and joint contribution for shared benefits, that is, global affairs must be discussed by all, governance systems built by all, and benefits of governance shared by all, so that every country is a participant, contributor, and beneficiary of world peace and development.

5. Promoting the common values of humanity

China advocates peace, development, equity, justice, democracy and freedom, the common values of humanity. With an open mind, China understands that different civilizations have different understandings of the nature of these values, and respects the efforts of people in different countries to explore their own development paths. It goes beyond the narrow historical limitations of the so-called universal values, and promotes the common values of humanity embedded in Chinese civilization. These are the values embodied in pursuing a global community of shared future.

Peace and development are a common cause. A tree of peace cannot grow on barren land, nor can it bear the fruits of development amidst the flames of war. The fundamental solution to various global challenges lies in seeking peace and achieving development. Equity and justice are common ideals. No country should act as it pleases, or ride roughshod over others. Democracy and freedom are the common goals of humanity. There is no single model of democracy that is universally applicable, far less a superior one. Democracy is not Coca-Cola, tasting the same across the world as the syrup is produced in one single country. Democracy is not an ornament, but a solution to real problems. Attempts to monopolize the "patent" of democracy, arbitrarily define the "standards" of democracy, and fabricate a false narrative of "democracy versus authoritarianism" to provoke confrontation between political systems and ideologies are practices of fake democracy. Promoting the common values of humanity is not about canonizing the values of any particular country, but about seeking common ground while reserving differences, harmony without uniformity, and fully respecting the diversity of civilizations and the right of all countries to independently choose their social systems and development paths.

The more advanced human society becomes, the more important it is to strengthen exchanges and mutual learning among civilizations. All countries should treat each other with respect and as equals, discard arrogance and prejudice, deepen understanding of the differences between its own civilization and others, and promote dialogue and harmonious coexistence between different civilizations. Every country should value its own civilization, appreciate others, and facilitate their common progress. We should keep our own civilizations dynamic and create conditions for other civilizations to flourish. Together we can make the garden of world civilizations colorful and vibrant. All countries should be open and inclusive, promote mutual learning, strive to remove all barriers to cultural exchanges, and seek nourishment from other civilizations to promote the common development of all civilizations. All countries should progress with the times, explore new ground in development, take in the best of the present age, and sustain the development of civilizations through innovation.

V. China's Action and Contribution

A journey of a thousand miles begins with a single step. Over the past decade, China has contributed its strength to building a global community of shared future with firm conviction and solid actions.

1. Promoting high-quality Belt and Road cooperation

The Belt and Road Initiative (BRI) is a vivid example of building a global community of shared future, and a global public good and cooperation platform provided by China to the world. Since introducing the BRI ten years ago, based on extensive consultation and joint contribution for shared benefits, China has pursued open, green, clean, and high-standard cooperation to promote sustainable development and improve people's lives, and advanced high-quality Belt and Road cooperation. It has laid the groundwork and set up the frameworks of BRI cooperation, delivering tangible results and achieving sustainable

---

Panel 1   The Greek Port of Piraeus Getting a New Life

Located strategically at the "Southern Gate" of Europe, Piraeus, the largest port in Greece, has played an important role since its opening in around 400 BC. More than a decade ago, the port was in crisis, suffering huge losses. In 2010, China COSCO Shipping Corporation Limited officially became involved in the operation of the port, injecting new vitality to it. The annual handling capacity of the port has now reached 7.2 million TEUs, and its global ranking has jumped from No. 93 in 2010 to No. 33 in 2022. It has created more than 3,000 direct jobs and more than 10,000 indirect jobs locally, resulting in direct social contributions of more than 1.4 billion euros to the area.

> **Panel 2   Chinese Juncao Is Our "Grass of Happiness"**
>
> Juncao technology, which uses grass instead of wood to cultivate edible fungi, has solved a significant challenge – that the production of edible fungi had to rely on felling trees. Over the past 20 years, China has held 270 international training sessions on Juncao technology that trained over 10,000 people from 106 countries. It has set up demonstration centers or bases in 16 countries, creating hundreds of thousands of green jobs. In Fiji, Juncao technology is seen as a new hope of agriculture for island states; in Lesotho, farmers call Juncao "the grass of prosperity" because it makes quick returns; in Rwanda, more than 3,800 poor households have seen their annual incomes double or quadruple after they began Juncao production.

progress. Together, participants in the initiative have jointly advanced "hard connectivity", "soft connectivity" and "people-to-people connectivity", setting up an important platform that has enabled wide participation, built international consensus and pooled the strengths of all parties.

Policy connectivity continues to deepen. By July 2023, more than three-quarters of countries in the world and over 30 international organizations had signed agreements on Belt and Road cooperation with China. China has successfully hosted the first Belt and Road Forum for International Cooperation in 2017 and the second in 2019, and will host the third this year, maximizing synergy for advancing high-quality Belt and Road cooperation. Infrastructure connectivity continues to strengthen. A general connectivity framework consisting of six corridors, six routes, and multiple countries and ports is in place. The overall layout of land, sea, air and cyberspace connectivity continues to improve, centered on economic corridors such as the New Eurasian Land Bridge, supported by routes like the China-Europe Railway Express and the New International Land-Sea Trade Corridor and the information expressway, and underpinned by major railways, ports, and pipelines. Trade connectivity continues to increase. According to Belt and Road Economics, a report released by the

World Bank, the BRI, when fully implemented, will increase intra-BRI trade by 4.1 percent. By 2030, the BRI will generate US$1.6 trillion in annual global revenues. Financial connectivity continues to expand. The Asian Infrastructure Investment Bank and the Silk Road Fund have been set up, providing financing support for hundreds of projects. People-to-people connectivity continues to strengthen. Roads, bridges and development belts that lead to a happier and better life are constantly emerging in participating countries, and solid progress is being achieved in Juncao, wells, hybrid rice and other small projects that work faster in improving people's lives, giving local people of BRI countries a stronger sense of gain and fulfillment.

The BRI originated in China, but the opportunities and achievements it creates belong to the whole world. The China-Pakistan Economic Corridor, since its launch ten years ago, has lent strong impetus to the economic and social development of Pakistan. The China-Laos Railway has realized the long-cherished wish of the Lao people to convert Laos from a landlocked country to a land-linked hub. The Jakarta-Bandung High-speed Railway has become the first railway in Southeast Asia to reach a

---

Panel 3 China-Laos Railway and Jakarta-Bandung High-Speed Railway

The China-Laos Railway began operation on December 3, 2021, with 167 tunnels and 301 bridges built in 11 years along its total length of 1,035 kilometers. The railway construction created more than 110,000 local jobs, and helped build about 2,000 km of roads and canals for villages along the railway, bringing many visible and tangible benefits to local people. As of January 31, 2023, the China-Laos Railway had run 20,000 passenger train journeys and handled 10.3 million passenger trips.

The Jakarta-Bandung High-speed Railway, with a maximum designed speed of 350 kilometers per hour, is the first high-speed rail service in Southeast Asia. Now that the railway is in service, the commute time from Jakarta to Bandung has been reduced from more than three hours to just 40 minutes.

speed of 350 kilometers an hour. The Mombasa-Nairobi Railway has added more than two percentage points to local economic growth. Malawi's 600 wells built with Chinese assistance have become "wells of happiness" serving 150,000 local people. The China-Europe Railway Express serves as a "steel camel fleet" between China and Europe. Luban workshops help young people in Tajikistan and other countries acquire vocational skills. Cooperation in the fields of health, green development, digital economy, and innovation is thriving.

The BRI is an initiative for economic cooperation, not for geopolitical or military alliances. It is an open and inclusive process that neither targets nor excludes any party. Rather than forming exclusionary cliques or a "China club", it aims to help China and the rest of the world to seize opportunities and pursue common development. Rather than a private route for any one party, it is a broad path that can be joined by all interested countries to work together for shared benefits.

The international community speaks highly of the BRI, praising it not simply as some random road or economic belt, but as an initiative to achieve common progress for humanity, an initiative that has opened up new paths for the common development of all countries. The BRI has facilitated the modernization drive of developing countries, leading the world into a new era of transcontinental cooperation.

Panel 4   900 Days of Hard Work Leading to a 900-Second Miracle
The Qamchiq Tunnel on the Angren-Pap Railway line is the first ever railway tunnel built in Uzbekistan, and one of the most important cooperation projects between China and Uzbekistan under the BRI framework. Construction started on September 5, 2013, and was completed on February 25, 2016. Chinese builders spent 900 days creating the miracle of a train passing through the mountains in only 900 seconds. The locals were astonished: "In the global bidding for the project, the European and American companies offered a construction period of five years. But the Chinese company did it in 900 days. How did you make it?"

2. Implementing the three global initiatives

It is widely recognized that peace and stability, material sufficiency, and cultural-ethical enrichment represent the basic goals of human society. Development serves as the material foundation for security and civilization, security acts as the fundamental prerequisite for development and civilization, and civilization provides the cultural-ethical support for development and security. The Global Development Initiative, Global Security Initiative, and Global Civilization Initiative proposed by China guide the advance of human society across these three dimensions. Resonating and complementing each other, they have evolved into a crucial cornerstone for building a global community of shared future, offering China's solutions to major challenges pertaining to peace and development for humanity.

— Through the Global Development Initiative, China has issued a resounding call for commitment to development and reinvigorated cooperation, and made its contribution to resolving challenges to development and advancing global development. The fundamental aim of the initiative is to accelerate the implementation of the UN's 2030 Agenda for Sustainable Development. Its core requirement is a people-centered approach, its foremost philosophy is united, equal, balanced, and inclusive global development partnerships, and its pivotal measure entails results-oriented actions to bolster stronger, greener, and healthier global development and jointly build a global community of development.

China has hosted the High-level Dialogue on Global Development and presented 32 major measures to implement the initiative, such as creating the Global Development and South-South Cooperation Fund totaling US$4 billion, launching the China-FAO South-South Cooperation Trust Fund (Phase III), and strengthening support for the China-UN Peace and Development Fund. Over the past two years, the international community has extensively responded to the initiative and jointly tackled prominent issues including food security, poverty reduction, and energy security as the implementation mechanism steadily improves and practical cooperation delivers progress. The Global Development Promotion Center is running smoothly, and the library of the Global Development Initiative projects is expanding, with over 200 projects achieving good results. At the same time, China has issued the Global Development Report, and established the Global Knowledge Network for Development, contributing Chinese wisdom to the resolution of developmental challenges. Currently, more than 100 countries and international organizations have expressed support for the Global Development Initiative, with over 70 countries participating in the Group of Friends of the Global Development Initiative established at the UN.

China is committed to propelling global development through its own development. It has thoroughly applied the new development philosophy, with a focus on promoting high-quality development to foster a new development paradigm. Modernization of the more than 1.4 billion Chinese people will create a market rivaling the aggregated size of all developed countries. This will open up more opportunities for all countries and stakeholders to partake in China's huge market. China has also pioneered major expos and fairs, exemplified by the China International Import Expo, China International Fair for Trade in Services, China Import and Export Fair, and China International Consumer Goods Expo. It has encouraged all countries and stakeholders to share the opportunities presented by China's institutional opening up and steadily expanded institutional opening up with regard to rules, regulations, management, and standards. It has enforced the Foreign Investment Law and its supporting rules and regulations, implemented the new catalogue for encouraging foreign investment, continued to remove items from the negative list of market access for foreign investment, advanced high-quality development of pilot free trade zones, and accelerated the development of the Hainan Free Trade Port.

China is committed to win-win cooperation and common development. As the largest developing country in the world and a member of the Global South, China has made every effort to aid other developing countries and help recipient countries expand their capacity for development.

China is actively engaged in international exchanges and cooperation. It has cooperated with almost 20 international organizations, including the UN World Food Programme, the UN Development Programme, the UN Children's Fund, the UN Refugee Agency, the World Health Organization, and the International Committee of the Red Cross, and executed over 130 projects in nearly 60 countries including Ethiopia, Pakistan, and Nigeria. "Small but beautiful", these projects span fields such as poverty reduction, food security, Covid-19 response, and climate change, and have benefited more than 30 million individuals. China worked actively for the adoption of and has comprehensively acted on the Debt Service Suspension Initiative of the Group of Twenty (G20), contributing more than any other G20 member to its implementation. China has signed agreements or reached understandings on the suspension of debt repayments with 19 African countries, helping Africa alleviate debt pressure.

China is committed to building an open world economy. It has become the main trading partner of more than 140 countries and regions, and signed 21 free trade agreements with 28 countries and regions. It has worked for high-quality implementation of the Regional Comprehensive Economic Partnership, actively worked to join the Comprehensive and Progressive Agreement for Trans-Pacific Partnership and the Digital Economy Partnership Agreement, and expanded its globally-oriented network of high-standard free trade areas. It has also promoted the internationalization of the Renminbi, and reinforced financial standards and its level of internationalization, thereby converging its interests closer with other countries.

– Through the Global Security Initiative, China seeks to work with the international community in upholding the spirit of the UN Charter, and calls for adapting to the profound changes in the international landscape through solidarity, addressing traditional and non-traditional security risks and challenges with a win-win mindset, and creating a new path to security that features dialogue over confrontation, partnership over alliance, and win-win results over zero-sum game.

| Panel 5 | Six Proposals of the Global Development Initiative |

— **Staying committed to development as its first priority.** Putting development front and center in the global macro policy framework, boosting policy coordination among major economies, ensuring policy continuity, consistency, and sustainability, fostering global development partnerships featuring greater equality and balance, coordinating multilateral development cooperation to generate synergy, and accelerating the implementation of the UN's 2030 Agenda for Sustainable Development;

— **Staying committed to a people-centered approach.** Ensuring and improving people's wellbeing and protecting and promoting human rights through development, ensuring that development is for the people and by the people and that its fruits are shared by the people, ensuring a stronger sense of fulfillment, happiness, and security for the people, and pursuing the people's well-rounded development;

— **Staying committed to inclusiveness and benefits for all.** Addressing the special needs of developing countries, supporting developing countries – especially vulnerable countries facing exceptional difficulties – by means such as debt suspension and development aid, and addressing imbalanced and inadequate development among and within countries;

— **Staying committed to innovation-driven development.** Seizing the historic opportunities created by the latest round of revolution in science and technology and industrial transformation, speeding up efforts to harness scientific and technological achievements to boost productivity, creating an open, fair, equitable, and non-discriminatory environment for scientific and technological advances, unleashing new impetus for post-pandemic economic growth, and joining hands to achieve leapfrog development;

— **Staying committed to harmony between humanity and nature.** Improving global environmental governance, actively responding to climate change, building a community of life for humanity and nature, accelerating the transition to green and low-carbon development, and achieving green recovery and development;

— **Staying committed to results-oriented actions.** Increasing the input of development resources, prioritizing cooperation in areas such as poverty reduction, food security, pandemic response and vaccines, financing for development, climate change and green development, industrialization, the digital economy, and connectivity, and building a global community of development.

In February 2023, China officially released The Global Security Initiative Concept Paper. The document further elaborates the core concepts and principles of the initiative, elucidates its key avenues for cooperation, and presents recommendations and ideas concerning its cooperation platforms and mechanisms. This has demonstrated China's awareness of its duty to maintain world peace and its firm determination to safeguard global security. As an international public good, the Global Security Initiative serves the interests of and maintains peace for people throughout the world.

Panel 6   Six Proposals of the Global Security Initiative

– Staying committed to the vision of common, comprehensive, cooperative, and sustainable security, and working together to maintain world peace and security;

– Staying committed to respecting the sovereignty and territorial integrity of all countries, upholding non-interference in others' internal affairs, and respecting the independent choices of development paths and social systems made by people in different countries;

– Staying committed to abiding by the purposes and principles of the UN Charter, rejecting the Cold War mentality, opposing unilateralism, and saying no to bloc politics and camp-based confrontation;

– Staying committed to taking the legitimate security concerns of all countries seriously, upholding the principle of indivisible security, building a balanced, effective, and sustainable security architecture, and opposing the pursuit of one's own security to the detriment of others' security;

– Staying committed to peacefully resolving differences and disputes between countries through dialogue and consultation, supporting all efforts conducive to the peaceful settlement of crises, rejecting double standards, and opposing the arbitrary use of unilateral sanctions and long-arm jurisdiction;

– Staying committed to maintaining security in both traditional and non-traditional domains, and working together to address regional disputes and global challenges such as terrorism, climate change, cybersecurity, and biosecurity.

China is a pillar in maintaining world peace. It is committed to handling disputes with relevant countries over territorial sovereignty and maritime rights and interests through negotiation and consultation. It has settled land boundary issues peacefully with 12 of its 14 neighbors along its land borders through negotiation and consultation, and delimited the maritime boundary in the Beibu Bay with Vietnam. China has faithfully fulfilled its responsibilities and missions as a permanent member of the UN Security Council. It is the second largest contributor to the UN regular budget and peacekeeping assessment, and the largest contributor of peacekeeping troops among the permanent members of the Security Council. Over the past three decades and more, having sent more than 50,000 personnel to UN peacekeeping operations in over 20 countries and regions, China has become a key force in UN peacekeeping. China has dispatched more than 100 naval vessels in 45 taskforces to the Gulf of Aden and waters off the coast of Somalia to provide escort for over 7,000 Chinese and foreign ships.

Facing constant flare-ups of hotspot issues, China has been committed to fulfilling its role as a responsible major country, pushing for the resolution of international and regional flashpoints, such as the Korean Peninsula, Palestine, the Iranian nuclear issue, Syria, and Afghanistan. On the Ukraine issue, China has actively promoted talks for peace, put forth four key principles, four things that the international community should do together and three observations, and released China's Position on the Political Settlement of the Ukraine Crisis. China has dispatched the Special Representative of the Chinese Government on Eurasian Affairs to engage in extensive interactions and exchanges with stakeholders on the political settlement of the Ukraine crisis.

Through the mediation of China, Saudi Arabia and Iran have achieved historic reconciliation, setting a fine example for countries in the region to resolve disputes and differences and achieve good neighborly relations through dialogue and consultation, and catalyzing a wave of reconciliation in the Middle East.

China has actively cooperated with other parties in non-traditional security domains such as anti-terrorism, biosecurity, and food security. It has proposed the International Cooperation Initiative on Global Food Security within the framework of the G20, and pushed for the adoption of the Strategy on Food Security Cooperation of the BRICS Countries. It

---

Panel 7   China's Major Propositions on Political Settlement of the Ukraine Crisis

Four key principles:
- The sovereignty and territorial integrity of all countries should be upheld;
- The purposes and principles of the UN Charter should be observed;
- The legitimate security concerns of all parties should be taken seriously;
- All efforts conducive to the peaceful settlement of the crisis should be supported.

Four things that the international community should do together:
- The international community should jointly support all efforts to peacefully settle the Ukraine crisis, call on the parties concerned to stay rational, exercise restraint, and conduct direct engagement as quickly as possible, and create conditions for the resumption of negotiations;
- The international community should jointly oppose the threat or use of nuclear weapons and advocate that nuclear weapons must not be used and nuclear wars must not be fought, to avoid a nuclear crisis on the Eurasian continent;
- The international community should jointly work to keep global industrial and supply chains stable and prevent disruptions to international cooperation in energy, food, and finance that could undermine the global economic recovery, especially the economic and financial stability of developing countries;
- The international community should jointly provide winter relief to civilians in conflict zones, and improve humanitarian conditions, with a view to preventing a humanitarian crisis on a larger scale.

Three observations:
- Conflicts and wars produce no winner;
- There is no simple solution to a complex issue;
- Confrontation between major countries must be avoided.

has also officially launched the China-Pacific Island Countries Disaster Prevention and Mitigation Cooperation Center, representing yet another robust action to help developing countries tackle non-traditional security challenges within the context of the Global Security Initiative.

– Through the Global Civilization Initiative, China calls for jointly advocating respect for the diversity of civilizations, jointly advocating the common values of humanity, jointly advocating the importance of continuity and evolution of civilizations, and jointly advocating closer international people-to-people exchanges and cooperation. The Global Civilization Initiative makes a sincere call for the world to enhance inter-civilization exchanges and dialogue, and promote human progress with inclusiveness and mutual learning, inspiring the building of a global community of shared future.

China has hosted gatherings including the CPC in Dialogue with World Political Parties High-level Meeting, the CPC and World Political Parties Summit, and the Conference on Dialogue of Asian Civilizations. It has engaged in extensive bilateral and multilateral activities for political party exchanges and cooperation, and promoted diverse forms of civil diplomacy, city diplomacy, and public diplomacy. China has continued to deepen cooperation with the UN Educational, Scientific, and Cultural Organization (UNESCO) and the UN World Tourism Organization. It now has 43 items inscribed on the intangible cultural heritage lists of UNESCO.

China has celebrated over 30 large-scale cultural and tourist "years" (festivals), such as the China-Italy Year of Culture and Tourism, the China-Greece Year of Culture and Tourism, and the China-Spain Year of Culture and Tourism. It has promoted the steady development of 16 multilateral exchanges and cooperation mechanisms, such as the meeting of BRICS ministers of culture, as well as 25 bilateral cooperation mechanisms. It regularly hosts cultural activities at home, such as the Arabic Arts Festival and the Meet in Beijing International Arts Festival, and has held "Happy Spring Festival" celebrations outside China for more than

20 years in a row. It hosted approximately 2,000 events across over 130 countries in 2017, and has organized activities around the world under such brands as "Tea for Harmony" Yaji Cultural Salon. It has advanced cultural and tourism exchanges under the Belt and Road Initiative, carried out the Cultural Silk Road program, and established the Silk Road international theater, museum, art festival, library, and art museum alliances. It has also established approximately 3,000 pairs of sister cities or provinces with various countries, and launched the "Nihao! China" inbound tourism promotion program.

The international community has spoken highly of these three global initiatives, acknowledging that they reflect China's global vision and growing international influence and provide comprehensive solutions to

---

Panel 8   Four Proposals of the Global Civilization Initiative

— **Jointly advocating respect for the diversity of civilizations.** Countries should uphold equality, mutual learning, dialogue, and inclusiveness among civilizations, and let cultural exchanges transcend estrangement, mutual learning transcend conflict, and inclusiveness transcend supremacy.

— **Jointly advocating the common values of humanity.** Peace, development, equity, justice, democracy and freedom are shared aspirations of people across the world. Countries should be open to appreciating different perceptions of values by different civilizations, and refrain from imposing their own values or models on others and from stoking ideological confrontation.

— **Jointly advocating the importance of continuity and evolution of civilizations.** Countries should fully harness the relevance of their histories and cultures to the present times, and push for creative transformation and innovative development of their fine traditional cultures in the course of modernization.

— **Jointly advocating closer international people-to-people exchanges and cooperation.** Countries should explore the building of a global network for inter-civilization dialogue and cooperation, enrich the contents of exchanges and expand avenues of cooperation to promote mutual understanding and friendship among people of all countries, and jointly advance the progress of human civilization.

---

the challenges confronting humanity. The Global Development Initiative is highly compatible with the UN's 2030 Agenda for Sustainable Development, and resonates, in particular, with the aspirations of developing countries for greater development. The Global Security Initiative upholds the principle of common security, emphasizes comprehensive approaches, pursues sustainable security through cooperative efforts, and makes a valuable contribution to addressing international security challenges. The Global Civilization Initiative calls on all countries to respect the diversity of civilizations in the world, which is conducive to facilitating exchanges and mutual learning among different civilizations.

3. Working with more countries and regions

China has proposed a range of regional and bilateral initiatives on building communities of shared future, and is working with stakeholders to build consensus and expand cooperation, thereby playing a constructive role in promoting regional peace and development.

The China-Africa community of shared future was the first regional proposal. It values sincerity and equality, pursues both friendship and interests and puts friendship first, takes a people-oriented approach in pursuing practical and efficient cooperation, and follows an open and inclusive approach to cooperation. It has set a good example of China and African countries building a community of shared future. The China-Arab community of shared future, China-Latin America and the Caribbean community of shared future, and China-Pacific Island Countries community of shared future have all made swift and steady progress. They are vivid illustrations of solidarity, cooperation, and common progress among developing countries.

The community of shared future among neighboring countries has taken firm root. As the China-ASEAN community of shared future continues to make advances, China-ASEAN cooperation has evolved into the most fruitful, dynamic, and substantive cooperation in East Asia. The two sides have seen a steady increase in mutual trust, engaged in frequent high-level exchanges, and established dialogue and cooperation mechanisms in nearly 50 domains and institutions. The community of shared future of Lancang-Mekong countries continues to make progress. The Shanghai Cooperation Organization community of shared future has yielded substantial outcomes. The building of the China-Central Asia community of shared future has made solid steps forward. The first China-Central Asia Summit was a success and a meeting mechanism at the heads-of-state level between China and Central Asian countries has been established. These efforts have contributed to enduring peace and shared prosperity in the region and the wider world.

At the bilateral level, China is building communities of shared future with an increasing number of partners in different forms. China and countries including Laos, Cambodia, Myanmar, Indonesia, Thailand, Malaysia, Pakistan, Mongolia, Cuba and South Africa have published action plans, released joint statements, or reached important agreements on building bilateral communities of shared future. China has also implemented the vision of building a global community of shared future on a bilateral level with all the five Central Asian countries. As this vision gains greater traction among the people, substantial outcomes have been delivered, significantly boosting local development and improving people's lives.

The global community of shared future is a dynamic, open, and inclusive system. However different countries may be in geographical location, history, culture, social system, size of economy, and development stage, alignment with the core idea of a global community of shared future enables them to seek common ground while shelving differences, achieve harmony in diversity, reinforce cooperation, and pursue win-win outcomes. China will work with more and more regions and countries to build a global community of shared future and contribute to the development of all countries and the progress of human civilization.

4. Boosting international cooperation in all areas

The vision of a global community of shared future addresses the deficits in peace, development, security, and governance facing the world today. As China's unique contribution to solving global problems, it also offers solutions which have been translated into concrete actions in areas such as health, climate change, and cybersecurity.

Confronted by the rampant Covid-19 pandemic, China proposed to build a community of health for all. It has stood in the frontline of international anti-pandemic cooperation, carrying out global emergency humanitarian relief and providing assistance and support to more than 150 countries and international organizations. China has advocated that vaccines must first and foremost be a global public good, and was among the first countries to make a commitment to supply Covid-19 vaccines as a global public good, to support waiving intellectual property rights on the vaccines, and to start joint production with other developing countries. It has also played a pioneering role in the equitable distribution of vaccines, contributing China's strength to the global health cause through firm commitment and practical actions.

To address disorder in cyberspace governance, China has proposed the concept of a community of shared future in cyberspace. It actively participates in UN cybersecurity processes and supports the UN in playing a core role in global cyberspace governance. China has hosted the World Internet Conference and established the World Internet Conference Organization as a platform for global internet sharing and governance.

To advance the development of a set of rules for global digital governance, it has launched the Global Data Security Initiative, and released the China-LAS Cooperation Initiative on Data Security together with the League of Arab States and the Data Security Cooperation Initiative of China + Central Asia together with the five Central Asian countries. To ensure that rights and responsibilities are shared among all countries, it promotes the improvement of governance rules in the deep sea, polar regions, outer space, and other new frontiers. Efforts are made to ensure that in formulating new rules for governance in new frontiers, the interests and expectations of emerging market countries and developing countries are fully reflected.

Concerning the fundamental issues in global nuclear security governance, China proposes to build a community of shared future on nuclear security. It firmly safeguards the international nuclear nonproliferation regime, promotes the peaceful use of nuclear energy, and upholds a rational, coordinated and balanced approach to nuclear security. In response to the increasing risk of nuclear conflict, China has pushed for the conclusion of a joint statement among the leaders of the five nuclear-weapon states, reaffirming that "a nuclear war cannot be won, and must never be fought". China actively advocates the complete prohibition and thorough destruction of nuclear weapons, and it is the only nuclear country that has publicly committed to no-first-use of nuclear weapons, and not using or threatening to use nuclear weapons against non-nuclear-weapon states and nuclear-weapon-free zones.

Faced with increasingly complex maritime issues, China has proposed to form a maritime community of shared future and has always been committed to peaceful resolution of territorial sovereignty and maritime rights and interests disputes through dialogue and consultation. China has signed and fully and effectively implemented the Declaration on the Conduct of Parties in the South China Sea with ASEAN countries, and continues to advance consultations on the code of conduct in the South China Sea. China has proposed to jointly build a partnership on blue economy and strengthen maritime connectivity. It adheres to the path of pursuing joint development while setting aside disputes, and actively explores joint resource development with maritime neighbors at sea.

Faced with the severe and growing global climate challenge, China has proposed important concepts such as building a community of life for humanity and nature and a community of all life on Earth. China actively promotes economic development and transformation, and undertakes to strive to achieve peak carbon dioxide emissions before 2030 and carbon neutrality before 2060. It has introduced a "1+N" policy system for carbon peaking and neutrality. China has built the world's largest clean power generation network, contributed 25 percent of the world's newly added green area since 2000, and enabled an annual economic growth rate of over 6 percent with an average annual energy consumption growth rate of 3 percent. It has the largest installed capacity of hydropower, wind power, and solar power in the world. It actively participates in global environmental governance, advocates the comprehensive and effective implementation by the international community of the United Nations Framework Convention on Climate Change and the Paris Agreement, and adheres to the principle of "common but differentiated responsibilities". China tries its best to help developing countries improve their ability to address climate change, and vigorously supports their green and low-carbon energy development. It has inked 46 South-South cooperation documents with 39 developing countries to address climate change, and trained approximately 2,300 officials and technical personnel in the field of climate change for more than 120 developing countries. Holding the presidency of the 15th Meeting of the Conference of the Parties to the UN Convention on Biological Diversity (COP15), China made every effort to ensure the success of the meeting, taking the lead in funding the

---

Panel 9   The Northern Trek of Wandering Elephants

In March 2020, a group of wild Asian elephants from the Xishuangbanna National Nature Reserve in Yunnan Province traveled north, passing through multiple places in the province. After traveling for about a year and a half, they safely returned home under the care and meticulous protection of the local government and people. The collective migration of Asian elephants made regular headlines in China, and attracted the attention of netizens around the world, sparking lively domestic and international discussions on building a home on Earth featuring harmony between man and nature.

establishment of the Kunming Biodiversity Fund and contributing to the Kunming-Montreal Global Biodiversity Framework.

Whether dealing with the current crises or creating a better future together, all countries need to unite and cooperate. Faced with profound changes unseen in a century, China has proposed the building of a global community of shared future, calls on all countries to uphold the concept of a shared future, fully communicate and consult with each other, share governance responsibilities, and form broad consensus and take concerted actions to address global issues, so as to inject confidence and momentum into humanity's drive towards a bright future.

Conclusion

All good principles should adapt to changing times in order to remain relevant. A broad consensus of solidarity and cooperation has developed in the international community behind the proposal and the implementation of the concept of a global community of shared future to address the challenges facing humanity. Looking to the future, it is bound to shine as a pioneering thought with the power of truth that transcends time and space, opening up a beautiful prospect of common development, long-term stability, and sustained prosperity for human society. The future of humanity is bright, but it will not come without effort. Building a global community of shared future is both a salutary vision and a historical process that calls for generations of hard work.

To realize this goal, confidence and determination are of foremost importance. The trend of our times for peace, development and win-win cooperation cannot be halted. Building a global community of shared future is the way forward for all the world's peoples. However, it is not a goal to be accomplished overnight, and there will be no plain sailing. We need to make unremitting efforts and forge ahead with perseverance. We should never give up on our dreams because of harsh realities; we should never stop pursuing our ideals because they seem out of reach.

To realize this goal, a broad mind and a global vision are central as we live in great times. In the face of common challenges, no person or country can remain isolated. The only response is to work together in harmony and unity. Only by strengthening coordination and cooperation, and ensuring that the interests of the people of every country will be kept in line with those of all others, can all countries move forward towards a global community of shared future.

To realize this goal, a sense of responsibility and a will to act hold the key. The key to success is simple and boils down to action. Building a global community of shared future depends on the joint actions of all countries. All countries should take a sense of responsibility that treats the task as a bound duty, and take concrete actions instead of being bystanders. We should strengthen dialogue, build consensus, promote peace and development, improve governance, and carry out global actions, global responses, and global cooperation.

Our journey ahead will be a lengthy and arduous one. But as long as we press ahead with perseverance, there will be much to expect. Successes and setbacks await us, but hopes abound. When all countries unite in pursuing the cause of common good, plan together, and act together day by day towards the right direction of building a global community of shared future, we can build an open, inclusive, clean, and beautiful world of lasting peace, universal security and shared prosperity, and jointly create a better future for all of humanity.

The Belt and Road Initiative: A Key Pillar of the Global Community of Shared Future

The State Council Information Office of
the People's Republic of China

October 2023

Preamble

Over two millennia ago, inspired by a sincere wish for friendship, our ancestors travelled across grasslands and deserts to create a land Silk Road connecting Asia, Europe and Africa, leading the world into an era of extensive cultural exchanges. More than 1,000 years ago, our ancestors set sail and braved the waves to open a maritime Silk Road linking the East and the West, beginning a new phase of closer communication among peoples.

Spanning thousands of miles and years, the ancient silk routes were not only routes for trade but also roads for cultural exchanges. They made a great contribution to human progress. In the 1980s, the United Nations and some countries began to envisage the Eurasian Land Bridge, the Silk Road Initiative, and other plans, reflecting a common wish to engage in communication and cooperation.

In March 2013, President Xi Jinping proposed the vision of a global community of shared future; in September and October that year, he raised the initiatives of joining with others to build a Silk Road Economic Belt and a 21st Century Maritime Silk Road (Belt and Road Initiative, or BRI). The Belt and Road Initiative is a creative development that takes on and carries forward the spirit of the ancient silk routes – two of the great achievements in human history and civilization. It enriches the ancient spirit with the zeitgeist and culture of the new era, and provides a platform for building a global community of shared future.

Since its launch 10 years ago, thanks to the combined efforts of all parties, cooperation under the BRI framework has expanded beyond the borders of China to become an international effort. It has evolved from ideas into actions, from a vision into reality, and from a general framework into concrete projects. It has been welcomed by the international community both as a public good and a cooperation platform, and has achieved solid results.

Over the past decade, BRI cooperation has delivered real gains to participating countries. It has contributed to the sound development of economic globalization and helped to resolve global development challenges and improve the global governance system. It has also opened up a new path for all humanity to realize modernization, and ensured that the efforts of building a global community of shared future are delivering real results.

The Chinese government is publishing this white paper to present the achievements of the BRI during the past 10 years. It will give the international community a better understanding of the value of the initiative, facilitate high-quality cooperation under it, and ultimately deliver benefits to more countries and peoples.

I. Proposed by China but Belonging to the Whole World

The world today is going through profound change on a scale unseen in a century. Problems and challenges continue to threaten the progress of human civilization. In response to a changing global situation and the expectations of the international community, and with the future and overall interests of humanity in mind, China proposed the Belt and Road Initiative (BRI). Committed to the Silk Road spirit, a great heritage of human civilization, the BRI connects the past, the present, and the future. This initiative was launched by China, but it belongs to the world and benefits the whole of humanity.

1. Rooted in history, the BRI carries forward the Silk Road spirit

At around 140 BC during China's Han Dynasty, Zhang Qian, a royal emissary, made a journey to the West from Chang'an (present-day Xi'an in Shaanxi Province), opening an overland route linking the East and the West. Centuries later, in the years of the Tang, Song and Yuan dynasties, silk routes boomed both over land and at sea, facilitating trade between the East and the West. In the early 15th century, Zheng He, the famous Chinese navigator of the Ming Dynasty, made seven voyages to the Western Seas, which boosted trade along the maritime silk routes.

For thousands of years the ancient silk routes served as major arteries of interaction, spanning the valleys of the Nile, the Tigris and Euphrates, the Indus and Ganges, and the Yellow and Yangtze rivers. They connected the birthplaces of the Egyptian, Babylonian, Indian and Chinese civilizations, the lands of the believers of Buddhism, Christianity and Islam, and the homes of peoples of different nationalities and races. These routes increased connectivity among countries on the Eurasian continent, facilitated exchanges and mutual learning between Eastern and Western civilizations, boosted regional development and prosperity, and shaped the Silk Road spirit characterized by peace and cooperation, openness and inclusiveness, mutual learning and mutual benefit.

Symbolizing communication and cooperation between the East and the West, the millennia-old silk routes demonstrated that by upholding solidarity and mutual trust, equality and mutual benefit, inclusiveness and mutual learning, and win-win cooperation, countries of different ethnic groups, beliefs and cultural backgrounds could share peace and achieve development together. The Silk Road spirit is consistent with the ideal of "all states joining together in harmony and peace" long upheld by the Chinese nation, with the Chinese people's principles of amity, good neighborliness and "helping others to succeed while seeking our own success", and with the call of the times for peace, development and win-win cooperation.

The Communist Party of China is a major political party with a global vision, and China is a major country pursuing peaceful development. The BRI, which carries forward the Silk Road spirit in the new era, evokes the pleasant memories of the past and has fired many countries' enthusiasm for connectivity.

The BRI pays respect to history and tries to recreate the bustling scenes of untiring envoys and businessmen over land and countless ships calling at ports along the ancient silk routes. It is also navigating a way to the future by drawing wisdom and strength from the ancient silk routes and the Silk Road spirit. Enlightened by history, we will continue to move forward and integrate the Chinese Dream with the world's dreams, in order to realize the aspiration of all peoples for exchanges between civilizations, peace and tranquility, common development, and better lives.

2. In response to reality, the BRI resolves problems in development

Development holds the master key to solving all problems. Economic globalization has given strong momentum to the world economy. Over 500 years ago, after the ancient silk routes had been interrupted for more than a half century, the Age of Discovery arrived, fundamentally changing the course of human society. Since the advent of modern times, technological revolutions and development of the productive forces have made economic globalization a surging historical trend. In particular, since the 1990s, the rapid advance of economic globalization has greatly facilitated trade, investment, flows of people, and technological progress, making an important contribution to the progress of human society.

However, the economic globalization dominated by a few countries has not contributed to the common development that delivers benefits to all. Instead, it has widened the wealth gap between rich and poor, between developed and developing countries, and within developed countries. Many developing countries have benefited little from economic globalization and even lost their capacity for independent development, making it hard for them to access the track of modernization. Certain countries have practiced unilateralism, protectionism and hegemonism, hampering economic globalization and threatening a global economic recession.

It is imperative to address such global problems as sluggish economic growth, shortcomings in economic governance, and imbalanced economic development. It is no longer acceptable that only a few countries dominate world economic development, control economic rules, and enjoy development fruits.

The BRI targets development not only for China but for the world at large. Economic globalization remains an irreversible trend. It is unthinkable for countries to return to a state of seclusion or isolation. However, economic globalization must undergo adjustments in both form and substance. It should be made more open, inclusive, balanced and beneficial to all.

China has not only benefited from economic globalization but also contributed to it. As an active participant in economic globalization, China has achieved rapid economic growth through positive interactions with the rest of the world and explored a unique path towards modernization, expanding the options for other developing countries to achieve modernization. China's rapid economic growth and steady progress in reform and opening up has provided a strong driving force for global economic stability and growth as well as an open world economy.

China has been a firm advocate and defender of economic globalization. The BRI dovetails with the UN 2030 Agenda for Sustainable Development in concept, measures and goals. A major step taken by China, the BRI aims to promote higher-quality development through higher-standard opening up, and share China's development opportunities with the rest of the world. The BRI is also a Chinese solution to global development issues, which aims to advance modernization in participating countries in tandem, make economic globalization more dynamic, inclusive and sustainable, and ensure that more of the fruits will be shared more equitably by people across the world.

3. Oriented towards the future, the BRI creates a better world

Today, the world is moving ever closer towards greater multipolarity, economic globalization, and cultural diversity, and becoming increasingly information-orientated in the process. Countries are more frequently connected and closely interdependent than at any time in the past. It is increasingly clear that humanity is a community of shared future in which everyone's interests are inseparably entwined.

However, a growing deficit in peace, development, security and governance, together with interwinding conventional and non-conventional security issues such as regional conflicts, arms races, food security, terrorism, cyber-attacks, climate change, energy crises, major infectious diseases, and artificial intelligence problems, poses a grave threat to the beautiful planet on which all humans live.

In the face of emerging global difficulties and challenges, human society needs new ideas, new concepts, and a more just, equitable, balanced, resilient and effective global governance system. What kind of world to build and which way to take to create a brighter future are issues that have a bearing on every country and every person. We must respond to the challenges presented by the times and make the right historic choice.

As a major developing country that meets its responsibilities, China keeps in mind the future and the common interests of humanity. China has therefore proposed building a global community of shared future, with the goal of creating an open, inclusive, clean and beautiful world that enjoys lasting peace, universal security and common prosperity, charting a bright future for human development.

The ultimate goal of the BRI is to help build a global community of shared future. As an important public good for improving global governance, the initiative provides a platform for turning the vision into reality. The BRI involves countries in different regions, at different development stages, and with different cultures. It transcends differences in ideologies and social systems. It enables different countries to share opportunities, realize common development and prosperity, and build a community of shared interests, responsibility and destiny characterized by mutual political trust, economic integration and cultural inclusiveness. As a practical means of building a global community of shared future, the BRI has created new understanding and inspired the imagination of the world, and contributed new ideas and new approaches to international exchanges. It will produce a fairer and more equitable global governance system, and take humanity to a better future.

II. Paving the Way Towards Shared Development and Prosperity

The BRI is in alignment with the concept of a global community of shared future. It promotes and puts into action ideas that are relevant to the present era, the world, development, security, openness, cooperation, civilization, and governance. It provides not only a conceptual framework but also a practical roadmap for all nations to achieve shared development and prosperity.

1. Principles: extensive consultation, joint contribution, and shared benefits

The BRI is founded on the principles of extensive consultation, joint contribution, and shared benefits. It advocates win-win cooperation in pursuit of the greater good and shared interests. It emphasizes that all countries are equal participants, contributors and beneficiaries, and encourages economic integration, interconnected development, and the sharing of achievements.

The principle of extensive consultation signifies that the BRI is not a solo endeavor by China, but a collaborative effort involving all stakeholders. This principle promotes and activates authentic multilateralism, encouraging collective decision-making while fully respecting the varying levels of development, economic structures, legal systems, and cultural traditions of different nations. It emphasizes equal participation, effective communication, collective wisdom, freedom from any political or economic preconditions, and voluntary engagement to foster maximum consensus. Irrespective of size, strength and wealth, all countries participate on an equal footing and can provide opinions and proposals in bilateral and multilateral cooperation.

Under this principle, economies at different stages of development will reinforce bilateral or multilateral communication, jointly identify and establish innovative cooperation mechanisms, and provide a platform for dialogue, cooperation and participation in global governance.

The principle of joint contribution highlights that the BRI is not one of China's international aid programs or geopolitical tool, but a collaborative effort for shared development. It aims to align with existing regional mechanisms rather than becoming their substitute and leverage complementary strengths. This principle emphasizes the participation of all parties involved, substantial coordination with the development strategies of relevant countries and regions, and the identification and utilization of their respective development potential and comparative strengths. The objective is to collectively create new opportunities, driving forces, and development space while achieving complementary and interactive growth by capitalizing on each party's strengths and capabilities.

To promote extensive participation, this principle encourages countries and businesses to engage through various forms such as bilateral cooperation, third-party market cooperation and multilateral cooperation, thereby creating synergy for development. This principle values market forces and promotes market-oriented operations to further the interests and meet the expectations of all parties involved. In this context, businesses play a central role as the main actors, while the government's responsibility lies in building platforms, establishing mechanisms, and providing policy guidance. China's key role in BRI cooperation stems from its economic size, market scale, experience in infrastructure construction, capacity to produce low-cost, high-quality, high-performance equipment, and comprehensive strengths in industry, capital, technology, talent and management.

The principle of shared benefits underscores the importance of win-win cooperation. It aims to identify common interests and grounds for cooperation, meet the development needs of all parties, and address the real concerns of the people. This principle emphasizes sharing development opportunities and outcomes among all participating countries, ensuring that none of them is left behind. Most participants are developing countries, all seeking to leverage collective strengths to address challenges such as inadequate infrastructure, lagging industrial development, limited industrialization, insufficient capital and technology, and a shortage of skilled workers, to promote their own economic and social development.

Under the BRI framework, China pursues the greater good and shared interests, with the former taking precedence, by providing assistance to partner countries within its capabilities and genuinely supporting other developing countries to accelerate development. Simultaneously, through BRI cooperation, China aims to foster all-round opening up by building connections with other countries over land and sea while creating synergy between its eastern and western regions. It seeks to build a more advanced open economy and create a double development dynamic with the domestic economy as the mainstay and the domestic economy and international engagement providing mutual reinforcement.

2. Concepts: open, green and clean cooperation

The BRI is committed to open, green and clean cooperation towards inclusive and sustainable development. It has zero tolerance for corruption and promotes steady and high-quality growth.

The BRI is a public road open to all, not a private path owned by any single party. It is free from geopolitical calculations. It does not aim to create an exclusive club, nor does it target at any party. It does not form cliques based on specific ideological standards. It has no intention of establishing military alliances. Countries from Eurasia, Africa, the Americas, and Oceania are all welcome to participate in the initiative, regardless of their political system, historical background, culture, development stage, ideology, or religious beliefs, as long as they seek common development. All participants uphold principles of openness and inclusiveness, while firmly opposing protectionism, unilateralism and hegemonism, and working together to create an all-round, three-dimensional landscape of interconnectivity. The goals are to develop a new model of cooperation based on win-win outcomes, shared responsibility, and collective participation, build a global network of partnerships, and nurture a harmonious coexistence for humanity.

The BRI embraces the global trend of green and low-carbon development, emphasizes respecting and protecting nature and following its laws, and respects the right of all parties to pursue sustainable and eco-friendly growth.

Based on a shared commitment to eco-environmental considerations, the parties involved have carried out policy dialogues, and shared ideas and achievements in green development. Through closer cooperation in areas such as green infrastructure, renewable energy, eco-friendly transport, and sustainable finance, all parties work together to broaden consensus and take concrete steps towards green development. The ultimate goal is to establish a resource-efficient, eco-conscious and low-carbon Silk Road, thereby making a significant contribution to protecting the eco-environment, achieving peak carbon and neutrality goals and addressing climate change.

Leveraging its expertise in renewable energy, energy conservation, environmental protection and clean production, and employing Chinese technology, products and experience, China actively promotes BRI cooperation in green development.

Clean governance is considered an intrinsic and necessary condition for the steady and sustained development of the BRI, with a commitment to transparency in cooperation. All participants joined to combat corruption, strengthening their legal systems and mechanisms, harmonizing their laws and regulations, and fostering international cooperation. Furthermore, all participants stand united against all forms of corruption and other international criminal activities, and work consistently to combat commercial bribery. This ensures that financial resources and projects are managed with integrity and efficiency, leading to greater outcomes and making BRI cooperation an example of clean governance.

In April 2019, together with relevant countries, international organizations, and representatives from the business and academic communities, China launched the Beijing Initiative for the Clean Silk Road. This initiative calls for a clean Silk Road characterized by extensive consultation, joint contribution, and shared benefits. Chinese companies expanding globally are committed to compliance and lawful operations, adhering to the laws of both China and the host countries and to international norms. They have particularly heightened their capacity to mitigate overseas operational risks, strengthening project supervision and management to ensure the delivery of clean, cost-efficient and high-quality projects.

State-owned enterprises (SOEs) directly under the central government have released 868 guidelines of compliance in key areas, and defined 5,000-plus job compliance responsibilities; SOEs and financial institutions directly under the central government and their branches have formulated and updated more than 15,000 rules for managing overseas operations. In November 2020, more than 60 Chinese enterprises engaged in extensive BRI cooperation joined in launching the Integrity and Compliance Initiative for BRI Enterprises.

3. Objectives: high standards, sustainability, and better lives

The BRI aims at high standards, sustainability, and better lives by raising cooperation standard, investment effectiveness, supply quality, and development resilience, delivering real and substantive results for all participants.

The BRI introduces universally accepted rules and standards to guide business practices in project tendering, procurement, development and operation. It promotes high-standard cooperation and construction in various sectors. It advocates establishing free trade zones in alignment with international rules and standards, and implementing policies to promote trade and investment liberalization and facilitation to a higher level. This will ensure safe, smooth and orderly flows of people, goods, funds and data, and enable greater interconnectivity and deeper exchanges and co-operation. The approach emphasizes world-class standards, practicality, and cost-effectiveness. Pilot projects precede wider implementation, and participating countries are encouraged to adopt rules and the path adapted to their national conditions. China has established a high-level leadership organization and issued policy documents to consistently improve BRI design and implementation.

In alignment with the UN 2030 Agenda for Sustainable Development, the BRI promotes coordinated economic, social, and eco-environmental development. Its aims are to address the root causes and obstacles that hinder development and boost the self-driven development of participating countries. It strives to achieve lasting, inclusive and sustainable economic growth, integrating sustainable development principles into project selection, implementation and management. Following international practices and debt sustainability principles, it is working to create a long-term, stable, sustainable and risk-controlled investment and financing system with innovative models and diverse channels in order to establish a stable, transparent and high-quality funding guarantee system that ensures commercial and fiscal sustainability. No participating country has fallen into a debt crisis as a result of BRI cooperation.

The BRI takes a people-centered approach, with the focus on poverty eradication, job creation, and improvement of people's wellbeing to ensure that the benefits of cooperation reach all individuals. Deeper cooperation is encouraged in areas such as public health, poverty reduction, disaster mitigation, green development, science and technology, education, culture, arts, and health care. Closer exchanges are promoted among political parties, social organizations, think tanks, youth, women, and sub-national communities. These efforts aim to create projects that are grounded in the needs of the people, increasing their sense of gain and fulfillment. China actively promotes small-scale yet impactful projects through foreign aid, benefiting people's lives. From Asia to Africa, Latin

America to the South Pacific, the construction of roads, railways, schools, hospitals and agricultural facilities contributes to poverty reduction and improves the people's wellbeing in participating countries.

4. Vision: a path to global wellbeing

An initiative towards progress, cooperation and inclusiveness, the BRI pursues development, promotes win-win outcomes, and inspires hope. It aims to deepen understanding and trust, strengthen comprehensive exchanges, and ultimately achieve common development and shared prosperity.

A path to peace. Peace is a prerequisite for development, while development serves as the foundation for peace. The BRI goes beyond the law of the jungle and the hegemonic order based on power struggles. It rejects zero-sum thinking and discards the Cold War mentality of ideological rivalry and geopolitical competition. Instead, it paves the way for peaceful development, and aims to offer a fundamental approach to lasting peace and universal security. Under the BRI, nations respect each other's sovereignty, dignity, territorial integrity, development path, social system, core interests, and major concerns. As the initiator of the BRI, China passionately campaigns for the establishment of a new model of international relations characterized by mutual respect, equity, justice, and win-win cooperation. It is committed to building partnerships based on dialogue rather than confrontation, and friendship rather than alliance, and to fostering a new vision of common, comprehensive, cooperative and sustainable security. These efforts help to create a peaceful and stable development environment.

A path to prosperity. The BRI is committed to building a prosperous future that diverges from the exploitative colonialism of the past, avoids coercive and one-sided transactions, rejects the center-periphery model of dependency, and refuses to displace crisis onto others or exploit neighbors for self-interest. Instead, it aims to achieve win-win outcomes and shared development and prosperity. Under the BRI, all parties will prioritize development as the common goal, leveraging their respective resources and potential advantages, igniting their own growth engines, growing their capacity for independent development, and collectively creating more opportunities and space for development. This collaborative effort aims to foster new centers and impetus for global economic growth, drive inclusive growth, and bring global development into a balanced, coordinated and inclusive new stage.

A path to openness. The BRI represents an open and inclusive collaborative process that transcends national borders, ideological differences, developmental disparities, social system variations, and geopolitical conflicts. It is not aimed at designing a new international system, but rather supplementing and improving the existing mechanisms. All parties involved uphold the core values and fundamental principles of the multilateral trading system. Together, participants will establish an open and cooperative platform, safeguard and promote an open global economy, create an environment conducive to open development, construct a fair, equitable and transparent system of international trade and investment rules, and advance cooperation based on win-win outcomes, shared responsibility and collective participation. The BRI facilitates the orderly flow of production factors, the efficient allocation of resources, deep integration of markets, and liberalization and facilitation of trade and investment, and ensures the stable performance and smooth operation of global industrial and supply chains. It aims to build an economic globalization that is open, inclusive, balanced, and beneficial to all.

A path to innovation. Innovation serves as a critical driving force for progress. The BRI is dedicated to innovation-led development, harnessing the opportunities presented by digital, internet-based and smart development. It explores new business forms, technologies and models, seeking out fresh sources of growth and innovative development pathways to propel transformative advancements for all involved. Participants collaborate to connect digital infrastructure, build the Digital Silk Road, strengthen innovative cooperation in cutting-edge fields, and promote the deep integration of science, technology, industry and finance. These efforts aim to optimize the environment for innovation, gather innovative resources, foster a regional ecosystem of collaborative innovation, and bridge the digital divide, injecting strong momentum into common development.

A path to social progress. The BRI champions equality, mutual learning, dialogue, and inclusiveness among civilizations. It upholds the shared values of peace, development, equity, justice, democracy and freedom. It transcends barriers between cultures through exchanges, resolves conflicts through mutual understanding, and rejects superiority while promoting coexistence. It encourages civilizations to appreciate their differences, seek common ground, and learn from one another. Parties involved will establish multitiered mechanisms for people-to-people cooperation, create more platforms and channels, and facilitate exchanges across various fields. These efforts aim to reinforce mutual understanding, respect and trust among nations, broaden consensus on ideas and values, and achieve new human progress.

III. Promoting All-Round Connectivity in Multiple Fields

To promote greater connectivity through BRI cooperation, we have continued to facilitate policy coordination, infrastructure connectivity, unimpeded trade, financial integration, and closer people-to-people ties, by orienting towards "hard connectivity" in infrastructure, bolstering "soft connectivity" through harmonized rules and standards, and strengthening people-to-people bonds. As its scope expands, the BRI has become the world's largest platform for international cooperation, with the broadest coverage.

1. Extensive and in-depth policy coordination

Policy coordination underpins BRI cooperation. China has worked with participating countries and international organizations to establish a multilevel policy coordination and communication mechanism for aligning development strategies, technological and economic policies, and administration rules and standards. Under this mechanism, plans and measures for regional cooperation have been formulated through joint efforts to facilitate and speed up cooperation, making the BRI an important collaborative framework for international exchanges.

Strategy and policy coordination is expanding in scope. At the global level, the 193 UN member states unanimously agreed to incorporate the Belt and Road Initiative in the UN resolution passed at the 71st United Nations General Assembly in November 2016. In March 2017, the United Nations Security Council adopted Resolution 2344, calling for stronger regional economic cooperation through the BRI, among other initiatives. The United Nations Development Programme and the World Health Organization (WHO) have signed BRI cooperation agreements with China. At the World Trade Organization (WTO), China's efforts have facilitated the conclusion of the negotiations on the text of the Investment Facilitation for Development Agreement, with a view to establishing a co-ordinated and unified investment management system covering more than 110 countries and regions to encourage BRI cooperation on investment.

At regional and multilateral levels, the BRI has supported regional integration and global development by aligning with plans such as the UN 2030 Agenda for Sustainable Development, the Master Plan on ASEAN Connectivity 2025, the ASEAN Outlook on the Indo-Pacific, the African Union's Agenda 2063, and the European Union's Strategy on Connecting Europe and Asia.

At the bilateral level, the BRI has succeeded in coordinating with a wide range of strategies and initiatives, including Russia's Eurasian Economic Union framework, Kazakhstan's Bright Road economic policy, Turkmenistan's strategy of reviving the Silk Road, Mongolia's Steppe Road plan, Indonesia's Global Marine Fulcrum initiative, the Philippines' Build Better More program, Vietnam's Two Corridors and One Economic Circle plan, South Africa's Economic Reconstruction and Recovery Plan, Egypt's Suez Canal Corridor Project, and Saudi Arabia's Vision 2030. By June 2023, China had signed more than 200 BRI cooperation agreements with more than 150 countries and 30 international organizations across five continents, yielding a number of signature projects and small-scale yet impactful projects.

A long-term mechanism for policy coordination is largely in place. Multilevel channels for regular communication among different parties have been opened up on different platforms. This has been made possible through top-down driven diplomatic efforts led by heads of state, with support from intergovernmental strategic communication and local and interdepartmental policy coordination, and with cooperation projects carried out by enterprises and social organizations.

China has hosted the Belt and Road Forum for International Cooperation twice, providing an important platform for participating countries and international organizations to expand exchanges, increase mutual trust, and strengthen ties. The first forum in 2017 welcomed heads of state and government from 29 countries, and more than 1,600 representatives from 140-plus countries and 80-plus international organizations, yielding a total of 279 deliverables in five categories. At the second forum held in 2019, 40 leaders, including heads of state and government from 38 countries, the UN secretary-general and the International Monetary Fund's managing director, attended the Leaders' Roundtable. More than 6,000 representatives participated, from over 150 countries and 92 international organizations, yielding 283 deliverables in 6 categories.

Multilateral cooperation is driving forward. Under the BRI framework, Chinese and foreign partners have launched 20-plus multilateral dialogue and cooperation mechanisms in professional domains such as railways, ports, energy, finance, taxation, environmental protection, disaster prevention and relief, think tanks, and the media, attracting a growing number of participants. BRI participating countries have also expanded practical cooperation through major multilateral platforms such as China-ASEAN (10+1) Cooperation, Forum on China-Africa Cooperation, China-Arab States Cooperation Forum, Forum of China and the Community of Latin American and Caribbean States, China-Pacific Island Countries Economic Development and Cooperation Forum, China-Central and Eastern European Countries Cooperation, World Economic Forum, Boao Forum for Asia, and CPC and World Political Parties Summit.

Rules and standards are being coordinated. Cooperation on standardization has advanced to new levels. As of June 2023, China had signed 107 documents with standardization bodies in 65 countries such as Pakistan, Russia, Greece, Ethiopia, and Costa Rica and also with regional and international organizations, in areas covering civil aviation, climate change, agri-food, building materials, electric vehicles, oil and gas pipelines, logistics, small hydropower stations, oceanography, and surveying and mapping.

The Standard Information Platform Contributed by the Belt and Road Countries provides overviews of standards information in 149 partner countries, and full-text search services for standards catalogues regarding 59 countries and 6 regional and international standardization organizations, serving as a bridge for participating countries. Chinese standards in foreign language versions have been supplied in larger quantities. Nearly 1,400 national standards and more than 1,000 industry standards have been published in foreign languages.

In May 2022, the Asian-African Legal Consultative Organization opened a regional arbitration center in Hong Kong, providing solutions for multilateral disputes in BRI cooperation.

China has continued to strengthen cross-border accounting and auditing regulatory cooperation with 22 countries and regions including Russia, Malaysia and Singapore, providing institutional guarantees for expanding cross-border investment and financing channels.

2. Growing connectivity of infrastructure

The BRI prioritizes connectivity of infrastructure. Based on a framework comprising "six corridors, six routes, and multiple countries and ports", a multitiered and multidimensional infrastructure network is taking shape. Basic connectivity over land, maritime, air and cyberspace is in place, laying solid foundations for deeper cooperation in trade and industrial capacity, and strengthening cultural and people-to-people exchanges.

The construction of economic corridors and international routes is making substantial progress. Participating countries have pressed forward with the creation of international arterial routes, building an infrastructure network that connects subregions in Asia as well as the continents of Asia, Europe and Africa.

Major projects along the China-Pakistan Economic Corridor are under way. The Peshawar-Karachi Motorway (Sukkur-Multan section), the

Karakoram Highway Phase II (Havelian-Thakot section), and the Lahore Orange Line Metro are all open to traffic. Coal-fired power plants such as Sahiwal, Port Qasim, Thar, and Hub are operating safely and steadily; the Mehra DC transmission project is operational; and the Kalot Hydropower Station is connected to the power grid. Rashakai Special Economic Zone has reached the stage of comprehensive development.

Along the New Eurasian Land Bridge, the Belgrade-Novi Sad section of the Hungary-Serbia Railway in Serbia became operational in March 2022, and track-laying has started on the Budapest-Kelebija section in Hungary. The Peljesac Bridge in Croatia has celebrated its first anniversary of opening to traffic. The Western Europe-Western China Highway has been completed. The Smokovac-Matesevo section of the Bar-Boljare Highway in Montenegro has been completed and is open to traffic.

Along the China-Indochina Peninsula Economic Corridor, the China-Laos Railway has been completed and is providing sound service, and its role as a golden transport channel is becoming increasingly prominent. The Jakarta-Bandung High-speed Railway, the flagship project of BRI cooperation between China and Indonesia, has achieved an operational speed of 350 km per hour. The contract for the China-Thailand Railway Phase I (Bangkok-Nakhon Ratchasima section) was signed online, and 11 sections of the construction project have started, including one that has been completed.

Along the China-Mongolia-Russia Economic Corridor, the Heihe-Blagoveshchensk Highway Bridge and the Tongjiang-Nizhneleninskoye Railway Bridge, connecting China and Russia, have opened to traffic. The China-Russia eastern natural gas pipeline is fully operational. China, Russia and Mongolia have officially launched a feasibility study on the upgrading and development of the central-route railway of the China-Mongolia-Russia Economic Corridor.

Along the China-Central Asia-West Asia Economic Corridor, the China-Kyrgyzstan-Uzbekistan Highway is in full operation. The China-Central Asia Gas Pipeline is fully operational. The grain and oil rail transport lines between North Kazakhstan and China are operating in conjunction with the China-Europe Railway Express.

Along the Bangladesh-China-India-Myanmar Economic Corridor, the China-Myanmar Crude Oil and Gas Pipeline has been completed and entered service. The feasibility study on the Muse-Mandalay section of the

---

Panel 1   Mombasa-Nairobi Railway promotes Kenya's economic and social development

The Mombasa-Nairobi Standard Gauge Railway in Kenya connects Mombasa, the largest port in East Africa, and Nairobi, the capital of Kenya. It extends further northwest to Suswa. The line is 592 kilometers long. It utilizes Chinese standards, technology, equipment, and project management. It is an important success story in BRI cooperation between China and Kenya, and is hailed as a route of friendship, of win-win cooperation, of development and prosperity, and of eco-environmental protection.

The Mombasa-Nairobi Railway is the largest infrastructure project undertaken in Kenya since independence. Since it opened in 2017, the railway has had a positive impact on Kenya's economic and social development and the people's wellbeing; it has also significantly reduced the logistics costs of products from the inland regions of East Africa exported through the Mombasa Port. As of August 31, 2023, the railway is operating an average of 6 passenger trains per day; a total of 11 million passengers have been carried, and the average occupancy rate is above 95 percent; an average of 17 freight trains operate daily, and a total of 28 million tonnes of goods have been transported. According to Kenyan government estimates, the railway has added 2 percent to Kenya's economic growth.

In the construction and operation of the Mombasa-Nairobi Railway, Chinese enterprises have supported technology transfer and provided training to local employees. During the construction period, more than 30,000 local employees received orientation training, and every year a number of young Kenyans were selected to participate in training and academic education in China. Since the opening of the railway, Chinese companies have adopted tailored training methods for different people, professions and posts, and have trained 1,152 professionals for Kenya.

China-Myanmar Railway has been completed, and the feasibility study on the Mandalay-Kyaukphyu section has been launched. Construction projects in Bangladesh, including the Bangladesh-China Friendship Bridge and the Dohazari-Cox's Bazar rail route, have made good progress.

In Africa, railways such as the Mombasa-Nairobi Railway and the Addis Ababa-Djibouti Railway are now operational and have become important drivers of in-depth development not only in East Africa but across the entire continent.

Maritime connectivity is steadily improving. Cooperation is expanding in shipping among the ports of participating countries, and the efficiency of cargo transportation has seen notable increase.

The annual cargo throughput of the Port of Piraeus in Greece has increased to above 5 million twenty-foot equivalent units (TEUs), making it the fourth largest TEU port in Europe and a leading TEU port in the Mediterranean.

The Gwadar Port in Pakistan has seen major progress and is marching towards the goal of becoming a logistics center and industrial base.

Preliminary work is currently under way on the Kyaukphyu Deep-sea Port project in Myanmar, including geological exploration and environmental and social assessment.

The annual throughput of bulk cargo at Hambantota Port in Sri Lanka has increased to 1.21 million tonnes.

The Vado Gateway terminal has become the first semi-automatic terminal operating in Italy.

The Lekki Deep-sea Port in Nigeria has been completed and entered service, becoming a major modern deepwater port in Central and Western Africa.

The Silk Road Maritime network has continued to expand. By the end of June 2023, it had reached 117 ports in 43 countries, and more than 300 well-known Chinese and international shipping companies, port enterprises and think tanks, among other bodies, have joined the Silk Road Maritime association.

A marine environment forecast and support system that focuses on areas along the Maritime Silk Road offers services to more than 100 cities in participating countries.

The Air Silk Road has made notable progress. The aviation route network between participating countries is expanding rapidly, and the level of air connectivity is steadily improving.

China has signed bilateral air transport agreements with 104 BRI partner countries and opened direct flights with 57 partner countries to facilitate cross-border transport.

Chinese enterprises are active participants in civil aviation infrastructure cooperation with partner countries including Pakistan, Nepal and Togo, helping to develop the local civil aviation industry.

A BRI cooperation platform proposed by the Civil Aviation Administration of China was established in August 2020, improving mechanisms and platforms of civil aviation exchanges and cooperation among participating countries.

During the Covid-19 pandemic, a direct line of the Air Silk Road linking Zhengzhou in Henan Province and Luxemburg did not suspend its air or freighting services, and transported a large amount of supplies. It served as an air lifeline between China and Europe, and contributed to keeping international industrial and supply chains stable.

International inter-modality transport channels continue to enjoy stable development. These channels include the China-Europe Railway Express, the China-Europe Land-Sea Express Line, the New International Land-Sea Trade Corridor, and the Lianyungang-Khorgos New Eurasian Land-Sea Expressway.

The China-Europe Railway Express has now reached more than 200 cities in 25 European countries, comprising 86 routes passing through the main regions of the Eurasian hinterland at a speed of 120 km per hour. Its logistics distribution network covers the entire Eurasian continent. By the end of June 2023, the cumulative volume of the China-Europe Railway Express had exceeded 74,000 trips, transporting nearly 7 million TEUs and over 50,000 types of goods in 53 categories such as automobiles, mechanical equipment, and electronic products, to a total value of more than US$300 billion.

The China-Europe Land-Sea Express Line has emerged from scratch to become the third trade channel between China and Europe, after traditional sea routes and the China-Europe Railway Express. In 2022, more than 180,000 TEUs were transported through this line, with rail trips exceeding 2,600.

The routes of rail-sea freight trains of the New International Land-sea Trade Corridor cover 18 provinces and equivalent administrative units, in central and western China, transporting goods to 300-plus ports in more than 100 countries.

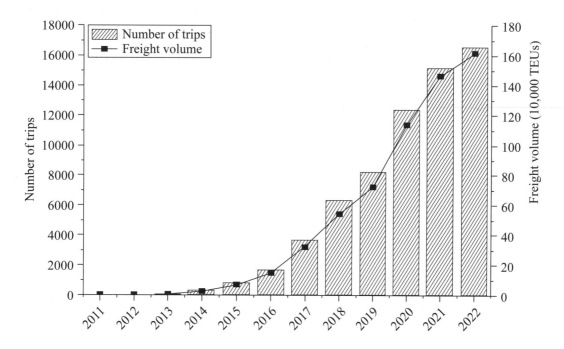

Figure 1: Number of trips and freight volume of China-Europe freight trains (2011-2022)

3. Unimpeded, convenient and efficient trade

Facilitating trade and investment is a major task in building the Belt and Road. The participating countries have worked hard to promote trade and investment liberalization and facilitation, remove investment and trade barriers, and improve the business environment within the region and in all related countries. Efforts have been made to build free trade zones, broaden trading areas, improve trade structure, expand areas of mutual investment and industrial cooperation, establish a more balanced, equal and sustainable trading system, and develop mutually beneficial economic and trade relations, so as to make the "pie" of cooperation bigger.

Trade and investment are expanding steadily. From 2013 to 2022, the cumulative value of imports and exports between China and BRI partner countries reached US$19.1 trillion, with an average annual growth rate of 6.4 percent. The cumulative two-way investment between China and partner countries reached US$380 billion, including US$240 billion from China. The value of newly signed construction contracts with partner countries reached US$2 trillion, and the actual turnover of Chinese contractors reached US$1.3 trillion. In 2022, the value of imports and exports between China and partner countries reached nearly US$2.9 trillion, accounting for 45.4 percent of China's total foreign trade over the same period, representing an increase of 6.2 percentage points compared with 2013; the total value of imports and exports of Chinese private enterprises

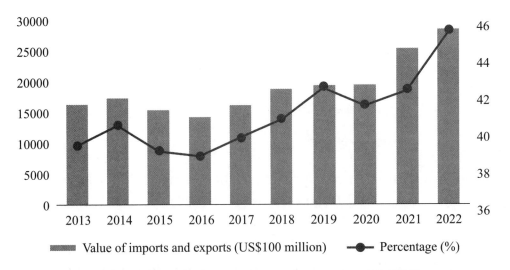

Figure 2: Value of China's imports and exports with BRI partner countries and its share in China's total trade (2013-2022)

to partner countries exceeded US$1.5 trillion, accounting for 53.7 percent of the trade between China and these countries over the same period.

Trade and investment liberalization and facilitation is improving. BRI participating countries continue to uphold multilateralism and free trade, working hard to create a sound institutional environment for closer economic and trade relations. Positive progress has been made in the alignment of working systems, coordination of technical standards, mutual recognition of inspection results, and online verification of electronic certificates.

By the end of August 2023, more than 80 countries and international organizations had subscribed to the Initiative on Promoting Unimpeded Trade Cooperation Along the Belt and Road, proposed by China. China had signed 21 free trade agreements with 28 countries and regions. On January 1, 2022, the Regional Comprehensive Economic Partnership (RCEP) agreement entered into force, creating the world's largest free trade zone in terms of population size and trade volume. The RCEP and the BRI overlap and complement each other in terms of participating countries and regions, as well as areas and contents of cooperation, forming a new dynamic of economic and trade cooperation in Asia.

China also works actively towards joining the Comprehensive and Progressive Agreement for Trans-Pacific Partnership and the Digital Economy Partnership Agreement.

China has signed bilateral investment agreements with 135 countries and regions, and conventions for the avoidance of double taxation (including arrangements and agreements) with 112 countries and regions. It has achieved Authorized Economic Operator mutual recognition with 35 partner countries, and has signed third-party market cooperation documents with 14 countries.

China has established a "single-window" cooperation mechanism with Singapore, Pakistan, Mongolia, Iran and other partner countries, and signed cooperation documents on customs inspection and quarantine, effectively improving the efficiency of customs clearance at border ports.

Trade and investment platforms are playing a growing role. China International Import Expo (CIIE) is the world's first import-themed national-level expo and has been held for the past five years. It has resulted in a cumulative intended turnover of nearly US$350 billion, and about 2,000 launches of new products. With diverse participants from many countries and regions, the CIIE has become a global platform for international procurement, investment promotion, cultural exchanges, and open cooperation.

The influence of key exhibitions continues to expand; these include China Import and Export Fair (Canton Fair), China International Fair for Trade in Services, China International Fair for Investment and Trade, China International Consumer Products Expo, Global Digital Trade Expo, China-Africa Economic and Trade Expo, China-Arab States Expo, China-Russia Expo, China-CEEC Expo & International Consumer Goods Fair, China-ASEAN Expo, and China-Eurasia Expo. All of these have provided a strong boost to trade and investment cooperation among participating countries.

The Hong Kong SAR has held the Belt and Road Summit eight times, and the Macao SAR has held the International Infrastructure Investment and Construction Forum 14 times, which have played an important role in advancing economic, trade and investment cooperation along the Belt and Road.

Industrial cooperation is deepening. BRI participating countries have worked hard to foster a paradigm of cooperation based on coordinated development, mutual benefit, and win-win outcomes, which has given a strong boost to upgrading industrial structures and optimizing industrial chains in the countries involved.

The participating countries have jointly promoted cooperation on industrial capacity, expanded cooperation in traditional industries including steel, non-ferrous metals, building materials, automobiles, engineering machinery, resources and energy, and agriculture, explored cooperation in emerging industries such as the digital economy, new energy vehicles, nuclear energy and technology, and 5G, and carried out tri-party and multiparty market cooperation, thus advancing mutual complementarity and providing mutual benefits to all parties.

By the end of June 2023, China had signed agreements on industrial capacity cooperation with more than 40 countries. China Mining Conference & Exhibition and China-ASEAN Mining Cooperation Forum & Exhibition serve as important platforms for participating countries to conduct mining capacity cooperation.

The Shanghai Cooperation Organization (SCO) Demonstration Base for Agricultural Technology Exchange and Training has supported advances in agricultural science and technology under the BRI, and promoted economic and trade cooperation in agriculture among participating countries.

Jointly constructed by China and Pakistan, the K2 and K3 units of the Karachi Nuclear Power Plant have been completed and are in operation, utilizing China's Hualong One nuclear technology.

The Ulba Fuel Assembly Plant, a successful joint venture between China and Kazakhstan, is now operational.

The China-ASEAN Forum on Peaceful Uses of Nuclear Technology has served as a bridge to establish connectivity, enabling BRI participating countries to cooperate on nuclear technology and promote growth and people's wellbeing.

More than 70 overseas industrial parks have been built by Chinese enterprises together with governments and enterprises in partner countries. The China-Malaysia and China-Indonesia "Two Countries, Twin Parks" projects, the China-Belarus Great Stone Industrial Park, the China-UAE Industrial Capacity Cooperation Demonstration Zone, and the China-Egypt TEDA Suez Economic and Trade Cooperation Zone are making steady progress.

4. Diverse dynamics of financial integration

Financial integration is an important pillar of BRI cooperation. Participating countries and relevant institutions have carried out multiple forms of financial cooperation, created new models, expanded the channels, diversified the parties involved, and improved the mechanisms for investment and financing. They have promoted policy-based finance, development finance, commercial finance, and cooperative finance to support BRI cooperation, and worked to build a long-term, stable and sustainable investment and financing system that keeps risk under control.

The financial cooperation mechanisms are maturing. China Development Bank (CDB) has promoted the establishment of multilateral financial cooperation mechanisms such as China-Central and Eastern Europe Interbank Consortium, the China-Arab Countries Interbank Association, China-ASEAN Interbank Association, the ASEAN Plus Three Interbank Cooperation mechanism, China-Africa Interbank Association, and the Association of China-LAC Development Financial Institutions. The Industrial and Commercial Bank of China (ICBC) has promoted the Belt and Road Interbank Regular Cooperation (BRBR) mechanism.

As of the end of June 2023, a total of 13 Chinese-funded banks had established 145 first-tier offices and branches in 50 BRI partner countries; some 17.7 million businesses in 131 partner countries had opened Union-Pay services, and 74 partner countries had opened UnionPay mobile payment services. The Belt and Road Innovation and Development Center, the Research Center for Belt and Road Financial and Economic Development, and the China-IMF Capacity Development Center have been established.

China has signed bilateral currency swap agreements with 20 partner countries and established renminbi (RMB) clearing arrangements in 17 partner countries. The number of participants, business volume, and influence of the RMB cross-border payment system have gradually increased, effectively facilitating trade and investment.

Financial regulation cooperation and exchanges have continued to move forward. China Banking and Insurance Regulatory Commission (now National Administration of Financial Regulation), China Securities Regulatory Commission (CSRC), and regulatory agencies from multiple other countries have signed memorandums of understanding (MoUs) for regulatory cooperation, facilitating the establishment of regional regulatory coordination mechanisms, promoting efficient allocation of funds, strengthening risk control, and creating sound investment conditions for various financial institutions and investment entities.

The channels and platforms for investment and financing are constantly expanding. China has funded the establishment of the Silk Road Fund (SRF) and established the Asian Infrastructure Investment Bank (AIIB) with other participating countries. The SRF specifically serves BRI cooperation. By the end of June 2023, the fund had signed agreements on 75 projects with committed investment of about US$22 billion; the number of AIIB members had reached 106, and the bank had approved 227 projects with a total investment of US$43.6 billion. The projects involve transport, energy, public health and other fields, providing investment and financing support for infrastructure connectivity and sustainable economic and social development.

China has actively participated in various existing financing arrangements. It has signed memorandums of cooperation with international financial institutions such as the World Bank and the Asian Development Bank, worked with international financial institutions to establish a multilateral development financing cooperation center, strengthened third-party market cooperation in investment and financing with the European Bank for Reconstruction and Development, and carried out joint financing with the International Finance Corporation, the African Development Bank and others. These moves have effectively mobilized market capital.

China has initiated the establishment of international economic cooperation funds such as the China-Eurasian Economic Cooperation Fund, the China-LAC Cooperation Fund, the China-Central and Eastern Europe Investment Cooperation Fund, the China-ASEAN Investment Cooperation Fund, the China-LAC Industrial Cooperation Investment Fund, and the China-Africa Fund for Industrial Cooperation. These have effectively expanded investment and financing channels for partner countries.

The CDB and the Export-Import Bank of China (China Eximbank) have each set up special loans for the BRI to pool resources to increase financing support for BRI cooperation. By the end of 2022, the CDB has provided direct high-quality financial services for more than 1,300 BRI projects, playing a leading role in guiding development finance, and pooling all kinds of domestic and foreign funds for BRI cooperation. The balance of loans of China Eximbank for BRI projects reached RMB2.2 trillion, covering 130-plus participating countries and driving more than US$400 billion of investment and more than US$2 trillion of trade. China Export & Credit Insurance Corporation has fully applied export credit insurance and actively provided comprehensive guarantees for building the Belt and Road.

Innovative investment and financing methods are steadily being explored. Various models such as funds and bonds have been developed, and BRI financial cooperation is improving.

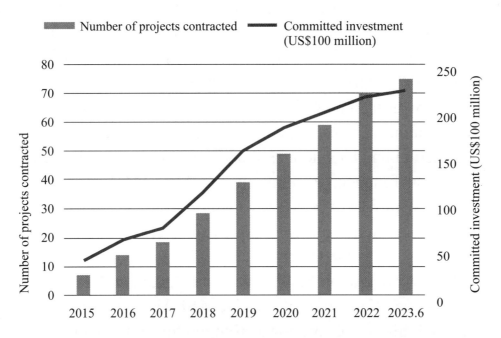

Figure 3: Number of projects contracted and committed investment by the Silk Road Fund since 2015

China's securities industry has set up a number of BRI-themed funds and indexes. In December 2015, the CSRC officially launched a pilot project for overseas institutions to issue RMB-denominated bonds (panda bonds) in China's exchange-traded bond market. By the end of June 2023, overseas issuers in total had issued 99 panda bonds in China's exchange-traded bond market, with a total value of RMB152.54 billion; 46 BRI-themed bonds had been issued, with a total value of RMB52.72 billion.

Green finance is steadily developing. In May 2019, the ICBC issued the first green BRBR bond that conformed to both international and domestic green bond standards. By the end of 2022, more than 40 large global institutions had signed the Green Investment Principles for the Belt and Road. In June 2023, China Eximbank issued financial bonds for promoting international cooperation in building the Belt and Road and supporting infrastructure construction of partner countries. China's domestic stock and futures exchanges have steadily promoted practical cooperation in equity, products, technology and other fields with the exchanges in partner countries, and actively supported the development of exchanges participating in or holding shares in BRI projects, such as the Astana International Exchange in Kazakhstan, the Pakistan Stock Exchange, and the Dhaka Stock Exchange in Bangladesh.

Debt sustainability has continued to improve. Based on the principle of equal participation and benefit and risk sharing, China and 28 countries approved the Guiding Principles on Financing the Development of the Belt and Road, encouraging the governments, financial institutions and enterprises of participating countries to attach importance to debt sustainability and improve their debt management capability. Drawing on the debt sustainability framework of low-income countries endorsed by the International Monetary Fund and the World Bank, China has developed tools based on the actual conditions of participating countries, and issued the Debt Sustainability Framework for Participating Countries of the Belt and Road Initiative. All parties are encouraged to use it on a voluntary basis.

To avoid causing debt risk and financial burden to the countries where BRI projects are located, China has prioritized economic and social benefits and provided loans for project construction based on local needs and conditions. The key areas of investment are infrastructure projects designed to increase connectivity, and projects for public wellbeing urgently needed in participating countries. These have brought effective investment, increased high-quality assets, and boosted development momentum.

Many think tank experts and international institutions have pointed out that almost all the BRI projects are initiated by the host countries with the goals of growing their economies and improving their people's lives. In the process, the logic of economics has taken precedence over geopolitics.

5. Solid foundations for people-to-people ties

People-to-people ties are the social foundations of BRI cooperation. The participating countries have passed on and carried forward the spirit of friendly cooperation of the ancient Silk Road, cooperated on exchanges in culture, tourism, education, think tank and the media, and promoted mutual learning among civilizations and cultural integration and innovation. A model of people-to-people exchanges characterized by dynamic interactions and diversity has underpinned public support for furthering the initiative.

Cooperation on culture and tourism is rich and colorful. By the end of June 2023, China had signed cultural and tourism cooperation documents with 144 BRI partner countries.

China has created cooperation platforms together with participating countries, including the Silk Road International League of Theaters, the Silk Road International Museum Alliance, the Network of Silk Road Arts Festivals, the Silk Road International Library Alliance, and the Silk Road International Alliance of Art Museums and Galleries. These platforms have a total of 562 members, including 326 cultural institutions from 72 partner countries.

China is steadily expanding international cultural exchanges. China has launched the Cultural Silk Road program, and organized signature events such as the Happy Chinese New Year celebrations, the Nihao China tourism promotions, and the Silk Road: Artists' Rendezvous art exhibition.

It has worked with Brunei, Cambodia, Greece, Italy, Malaysia, Russia and ASEAN to co-host cultural and tourism activities at designated years. China and BRI partner countries have hosted events in a reciprocal manner, ranging from cultural relics exhibitions, film festivals, arts festivals, book fairs and music festivals, and jointly translated and promoted each other's publishing, radio, film and television programs. They have also implemented the BRI-themed theater arts creation and promotion project, the Belt and Road International Art Project, and the Belt and Road good-neighborliness cultural project, and worked to protect Asian cultural heritage. China has established 46 China cultural centers in 44 countries, of which 32 are partner countries. China has established 20 tourism offices in 18 countries, eight of which are in partner countries.

Educational exchanges and cooperation are extensive and profound. China has released the Education Action Plan for the Belt and Road Initiative to promote international education exchanges and cooperation. By the end of June 2023, China had signed agreements with 45 participating countries on the mutual recognition of higher education degrees.

China has set up the Silk Road Program under the Chinese Government Scholarship scheme. Some of China's provinces and Hong Kong and Macao SARs, as well as universities and research institutions have also set up scholarships for students from BRI partner countries.

Chinese universities and colleges have opened 313 Confucius Institutes and 315 Confucius Classrooms in 132 partner countries. The "Chinese Bridge" Summer Camp has invited nearly 50,000 young people from more than 100 partner countries to come to China for academic visits, and supported 100,000 Chinese language enthusiasts from 143 partner countries to learn Chinese and experience Chinese culture online.

Chinese universities and colleges have worked with more than 20 counterparts in partner countries from Asia, Africa and Europe to build a number of Luban Workshops – a professional training program dedicated to the sharing of expertise by China's vocational education institutions.

China and UNESCO have jointly held the International Youth Forum on Creativity and Heritage Along the Silk Roads and relevant activities in seven consecutive years, and established the Silk Roads Youth Research Grant which has funded 24 youth research projects. The Atomic Energy Scholarship of China has funded the education of nearly 200 Master's and Doctoral students in the field of peaceful use of nuclear energy for 26 BRI partner countries.

Participating countries have capitalized on the demonstration and driving role of the University Alliance and the Alliance of International Science Organizations (ANSO) under the BRI framework, and expanded international exchanges and cooperation in talent training and scientific research.

Media and think tank cooperation has yielded fruitful results. BRI participating countries have held the Media Cooperation Forum on Belt and Road six times, and established the Belt and Road Media Community. The China-Arab States Forum on Radio and Television Cooperation, the Forum on China-Africa Media Cooperation, the China-Cambodia Radio and Television Annual Regular Cooperation Conference, the ASEAN-China Media Cooperation Forum, the Lancang-Mekong Audiovisual Week, and other bilateral and multilateral cooperation mechanisms have been set up. International organizations such as the Asia-Pacific Broadcasting Union and the Arab States Broadcasting Union have become active and important platforms for building consensus among participating countries.

Media outlets in China and partner countries have jointly established the Belt and Road News Network, which launched the Silk Road Global News Awards. By the end of June 2023, the network's members had increased to 233 media outlets in 107 countries.

Think tank exchanges have become more frequent. The Advisory Council of the Belt and Road Forum for International Cooperation was established in 2018. The Silk Road Think Tank Association has recruited 122 partners in Asia, Africa, Europe, and Latin America. Sixteen Chinese and foreign think tanks have established the Belt and Road Studies Network.

People-to-people exchanges are constantly expanding. Non-governmental organizations (NGOs) continue to strengthen cooperation with the goals of benefiting the people, improving their lives, and connecting their hearts. At the people-to-people ties sub-forum of the Second Belt and Road Forum for International Cooperation, Chinese and foreign NGOs, including China NGO Network for International Exchanges, combined to launch the Silk Road Community Building Initiative, encouraging Chinese and foreign NGOs to establish nearly 600 cooperative partnership pairings and carry out more than 300 cooperation projects for improving people's lives. Of these, some brand projects have achieved a wide impact, including the Shenzhen-Lancang-Mekong Cooperation to benefit the people in the Lancang-Mekong region with Shenzhen's advanced products and technology, the Panda Pack Project to provide primary school students with learning supplies, and the Brightness Journey program to provide free cataract surgery to those in need.

Cities from 60-plus BRI partner countries have formed more than 1,000 pairs of friendly cities with their Chinese counterparts. A total of 352 NGOs from 72 countries and regions have formed a Silk Road NGO Cooperation Network, carrying out over 500 projects and various other activities, and becoming an important platform for exchanges and cooperation between NGOs in participating countries.

6. Steady progress in new areas

Leveraging their respective strengths, participating countries have continued to expand BRI cooperation into new fields and created innovative cooperation models, achieving great progress in building a healthy, green, innovative and digital Silk Road and further broadening the space for international cooperation.

Notable achievements have been made in health cooperation. To establish closer partnerships in health cooperation, participating countries are working hard to build a Health Silk Road and a global community of health for all. By the end of June 2023, China had signed an MoU with the

WHO on health cooperation in BRI partner countries, inked health cooperation agreements with more than 160 countries and international organizations, and initiated or participated in nine international and regional health cooperation mechanisms, including China-Africa Health Cooperation, China-Arab States Health Cooperation, and China-ASEAN Health Cooperation.

Relying on mechanisms and platforms such as the Belt & Road Health Professionals Development Alliance, the Belt & Road Hospital Cooperation Alliance, the Belt & Road Health Policy Research Network, and the China-ASEAN Human Resources Training Program of Health Silk Road (2020-2022), China has helped BRI partner countries to train tens of thousands of professionals in health management, public health and medical research. It has also dispatched medical teams to 58 partner countries, and provided free treatment for nearly 10,000 cataract patients in more than 30 partner countries through the Brightness Journey program. In addition, China has sent several rounds of medical aid to island states of the South Pacific, and carried out international medical cooperation with neighboring countries, including countries of the Greater Mekong Subregion, Central Asian countries, and Mongolia.

After the outbreak of Covid-19, China provided assistance to more than 120 BRI partner countries to combat the pandemic, and sent 38 expert medical teams to 34 countries. It started the Initiative for Belt and Road Partnership on Covid-19 Vaccines Cooperation together with 31 countries, delivered more than 2 billion doses of vaccines to partner countries, and conducted joint vaccine production with more than 20 countries, improving vaccine affordability and accessibility in developing countries.

In addition, China has signed documents on traditional medicine cooperation with 14 BRI partner countries; eight partner countries have taken measures to support the development of traditional Chinese medicine (TCM) within the framework of their respective legal systems; 30 overseas TCM centers have been built; and 100-plus TCM drugs have been registered and marketed in partner countries.

Remarkable progress has been achieved in green and low-carbon

development. China is working together with partner countries and international organizations to build a cooperation mechanism for green and low-carbon development under the BRI framework, promote green development, and address climate change.

China has issued documents such as the Guidance on Promoting Green Belt and Road and the Guidelines on Jointly Promoting Green Development of the Belt and Road, and set itself the ambitious goal of forming a basic framework of green development through BRI cooperation by 2030. China has also signed an MoU with the United Nations Environment Programme on building a green Belt and Road for 2017-2022, reached environmental cooperation agreements with more than 30 countries and international organizations, launched the Initiative for Belt and Road Partnership on Green Development together with 31 countries, formed the Belt and Road Initiative International Green Development Coalition with more than 150 partners from 40-plus countries, and established the Belt and Road Energy Partnership with 32 countries.

China has pledged to stop building new coal-fired power stations overseas, and to actively build green finance platforms and international cooperation mechanisms. It stands ready to cooperate with partner countries on research into biodiversity conservation, safeguarding the eco-environmental security of the Maritime Silk Road, building the Belt and Road Big Data Service Platform on Ecological and Environmental Protection and the Belt and Road Environmental Technology Exchange and Transfer Center, and implementing the Green Silk Road Envoys Program.

China is actively promoting the Belt and Road South-South Cooperation Initiative on Climate Change. It has signed 47 South-South MoUs on climate change with 39 partner countries, built low-carbon demonstration zones with Laos, Cambodia, and Seychelles, carried out more than 70 climate change mitigation and adaptation projects with 30-plus developing countries, and trained more than 3,000 environment management personnel and experts from more than 120 countries.

In May 2023, China Eximbank, together with a dozen financial institutions including China Development Bank, and China Export & Credit Insurance Corporation, released the Initiative for Supporting Belt and Road Energy Transition with Green Finance, calling on all parties involved to strengthen support for green and low-carbon energy transition in BRI participating countries.

Cooperation in scientific and technological innovation is gathering speed. BRI participating countries are strengthening cooperation on innovation, facilitating technology transfer and knowledge sharing, optimizing the innovation-enabling environment, and pooling innovation resources. They are also building up their capacity for scientific and technological innovation through cooperation in major projects and talent training.

In October 2016, China released the Special Plan on Advancing Belt and Road Cooperation in Scientific and Technological Innovation. In May 2017, the Action Plan on Belt and Road Cooperation in Scientific and Technological Innovation was implemented, to increase the capacity for innovation in BRI participating countries through pragmatic measures such as joint research, technology transfer, exchanges in science, technology and culture, and cooperation between high-tech industrial parks.

By the end of June 2023, China had signed intergovernmental agreements on scientific and technological cooperation with more than 80 BRI partner countries, and 58 members had joined the ANSO. Since 2013, China has hosted more than 10,000 young scientists from partner countries in carrying out short-term research and exchanges in China, and trained more than 16,000 technicians and management professionals for partner countries; China has established nine cross-border technology transfer platforms targeting ASEAN, South Asia, Arab states, Africa, Latin America, and other regions; China has assisted 22 African countries to build 23 agricultural technology demonstration centers, and set up 50-plus BRI joint laboratories in areas such as agriculture, new energy, and health.

China has signed an agreement with the World Intellectual Property

Organization (WIPO) on strengthening BRI cooperation on intellectual property and additional agreements on subsequent revision and prolongation of the said agreement. China and the WIPO have jointly hosted twice the High-level Conference on Intellectual Property for Countries Along the Belt and Road, and released a joint initiative and a joint statement on strengthening cooperation on intellectual property. To date, China has established intellectual property cooperation relationships with more than 50 partner countries and international organizations, whose goal is to create an innovation and business environment in which the value of knowledge is duly respected.

Digital silk road cooperation presents numerous highlights. BRI participating countries have joined to create an open, fair, equitable and non-discriminatory environment for digital development by strengthening facilitation of and cooperation on rules and standards and promoting regional policy coordination.

By the end of 2022, China had signed MoUs on building the Digital Silk Road with 17 countries, MoUs on e-commerce cooperation with 30 countries, and MoUs on closer investment cooperation in the digital economy with 18 countries and regions. It has proposed and worked to launch the Global Initiative on Data Security, the Belt and Road Digital Economy International Cooperation Initiative, the initiative for building the ASEAN-China Partnership on Digital Economy Cooperation, the China-League of Arab States Cooperation Initiative on Data Security, the China + Central Asia Data Security Cooperation Initiative, and the BRICS Digital Economy Partnership Framework, among others. It also took lead in formulating the Framework of Standards on Cross-border E-commerce.

China is active in strengthening digital infrastructure connectivity and is stepping up work on digital corridors. Several international submarine cables have made positive progress, and 130 cross-border terrestrial cable systems have been built.

China has built many 5G base stations, data centers, cloud computing centers and smart cities, and promoted digital upgrading and transformation of traditional infrastructure such as ports, railways, highways, energy networks and water conservancy facilities.

A number of key projects such as the China-ASEAN Information Harbor, and the digital platform of China-Europe Railway Express and the China-Arab Online Silk Road is making good progress, and the DBAR Big Earth Data Platform has realized multilingual data sharing.

The construction of the Belt and Road Initiative Space Information Corridor has been a resounding success. China has built teleports connecting South Asia, Africa, Europe, and the Americas. The data from

---

Panel 2   Silk Road E-commerce expands new channels for economic and trade cooperation

Thriving new business models of international trade, represented by cross-border e-commerce and overseas warehouses, are providing better services and more choice to global consumers, and promoting global trade innovations. Silk Road E-commerce is an important means by which China can capitalize on its strengths in e-commerce technology application, model innovation and market size, expand economic and trade cooperation, and share the opportunities of digital development with BRI participants.

By the end of September 2023, China had established bilateral mechanisms of e-commerce cooperation with 30 countries on five continents; multilateral mechanisms had been built under the China-CEEC and China-Central Asia frameworks.

Activities such as the Silk Road E-commerce Platform of the Brand and Quality Online Shopping Festival and the Quality African Products Online Shopping Festival have yielded substantial results, and virtual country pavilions help partner countries to export their high-quality specialty products to the Chinese market.

The innovative Cloud Classroom program has provided livestreamed training sessions for more than 80 participating countries to reinforce their digital literacy.

Through consistently enriching the content and elevating the level of cooperation, Silk Road E-commerce has become a new platform for bilateral and multilateral economic and trade cooperation and a new strength in high-quality BRI cooperation.

remote sensing satellites under the China-Brazil Earth Resources Satellite (CBERS) program is widely used in multiple countries and fields. The BeiDou navigation satellite system (BDS-3) provides comprehensive services for China-Europe Railway Express, and in maritime transport and other fields.

China and a number of BRI partner countries and regions have combined to develop and launch communication or remote sensing satellites, and constructed satellite ground stations and other space infrastructure. Through the Regional Centre for Space Science and Technology Education in Asia and the Pacific (China) affiliated to the United Nations, China has trained a large number of space professionals for partner countries. Together with other countries and regions, China has built the China-GCC Joint Center for Lunar and Deep Space Exploration, the China-UAE Space Debris Joint Monitoring Center, the Lancang-Mekong Cooperation Center for Earth Observation Data, the China-ASEAN Satellite Remote Sensing Application Center, and the China-Africa Cooperation Center on Satellite Remote Sensing Application. The CNSA-GEO platform, the Belt and Road Analysis and Early Warning Platform for Typical Meteorological Disasters, and the Natural Resources Satellite Remote Sensing Cloud Service Platform now serve many partner countries.

IV. Injecting Positive Energy into World Peace and Development

Over the past decade, BRI cooperation has witnessed remarkable results. It has opened up new space for world economic growth, built a new platform for international trade and investment, reinforced the development capacity of relevant countries and improved people's lives, sought ways to improve the global governance system, and brought greater certainty and stability to a world fraught with turbulence and change. The BRI has boosted China's development and benefited the rest of the world.

1. Bringing tangible benefits to participating countries

Development is an eternal theme for humanity. The BRI has focused on the fundamental issue of development, addressing the weaker links and bottlenecks that hinder development, building new engines for economic development, and creating a new development environment and space for participating countries. This has strengthened their confidence and their capacity for development, and improved their people's lives. The initiative has contributed to addressing global development imbalance and advancing modernization in all countries.

Boosting development in participating countries. Over the last 10 years, the BRI has addressed the major bottlenecks restricting connectivity and economic growth in most of the developing countries. A large number of infrastructure projects have been built, with significant progress for participating countries in the construction of railways, highways, pipelines, shipping, energy, communications and other basic public service facilities. This has improved local living and working conditions and the development environment, and boosted their capacity for independent economic development.

Some engineering projects with a long construction cycle are like seeds sown in a field, gradually generating comprehensive benefits for the long term. Connectivity in infrastructure has effectively reduced the cost for countries to participate in international trade, increased their access to the global economy, and stimulated the potential and impetus for their development. Research by the Asian Development Bank shows that lowering a land-locked country's trade costs by 10 percent through improvement in infrastructure could increase its exports by 20 percent.

Industrial capacity cooperation has promoted industrialization, digitization, informatization, and the structural upgrading of industries in participating countries. It has helped them to form competitive industrial systems and expand the breadth and depth of their participation in the international division of labor and cooperation, creating more opportunities and greater space for development.

China has actively conducted international cooperation in emergency management. It has sent rescue teams to Nepal, Mozambique, Türkiye and other countries to carry out humanitarian operations following earthquakes and floods, and provided emergency supplies and technical support to Tonga and Madagascar, among other countries.

Building poverty reduction capacity in participating countries. Developing countries still face the challenge of problems related to food. China has taken an active part in global food and agriculture governance. It has released the Vision and Action on Jointly Promoting Agricultural Cooperation Along the Belt and Road with partner countries, and signed more than 100 agricultural and fishery cooperation documents with almost 90 partner countries and international organizations. Its trade in agricultural products with BRI partners has reached US$139.4 billion. China has sent more than 2,000 agricultural experts and technicians to over 70 countries and regions, and introduced more than 1,500 agricultural technologies such as *Juncao* and hybrid rice to many of these countries. It has helped with rural poverty reduction in Asia, Africa, the South Pacific, Latin America, and the Caribbean, developing modern agriculture and helping to increase farmers' incomes.

Boosting employment is an important element of poverty reduction. In the process of BRI cooperation, China has helped to construct industrial parks with participating countries and provided guidance for Chinese enterprises to create jobs for local residents through high-level industrial cooperation. The jobs provided to locals have helped to lift their families out of poverty. A McKinsey survey revealed that Chinese firms in Africa recruited 89 percent of their employees locally, contributing to local employment in an effective way.

The World Bank has estimated that by 2030, BRI-related investments could lift 7.6 million out of extreme poverty and 32 million out of moderate poverty.

Panel 3   *Juncao* poverty alleviation wins worldwide acclaim

China's *Juncao* technology makes comprehensive and efficient utilization of three major agricultural resources – light, heat and water. It makes circular production based on plants, animals, and fungi possible, combines economic, social and environmental benefits, and supports food, energy, and eco-environmental security.

Juncao technology was first launched as an official assistance project in 2001, in Papua New Guinea. Over the last two decades, China has hosted more than 270 international training courses on *Juncao* technology, for more than 10,000 trainees from 106 countries. It has also established *Juncao* technology demonstration centers or bases in 13 countries in Asia, Africa, Latin America, and the South Pacific region. Today, *Juncao* technology is being applied in more than 100 countries, creating hundreds of thousands of green jobs for local youth and women. A former cabinet minister of Papua New Guinea named his daughter Juncao. The people of Lesotho have produced folk songs in praise of *Juncao* which are still popular today. In 2017, *Juncao* technology was listed as a key project of the China-UN Peace and Development Fund, contributing more Chinese know-how to the cause of international poverty reduction.

Delivering notable results in projects that improve people's lives. Chinese firms have repaired and maintained bridges to make it easier for local residents to travel. They have drilled wells to meet local villagers' needs for drinking water. They have installed street lamps for pedestrians to see clearly on their way home at night. Many such seemingly small projects have solved urgent problems for local people and improved their daily lives. They have brought tangible benefits to the people of participating countries, and increased their sense of gain, fulfillment and security.

Over the last 10 years, Chinese firms have launched more than 300 poverty alleviation, health care and rehabilitation, and Happy Home projects in participating countries. They have helped with the construction of the headquarters of Africa Centres for Disease Control and Prevention and the China-Pakistan Fraternity Emergency Care Center in Gwadar, Pakistan. They have also helped Cameroon, Ethiopia, Djibouti and other countries to provide clean drinking water for the local people.

The Silk Road Community Building Initiative has promoted projects in more than 20 areas, including poverty alleviation and disaster relief,

---

**Panel 4   The Sweet Spring Project improves people's wellbeing
in the Lancang-Mekong Region**

In January 2020, China launched the Lancang-Mekong Sweet Spring Project, a project demonstrating rural water supply safety technology in the Lancang-Mekong region. Water supply facilities were built in rural areas of Cambodia, Laos, and Myanmar, markedly improving local water supply capacity and safety. Through this project, China has helped to improve the lives of local people and played an active role in helping the Lancang-Mekong region to access clean water and sanitation, one of the United Nations 2030 Sustainable Development Goals.

As of December 2022, 62 demonstration sites had been built in the project area, ensuring safe drinking water for more than 7,000 local people. China had also trained over 400 personnel from the region in rural water supply management and project management.

humanitarian assistance, environmental protection, and women's exchanges and cooperation. Related activities have had an extensive impact.

2. Adding vitality to economic globalization

Against a rising tide of de-globalization, the BRI is committed to global connectivity and interconnected development. It has further opened up the main arteries of economic globalization, facilitated the flow of information, capital, technology, product, industry and people, and promoted closer and broader international cooperation. By expanding economic globalization and distributing its benefits fairly, the BRI aims to promote global development that is balanced, coordinated, inclusive and shared by all, and that brings win-win cooperation and common prosperity.

Boosting the momentum for global development. The BRI has connected the vibrant East Asia economic circle at one end, the developed European economic circle at the other, and the countries in between with huge potential for economic development, and fostered closer economic cooperation with African and Latin American countries. It has formed a new global development dynamic in which the Eurasian continent is fully connected with the Pacific, Indian and Atlantic oceans, and the land is integrated with the sea. It has expanded the scope and coverage of the international division of labor in a broader economic and geographical space, and enlarged the global market, which ultimately promoted new global economic growth.

At the same time, through infrastructure connectivity, the BRI has proved a catalyst to international investment and boosted global interest in and enthusiasm for investment in infrastructure, which provides economic growth and rapid development in participating countries. These efforts have effectively addressed the shortage of international public goods and provided sustained impetus for world economic growth.

Encouraging deeper regional economic cooperation. In strengthening infrastructure connectivity, the BRI promotes connectivity between countries in many directions and various fields. The BRI turns dots into lines and lines into fields, gradually amplifying the radiation effect of development. It encourages countries to coordinate economic policies, systems and mechanisms, and innovate cooperation models, conduct broader, deeper and closer regional cooperation, and jointly create an open, inclusive and balanced regional economic cooperation architecture that benefits all. It has facilitated a freer and more orderly flow of economic factors, more efficient allocation of resources, and deeper integration of markets, and upgraded economic and trade connectivity and vitality between countries and regions, and the overall position of participating countries in global industry chains, supply chains, and value chains.

Participating countries have made full use of their own factor endowments to integrate, coordinate, and upgrade their industry chains, promote industrial complementarity, and improve the efficiency of division of labor. They have broken down trade barriers and market monopolies, unleashed internal and cross-border consumption potential, and expanded the scale of regional markets. Through technology transfer and cooperation in industrial cooperation, they have established technology interaction and interdependence, strengthened capacity for innovation, and promoted leapfrog development.

Promoting global trade. The BRI supports the liberalization and facilitation of trade and investment by building transport and information infrastructure in a planned and progressive manner. It has eliminated internal, transnational, and inter-regional transport bottlenecks and barriers to trade and investment cooperation, made cross-border logistics and foreign trade easier and more convenient, and increased the efficiency of domestic and international cooperation. It has built up an all-round, multi-level and complex network of unimpeded trade, creating a new dynamic and greatly facilitating global trade.

At the same time, the BRI has made participating countries more attractive to quality global capital, and contributed to rising direct cross-border investment in these countries. In 2022, cross-border direct investment inflows in Southeast Asia accounted for 17.2 percent of the global total, 9 percentage points higher than in 2013. The inflow of FDI into Kazakhstan grew by a historical high of 83 percent year on year.

World Bank study – "Belt and Road Economics: Opportunities and Risks of Transport Corridors" – estimates that prior to the BRI, the six corridor economies undertrade with each other and the rest of the world by 30 percent on average and they fall short of their absorptive potential of FDI by 70 percent. Transport infrastructure projects under the BRI would reduce trade costs for the world by 1.8 percent, and reduce trade costs along the China-Central Asia-West Asia economic corridor by 10 percent. This has greatly facilitated global trade and boosted economic growth. The study projects that trade growth would range between 2.8 and 9.7 percent for corridor economies and between 1.7 and 6.2 percent worldwide, and global real income is expected to increase by 0.7 to 2.9 percent.

Maintaining the stability of global supply chains. An efficient and interconnected international transport corridor established under the BRI framework plays an important role in maintaining the stability and smooth flow of global supply chains.

During the Covid-19 outbreak, ports and logistics companies canceled or reduced services for shipping and freight transport, which had dealt a hard blow to those global supply chains which were highly dependent on shipping.

Panel 5　China-Laos Railway
turns land-locked Laos into a land-linked country

The China-Laos Railway is an electrified railway directly connecting Kunming City of China with Vientiane City of Laos. It is the first transnational railway built under the BRI, funded mainly by Chinese investment, operated jointly by the two sides, and connected directly with China's railway network. The 1,035-km-long railway officially opened for business on December 3, 2021. On April 13, 2023, the China-Laos Railway started cross-border passenger services, with bullet trains running directly in both directions between Kunming and Vientiane.

As an important part of the central section of the pan-Asia railway network, the China-Laos Railway has helped Laos to realize its long-cherished dream of becoming a land-linked country from a landlocked one. It has promoted transport, investment, logistics and tourism, and injected new impetus into the economic development of Laos and areas along the line. By August 31, 2023, the railway had recorded a total of 20.79 million passenger trips and carried 25.22 million tonnes of cargo. It has become a safe and efficient international passageway connecting Laos with its neighboring countries and regions and generating mutual benefits.

The China-Laos Railway is a project that wins the heart of the people and an example of clean management. The leaders of China and Laos reached an important agreement on making the China-Laos Railway a clean project. The discipline inspection and supervision departments of the two countries established a government-level supervision and coordination mechanism, and the enterprises involved in construction had taken incorruptibility as a top priority from project design and deployment through to implementation and review. Effective systems were in place to enforce this principle throughout construction, and new methods of cooperation to fight corruption were tested. Through the efforts of both parties, the China-Laos Railway has become a road of friendship, integrity and happiness.

According to a World Bank study – "From Landlocked to Land-Linked: Unlocking the Potential of Lao-China Rail Connectivity" – the China-Laos Railway could raise Laos' aggregate income by up to 21 percent over the long term. The transit trade through Laos along the line is estimated to reach 3.9 million tonnes per year by 2030, which would include a shift of an estimated 1.5 million tonnes of trade from maritime transport to the railway.

As a key output of BRI cooperation, the China-Europe Railway Express effectively sustained rail connectivity on the Eurasian continent, boosted sea-rail, road-rail, air-rail, and other forms of multi-modal transport, and opened up a new transport corridor for the Eurasian continental supply chain. Together with the innovations in customs clearance such as the Customs-Train Operators Partnership for Secure and Expedited Clearance of CR Express Carried Goods (C-TOP), Rapid Customs Clearance for rail service, China made an important contribution to stabilizing the global economy.

Several well-known international logistics associations have stated publicly that the China-Europe Railway Express has provided the world with a reliable logistics solution that can effectively alleviate tensions in the global supply chain and strengthen international logistics.

3. Providing new solutions for improving global governance

The deficit in global governance presents a severe challenge to the whole world. The BRI supports genuine multilateralism, and cherishes shared growth through consultation and collaboration in global governance. It advocates dialogue rather than confrontation, removing walls rather than erecting walls, integration rather than decoupling, and inclusiveness rather than exclusion. This is a new paradigm for state-to-state relations that shapes the international order towards greater justice and equality.

Gaining more recognition for the concept of global governance. The BRI's core principles of "extensive consultation, joint contribution, and shared benefits" have appeared in important documents from international organizations and mechanisms, including the UN and the Forum on China-Africa Cooperation.

The vision of a global community of shared future has developed deep roots. A number of bilateral communities have been built between China and other countries, including Laos and Pakistan. Steady progress has been made in building multilateral communities, including those between China and Africa, the Arab States, Latin America, ASEAN, Central Asia and Pacific Island countries. Practical results have been achieved in building communities in functional areas, including cyber space, maritime cooperation, and health for all.

According to the China's National Image Global Survey released by the Academy of Contemporary China and World Studies in 2020, the BRI is the Chinese proposal with the highest level of acceptance overseas, with more than 70 percent of respondents recognizing the positive impact of the BRI on individuals, states and global governance. European think tank Bruegel released a paper titled "Global Trends in Countries' Perceptions of the Belt and Road Initiative" in April 2023, which noted that the BRI is generally positively received in the world, and Central Asia and sub-Saharan Africa, in particular, exhibit strongly positive sentiment towards the BRI.

Improving multilateral governance mechanisms. The BRI upholds the principles of mutual respect and equality, openness, inclusiveness, and win-win results. It enshrines multilateralism by securing international fairness and justice, and protecting the rights and interests of developing countries.

The BRI helps improve the existing multilateral governance mechanisms by firmly upholding the authority and status of the UN, and striving to consolidate and strengthen the stature and effectiveness of global multilateral governance platforms such as the WTO. It actively promotes new multilateral governance mechanisms such as the Asian Infrastructure Investment Bank, and works with participating parties to promote governance mechanisms in emerging areas such as the deep sea, polar regions, outer space, internet and artificial intelligence.

The BRI has strengthened the position and role of developing countries and emerging economies in the world market system, and increased their discourse power in regional and global economic governance. As a result, the aspirations and concerns of developing countries are increasingly included in the global agenda – a significant improvement in global governance.

Innovating and optimizing global governance rules. Taking into account the differences in the level of economic development, factor endowments, and cultural and religious traditions of relevant parties, the BRI has not preset any rules and standards, nor does it draw ideological lines. Instead, it formulates new rules to solve new problems through full consultation and in-depth exchanges, based on the wishes and needs of the parties involved.

BRI participating countries seek synergy in their strategies, plans, mechanisms, projects, and rules and standards, which helps to optimize the rules for BRI cooperation, and supports the transition from opening up based on the flow of goods and factors of production to opening up based on rules and related institutions. Some rules and standards with strong potential for universal application have been formulated in this process, which has effectively filled in gaps in the global governance system in these areas.

4. Garnering strength for the progress of human civilization

Exchanges and mutual learning among civilizations drive human progress and global peace and development. In contrast to those who persist with black and white thinking, concoct such concepts as the "clash of civilizations" and "superiority of Western civilization", and provoke large-scale ideological confrontation, the BRI advocates equality, mutual learning, dialogue, and inclusiveness among civilizations, and promotes the shared values of humanity. It has charted a path of exchanges and mutual learning among civilizations for all to prosper individually and collectively, in order to achieve closer ties among peoples and link up the cultures and hearts of all countries.

Improving the mechanisms for people-to-people exchanges. People-to-people exchanges cover a wide range of areas, including politics, culture, the arts, sports, and education. The global influence of various multilateral and bilateral political party exchange mechanisms has increased with the creation of mechanisms such as the CPC and World Political Parties Summit, and the CPC in Dialogue with World Political Parties High-level Meeting. The leading role of high-level inter-party exchanges garners consensus and strengths for stronger people-to-people ties.

Various BRI cooperation mechanisms have emerged, including the Silk Road Think Tank Association, the Belt and Road Initiative Tax Administration Cooperation Mechanism, the ANSO, the Belt and Road Health Professionals Development Alliance, the Silk Road International League of Theaters, and the Silk Road International Museum Alliance.

The emergence of such mechanisms has facilitated people-to-people exchanges in diverse forms, promoting mutual understanding, mutual respect, and mutual appreciation among the peoples of all countries.

China, Kyrgyzstan, Iran and other Central and West Asian countries jointly launched the Alliance for Cultural Heritage in Asia – the first international cooperation mechanism regarding Asian cultural heritage – to protect cultural heritage, the tangible carriers of civilization. The projects under the framework of the alliance, for example the protection and restoration of Uzbekistan's ancient city of Khiva, have been highly commended by UNESCO.

Creating quality brand projects and activities. Several projects and activities have become popular and attracted widespread public participation. Examples include the Silk Road (Dunhuang) International Cultural Expo, the Belt and Road/Great Wall International Folk Culture and Arts Festival, the Silk Road International Arts Festival, the Maritime Silk Road International Arts Festival, the Belt and Road Youth Story, and the Tea Road Cultural Tourism Expo.

Cultural and people-to-people exchange programs have won wide acclaim, including the Silk Road Community Building Initiative, the Kit of Love of medical supplies, Luban Workshops of technical vocational training, the Happy Spring well-drilling project, the Brightness Journey program of free cataract surgeries, the Panda Pack Project of school supplies, the Amity Torch Program of educational assistance, the Belt and Road Tour of Acupuncture-Moxibustion promoting traditional Chinese medicine therapies, and the Confucius Classroom of cultural exchanges.

As these goodwill activities, quality brands, and signature projects continue to emerge, they have become an important means through which all parties can join to strengthen people-to-people ties. This reinforces the sense of identity and belonging of the peoples of all BRI participating countries.

Galvanizing the power of youth. The future of the BRI belongs to the youth. Over the last 10 years, young people in participating countries

Panel 6　Luban Workshops

Lu Ban was an ancient Chinese woodcraft master and inventor. The Luban Workshop, an international exchanges platform for vocational education named after the master, has become a well-known Chinese initiative for introducing Chinese vocational education internationally. Luban Workshops are mainly opened in ASEAN, SCO and African countries.

The workshops offer a combination of academic education and vocational training, and share the approach, technology, and standards of Chinese vocational education. The project has built training centers, provided advanced teaching equipment, and sent Chinese teachers and technicians to help train technical personnel for participating countries.

Since the first Luban Workshop opened in Thailand in 2016, Chinese universities and colleges have established dozens of Luban Workshops with more than 20 participating countries in Asia, Africa, and Europe, which offer courses in more than 70 directions, including industrial robots, new energy, and the Internet of Things. The workshops have trained tens of thousands of technical personnel for participating countries, helping more young people to find work.

Though small in scale, the workshops respond to people's desire for a better life, and facilitate the realization of the dream of common development.

have engaged proactively in people-to-people exchanges and programs that create a better life. The younger generation has galvanized the tremendous power of youth for strengthening people-to-people bonds and realizing common development.

The Chinese Youth Global Partnership has received a positive response from all over the world. More than 100 national youth organizations and international organizations have established ties and cooperative relations with China.

Sixteen events of the Belt and Road Youth Story have attracted more than 1,500 young people from participating countries. Focusing on poverty alleviation and reduction, climate change, and pandemic response cooperation, participants shared with the audience their stories and experience in promoting social development and their own development, which vividly demonstrated the right way to view the world from the perspective of appreciation, mutual learning, and sharing.

Other successful activities have also taken place, including the Silk Road Incubator Youth Entrepreneurship Program and the China-Central and Eastern Europe International Forum for Young Innovators, which have become important platforms for the youth of participating countries to strengthen friendly exchanges and cooperation.

V. Pursuing Steady and Sustained Progress in High-Quality BRI Cooperation

Experience over the past 10 years has proved that BRI cooperation responds to the call of the times and benefits the peoples in participating countries. It thus enjoys popular support. It is a path for all participating countries to achieve modernization and a path of hope leading to a bright future. It is resilient and vigorous, and offers broad prospects.

Currently, the world is in a period of turbulence and transformation. Rivalry and competition between major countries is escalating; the geopolitical situation remains tense; global economic recovery is yet to appear over the horizon; cold-war and zero-sum mentalities are resurgent; unilateralism, protectionism and hegemonism are proliferating; populism is making a noticeable resurgence. A new round of technological revolution and industrial transformation has given rise to ever fiercer competition; the deficit in peace, development, security and governance is growing; foreseeable and unforeseeable risks are rising rapidly around the globe. All of this presents unprecedented challenges to humanity.

Certain countries overstretch the concept of national security and seek "decoupling" in the name of "derisking"; they trample international economic and trade order and market rules, and endanger the security and stability of international industrial supply chains; they also impede international humanistic and technological exchanges and cooperation. Their actions raise obstacles to the long-term development of humanity. In a world full of uncertainties and instabilities, all countries should urgently bridge differences through dialogue, oppose rifts with unity, and promote development through cooperation. Against this backdrop, the BRI becomes more meaningful and is an initiative to be welcomed.

In the long term, the trends towards multipolarity and economic globalization, the trend of our times towards peace, development, cooperation and win-win outcomes, and the desire of the people of all countries for a better life will remain unchanged. So will the momentum behind the rise of developing countries as a whole and the status and responsibilities of China as the largest developing country in the world. The BRI faces some difficulties and challenges; however, its future is promising, as long as all countries can manage threats, address challenges, and advance cooperation by considering both their own long-term interests and the overall interests of humanity.

As a large and developing country that meets its responsibilities, China will continue to promote the BRI as its overarching plan and its top-level design for opening up and win-win international cooperation. It will open up on a larger scale, across more areas, and in greater depth. It will steadily expand institutional opening up with regard to rules, regulations, management and standards, and establish new mechanisms for a more open economy. It will achieve high-quality new development through opening up, and provide new opportunities for the world with that development.

China is ready to increase its resource input in global cooperation and do its best to support and help other developing countries to progress faster. It will work to achieve a greater say for emerging economies and developing countries in global governance, and contribute to the common development of all countries. China sincerely welcomes more countries and international organizations to join in cooperation under the BRI, and will support any initiative that can genuinely help developing countries build infrastructure and achieve shared progress, thereby promoting global connectivity and sustainable development.

All countries involved in high-quality BRI cooperation are equal participants, contributors and beneficiaries. China is willing to work with all other parties to strengthen confidence, maintain resolve, and advance

BRI cooperation in the spirit of extensive consultation, joint contribution and shared benefits. China hopes that all parties can consolidate the foundations, expand the reach, and optimize the projects of cooperation. Working together, all can create new opportunities, seek new drivers, create new space, and share new fruits of development. All can form closer partnerships in health, connectivity, green development, opening up, inclusiveness, innovation and clean government, and all can thereby participate in fruitful BRI cooperation and provide new and powerful impetus for building a global community of shared future.

Conclusion

The Belt and Road Initiative has given new life to a history of cultural exchanges that dates back more than two millennia, and has inspired more than 150 countries with the zeal to realize new dreams.

In the 10 years that have passed since its launch, cooperation under the BRI framework has brought remarkable and profound change to the world and become a major milestone in the history of humanity.

The BRI is a long-term, transnational and systematic global project of the 21st century. It has succeeded in taking its first step on a long journey. Continuing from this new starting point, the BRI will demonstrate greater creativity and vitality, become more open and inclusive, and generate new opportunities for both China and the rest of the world.

In the future, the BRI will find itself confronted by new difficulties. But as long as all parties involved combine their forces, work together and persevere, we will be able to overcome these problems and raise our extensive consultation, joint contribution, and shared benefits to new heights. Cooperation will thrive, and the BRI can look forward to an even brighter future.

China stands ready to work with other countries to pursue closer and more fruitful cooperation under the BRI framework, implement the Global Development Initiative, the Global Security Initiative and the Global Civilization Initiative, and build an open, inclusive, clean and beautiful world that enjoys lasting peace, universal security and common prosperity. Our goals are to pass on the torch of peace from generation to generation, sustain development, ensure that civilizations flourish, and build a global community of shared future.

Development of China's Distant-Water Fisheries

The State Council Information Office of
the People's Republic of China

October 2023

Preamble

Sustainable utilization of the ocean is essential to the survival and development of humanity. China was one of the first countries to utilize the ocean's resources. More than 4,000 years ago, people in coastal areas of China were already living off the sea and fishing and had started exploring the ocean and utilizing its resources along with the people of other countries.

Since its distant-water fisheries industry (DWF) first emerged in 1985, China has been conducting practical and mutually beneficial cooperation with other countries in accordance with relevant bilateral fisheries agreements or arrangements. Conforming to the United Nations Convention on the Law of the Sea and other applicable international laws, it is deeply involved in multilateral fisheries governance and regional fisheries management under the framework of the United Nations (UN). It actively exercises the right to utilize high seas fisheries resources, and it fulfills to the letter the relevant obligations concerning resource conservation and management.

Since the 18th National Congress of the Communist Party of China in 2012, under the guidance of Xi Jinping Thought on Socialism with Chinese Characteristics for a New Era, China has earnestly advanced the vision of a global community of shared future and a maritime community of shared future, steadily strengthened the conservation of the marine eco-environment, and consistently followed the path of green and sustainable development of the DWF sector. In order to realize scientific conservation and sustainable utilization of fisheries resources and achieve high-quality DWF development, China is committed to optimizing the industrial structure, promoting transformation and upgrading, improving quality and efficiency, strictly controlling the scale of development, strengthening standardized management, and combating illegal fishing.

The Chinese government is publishing this white paper to present a complete picture of China's philosophy, principles, and policies in the DWF sector and its success in honoring international agreements, to share with the world its experience in DWF administration, and to promote international cooperation and exchanges in this field.

I. High-Quality Development of China's DWF Sector

DWF is an important part of China's fishing industry. Based on win-win cooperation, security, stability, green and sustainable development, China has expanded international exchanges, conducted mutually beneficial cooperation through multiple channels and in multiple forms, kept to the path of high-quality development of the industry, and contributed to the development of the global DWF industry and the supply of aquatic products.

1. Steady development of international aquatic production and trade

Aquatic products are globally recognized as healthy foods and play a key role in global food and nutrition security. Sustainable aquaculture development and effective fisheries management are essential to ensuring the supply of aquatic products in the international market.

In recent years, international trade in aquatic products has grown significantly. According to statistics from the Food and Agriculture Organization of the United Nations (FAO), in 2020, the European Union (EU) was the largest single importing market, accounting for 16 percent of the global value of aquatic imports (excluding intra-EU trade), and the United States (US) was the largest importing country, accounting for 15 percent of the global value of aquatic imports. The top three exporting countries were China, Norway and Vietnam, with their exports accounting for 25 percent of the global total export value. According to statistics from the General Administration of Customs of China, China exported almost 3.75

million tonnes of aquatic products in 2020, and the worth of its exported aquatic products accounted for 12 percent of the global total. The main destinations included countries and regions such as the EU, the Association of Southeast Asian Nations, Japan, and the US. As the world's largest exporter of aquatic products, China has made a significant contribution to the global supply and consumption of aquatic products.

According to The State of World Fisheries and Aquaculture 2022 released by the FAO, global fisheries and aquaculture production reached an all-time record of 214 million tonnes in 2020. Within this figure, aquaculture production was 122.6 million tonnes, accounting for 57 percent. China is the world's largest source of aquatic products, with a total output of 65.5 million tonnes in 2020. Its aquaculture production – which reached 52.2 million tonnes in the year, or about 80 percent of its total aquatic products – also led the world, accounting for about 40 percent of the global total. The development of China's fisheries and aquaculture industry has made an important contribution to meeting its own and the world's demand for aquatic products, reducing the use and dependence on natural marine fisheries resources, and promoting the scientific conservation and sustainable use of global fisheries resources.

2. China's contribution to the world's DWF development

The world's DWF has a long history, with detailed fisheries statistics dating back to the 1950s. Different countries and regions played a greater or lesser role in different historical periods. These countries and regions, along with other coastal countries, have played a positive role in developing and utilizing global marine fisheries resources, promoting the supply of marine foods and nutrition, and ensuring the livelihoods and development of coastal communities.

China's DWF sector began in 1985. Although it started relatively late, after more than 30 years of hard work, China has made significant progress. For many years, it has signed reciprocal cooperation agreements with relevant countries and regions in Asia, Africa, South America, and

Oceania. In accordance with these agreements and the laws and regulations of the relevant countries, China has established orderly fisheries cooperation with more than 40 countries and regions.

In accordance with the United Nations Convention on the Law of the Sea and other international laws, China has joined the International Commission for the Conservation of Atlantic Tunas, the Indian Ocean Tuna Commission, the Western and Central Pacific Fisheries Commission, the Commission for the Conservation of Antarctic Marine Living Resources, the Inter-American Tropical Tuna Commission, the South Pacific Regional Fisheries Management Organisation, the North Pacific Fisheries Commission, the Southern Indian Ocean Fisheries Agreement and other organizations, and approved the International Agreement to Prevent Unregulated Fishing in the High Seas of the Central Arctic Ocean. China attaches great importance to honoring the international DWF agreements. It actively fulfills the obligations of member states under multilateral fisheries treaties and regional fisheries management organizations (RFMOs), and carries out the due diligence obligations of flag states[1] for high seas fisheries that are not yet managed by RFMOs. It actively promotes the establishment of relevant RFMOs, continuously strengthens the regulation of the DWF sector, and champions the scientific conservation and sustainable utilization of global fisheries resources.

In 2022, China had 177 approved DWF enterprises and 2,551 DWF vessels (including 1,498 high seas fishing vessels) operating in the high seas of the Pacific, Indian and Atlantic oceans, and the seas around Antarctica, as well as in the waters under the jurisdiction of cooperating countries. The total catch for the year was around 2.33 million tonnes.

3. Achieving better development of China's DWF sector

As a developing country, China still lags somewhat behind developed countries in terms of fishing vessels and equipment, detection of fisheries

---

[1] A flag state refers to the country where a vessel is registered and whose flag the vessel flies.

resources, and the contribution of science and technology to industrial development. To adapt to and fulfill the new requirements of international fisheries governance, and based on its own development needs, China has released successive policy documents for DWF development, such as the National Plan for Fisheries Development in the 14th Five-Year Plan Period, the Guidelines on Promoting the High-Quality Development of Distant-Water Fishery in the 14th Five-Year Plan Period, the Action Plan for the "Regulation Improvement Year" of Distant-Water Fishery, and the Three-Year Action Plan for the Personnel Training of Distant-Water Fishery.

In the 14th Five-year Plan period (2021-2025) and beyond, China will make sustained efforts to promote the concentration and development of the entire DWF industrial chain, consolidate the foundations, increase the comprehensive governance capacity, and provide effective support. By optimizing the industrial structure, strengthening scientific and technological foundations, increasing regulatory capabilities, participating extensively in international fisheries governance, and improving the policy system, China aims to achieve high-quality development of its DWF sector. By 2025 China's total DWF output and the size of its DWF fleet will be stable, the overall quality and production efficiency of the industry will be much higher, the number of violations and accidents will be much lower, regional and industrial configuration will be further optimized, supervision and administration will be more effective, and a significant effort will be directed towards the implementation of international agreements.

II. Coordinating Resource Conservation and Sustainable Use

China puts equal emphasis on the protection and development of fisheries resources, and takes key measures such as voluntary moratoria on the high seas. It continuously strengthens fisheries resource conservation and management of the ecosystem, and pays close attention to climate change and biodiversity conservation. It has achieved remarkable results in promoting long-term sustainable use of fisheries resources.

1. Committing to long-term sustainable use of resources

Fisheries resources are renewable, and setting the allowable catch based on scientific assessment is therefore key to the sustainable use of these resources. China follows the path of green and sustainable development, balances conservation with exploitation of fisheries resources, and consistently advocates reasonable conservation and long-term sustainable use of resources on the basis of scientific assessment. China supports the fishing strategies set by the Western and Central Pacific Fisheries Commission, the Indian Ocean Tuna Commission and other relevant RFMOs. It manages fisheries resources properly and controls total fishing capacity. It strictly abides by the fishing quota systems and resource recovery plans adopted by RFMOs such as the International Commission for the Conservation of Atlantic Tunas, maintains the catches of relevant species within the quota, and supports the rational transfer of quotas and related fishing capacity.

Moratorium is a crucial tool for managing international fisheries and conserving resources. China began to implement voluntary moratoria on some high seas from 2020 onwards, with squid as the target species – this is an important measure to further strengthen the scientific conservation and sustainable use of high seas fisheries resources. This is in addition to the moratoria set by the regulations of RFMOs such as the seasonal moratorium measure for tuna purse seine in the West and Central Pacific Ocean.

Panel 1   Voluntary Moratoria on the High Seas

For the purpose of conservation and long-term sustainable use of fisheries resources on the high seas, in 2020 China tried out three-month voluntary fishing moratoria in parts of the high seas in the Southwest Atlantic Ocean and the East Pacific Ocean, and officially implemented the measure in 2021. Fishing bans were observed from July 1 to September 30 in the high seas of the Southwest Atlantic Ocean between 32 degrees and 44 degrees south and 48 degrees and 60 degrees west; while from September 1 to November 30, fishing bans covered the high seas in the East Pacific Ocean between 5 degrees north and 5 degrees south and 95 degrees to 110 degrees west. During this period, all Chinese squid jiggers and trawlers in the areas suspended operations.

In 2022, China further included the North Indian Ocean high seas into the scope of voluntary moratoria. Fishing bans were observed from July 1 to September 30 in parts of the high seas in the North Indian Ocean between the equator to 22 degrees north, and 55 degrees to 70 degrees east (excluding the jurisdictional waters under the Southern Indian Ocean Fisheries Agreement). During the moratorium period, Chinese squid jiggers and light purse seiners suspended fishing operations. Since then, high seas areas (or species) covered by China's DWF but not yet subject to the jurisdiction of RFMOs have been included in the scope of voluntary moratoria.

The Chinese government has strictly supervised the voluntary moratoria, and the relevant distant-water fishing vessels have strictly observed the moratoria. According to the resource monitoring data, the relative resource abundance of squid species in the Southwest Atlantic and Southeast Pacific has improved. As an innovative measure of China to actively conserve fisheries resources on the high seas, the voluntary moratorium mechanism has achieved remarkable results. The time and scope of the moratoria will be adjusted according to expert argumentation and public consultation based on the actual situation and resource conditions.

2. Strengthening the protection and management of bycatch species

China pays close attention to the sustainable development of bycatch species related to the target species, emphasizes the assessment and monitoring of bycatch species resources, and encourages and participates in information collection and scientific research. China effectively protects sharks, manta rays, sea turtles, seabirds and related marine mammals. It actively implements the FAO International Plan of Action for Conservation and Management of Sharks, and strictly abides by the conservation and management measures of RFMOs on sharks and other species. China has formulated and implemented the Action Plan of Sea Turtle Conservation (2019-2033), and has prepared an overall plan of sea turtle conservation and management at national level. China further strengthens conservation and management of marine mammals, requiring distant-water fishing vessels to strictly comply with the conservation and management measures of RFMOs, and to make sure safe release, data collection, information reporting, scientific research, and supervision and management of marine mammals and other bycatch species are well-conducted. China prohibits large-scale driftnet fishing on the high seas. It refuses to approve the construction of any new pair trawlers and large-scale lighting purse seiners with cod-end that have destructive effects on fisheries resources. It actively develops and puts into use eco-friendly fishing boats, fishing gears, and fishing technologies. It also offers more fishing gear options, promotes energy-saving attracting-fish lamp in squid jigging fishery and eco-friendly fishing gear and methods in tuna longline fisheries, and develops non-entanglement and biodegradable fish aggregation devices in tuna purse seine fishery. China carries out experiments to reduce the harm caused to seabirds and experiments on the safe release of marine mammals incidentally caught in Antarctic krill fishing, so as to protect bycatch species and rare and endangered species.

3. Focusing on climate change responses and biodiversity conservation

China attaches great importance to climate change responses and biodiversity conservation, and actively conducts research on the impact of climate change on the distribution, migration, and regeneration capacity of fish and other marine species. Research into the relations between climate change, fisheries resources, and the ecosystem and their management is also highly valued. In 2019, China supported the adoption of a climate change research proposal by the Western and Central Pacific Fisheries Commission and supported the Indian Ocean Tuna Commission in adopting a proposal to focus on climate change in the management of tuna fisheries in 2022. Marine biodiversity is closely related to marine ecosystem protection and marine sustainable development. China successfully chaired the 15th Meeting of the Conference of the Parties to the Convention on Biological Diversity, which was held in two phases, first in Kunming and then in Montreal. Thanks to its leadership efforts, the Kunming-Montreal Global Biodiversity Framework was agreed at the meeting. China actively participates in the negotiation of agreements on the conservation and sustainable use of marine biodiversity of areas beyond national jurisdiction and makes a significant contribution to global biodiversity conservation.

4. Stepping up resource conservation and international compliance efforts

In an effort to facilitate high-quality development, China implements policies to support both the conservation of fisheries resources and industrial restructuring in the new era. It promotes the high-quality development and modernization of its fisheries, creating a new dynamic for development. At the beginning of the 14th Five-year Plan period (2021-2025), China cancelled fuel subsidies for distant-water fishing vessels. It supports the construction of fisheries infrastructure and the green and circular development of the industry. It has worked to promote the research and conservation of fisheries resources and international compliance capabilities. China observes international conventions to protect international fisheries resources, and to research, monitor and evaluate fisheries resources. These efforts aim to promote the long-term sustainable use of fisheries resources and create a new dynamic for green and sustainable DWF development.

DWF enterprises and fishing vessels are the main entities that must comply with international conventions and operate in accordance with laws and regulations. In 2022, China formally implemented a compliance evaluation system for DWF enterprises. The performance of enterprises will directly influence administrative approval and policy support. Through a system of incentives and sanctions, China guides enterprises to continuously improve their management systems, strictly implement management measures, avoid violations, and effectively improve their performance. This system, which has attracted the attention of all sides, has effectively promoted the standardized management and international compliance capability of DWF enterprises, and won widespread recognition.

Panel 2   Compliance Evaluation System for DWF Enterprises

In order to increase the international compliance capability of DWF enterprises, to promote the high-quality development of DWF, and to promote the conservation and long-term sustainable use of global fisheries resources, China began to pilot a compliance evaluation system in 2019, which was fully implemented in 2022. The system includes quantitative indicators to measure management systems, implementation status, resource conservation, scientific and technological innovation, social responsibility, and violation of laws and regulations. It includes 3 first-level indicators, 10 second-level indicators, and 60 third-level indicators. The annual performance score of an enterprise is determined based on self-evaluation, preliminary examination by local authorities, and examination by the national fisheries authority.

In 2022, the overall compliance of enterprises engaged in DWF was good. The evaluation has increased the companies' awareness and capabilities in terms of compliance. Enterprises are making more active use of green and environmentally friendly fishing gears and methods. Additionally, they are engaging more actively in tasks related to electronic logbook, electronic monitoring, national fisheries observer, and they have improved various work practices related to operation safety and environmental protection.

III. Fulfilling the Flag State Duties in All Respects

As a responsible fishing nation, China strictly observes the United Nations Convention on the Law of the Sea and other multilateral agreements on fisheries it has joined. It performs its duties as a flag state[1] in terms of the controls over total output and the number of fishing vessels, data collection and reporting, national fisheries observer program, etc., producing positive outcomes.

1. Continuing to improve the DWF licensing system

China has put in place a comprehensive DWF licensing system and relevant measures. No Chinese DWF vessel is permitted to work before going through registration and examination procedures and getting the authority's approval in accordance with China's Fisheries Law and the Administrative Regulations for Distant-Water Fisheries. Chinese DWF fleets fishing in certain sea areas have fulfilled registering procedures as required by authorized RFMOs. Multiple government departments have strengthened the management of DWF vessels by measures including examination and approval, registration and decommissioning, and fishing licensing. They have also issued standard format documents for fishing vessels such as the Fishing License of the People's Republic of China (High Seas).

---

[1] The flag state is obliged to fulfill certain duties when allowing ships to fly its flag, including: exercise its control on technical matters, perform competency management of masters, officers and other crew members, restrict and protect the ships in accordance with internal laws, ensure the ships conform to international conventions, and others.

2. Implementing input and output control

China rigorously abides by the restrictions on the number and tonnage of fishing vessels and the species-based fishing quotas imposed by RFMOs. Its DWF sector remained stable during the 13th Five-year Plan period (2016-2020), and will continue to be under strict control during the 14th Five-year Plan period (2021-2025), with the goals of keeping the number of DWF vessels below 3,000 and their output around 2.3 million tonnes. The Chinese government announced in 2021 that China will not increase squid jiggers nor expand its squid fleets on the high seas, and formulated and implemented an individual vessel quota program on Pacific saury; these have been effective in regulating fishing activity. China strictly conforms to conservation and management measures such as seasonal and area fishing ban imposed by RFMOs, and has put in place voluntary ban for its fishing fleets on the high seas.

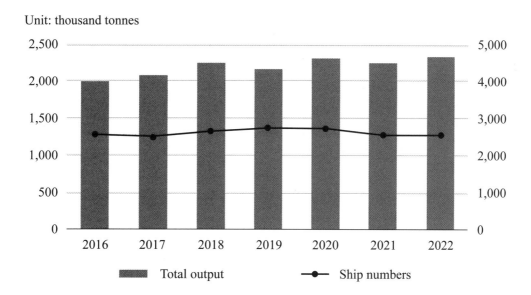

Figure 1 Total output and ship numbers of China's DWF sector since the 13th Five-year Plan period

Source of data: National Data Center for Distant-Water Fisheries of China

3. Gradually establishing a complete data collection and reporting system

China has intensified its efforts to collect and report basic statistics in the DWF sector, raise data quality, and promote sharing and integration. It has set up an inclusive DWF data collection framework, covering enterprise information, ship information, position monitoring, fishing logbook, transshipment of catches, national fisheries observers, port sampling, scientific survey and trial fishing, and reported data on fisheries to respective RFMOs in line with their requirements. China advocates sufficient and fair data sharing and research, maximizes the role of science-based data in decision making, protects data security, and makes its due contribution to conservation and sustainable use of fisheries resources in all regions.

4. Rolling out electronic fishing logbook

China has imposed requirements for keeping fishing logbook for tuna, squid, jack mackerel, Pacific saury, and other species on the high seas, and retrieved logbooks from all fishing vessels, whose reporting quality continues to rise. Chinese ships also report to other countries as required when fishing in their waters. In order to acquire accurate data in real time, China is advancing the research, testing, and application of electronic reporting to cover all Chinese high seas fishing vessels, and has participated in RFMOs' electronic reporting programs. In July 2022, the Chinese government issued administrative measures for electronic reporting, and announced the full implementation of the system as from January 2024 for all China-approved fishing vessels on the high seas.

5. Promoting the national fisheries observer program

China has implemented a national fisheries observer program to regulate and standardize the dispatch of observers. Its observer programs in the West and Central Pacific Ocean and the South Pacific Ocean have been reviewed or approved by respective RFMOs. After satisfying the RFMO mandated observer coverage rate of five percent, China has en-

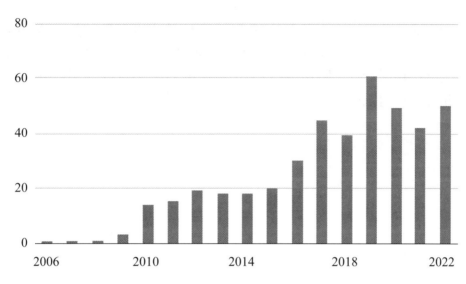

Figure 2　Number of trips made by Chinese DWF observers between 2006 and 2022

Source of data: National Data Center for Distant-Water Fisheries of China

couraged the use of electronic observers. It launched its high seas transshipment observer program in 2021 to oversee transshipment activities that do not fall under the management of RFMOs. China continues to reinforce its contingent of competent observers, and has incorporated this profession into the General Code of Occupational Classification of the People's Republic of China (2022 Edition), laying institutional foundations for observer programs.

6. Strengthening management of high seas fishing vessels

China has rigorously complied with the conservation and management measures imposed by RFMOs. It has formulated and implemented special administrative measures for fishing activities in the North and South Pacific Ocean regions and for tuna, squid and other major species, and strengthened supervision and management of high seas fisheries and compliance with international treaties. In the high seas areas where Chinese DWF vessels concentrate, China has applied quota controls to squid fishing since 2021, focusing on the management of DWF squid jigging vessels that work in areas without RFMOs. It has optimized the regional distribution of fishing vessels, regulated their activities, and performed its duty of care as a flag state.

IV. Strictly Regulating the DWF Sector

China executes the world's strictest management measures and regulations to monitor and position distant-water fishing vessels, and adopts a "zero tolerance" attitude towards illegal fishing. By reinforcing monitoring and management mechanisms and capabilities, China has made notable progress on critical issues and in priority areas such as monitoring and managing distant-water fishing vessels, managing crews, conducting monitoring and control over key sea areas, reinforcing capacity to regulate DWF, and ensuring overall stability in production of the sector.

1. Actively monitoring and regulating transshipments on the high seas

Based on the effective implementation of regulations formulated by RFMOs, China has begun to fully and independently monitor and regulate transshipments conducted by distant-water fishing vessels on the high seas since 2020. It has established a new platform that manages all distant-water fishing vessels, requiring a permit before and a report after a transshipment, and has begun to dispatch onboard observers or install onboard video surveillance systems. In April 2021, for the first time observers authorized by the Chinese government boarded distant-water fishing vessels to supervise transshipments on the high seas. In May 2022, China attended the Technical Consultation on the FAO Voluntary Guidelines for Transshipment, and contributed to the successful conclusion of the consultation and the adoption of the guidelines.

2. Further regulating seafood imports and exports

China always strictly regulates seafood imports and exports, and actively fulfills its obligations as a market state. In accordance with the conservation and management measures stipulated by relevant RFMOs, China verifies the legitimacy of imports and exports of bigeye tuna, swordfish, bluefin tuna and Antarctic toothfish, including products caught by Chinese DWF vessels. As requested by importing countries and regions such as the Republic of Korea (ROK), Chile and the EU and by exporting countries such as Russia, China verifies the legitimacy of imported and exported seafood, and conducts investigations and gives feedback in line with the verification requirements of relevant countries to ensure that all imported and exported catches are obtained through legal and regulated fishing. For species listed in the Convention on International Trade in Endangered Species of Wild Fauna and Flora (CITES), China conducted introduction from the sea according to the requirements.

3. Resolute action against illegal fishing

China strictly regulates DWF, shows "zero tolerance" for illegal fishing, and severely punishes via legislation and administrative means any distant-water fishing vessel and company that has engaged in illegal fishing. China will carry out full-scale investigations on any report made by other countries and international organizations against suspicious activities conducted by Chinese distant-water fishing vessels. Should a violation be confirmed, the vessel responsible and the vessel owner(s) will be severely punished, and the result will be announced appropriately. Since 2016, six fishing companies have had their distant-water fishing enterprise qualification revoked, and 22 companies have been suspended from distant-water fishing. Punishments resulting from different violations imposed on vessels and skippers have included cancellation of all DWF projects, suspension of all DWF projects, a ban on applying for new DWF projects, and the imposition of fines, with total financial penalties exceeding RMB1 billion.

China resolutely supports and actively joins in the efforts made by the international community to curb illegal fishing. Starting from 2020, China dispatches law enforcement vessels every year to conduct fishery patrols and deal with illegal fishing activities on the high seas of the North Pacific. In 2016, along with the Commission for the Conservation of Antarctic Marine Living Resources (CCAMLR), China impounded and penalized a foreign vessel that conducted an illegal transshipment of Antarctic toothfish. Since 2018, China has begun to inform its domestic ports of vessels blacklisted for illegal, unreported and unregulated (IUU) fishing by RFMOs to which China belongs, to ban these vessels from entering ports to land their catches, obtain supplies and refuel.

Panel 3   The Capture of the *Andrey Dolgov*

China is actively seeking to join the FAO Agreement on Port State Measures to Prevent, Deter and Eliminate Illegal, Unreported and Unregulated Fishing, and applies the agreement and other relevant measures to conduct port inspections in order to combat illegal fishing. It has achieved considerable success. In May 2016, after receiving a tip-off from the CCAMLR, the Chinese authorities carried out an inspection on the *Andrey Dolgov*, a foreign refrigerated transport vessel which had docked at a harbor in China's Shandong Province and was suspected of transshipping illegal catches. Ultimately the vessel was convicted of illegally transshipping Antarctic toothfish. The CCAMLR placed the vessel on the IUU vessel list and requested the Chinese authorities to deal with the illegal catches. The Ministry of Agriculture and Rural Affairs of the People's Republic of China, the Ministry of Foreign Affairs of the People's Republic of China, and local authorities carried out a joint law enforcement operation, seizing and auctioning the 110-tonne illegal catch. After deducting necessary expenses, the proceeds of the total sales were donated to the CCAMLR to fight against illegal fishing around Antarctica and conserve Antarctic marine living resources. China's successful action against this illegal transshipment of Antarctic toothfish manifests its resolute determination to carry out port inspections and combat illegal catches.

---

4. Championing the high seas boarding and inspection regime

China systematically supports the high seas boarding and inspection performed within the frameworks of RFMOs, with the aim of combating illegal fishing and effectively implementing conservation and management measures. China requires all Chinese fishing vessels to accept the high seas boarding and inspection carried out pursuant to regulations formulated by RFMOs.

In 2020, China began to register China Coast Guard (CCG) vessels with the North Pacific Fisheries Commission to obtain the right to board and inspect vessels on the high seas of the North Pacific to fulfill its obligations as a member state. Starting from 2021, China has sent the CCG vessels to carry out boarding and inspection on the high seas of the North Pacific and has taken steps pursuant to legitimate procedures to dispatch law enforcement vessels to sea areas under the jurisdiction of other RFMOs, working with the international community to play its part in combating illegal fishing on the high seas.

V. Reinforcing Scientific and Technological Support for the DWF Sector

China engages in scientific surveys of high seas fisheries resources, participates in research initiatives led by RFMOs, and progressively upgrades fishing vessels and equipment. These efforts reflect China's commitment to scientific and technological innovation, transformation and upgrading, and high-quality development and efficiency in the fishing sector. The National Plan for Fisheries Development in the 14th Five-Year Plan Period sets a target to increase the contribution rate of scientific and technological progress in the sector from 63 percent in 2020 to 67 percent by 2025.

1. Improving scientific and technological support framework

China's DWF management is based on scientific principles. It aims to establish and improve a comprehensive management and compliance technology support system, where competent authorities, industry associations, and scientific research institutes collaborate to develop management strategies, implement effective management measures, and evaluate their outcomes. Industry associations play a crucial role in organizing and coordinating fisheries operation, standardizing corporate behavior, providing employee training, strengthening industry self-discipline, and promoting best practices. To further ensure compliance, China has established a DWF compliance research center and a DWF data center. Additionally, efforts have been made to improve the mechanism for compliance and to strengthen scientific research institutions and think tanks, steadily improving the capacity and effectiveness of compliance.

Panel 4　Training for Compliance in DWF Companies

China places great importance on the training for compliance in DWF companies. Each year, authorities at various levels, industry associations, and scientific research institutes organize training sessions in diverse forms, focusing on different aspects of compliance. Some companies proactively conduct training programs on management measures and compliance. Notably, key management personnel receive special training. Since 2014, China has implemented strict regulations governing the credentials of DWF employees. A mechanism has been implemented for the admission of DWF personnel. A qualification training program for practitioners, conducted by the DWF Training Center under the Ministry of Agriculture and Rural Affairs, is mandatory for enterprise legal persons or general managers, specific project leaders, and other middle and high-level management personnel. Participants must complete designated courses, pass assessments, and obtain qualification certificates. As of the end of 2022, more than 4,000 middle and high-level management personnel have been trained through various programs.

These training initiatives, including qualification training for employees, have effectively increased the knowledge of DWF company management personnel in areas such as international fisheries laws and regulations and management systems, China's DWF policies and management systems, and the handling of foreign-related fisheries issues. DWF companies have improved their ability to operate and implement management measures in compliance with laws and regulations. China will further strengthen the training of personnel engaged in the DWF industry, particularly focusing on company managers, captains of distant-water fishing vessels, and professional crew members.

---

2. Advancing information technology in the DWF sector

China actively promotes the mechanization, automation, and digitalization of distant-water fishing vessels. It invests in the research and development and application of technologies such as the Internet of Things (IoT) and artificial intelligence (AI) in the sector. Work is under way to adapt the BeiDou intelligent monitoring application system specifically for use in the sector. China is also participating in the research and testing of video surveillance systems for distant-water fishing vessels and contributing to the formulation of standards and specifications for the installation of video surveillance equipment on such vessels. The gradual rollout of pilot programs on key fish species and regional fishing vessels is being carried out. Furthermore, China actively engages in sharing its experimental experience in developing electronic monitoring/observation standards for RFMOs. In May 2023, China supported the Indian Ocean Tuna Commission's resolution on electronic monitoring standards, marking the first management measure of its kind in regional tuna fisheries management organizations. Currently, more than 100 tuna fishing vessels – accounting for approximately 20 percent of all tuna fishing vessels in China – have been equipped with electronic monitoring systems.

3. Improving the survey and monitoring of DWF resources

Fisheries resource assessment and management recommendations depend on scientific data, and conducting resource surveys and monitoring is an internationally recognized method of obtaining reliable first-hand scientific data. From the 14th Five-year Plan period (2021-2025), China has implemented a systematic plan for surveying and monitoring DWF resources. The objective is to provide scientific and data support for the conservation and sustainable development of resources. This involves deploying professional scientific survey vessels to conduct comprehensive scientific surveys of fisheries resources in the high seas of the Northwest Pacific and the West and Central Pacific Ocean. Additionally, China encourages scientific research institutions to collaborate with DWF companies to conduct trial fishing on fisheries resources. The survey findings are shared with the Western and Central Pacific Fisheries Commission, and the survey research results continue to be submitted to provide a scientific foundation for resource assessment and the formulation of management measures. China actively cooperates with other countries involved to conduct scientific surveys of fisheries resources, thereby promoting the conservation and long-term sustainable use of fisheries resources in such countries' waters. Furthermore, China is conducting a monitoring and evaluation project for significant global fish species resources. Research and monitoring activities focus on the population status of economically important fish species, bycatch species, and protected species. A database system is in place to provide scientific references for production management and resource conservation.

4. Conducting innovative research to formulate independent conservation management measures

China combines domestic and foreign research results with up-to-date information on its DWF development. Through collaborative efforts involving the government, industry, universities and research institutes, China actively conducts innovative research and formulates independent measures to conserve and manage fisheries resources. In June 2020, China issued management regulations to strengthen the conservation of high seas squid resources and promote the sustainable development of DWF. Measures included squid resource surveys and assessment, implementation of voluntary fishing moratoria for high seas squid fisheries, and research on the management system of the entire squid industry chain. China is actively exploring the compilation of DWF indexes to improve resource assessment capability, standardize practices, and guide sustainable industry development. Initiated with the squid as a pilot species, the oceanic squid index of China was developed and launched in 2020. This comprehensive index incorporates the squid resource abundance index, squid price index, and industry prosperity index, providing detailed and dynamic data to monitor squid products and the overall development of the distant-water squid fishery sector. In the next phase, work will be directed to studying and releasing the tuna fishery development index.

5. Carrying out timely research and adaptation of international conservation management measures

China emphasizes the importance of resource assessment and utilizing the best scientific evidence when making conservation management recommendations and formulating management measures. It actively engages in research on scientific management recommendations proposed by RFMOs. Additionally, China supports the participation of scientific researchers in various scientific conferences and their involvement in relevant scientific organizations. Focusing on resource assessment, China carries out research on fish population biology, ecosystem management, and the evaluation of fishing moratorium effects. China also actively participates in relevant research programs and submits a variety of research reports. In addition, it conducts in-depth studies on conservation and management measures adopted by RFMOs. China has issued documents on the conservation and management measures adopted by tuna fisheries organizations, the North Pacific Fisheries Commission and the South Pacific Regional Fisheries Management Organisation. These measures are promptly incorporated into relevant domestic management regulations to strengthen fisheries management and ensure compliance with international obligations.

VI. Ensuring Safety in the DWF Sector

China continues to upgrade its distant-water fishing infrastructure focusing on safety, eco-friendliness, sustainability, and worker protection. It is bringing the size of its distant-water fishing fleet under control. Vessel safety and the living environment of crews are being steadily improved.

1. Promoting safe and eco-friendly distant-water fishing vessels

China encourages and supports the upgrading of distant-water fishing vessels to make them safer and more eco-friendly. It has put strict restrictions on the tonnage of distant-water fishing vessels to minimize the impact of fishing on the marine environment and eco-systems. In accordance with the requirements of international conventions on pollution control and maritime safety such as the International Convention for the Prevention of Pollution from Ships of the International Maritime Organization (IMO) and relevant domestic regulations, in 2021, China amended the parameters for standard types of distant-water fishing vessels, improved their testing rules, standardized their scrapping procedures, and improved the reliability of newly-built distant-water fishing vessels and upgraded their safety and antipollution equipment.

2. Improving vessel position monitoring and surveillance

China attaches great importance to monitoring and observing the position of distant-water fishing vessels. It has upgraded the Distant-water Fishery Service Platform and the monitoring and surveillance system to cover all such vessels. To increase capacity and improve service, it has raised the frequency of position reporting, improved the collection of data and statistics, reinforced surveillance of key areas and trespassing alarms, and required electronic fishing logbooks and position monitoring and surveillance. The authorities have invested in the National Data Center for Distant-Water Fisheries of China, developed fishing data checking and quality control, and strengthened the scientific management of production reporting, fishing logbooks, and data from fisheries observers.

Panel 5   Position Monitoring and Surveillance of Distant-Water Fishing Vessels

In order to strengthen supervision over DWF and ensure compliance, China adopted a position monitoring and surveillance system of distant-water fishing vessels in 2006. In place for more than a decade, it has played a key part in China's distant-water fishing management. It covers all Chinese distant-water fishing vessels, monitoring their geographical range of daily activities and reporting their positions every hour to the authorities, higher than international industry standards.

Since 2021, with the support of specific technical departments, China has further adopted a daily statistical report system recording and reporting the change of position of all distant-water fishing vessels in the past 24 hours. Failing to report positions as required or reporting abnormal positions will be immediately reported to authorities for follow-up checks on the companies involved and in-time correction. Consistent improvements have been made to the position monitoring and surveillance system through additional functions such as trespassing alarms and navigation safety alerts. The system has played an important role in ensuring safe navigation and operation of distant-water fishing vessels, supervising their activities, guaranteeing that China fulfills its obligations as a flag state, and complying with international fisheries management measures.

---

3. Safeguarding the lawful rights and interests of the crew

As a founding member of the International Labor Organization, China attaches great importance to the protection of workers' rights and interests. By April 2023, it had ratified 28 international labor conventions including seven core conventions such as the Forced Labor Convention, 1930 and the Abolition of Forced Labor Convention, 1957. China prioritizes the protection of the rights and interests of distant-water fishing crew members. Consistent efforts have been made to regulate crew employment and management, enabling DWF companies to assume their full responsibilities, strengthening industry self-discipline and employment supervision, and ensuring satisfactory working conditions and proper remuneration for Chinese and international crew in accordance with the law. Companies are required to respect the following requirements:

- Pay the crew on time. Arrears of wages without justifiable cause are forbidden.
- Arrange reasonable working hours and provide sound living and working conditions for the crew.
- Properly handle the legitimate demands of the crew. Companies are required to understand, respect, and maintain an inclusive attitude towards their customs and religious beliefs and cultural differences. Discrimination, abuse or ill-treatment of the crew is strictly prohibited.
- Strengthen skills and workplace safety training and raise awareness of safety issues.
- Equip vessels with the necessary labor protection equipment and facilities to ensure a safe environment and working conditions.
- Equip vessels with essential medicines and rapidly provide all necessary medical treatment and psychological aid to crew members in need. Any illness or injury beyond the handling capacity of the vessel must be reported promptly to enable treatment.

4. Strengthening safety at work and rescue at sea

China has prioritized safe working conditions in DWF. It has strengthened safety checks and the identification of potential safety hazards to ensure safe navigation for the vessel and safe production for the crew. A 24-hour emergency rescue and service mechanism has been established by the industry association and efforts have been made to put in place a mechanism of mutual aid and support at sea. The country has also explored and established a DWF emergency response mechanism. The authorities take strict action against violations of laws and regulations by crew members. A score system is in place to manage crew members' violation of safe navigation and working practices, which helps to maintain production safety. China has also strengthened cooperation with other countries and organizations and played an active part in global marine rescue.

VII. Increasing International Cooperation on Fisheries

The sustainability of fisheries resources is currently threatened by climate and environmental change, creating new trends in cross-regional distribution, mobility, and migrations. International cooperation on fisheries management must therefore be strengthened. Committed to the vision of a maritime community of shared future, China has increased exchanges with other countries and regions in the DWF sector, launched mutually beneficial cooperation projects through multiple channels and in multiple forms, strengthened multilateral and bilateral intergovernmental fisheries cooperation mechanisms, and helped the fishing industry to develop in other countries and regions.

1. Participating in global fisheries governance

China has played an active role in multilateral fisheries governance within the framework of the UN, and supported calls for a fairer and more equitable global fisheries governance system. It is actively seeking to join the FAO Agreement on Port State Measures to Prevent, Deter and Eliminate Illegal, Unreported and Unregulated Fishing, and has engaged in the research of fisheries treaties like the IMO Cape Town Agreement of 2012 (on the Implementation of the Provisions of the Torremolinos Protocol of 1993 relating to the Torremolinos International Convention for the Safety of Fishing Vessels, 1977). In addition to registering its high seas fishing vessels in the FAO Global Record of Fishing Vessels, Refrigerated Transport Vessels and Supply Vessels, it has increased cooperation with the IMO and required its DWF vessels to apply and register for IMO identification numbers.

In recent years, the international community has paid close attention to fisheries subsidies. China firmly supports the multilateral trading system and conforms to the general trend of fisheries subsidies negotiations in the World Trade Organization (WTO). Over the years, China has actively participated in the fisheries subsidies negotiations of the WTO with the aim of facilitating talks, cooperation and solution. It tries its best to take care of the interests of all participants and the demands of developing members, strives to bridge the differences among members, puts forward suggestions for text revisions, actively responds to the opinions of other members, and demonstrates flexibility, making an active contribution to the final conclusion of the Agreement on Fisheries Subsidies. On June 27, 2023, China submitted its instrument of acceptance for the Agreement on Fisheries Subsidies to the WTO. It will fully implement its provisions and actively participate in the follow-up negotiations.

China attaches great importance to communication with NGOs like the World Wide Fund for Nature and Greenpeace on sustainable fisheries management, actions against illegal fishing, and other issues, and incorporated their sound proposals into its measures for voluntary fishing moratoria on the high seas and the conservation of squid resources.

2. Taking part in regional fisheries management

To show its commitment to expanding and strengthening regional fisheries cooperation, China has fulfilled its obligations as a member of RFMOs. It has made its due and voluntary financial contributions without delay to support their functions and efforts. To contribute Chinese solutions and strengths to their activities, it has organized relevant departments, scientific research institutes, industry associations, and representative companies to take part in the work of RFMOs, in the research and formulation of conservation and management measures, and in the exploration, evaluation and scientific research of fisheries resources. In order to improve fisheries governance in different regions, China has also increased communication and cooperation with RFMOs and their members.

3. Engaging in bilateral fisheries cooperation

China has made sustained efforts to increase bilateral cooperation through dialogue and exchanges, and set up a number of bilateral dialogue and negotiation mechanisms with Russia, the ROK, Japan, Vietnam, the US, Argentina, New Zealand, the EU and other countries and regions to promote mutual interests and combat illegal fishing. It has established communications with Indonesia, Panama, Peru, Ecuador and other countries and regions in terms of bilateral fisheries cooperation, regional fisheries governance, the fight against illegal fishing, protection of bycatch species, and ecological and environmental conservation in key sea areas like the Galapagos Islands. China has engaged in mutually beneficial fisheries cooperation with over 40 countries and regions in Asia, Africa, South America and Oceania, and encouraged Chinese enterprises to invest and start businesses in these countries, which has increased local jobs and boosted economic growth.

Panel 7   Increasing International Cooperation and Exchanges

China prioritizes international fisheries cooperation. Committed to the philosophy of innovative, coordinated, green, open and shared development, China has made active efforts to increase international cooperation and promote mutual benefit.

Increasing multilateral cooperation. China has played an active role in the negotiations and discussions on the agreement on conserving marine biological diversity in areas beyond national jurisdiction, the International Agreement to Prevent Unregulated Fishing in the High Seas of the Central Arctic Ocean, the UN General Assembly's resolution on sustainable fisheries, and the WTO fisheries subsidies agreement, and advocated an international fisheries governance mechanism that is fair, reasonable and sustainable. It participated in the IMO Ministerial Conference on Fishing Vessel Safety and Illegal, Unreported and Unregulated Fishing and

---

signed the Torremolinos Declaration. China has become a member to eight RFMOs, covering almost all ocean regions of application of RFMO conventions. Besides these, it has also taken part in the activities of over 30 international organizations concerning fisheries, including the UN, the FAO, the WTO, the Convention on International Trade in Endangered Species of Wild Fauna and Flora, the Asia-Pacific Economic Cooperation, and relevant RFMOs. In September 2021, together with the FAO and the Network of Aquaculture Centers in Asia-Pacific, it held the Fourth Global Conference on Aquaculture, aiming to increase pragmatic cooperation with other countries, promote global sustainable aquaculture development, and contribute to world food security.

Facilitating bilateral cooperation. China has established high-level dialogue mechanisms with the US, the EU, Norway, Canada, Australia, New Zealand and other major fisheries countries and regions, and implemented bilateral cooperation projects with many countries in Asia, Africa and Latin America. It held two China-Pacific Island Countries forums on fisheries cooperation and development in December 2021 and May 2023, and has provided further assistance to help these countries develop their fisheries and related industries.

4. Supporting other developing countries in fisheries development

Committed to the vision of a maritime community of shared future, China has implemented the Belt and Road Initiative and promoted South-South cooperation. It has always done all it can to provide technological and personnel assistance to other developing countries – especially small island developing states and the least developed countries – to help them develop their fisheries and local communities. Its assistance for developing countries covers fisheries infrastructure, resource exploration, skill training, artisanal and small-scale fisheries, and the development of aquaculture, processing and trade. China supports reasonable proposals from developing countries on multilateral issues, and defends their rights and interests.

5. Promoting sustainable development of global fisheries

The international community has a common understanding that

fisheries play an important role in safeguarding global food and nutrition security and providing a livelihood for the people living in coastal areas. China attaches great importance to the sustainable development of global fisheries. It believes that developing aquaculture can increase food supplies and protect food security in developing countries while reducing dependence on wild fisheries resources. China is the largest processor and exporter of aquatic products. Its aquaculture output has led the world for 32 years, making a contribution to world food security.

On the basis of equality and mutual benefit, China will work with other countries to improve multilateral consultation mechanisms, strengthen scientific and technological communication, expand economic and trade cooperation, combat illegal fishing, and promote scientific conservation and sustainable use of global fisheries resources. It will do all it can to safeguard global food security and contribute to the wellbeing of people living in coastal areas. It defends a fair and reasonable international maritime order, and firmly opposes unilateralism, protectionism, power politics, acts of bullying, and unilateral sanctions and long-arm jurisdiction that have no basis in international law.

Conclusion

Accessing the deepest oceans is the only way for humanity to better explore and protect the sea and use its resources. China will adhere to the philosophy of innovative, coordinated, green, open and shared development, carry out its Global Development Initiative, increase bilateral and multilateral fisheries cooperation and dialogue in accordance with relevant international laws and bilateral cooperation agreements, promote high-quality development of the DWF sector, increase its ability to implement international fisheries treaties and conservation and management measures, and meet those international obligations that are consistent with its development.

In the current era, international ocean governance is facing fresh challenges. At this new historical threshold, China will continue to work with the rest of the world on the basis of equality, mutual respect and mutual benefit to strengthen the conservation and sustainable use of the sea and its resources, and protect marine biodiversity. It will make further contribution to ensure success in completing the UN 2030 Agenda for Sustainable Development, promote a maritime community of shared future and facilitate the green and sustainable development of the sea.

CPC Policies on the Governance of Xizang in the New Era: Approach and Achievements

The State Council Information Office of
the People's Republic of China

November 2023

Foreword

Since the 18th National Congress of the Communist Party of China (CPC) held in 2012, the CPC Central Committee with Comrade Xi Jinping at its core has practiced a people-centered approach to development. With a strategic vision to rejuvenate the Chinese nation, and to ensure that the Xizang Autonomous Region will realize moderate prosperity and modernization together with the rest of the country, the CPC Central Committee has attached great importance to the development of Xizang and focused its attention on the people in the region. The CPC Central Committee held the sixth and seventh national meetings on Xizang in 2015 and 2020 respectively, at which it established the guiding principles, overall requirements and priority tasks, pointing the way to lasting stability and quality development, meeting the people's aspirations for a better life, and realizing socialist modernization in the region.

The seventh National Meeting on Xizang has outlined the CPC guidelines for governing Xizang in the new era as follows:

- Uphold CPC leadership, socialism with Chinese characteristics, and the system of regional ethnic autonomy;
- Adhere to the strategy that stability in Xizang is paramount in the governance of the border areas and the country as a whole;
- Focus on safeguarding national unification and strengthening ethnic unity;
- Govern Xizang in accordance with the law, bring prosperity to Xizang and its residents, unite them in one mind, and lay a solid foundation for its long-term growth;
- Address both domestic and international imperatives;
- Focus on improving people's lives and strengthening unity in

socio-economic development;

- Facilitate ethnic exchanges, communication and integration;
- Adapt religion to China's realities, and handle religious affairs in accordance with the law;
- Prioritize eco-environmental protection;
- Strengthen the Party, especially its political foundations.

These guidelines, grounded on the practice of socialism with Chinese characteristics and the actual situation of Xizang, demonstrate a keen understanding of work related to Xizang. They encapsulate the CPC's past successes in stabilizing Xizang and its plans for future development. Embodying Xi Jinping Thought on Socialism with Chinese Characteristics for a New Era, these guidelines provide answers to a series of questions on the future direction and strategy in governing Xizang and are to be followed in all undertakings related to the region.

Following the CPC's guidelines for governing Xizang in the new era, and with nationwide support, officials and the peoples of the various ethnic groups in the autonomous region have worked together and achieved all-round progress and historic success in various undertakings. Significant progress has been made in stabilizing the social environment, achieving rapid economic progress, and strengthening the Party organization in Xizang, which has led to a better life to its people, amity among all ethnic groups and religions, cultural prosperity, sound ecological systems, and secured borders. Together with the rest of the country, people in Xizang have witnessed the tremendous transformation of the Chinese nation from standing up and becoming prosperous to growing in strength, and are now embarking on a new journey of building a modern socialist country in all respects.

I. Full Implementation of the New Development Philosophy

The main driver of the CPC's endeavors is the people's aspirations for a better life. Xizang has followed the people-centered approach to development and applied the new development philosophy of innovative, coordinated, green, open and shared development in full. It is addressing imbalanced and insufficient development, optimizing the industrial structure, and boosting growth. Xizang had long been plagued by poverty, but absolute poverty has now been eradicated. The region has now achieved all objectives for development set in the 13th Five-year Plan (2016-2020) as scheduled, and the economy is robust.

– Sustainable, sound and rapid economic development

The economy has witnessed solid and steady growth. Seeing that the market plays the decisive role in the allocation of resources and the government better fulfills its functions, Xizang has extended the reform of the economic system, and coordinated the tasks of sustaining growth, promoting reform, making structural changes, improving people's lives, preventing risks, and ensuring social stability. As a result, the economy is growing more dynamic. In 2022 Xizang's GDP reached RMB213.26 billion, an increase by a factor of 2.28 compared with that in 2012 at constant prices, representing an average annual growth rate of 8.6 percent. Its economic growth rate ranked among the highest in China. The industrial structure is being rationalized and the capacity for endogenous development has been significantly increased.

High-quality development has been realized in agricultural

industries that leverage local strengths. Developing highland barley industry, high-quality animal husbandry, and protected agriculture have been treated as priorities. The days are gone when the Tibetan people lived at the mercy of the elements. A large number of industrial bases have been built for agriculture and animal husbandry adapted to local conditions, such as the cultivation of high-quality highland barley, the production of edible oil, pollution-free vegetable planting, standardized dairy cattle scale farming, and yak and Tibetan sheep farming. In 2022, the total output value of farm and livestock products processing reached RMB6 billion.

Progress has been made in industrial development. Secondary industry has achieved strong growth, and a modern industrial system with local characteristics has been established. From 2012 to 2022, the added value of industry increased by a factor of 2.77, and both the depth and breadth of industrial chains were extended. In 2022 the number of industrial enterprises of designated size (enterprises with a turnover exceeding RMB20 million per annum) expanded by 1.1 percent over the previous year, and the number of hi-tech firms reached 15.

There is greater vitality in the tertiary industry. With the support of the central government, Xizang is being transformed into a world-class tourist destination. The Tibetan Shoton Festival in Lhasa, Mount Qomolangma Cultural Tourism Festival in Xigaze, Yalong Cultural Tourism Festival in Shannan, Nyingchi Peach Blossom Festival, and Nagqu Horse Racing Festival have all become flagship tourist attractions. From 2012 to 2022, the number of tourists to Xizang climbed from 10.58 million to 30.03 million, with revenues from tourism surging by a factor of 3.2 from RMB12.65 billion to RMB40.71 billion. Zhaxi Qoiden community of Changzhu Township in the city of Shannan is a base for promoting Yalong Zhaxi Xoiba Tibetan Opera, an item on the national intangible cultural heritage list. As more tourists go to the community to appreciate the opera, locals have begun to operate household hotels, which have become a major source of income. Nima Tsering, a leading performer of

Tibetan Opera, said: "In the old days, we performed Tibetan Opera to please the serf owners. Today, we do it to help ourselves and others live a better life."

Further progress has been made in reform and innovation. To expand reform of the rural land system, a significant effort has been invested in improving the management systems of land contracts, the transfer of rural land use rights, and ownership registration. In 2014, farmers and herders in Baidui Village of Quxu County received their immovable property rights certificates, which means they have the right to use contracted land. This was the first time in the history of Xizang that land certificates had been issued to villagers. A project developing new types of agricultural business entity is under way, and the leading role of family farms and professional cooperatives has been given full play in rural reform.

Reform of state-owned enterprises and state capital has been extended and efforts have been made to strengthen, expand, and increase the returns on state capital. By 2022 the total assets of state-owned enterprises in Xizang had increased by a factor of 14.05 compared with 2012. The tax and business environment has been optimized. Reform of the system separating operating permits from business licenses has been advanced to simplify procedures and to reduce time for business registration. The number of different market entities in Xizang has grown from 124,400 in 2012 to 437,600 in 2022. Innovation drives development. The added value of Xizang's digital economy has increased by more than 10 percent.

Investment and financial services have brought more benefits to the people. From 2012 to 2022, a total of RMB1.73 trillion in financial subsidies from the central government went to Xizang. With the financial support of the state, investment in fixed assets increased by a factor of 3.33 times between 2012 and 2022. The investment focused on infrastructure, public services and other fields that could reinforce the foundations of Xizang's economic and endogenous development. A large number of major engineering projects related to long-term development have been set up over time, greatly improving the people's working and living conditions.

A total of RMB465 billion has been invested. Private investments are thriving. The system of financial institutions continues to improve, and a multi-level, diverse, and multi-functional financial system has taken shape for banking, securities, insurance, and other relevant activities. The role of finance in supporting economic and social development has expanded significantly.

Exchange and cooperation with other parts of the country and the world has been strengthened. Exchange and cooperation with neighboring regions has been strengthened. Xizang has actively integrated itself into regional economic circles, including the Chengdu-Chongqing Economic Circle, the greater Shangri-La Economic Circle, the Shaanxi-Gansu-Ningxia-Qinghai Economic Circle, and the Yangtze River Economic Belt. It has worked to transform itself into a vital channel for the country's increasing opening up towards South Asia. Integrated reform of customs clearance has been launched, and the South Asia Standardization (Lhasa) Research Center has been established. The Gyirong cross-border economic cooperation zone was set up with the approval of the State Council. The comprehensive bonded zone in Lhasa has passed acceptance review. Gyirong Port has been expanded as an international highway port, realizing the bilateral opening up of China and Nepal. In 2022, the total value of Xizang's foreign trade stood at RMB4.6 billion, and its trading partners covered 95 countries and regions. Events such as the Forum on the Development of Xizang, International Symposium of the Xizang Think Tank, China Xizang Tourism and Culture Expo, and the Trans-Himalaya International Extreme Cycling Race have become important platforms for promoting exchanges, mutual learning and cooperation between Xizang and the rest of the world.

Nationwide support for Xizang development has delivered remarkable results. Paired-up assistance from other parts of the country has made consistent progress. Between 1994 and 2022, a total of 11,900 officials and professionals were dispatched in ten groupings to assist Xizang. Coordination among provinces, cities and state-owned enterprises that assist Xizang has been intensified, and new models have been piloted in coordinated development, industrial cooperation, and management of paired-up assistance. Efforts have been made to coordinate assistance in the forms of financial aid, technical support, poverty alleviation, and facilitation of industrial development and employment, as well as sending teams of medical and educational professionals. The model of assistance has changed from one mainly relying on external support, such as providing funds and launching projects, to a self-sustaining model including developing industries, offering technical support, and nurturing talent. During the 13th Five-year Plan period (2016-2020), 17 provinces and municipalities launched 1,260 projects to assist Xizang, representing a total investment of RMB20 billion.

– Improved infrastructure

There has been considerable progress in transport infrastructure. Based on highways and supplemented by railways, aviation, and pipelines, a comprehensive transport system has been developed and steadily improved. By early 2022, the total road length exceeded 121,400 km, including 1,105 km of high-grade highway. A road network covering the whole of Xizang has been formed, with 20 national highways as the foundation, supported by 36 provincial highways together with many border roads and rural roads. The railway network was extended from 701 km in 2012 to 1,359 km in 2022. The Golmud-Lhasa section of the Qinghai-Xizang Railway has been renovated. The Ya'an-Nyingchi section of the Sichuan-Xizang Railway is under construction, and the Lhasa-Nyingchi section has entered service. The Fuxing high-speed train series is now operating in Xizang and reaches as far as Lhasa. The pipeline network transported 31 million tonnes-km in 2022. Tibet Airlines has been successfully launched, with 154 international and domestic routes connecting 70 cities. In 2022, passenger throughput handled by the Xizang Autonomous Regional Administration of CAAC reached 3.35 million. **Major breakthroughs have been made in the construction of the**

power grid. Xizang has made a historic shift in electrical power from rationing to surplus output. The Qinghai-Xizang, Sichuan-Xizang, central Xizang, and Ngari electric transmission lines have been built. Major electricity grid projects in western and southwestern regions have provided Xizang with ample supply of power. A safe and reliable power grid covers all counties/districts and main towns/townships in Xizang. The grid, described by the local people as a "grid of light, livelihood and happiness", has transmitted more than 13 billion kWh of clean energy-generated electricity. Now, 96.5 percent of villages have access to three-phase power supply. Electricity consumption increased from 2.88 billion kWh in 2012 to 11.98 billion kWh in 2022, recording one of the fastest rates of growth in China for many years. The Ngari power grid, operating in isolation for a long time, has now been connected with the central Xizang power network, and thus becomes part of the integrated regional network.

Further progress has been made in water conservation facilities. During the 13th Five-year Plan period (2016-2020), total investment increased by 52 percent compared with the previous period, and several landmark water conservancy projects were completed. The Lalho project was selected as one of the top 10 water conservancy projects in China. The Pondo and Lalho water conservation projects are generating electricity and providing irrigation. The Xianghe River water conservation project and the supporting irrigation facilities are under construction. More local people are benefiting from water conservation. Flood control and disaster reduction efforts have become more effective and the eco-environment of Xizang's rivers and lakes has steadily improved. Safe drinking water is now available in most rural areas. The capacity to provide secure water supplies in urban and rural areas has been significantly increased.

Digital infrastructure has made remarkable progress. The autonomous region's e-government websites, unified basic cloud platform and big data control center are largely complete. Xizang has actively participated in the national move to channel more computing resources from its eastern areas to its less developed western regions. It has built its first cloud computing center, and received the title of national green data center. A total of 8,099 5G base stations and nearly 312,600 km of fiber-optic cables have been built. 5G networks now cover all counties/districts and main towns/townships in Xizang. All 3A-level (and above) scenic spots now have mobile signal coverage. Optical fiber broadband, 4G, radio and TV signals cover almost all administrative villages. Modern cloud and network integration has enabled local people to connect with the world online.

– Eradication of absolute poverty

Xizang has eradicated absolute poverty. It has implemented five key measures – new economic activities, relocation from uninhabitable areas, recompense for eco-protection, education, and social assistance for basic needs – through which people have been lifted out of poverty. By the end of 2019, through the basic strategy of targeted poverty alleviation, the autonomous region had lifted 628,000 registered poor residents and 74 counties/districts out of poverty. This represented victory in the battle against extreme poverty that had plagued Xizang for thousands of years. The per-capita income of those lifted out of poverty reached RMB13,800 in 2022, growing faster than the per-capita disposal income of rural residents. Those people lifted out of poverty have reliable access to food, clothing, housing, education and medical care, more harmonious living and working conditions, more convenient infrastructure and basic public services, and a proper social security system.

Rural revitalization has accelerated. Since 2021, Xizang has built a total of 300 beautiful and livable villages and created and certified 505 demonstration villages. Efforts have been made to develop high-standard farmland through mechanical deep tillage, build state-level demonstration farms for standardized livestock and poultry husbandry, and provide all townships with comprehensive service centers for agriculture and animal husbandry. The number of new rural collective economic organizations reached 6,172, resulting in higher-level and larger-scale agricultural production. The region has developed local highland industries and green and organic farming. Xizang now hosts four special industrial clusters, seven modern agricultural industrial parks, and eighteen towns with strong farming industries. The region has consolidated and expanded the outcomes of the fight against poverty. More than 200,000 former victims of extreme poverty have found jobs outside their hometowns. A total of 173 intangible cultural heritage workshops have been built, offering opportunities for people who have been lifted out of poverty to work at or close to their homes. Xizang is turning a new page in all-around rural revitalization.

– Promotion of common prosperity

Xizang has seen a rapid rise in incomes. By 2022, the per-capita disposable income of urban residents has risen to RMB48,753 from RMB18,363 in 2012, representing a 2.7-fold increase. The per-capita disposable income of rural residents more than tripled from RMB5,698 in 2012 to RMB18,209 in 2022. The income ratio between urban and rural residents dropped from 3.22 in 2012 to 2.67 in 2022, narrowing the income gap. The per-capita disposable income of the region's residents as a whole rose to RMB26,675 in 2022 from RMB8,568 in 2012, representing the country's highest growth rate for eight consecutive years since 2015.

The consumer market has been more buoyant. The retail sales of consumer goods increased by a factor of 2.3 from RMB31.84 billion in 2012 to RMB72.65 billion in 2022. In 2022, total freight turnover reached 13.09 billion tonnes-km, effectively expanding links between centers of production and centers of consumption. The revenue of Xizang's postal services (excluding direct revenue of postal savings banks) reached RMB744 million, and 178.83 million courier delivery packages had been handled in 2022, including 12.19 million express delivery packages. Nineteen large national e-commerce and express delivery businesses have settled in Xizang, and cold chain storage space stands at 113,000 square meters. E-commerce services are available at city, county, township and village levels. In 2022, online retail sales reached RMB9.14 billion.

II. Notable Achievements in Cultural and Ethical Development

We must make a concerted effort to fully implement CPC policies on the governance of Xizang in the new era and boost the morale and confidence of all ethnic groups. To better meet the new expectations of the people of all ethnic groups for a rich intellectual and cultural life, Xizang has vigorously promoted mainstream socialist values, inherited and protected its fine traditional culture, and developed a system of public cultural services. As a result, its cultural undertakings have flourished, its cultural industries have developed, and the core socialist values have taken root in the hearts of the people.

– **Promotion of mainstream social values**

The guiding role of core values has been strengthened. Xizang has consistently built consensus and pooled strengths with the common ideal of building socialism with Chinese characteristics. It has issued the *Decision on Implementing the Guidelines on Cultivating and Practicing the Core Socialist Values*. The region has upheld the core socialist values, studied and implemented the essence of General Secretary Xi Jinping's speeches, and combined the core socialist values with the implementation of major policies, decisions and plans of the Party Central Committee, with the efforts in promoting reform, development and stability, and with major thematic publicity and educational campaigns. The region has increased educational activities on the history of the Party, the history of the PRC, the history of reform and opening up, the history of socialist development, and the history of the ties between Xizang as a region and the country as a whole, and helped officials and people of all ethnic groups in Xizang to develop a sound understanding of our nation and our country, and of history, culture and religion. This has all helped to inject strong impetus into the efforts to build a new socialist Xizang.

Revolutionary culture and education have been promoted. In 2021, the building of a new memorial hall dedicated to the liberation of the million serfs in Xizang was completed. A number of exhibitions, museums and sites have been designated as education bases for patriotism, providing more resources for cultivating the core socialist values. They include the Aid-Tibet Exhibition Hall, the Memorial Hall on the Spirit of Builders of the Two Plateau Highways, the Potala Palace Snow City Series Exhibition Hall, the Site of the Battle Against British Invaders in Gyangze, the Revolutionary Site of Linzhou Farm in Lhasa, the Revolutionary Martyrs Cemetery of Nyemo County, the Red Building of the Party Committee of Zamu County (today's Bomi County), Chamdo Revolutionary History Museum, the Site of the People's Liberation Army (PLA) 18th Army Barracks of Gamtog in Jomda County, the Memorial Hall of the Advance Company of the PLA in Gertse County.

– Revitalization of fine traditional culture

Historical and cultural heritage is under effective protection. Xizang now boasts three state-level historical and cultural cities, five such towns and four such villages. Eighty villages have been added to the List of Traditional Chinese Villages. Twenty-nine villages were awarded the title of ethnic-minority villages with cultural significance. A total of 4,468 sites of historical or cultural interest of all types have been examined, registered and protected by the local county or district government. Xizang has 2,373 cultural relics protection units under the protection of governments at different levels, 70 of which are key units under state protection. The Historic Ensemble of the Potala Palace, Lhasa (including the Potala Palace, Norbulingka, and Jokhang Temple) are registered on the World Heritage List. Xizang has formulated a protection plan for key cultural relics units under national-level protection including the Potala Palace, Norbulingka, Jokhang Temple, and Pala Manor. It has completed major protection projects including those on the Potala Palace and Norbulingka, and launched special actions to monitor cultural relics. A project dedicated to protecting important antiques in Sakya Monastery and Samye Monastery has been completed. Xizang is carrying out ongoing restorations to historical architecture and murals in Puncogling Monastery, Tolin Monastery, Khorzhak Monastery, among others. It also carries out projects to preserve precious sites of historical interest such as Tangkar Monastery, the main Hall of Riwoche Monastery, and Sera Monastery. Since 2013, over 100,000 precious cultural relics of all kinds have been carefully protected through digital archiving. The tea leaves and the brocade with characters meaning "marquis" and bird and animal patterns unearthed during archaeological excavations in the Gurujamu Cemetery in Gar County of Ngari Prefecture prove clearly that more than 1,800 years ago, western Xizang had already established close ties with other parts of the country through the ancient Silk Road. The archaeological excavation of Sangmda Lungga tomb site in Zanda County was named one of the top 10 new archaeological discoveries in China in 2020. The rich archaeological findings fully testify to the splendor of Chinese civilization.

Tibetan medicine has been protected and developed. In 2019, the state invested RMB1 billion in the construction of a new campus of the University of Tibetan Medicine, which has trained over 7,000 medicine professionals. As of early 2022, Xizang hosted 49 public institutions of Tibetan medicine; 94.4 percent of town/township health centers and 42.4 percent of village health clinics in the region provided Tibetan medicine services. Tibetan medicines are now being produced on a commercial basis, and the production of Tibetan medicine has been scaled up, standardized, and regulated. Over the years, more than 300 ancient documents on Tibetan medicine have been collated and published. More than 600 volumes of rare ancient books have been collected, and the *Four Medical Classics*, a masterpiece in Tibetan medicine, has been included in the Memory of the

World Asia Pacific Regional Register.

Tibetan classics and intangible cultural heritage (ICH) are under proper protection and utilization. In 2013, the state launched a priority cultural project – *Library of Chinese Classics: Tibetan Volume*. According to the plan, the project would take 15 years to collect and publish important Tibetan classics for the period from the Tubo Kingdom (618-842) to the peaceful liberation of Xizang in 1951. This is yet another landmark project in protecting and promoting Tibetan traditional culture. The central government and the Xizang local government had earmarked over RMB325 million between 2012 and 2022 for protecting ICH items on the national representative list in Xizang, recording the knowledge and skills of the bearers of ICH items on the national list, training ICH practitioners, and building facilities for ICH protection and utilization. There are 106 ICH items on the national representative list with 96 bearers, and 460 items on the regional list with 522 bearers. Three items – *Gesar*, Tibetan Opera, and the Lum medicinal bathing of Sowa Rigpa of Xizang – have been registered on the Representative List of the Intangible Cultural Heritage of Humanity.

The study and use of the Tibetan language and script are guaranteed by law. The Tibetan language is widely used in fields such as health, postal services, communications, transport, finance, and science and technology. Both standard Chinese and the Tibetan language can be found on public facilities, signage and advertisements. Radio and television programs in both languages are available at any time. Courses in both languages are taught in primary and secondary schools. By the end of 2022, Xizang had 17 periodicals and 11 newspapers in the Tibetan language, and had published 45.01 million copies of 7,959 Tibetan-language books. In 2015, the national standard *Information Technology – Vocabulary in the Tibetan Language* was officially released. In 2018, the National Committee for the Standardization of Tibetan Terminology issued *The New Tibetan Terms Approved Since the 18th National Congress of the Communist Party of China*, which contains nearly 1,500 new terms. Issued in 2022, *The New Tibetan Terms Approved Since the 19th National*

Congress of the Communist Party of China (Chinese-Tibetan) contains 2,200 new terms.

– Vigorous development of public cultural undertakings

The public cultural service system continues to improve. There is a five-tiered network of public cultural service facilities in place, at the levels of village/community, town/township, county/district, city/prefecture, and the autonomous region. There are now libraries, people's art halls and museums in all of Xizang's cities/prefectures, all-purpose cultural centers in the counties/districts, cultural activity stations in towns/townships, and cultural activity halls in villages/communities. Xizang boasts 10 professional performing art troupes, 76 art troupes at the county/district level, 153 part-time Tibetan Opera troupes, 395 performing teams at the township level and 5,492 at the administrative village level, with over 100,000 professional and amateur performers. Digitized movie projection is fully achieved in rural areas in Xizang. The region has 478 sets of digital movie projection facilities and holds more than 63,000 movie screenings every year. A total of 6,263 centers (stations) for promoting cultural and ethical progress in the new era have been set up at the village, township and county levels. The region has carried out programs to keep fine traditional Chinese culture alive and strong at the grassroots level, upgraded cultural facilities at the village/community level, and built 100 village-level cultural demonstration bases.

Cultural and artistic creation has flourished. With Chinese culture in mind, a number of outstanding literary and artistic works have been created, highlighting the spirit of the time and reflecting Tibetan features. They have proved popular with the general public. They include the song and dance gala *Bitter Turns Sweet when the CPC Comes*, *Tashidelek to Our Country*, and *Affection of the Tibetans for the CPC*, dramas such as *Our Common Home* and *The North Yard of Barkhor Street*, the Tibetan opera *Tsering Lhamo*, the *Story of Tibetan Incense,* and the musical theater *Galsang Flowers at the Roof of the World*. Among them, the drama *An*

Unblessed Birth, the song and dance gala *Affection of the Tibetans for the CPC,* the dance *Exuberant Plateau,* the square dance *Forging Ahead in the New Era,* and the Tibetan opera *Celebrating the New Year* performed by children have won national awards.

Xizang has seen rapid development in public sports. Various public sport events have taken place, with traditional ethnic sports promoted and mountain sports popularized. The region has gradually improved its performance in competitive sports. Athletes from Xizang won 231 medals at international and domestic events during the 13th Five-year Plan period (2016-2020). At the 2018 Jakarta Asian Games, athlete Dobjee won the bronze medal in the men's marathon – the best result that China had ever achieved in this event in the Asian Games. At the Lausanne 2020 Winter Youth Olympic Games, Sonam Chodron achieved the best result in China's history in two events: skiing and mountaineering women's individual cross-country race and short distance race. At the 14th National Games in 2021, the Tibetan delegation won three gold medals, one silver and two bronze. At the Beijing 2022 Winter Olympic Games, two athletes from Xizang qualified for the competition, representing a breakthrough in competitive sports for the region.

Radio, film, TV, and publishing are expanding rapidly. The coverage rates of radio and TV programs are both well over 99 percent of the population in Xizang. Movies like *Life of Budag, My Himalayas, Seventy-seven Days,* and *Fall in Love,* TV drama *Happy Home,* and documentaries *Hello, New Xizang, Our Stories in Xizang,* and *The Party Shines upon the Border* have been produced. By the end of 2022, Xizang had 74 digital cinemas with 191 screens in total. In 2022, cinemas in Xizang netted total box-office receipts of RMB37.23 million with around 879,700 tickets sold. Efforts have been made to build and make good use of integrated media centers in cities, prefectures, counties and districts, and to build and promote the use of the integrated media platform "Everest Cloud" of the Xizang Autonomous Region. Many excellent cultural documentaries have been produced and broadcast. More than 15,000 hours of radio programs,

7,300 hours of TV programs, and more than 80 movies are translated or dubbed from and into minority languages every year. There are 40 printing enterprises and 219 publishing institutions of various types, releasing nearly 2.32 million copies of periodicals and 2.71 million copies of books, with total sales exceeding RMB1.29 billion. Over 5,400 rural libraries and over 1,700 monastery libraries have been built. All this effectively promotes the prosperity and development of the press and publishing business in Xizang and continues to enrich the scientific and cultural knowledge of farmers and herders.

– Sound development of the cultural industry

The cultural industry is prosperous and dynamic. The Decision of the General Office of the Xizang Autonomous Region on In-Depth Integration of Culture and Tourism to Accelerate the Development of a Cultural Industry with Distinctive Characteristics has been made and implemented. The region has introduced preferential financing and taxation policies to attract investment and provided policy support to cultural enterprises of all categories registered in the region. The region offers incentive funds and supporting funds to help them. By the end of 2022, more than 8,000 cultural enterprises had registered in Xizang, employing over 70,000 people, and the added value of cultural and related industries reached RMB6.33 billion. A total of 344 cultural demonstration parks and bases had been set up at four levels across the region. Seven associated enterprises were listed among the 2021 Top 100 Private Enterprises in the Xizang Autonomous Region, and four among the 2021 Top 20 Private Employers in the Xizang Autonomous Region. One has been nominated four times for China's Top 30 Cultural Enterprises.

Key cultural programs have been launched. During the 13th Five-year Plan period (2016-2020), 91 key cultural projects were successfully implemented, with a total investment of nearly RMB50 billion. The cultural e-commerce platform Treasures in Xizang, Xizang Creative Culture and Tourism Industry Park, Xizang Publication and Cultural Industry Park, and

Mount Qomolangma Creative Culture and Tourism Industry Park, among others, have been instituted or built. Many characteristic cultural projects, such as the Tibetan epic drama *Princess Wencheng* and the stage play *Princess Jincheng*, have hit the market. Cultural products such as animations, films, television programs, and Thangka, which are rooted in Tibetan culture and capture distinct ethnic features and the characteristics of the times, have been well received by the public.

III. Solid Progress in Ethnic and Religious Undertakings

Developing a stronger sense of the Chinese nation as one community is the Party's top priority in managing ethnic affairs in the new era and a strategic task in governing Xizang. Committed to this mission, the region has strengthened its work related to ethnic affairs and consolidated the socialist ethnic relationship of equality, solidarity, mutual assistance, and harmony. It manages religious affairs in accordance with the law, fully guarantees freedom of religious belief, maintains harmony and stability in the religious field, and helps religion to adapt to the socialist society.

– Heightening the sense of Chinese identity

A shared sense of belonging for the Chinese nation has been consolidated. Xizang has compiled and published textbooks and readers on ethnic solidarity and progress, such as *The Readers on Building a Stronger Sense of National Identity*. Communication platforms featuring internet plus ethnic solidarity have been launched. The One Nation One Dream campaign was conducted in an effort to guide all ethnic groups to understand that they are in a community with shared joys and sorrows, and weal and woe. During major celebrations such as the Serf's Emancipation Day, the Peaceful Liberation Day of Xizang, and the Month for Promoting Ethnic Solidarity and Progress, Party and government departments, schools, enterprises, public institutions, and urban and rural communities organize popular activities such as knowledge contests and cultural performances on ethnic solidarity and progress. A theme park has been built to present a visual image of the Chinese nation as one community, creating a strong bond among all ethnic groups and inspiring them to move forward in unity and solidarity.

Exchanges, communication and integration among ethnic groups have been strengthened. Local communities in the region have formed multi-ethnic neighborhoods, where people of various ethnicities reside, learn from each other, and enjoy life together. A number of exemplary multi-ethnic harmonious neighborhoods (residential communities/families) mixing Han, Tibetan, Hui, and Mongolian people, such as the Wabaling community in Lhasa, have emerged. Puna Village in Qewa Township of Rinbung County, Xigaze City, is a newly established settlement of 59 households from diverse ethnic backgrounds. The villagers spontaneously included the term "solidarity" into the community regulations and agreed to host a solidarity forum annually for consultation on common development.

China has promoted mutual learning and common progress among students of all ethnicities. In 17 provinces and municipalities that provide assistance to Xizang, employment service and liaison offices have been set up for graduates of Xizang universities to find employment or business opportunities beyond their own region. The graduate employment rate has been maintained above 95 percent for years. Large household businesses in crop and animal farming, entrepreneurs, and agriculture-related businesses are encouraged to invest in Xizang. The autonomous region today is a place for unity, common prosperity and development among all ethnic groups.

– Further promoting ethnic solidarity and progress

Work to facilitate ethnic solidarity and progress has been carried out effectively. Efforts have been made to establish model communities of ethnic unity and progress to promote exchanges and integration of various ethnic groups. Tours have been organized to such cities and counties. In 2020, the region promulgated the Regulations on Building a Model Region for Ethnic Solidarity and Progress in the Xizang Autonomous Region. In 2021, the Plan for Building a Model Region for Ethnic

Solidarity and Progress in the Xizang Autonomous Region (2021-2025) was introduced. At the national level, 140 groups and 189 individuals in Xizang were honored by the State Council as models of ethnic solidarity and progress. Seven cities/prefectures including Lhasa were recognized as national demonstration cities. The story of Raidi, recipient of the national honorary title Outstanding Contributor to Ethnic Solidarity, was widely disseminated. People across the region were encouraged to emulate sisters Drolkar and Yangzom as models of the times for ethnic solidarity.

The fight against infiltration, subversion and secession continues. In accordance with the general requirements of safeguarding national security and the region's specific circumstances, and upholding the rule of law in the governance of the region, Xizang adopts a proactive approach to combat secessionism. The reactionary nature of the Dalai Group has been exposed and denounced, and the regional government relies closely on the people of all ethnicities to resist all forms of secession and sabotage. It is now deeply rooted in the people's minds across the region that unity and stability are a blessing, while division and unrest lead to disaster. They are ever more determined to safeguard the country's unity, national sovereignty, and ethnic solidarity.

– Fully guaranteeing the freedom of religious belief

Religious activities are carried out in an orderly manner. The region today hosts over 1,700 sites for Tibetan Buddhism activities, approximately 46,000 Buddhist monks and nuns, four mosques, about 12,000 native Muslims, and one Catholic church with over 700 believers. Over 1,700 religious and folk activities including the Shoton Festival, Butter Lamp Festival, Saga Dawa Festival, and the walks around lakes and mountains help to preserve the solemn traditional rituals and demonstrate new vitality with modern cultural elements. Reincarnation of living Buddhas is a practice recognized and respected by the government at all levels. In 2007, the State-Issued Measures on the Management of the Reincarnation of Living Buddhas of Tibetan Buddhism stipulated the principles that should be followed, the conditions that should be met, and the application and approval procedures that should be implemented. It also specified that reincarnated Tibetan living Buddhas, including Dalai Lamas and Panchen Rinpoches, must be looked for within the country, decided through the practice of lot-drawing from the golden urn, and receive approval from the central government. The reincarnation of living Buddhas has been carried out in an orderly manner ever since. In 2016, an online system has been launched to help obtain information about living Buddhas. By the end of 2022, 93 newly reincarnated living Buddhas have been approved and recognized.

Public services at monasteries and temples have been effectively guaranteed. Much work has been done since 2015 to promote the construction of medical clinics in monasteries and temples, train doctor-monks, improve the social security system for monks and nuns, raise their social security benefits year by year, and provide them with social public services. The government provides over RMB26 million per annum to cover medical insurance, pension schemes, subsistence allowances, accident injury insurance, and health check expenses for all registered monks and nuns. Great efforts have gone into improving infrastructure in monasteries and temples to modernize study and living conditions for monks and nuns; most monasteries and temples now have access to roads, telecommunications, electricity, water, radio and television.

– Conducting Tibetan Buddhist activities in an orderly manner

Law-based management of religious affairs has made steady progress. Fully implementing the Party's basic policy on religious affairs, Xizang has guided Tibetan Buddhism in adapting to socialist society, and moved faster to improve the institutions and standards for managing religious affairs in accordance with the law. Measures of the Xizang Autonomous Region on Implementing the Regulations on Religious Affairs, Measures of the Xizang Autonomous Region on the Management of Major Religious Activities and Detailed Rules for the Implementation of the

Measures on the Management of Living Buddha Reincarnation of Tibetan Buddhism have been issued and implemented to safeguard the legal rights and interests and order of religious society, properly resolve religion-related differences and disputes, improve monastery management, and promote religious harmony.

Tibetan Buddhist studies and the training of adepts have been strengthened. In the context of Xizang's actual situation, efforts have been made to raise awareness among religious groups that activities must be carried out in accordance with laws and regulations, and to promote efforts to standardize, institutionalize, and modernize the internal management of Tibetan Buddhist society. While promoting the integration of traditional and modern education, degrees and titles, new efforts have been made to standardize the three-level title system and cultivate patriotic and knowledgeable talent in monks and nuns. As of the end of 2022, 164 monks had been accredited as Geshe Lharampas and 273 monks had earned the highest Thorampa ranking. From 2016 to 2022, the Xizang branch of the Buddhist Association of China held annual meetings on the interpretation of Tibetan Buddhist sutras; the China Tibetology Research Center hosted annual seminars on the interpretation of Tibetan Buddhism doctrines and published 11 books, such as *Interpretive Notes for Tibetan Buddhism Doctrines (Trial Edition)* and *Collections of Studies on Interpretive Notes for Tibetan Buddhism Doctrines*, promoting in-depth study on the precepts and doctrines of Tibetan Buddhism.

IV. Sustained and Stable Social Development

The CPC policies on the governance of Xizang in the new era have emphasized the importance of accurately understanding the present work in Xizang, strengthening social governance, and safeguarding national security, social stability, and the people's wellbeing. With a focus on safeguarding national unification and strengthening ethnic unity, the local government of Xizang has constantly improved its working mechanisms and governance capacity. All of this is helping to lay a solid foundation for long-term development. As a result, Xizang has enjoyed sustained and steady social development, and the people's sense of gain, fulfilment and security continues to grow.

– **All-round progress of social undertakings**

Educational undertakings have achieved high-quality development. A modern education system encompassing preschools, primary and secondary schools, vocational and technical schools, institutions of higher learning, and continuing and special education institutions is in place. Progressively since 2012, Xizang has eliminated the problem of students dropping out of school. It has established a student financial assistance system covering all stages of education for every student from disadvantaged families. From 2012 to 2022, the central government invested more than RMB251.51 billion in Xizang's education. At present, the region has 3,409 schools of various types and at various levels, hosting over 944,000 students. The gross enrollment rate for preschool education has reached 89.52 percent. The completion rate for compulsory education has reached 97.73 percent. The gross enrollment rate in senior high schools is 91.07 percent. The results of the seventh national census showed that the number of college or university graduates per 100,000 inhabitants in Xizang had risen from 5,507 in 2010 to 11,019 in 2020. New entries into the region's workforce now have an average of 13.1 years of education.

Greater efforts have been made to ensure decent housing. Xizang has stepped up the construction of government-subsidized affordable homes in urban areas and the relocation of people in rural areas. It spares no effort in the renovation of dilapidated residential areas, shanty towns, and dilapidated rural houses. It is also increasing the supply of public rental houses. The region has launched a project to ensure heating in urban areas, especially in the five county seats located across cold and high-altitude areas and border areas. Since 2016, the central government has provided RMB1.71 billion in subsidies to help 43,600 households in farming and pastoral areas who fall into the four categories[1], including registered poor households, to renovate their sub-standard homes. It has also supported the renovation of sub-standard homes and improved the earthquake resistance of rural housing for key groups including the newly registered low-income group in rural areas. In 2022, the per-capita living space of urban residents in Xizang reached 44.82 square meters, and that of farmers and herders 40.18 square meters. The people enjoy a steady improvement in housing conditions.

Public health services have been strengthened. The region provides a comprehensive public healthcare system covering regular basic medical services, maternity and childcare, disease prevention and control, and Tibetan medicine and therapies. The assistance by medical professionals in groups to Xizang has made remarkable progress. Relevant provinces and municipalities have offered pairing-up assistance to Xizang, helping the region build six more Grade-A tertiary hospitals, train 1,165 medical teams with a total of 3,192 local medical workers, and plug 2,219

---

[1] The four categories are registered poor households, households entitled to subsistence allowances, severely impoverished rural residents cared for at their homes with government support, and impoverished families of individuals with disabilities. – *Tr.*

gaps in medical technology. Local patients can now obtain treatment for more than 400 serious diseases within the region and for more than 2,400 moderate diseases within the prefectural-level administrative units where they live; victims of minor diseases can receive timely treatment at county-level hospitals. The death rate of women in childbirth dropped to 45.8 per 100,000 in 2022 from 5,000 per 100,000 in the early 1950s, and the infant mortality rate declined from 430‰ to 7‰. Over the same period, average life expectancy has increased to 72.19 years. Endemic diseases such as hydatidosis and Kashin-Beck disease (KBD) and common diseases such as congenital heart disease and cataracts have been eradicated or brought under effective prevention and control. Xizang has effectively curbed the widespread occurrence of KBD through integrated prevention and control measures, such as improving water quality, changing diets, and relocating residents out of endemic areas. KBD has been eliminated in all of the region's 54 counties previously plagued by the disease. Since 2018, no new KBD cases have been detected among children. In 2012, the region launched a program to cure children with congenital heart disease. To date, the program has carried out over 3.66 million screenings. A total of 6,246 children have received interventional or surgical treatment at hospitals in Xizang and other places in the country. The overwhelming majority of those children have been cured.

A basic multi-tiered social security system has been established. Xizang has progressively integrated urban and rural social security networks, and established and improved a fair, unified, and sustained category-specific and multi-tiered social security system that covers all residents and coordinates urban and rural areas. The surveyed urban unemployment rate has remained below the national average and the number of families with no one in work has been steadily reduced to zero. A mechanism to set and regularly adjust the payment standard of basic pension schemes for urban and rural residents has been established, ensuring that it increases in parallel with economic growth. A total of 3.43 million people are covered by basic medical insurance, more than 95 percent of the total population in the region. The maximum reimbursement rate of inpatient medical expenses covered by basic medical insurance has surpassed 90 percent. More Tibetan medicines are being included in the National Essential Medicines List (Ethnic Medicines). A special treatment policy has been extended to cover 38 serious diseases. Patients can now settle their medical bills covered by medical insurance at one time on a cross-provincial basis.

– Steady achievements in building a safe Xizang

Concrete measures have been taken to achieve a higher standard of social stability. On a journey towards higher-level integrated governance, Xizang continues to strengthen social governance and makes every effort to build safe counties, safe townships, safe communities, safe institutions, safe monasteries, and safe schools. To forestall and defuse risks, Xizang has taken proactive action to meet people's rational demands and resolve their immediate concerns. In dealing with social complaints and disputes, law, fairness and compassion are all taken into consideration to ensure problems are settled in a manner acceptable to all stakeholders. By establishing the "Langza mediation offices", "Snow Lotus mediation offices", and "rural sages mediation teams", Xizang relies on and mobilizes the people to lay the social foundations allowing them to live and work in peace and contentment. Lhasa has been listed among "China's happiest cities" seven times. The safety index of people of all ethnic groups in the region has stayed above 99 percent for years.

– Considerable improvement in social governance

There has been a significant improvement in social governance. Xizang has made consistent innovations to the social governance system. It has released documents such as the Plan for the Pilot Project of Promoting the Modernization of Municipal Social Governance in Xizang, the Opinions on Improving Diversified Dispute Settlement Mechanisms, and the Implementation Plan of the Xizang Autonomous Region for Carrying out Special Campaigns to Improve Rural Governance. The region has made steady progress in establishing a multi-dimensional and intelligent public security system by accelerating the construction of integrated management centers, smart cities and intelligent border defense.

Xizang has implemented a social service and management model at both urban and rural communities known as "household groups" to help maintain social order and increase family income and has carried out a campaign to consolidate the development foundation and benefit the people. It has continued to guide the public towards participating in social governance. As a result, a new social governance pattern led by Party committees, implemented by government departments, based on consultation, coordination and broad participation, and underpinned by the rule of law and science and technology has been established. Efforts have been made to create a social governance community in which all participate and share.

– Steady progress in safeguarding and developing border areas
Efforts have been made to develop border areas and improve people's lives there. Xizang strives to build itself into a demonstration region for safeguarding, developing and bringing prosperity to border areas, with equal emphasis on stability and development. Plans and specific programs for developing villages and towns have been formulated. The measures for realizing moderate prosperity in all villages have been launched in line with the national strategy of rural revitalization. The region has improved infrastructure projects and public service facilities in border areas to ensure that people in farming and pastoral areas can find work near their homes. All these projects have contributed to reinforce the sense of the Chinese nation as one single community. Most villages and towns are enjoying improved infrastructure, flourishing businesses, better eco-environment, congenial living and working conditions, and economic prosperity and cultural development. Encouraged by notable improvement in their lives, the local residents are striving to become the conscientious guardians of the border areas and builders of happy homes.

V. Stronger Eco-Environmental Security Barrier

Xizang is one of China's important ecological barriers. Protecting the natural environment in Xizang will benefit the country and the people for thousands of years to come. In its efforts to become a national or even an international model in advancing eco-civilization, Xizang continues to prioritize eco-environmental conservation, follows a holistic approach to coordinating conservation and development, and pursues green and sustainable development. It will continue to deliver eco-environmental dividends while building a beautiful Xizang.

– Sound eco-environment

Orderly progress has been made in the development of eco-environmental function zones. Through proactive efforts, Changtang, Mount Qomolangma, Mount Kangrinboqe, Gaoligong Mountain and Yarlung Zangbo Grand Canyon have been included in China's Overall Plan of National Parks, and work to develop the system of nature reserves in Xizang has entered a new phase. Currently, there are 47 nature reserves of different types at all levels, which cover a total area of 412,200 square kilometers. According to the third national survey of territorial land, forests, grasslands, wetlands, water regions and other lands with stronger eco-environmental functions amount to 1.08 million square kilometers. The establishment of the Sanjiangyuan National Park (the section north of the Tanggula Mountain) has contributed to the protection and restoration of the river sources in China, such as the source areas of the Yangtze and Lancang rivers.

Biodiversity on the plateau has gradually improved. From 2016 to 2022, 8.32 million *mu* (554,666 hectares) of forests were planted in Xizang. It has achieved "double growth" in both forest and grassland vegetation coverage. There are 1,072 terrestrial wild vertebrate species in Xizang, including 65 species of wild animals under national Grade-I protection such as the snow leopard, wild yak, Tibetan antelope, black-necked crane and Yunnan golden snub-nosed monkey, and 152 species of wild animals under national Grade-II protection. Xizang has the largest population of large and medium-sized wild animal species in China. It has recorded 7,504 species of vascular plants; nine of these are under national Grade-I protection, including *Cupressus gigantea* and *Taxus wallichiana*, and 148 species are under national Grade-II protection. According to the second national survey on terrestrial animals and plants, the number of Tibetan antelopes increased from over 70,000 in the 1990s to over 300,000, wild yaks from under 10,000 to over 20,000, and black-necked cranes from under 3,000 to over 10,000. The Tibetan red deer, once considered extinct by the international community, has now come back, and its numbers have grown to over 800 from over 200 at the time of its rediscovery. Five new animal species such as the white-cheeked macaque, five new wildlife species in China, and one new wild plant species of *Chaetoseris iyriformis Shif* have been discovered.

The living environment continues to improve. Since 2016, the proportion of days with excellent or good air quality in Xizang has reached over 99 percent each year. The air quality in main towns and cities has, on the whole, remained excellent or good, and the concentrations of six pollutants in seven prefecture-level administrative units has reached the state Grade-II standards or above. The air quality in the Mount Qomolangma area continues to be rated as excellent or good, reaching the state Grade-I standards. In 2022, Lhasa ranked first among the 168 key cities in China in terms of air quality, and Nyingchi and Qamdo both enjoyed excellent air quality all year round. The major rivers and lakes report good water quality. The water quality of main streams of the Jinsha River, Yarlung Zangbo

River, Lancang River and Nujiang River has reached Grade-II standards, that of the Lhasa River, Nyangchu River and Nyang River that run through major towns and cities reached Grade-II standards or above, that of the Rongpo River that originates from Mount Qomolangma reached Grade-I standards, and that of the Pangong Tso, Yamzho Yumco and Nam Co lakes reached Grade-III standards. The quality of the drinking water sources in prefecture-level cities has all reached the required standards. Thanks to its comprehensive control of soil pollution, the soil environment in Xizang is generally maintained in its original natural state and is safe in quality.

– Complementary eco-environmental protection and economic development

The green, low-carbon industry has grown in strength. Xizang has accelerated the building of a national clean energy base, and clean energy now makes up 90 percent of the installed power generation capacity. It has thus contributed to China's targets for peak carbon emissions and carbon neutrality. Xizang has developed plateau green farming and animal husbandry, producing 1,014 different pollution-free, green or organic farm products or agro-products with geographical indications. Pagri yak and Yadong black fungus ranked among the Top 100 Farm Produce in China. Gyaca walnuts, Lhünze black highland barley, and Markam grapes have been listed as "pollution-free, green, organic farm products or agro-products with geographical indications", and are beginning to be recognized by more consumers.

Eco-environmental conservation has produced results. The Plan for Protection and Building of Ecological Security Barriers in Xizang (2008-2030) has been implemented. Greening projects for the basins of the Yarlung Zangbo, Nujiang, Lhasa, Nyangchu, Yalong and Shiquan rivers and for areas near residential houses, roads, farmlands and waters have been executed, with emphasis on eco-environmental restoration and green construction. During the construction of the Zam Hydropower Station on the Yarlung Zangbo River, a 2.6-kilometer-long fish migration channel was built, and fry breeding and release events were organized each year on a large scale. All these efforts have effectively secured the living and breeding conditions for rare plateau fish species. During the construction of the Lhasa-Xigaze Railway, fine tree species were selected to ensure the survival of turf and trees and efforts were made to stop and fix the sand dunes near the railway line. In addition, elevated passages were opened at major sections for the migration of wild animals. During the construction of the Lhasa-Nyingchi Railway, the largest winter habitat was well conserved for the black-necked cranes.

– New measures to accelerate eco-environmental progress

The autonomous region has continued to improve the eco-environmental governance system. A series of policies, regulations and statutes have been promulgated and implemented, including the Plan on Eco-environmental Protection and Sustainable Development on the Qinghai-Tibet Plateau, the Law of the People's Republic of China on Ecological Conservation on the Qinghai-Tibet Plateau, and Regulations on Developing National Eco-civilization Model in the Xizang Autonomous Region. Xizang follows a holistic approach to the integrated conservation and systematic management of mountains, rivers, forests, farmlands, lakes, grasslands, deserts and glaciers. A responsibility system has been introduced by which the responsibility for protecting rivers, lakes, forests and grasslands is assigned to specific persons with the title of chiefs. Since 2017, Xizang has enforced the strictest water resource administration system and established a "river/lake chief + procurator-general + police chief" coordinating mechanism, to strengthen the management of water bodies and shorelines, keep rivers and lakes healthy, and achieve their sustained utilization. A comprehensive system of forest chiefs has also been introduced across the region to establish a long-term mechanism for the protection and development of forest and grassland resources that addresses problems at source and covers the whole area. Under Party leadership, responsibilities are jointly assumed by local Party committees and governments supported by coordination of relevant departments. Cooperation with neighboring provinces and autonomous regions also has been reinforced in this regard. In 2020, Xizang signed a cooperation agreement with Qinghai and Yunnan provinces on establishing a joint prevention and control mechanism for water pollution emergencies in the upper and lower reaches of inter-provincial river basins. In 2021, it worked out an implementation document with Sichuan, Yunnan, Qinghai and Gansu provinces, Xinjiang Uygur Autonomous Region, and the Xinjiang Production and Construction Corps on establishing a cross-provincial cooperation mechanism for judicial eco-environmental protection of the Qinghai-Tibet Plateau and its surrounding areas, which will facilitate the coordinated protection of the Qinghai-Tibet Plateau. Xizang has also improved the monitoring and performance assessment system and strengthened the auditing of leading officials on their management responsibilities for natural resources. Thirty-five procuratorial liaison offices have been set up in 11 national nature reserves to handle public-interest litigation related to eco-environmental protection and to strengthen the capacity for law enforcement.

Great progress has been registered in scientific surveys and technological breakthroughs. The central government has launched the second comprehensive scientific survey on water, the eco-environment, and human activities on the Qinghai-Tibet Plateau, and conducted a thorough analysis of local environmental changes and their mechanisms. This has generated a number of original theories in international frontier fields of geoscience and life sciences and substantially increased knowledge about the plateau. It has also stepped up efforts to build platforms for scientific research on the Qinghai-Tibet Plateau, and built the Xizang Branch of the National Qinghai-Tibetan Plateau Data Center. Research results have provided technological support for protecting the plateau's eco-environment, addressing climate change, preventing and controlling natural disasters, and promoting green development.

Since 2012, the region has conducted research on core technologies and application demos in relation to climate change impact and biodiversity conservation, among others, and a number of innovative applications have emerged. Breakthroughs have been made in the treatment of degraded grassland vegetation – a key technology in research on restoring typical degraded plateau ecosystems. Ten new technologies, methods and techniques have been produced as a result. A demonstration project of a multi-dimensional network of the earth system for ecological conservation, restoration and governance was completed in Lhasa, providing a systematic plan for ecological conservation, restoration and governance. In order to optimize the national system of ecological security barriers and achieve the national goal of carbon neutrality, the region has taken systematic measures to protect and restore mountains, rivers, forests, farmlands, lakes, grasslands, deserts and glaciers, and investigated changes in the ecosystems of the Tibetan Plateau and its role as a carbon sink.

Xizang has established its first germplasm resource center and conserved 8,458 items of germplasm covering 2,047 species, a fundamental support to the protection of biodiversity. Researchers have worked out a system for utilizing solid waste and biomass on the plateau with low-carbon energy, which would reduce the costs of solid waste and biomass processing by 15 percent and environmental pollution by more than 75 percent. Research findings have been rolled out in neighboring provinces including Qinghai, generating an overall economic benefit of nearly RMB300 million.

– **Eco-environmental dividends**

Eco-environmental conservation mechanisms play an increasingly important role. Since 2018, more than RMB4.93 billion have been invested in the integrated protection and restoration of mountains, rivers, forests, farmlands, lakes, grasslands, deserts and glaciers. An eco-environmental conservation and compensation mechanism has been put in place that covers forest, wetland, grassland, and water ecosystems. The amount paid for eco-environmental compensation in 2012 was RMB3.7 billion and it quickly increased to RMB16.1 billion in 2022.

Xizang has shifted its focus from poverty alleviation to bringing prosperity to local people through eco-environmental conservation. From 2016 to 2022, 537,700 eco-environmental conservation jobs were created on average each year, and a total of RMB12.64 billion was paid in eco-environmental compensation. The development of eco-environmental businesses and the carbon sink economy has helped local people find green jobs or start green businesses. By the end of 2022, the number of rural family hotels and homestays had reached 2,377, receiving 12.74 million visits and generating revenues of almost RMB1.59 billion. Some 64,000 farmers and herders worked directly or indirectly for the rural tourism business, leading to a per capita rise of more than RMB4,500 in income.

An eco-friendly lifestyle has become popular. A new plateau eco-culture has taken shape in which people pursue harmony between humanity and nature and value sustainable development. Nyingchi City has been recognized as a national-level forest city, and 11 cities/counties including the Bomi County in Nyingchi City, the Qonggyai County in Shannan City and Jomda County in Qamdo City have become national eco-civilization demonstration zones. Bayi District in Nyingchi, Lhünze County in Shannan and Dagdong Village of Liuwu New District in Lhasa have been listed as bases for implementing the eco-environmental philosophy that "Lucid waters and lush mountains are invaluable assets". Since 2016, thanks to the Research and Development of Key Technologies for Afforestation and Greening Model Demonstration Project in Nagqu Prefecture (now Nagqu City), the region has selected and cultivated some high-resistance tree species, such as *Salix bangongensis*, *Salix cupularis*, dragon spruce, and *Hippophae gyantsensis*, which have been planted on more than 200 *mu* (about 14 hectares) of land. It is no longer the case that no tree could ever survive in the harsh conditions of Nagqu. Many farmers and herders now plant and protect trees rather than cutting them down. These rich eco-environmental resources are becoming the "real estate for a happy life" that the local people can see and keep.

VI. Strengthening Democracy
and the Rule of Law

To ensure that Xizang continues to achieve successful development, the rule of law must be upheld and socialist democracy strengthened across the board. Xizang has always been committed to the Party's leadership, the people's position as masters of the country, and law-based governance. Efforts have been made to ensure the effective implementation of the system of people's congresses, the system of CPC-led multiparty cooperation and political consultation, the system of regional ethnic autonomy, and the system of grassroots self-governance. Fresh progress has been made in strengthening the political development in the region, ensuring the right of all people of all ethnic groups to be masters of the region and the country. As a result, all undertakings have advanced in the region.

– Continuous progress in advancing socialist democracy
The strengths of the system of people's congresses have been given full play. Since the 18th CPC National Congress in 2012, two elections have been held in Xizang to elect the regional people's congress, in which more than 90 percent of eligible voters have participated in the county and township-level direct elections, and the participation rate in some places has even reached as high as 100 percent. The institutional mechanism for deputies to the people's congresses to fulfill their duties with due diligence has further improved. The People's Congress of the Xizang Autonomous Region has established and implemented a dual-contact system in which members of its standing committee maintain direct contact

with community-level deputies who in turn maintain direct contact with people in their constituencies. Dhawa, deputy from Naiyu Lhoba Township, Mainling City to the People's Congress of the Xizang Autonomous Region, believes that "as an elected deputy, one should do everything possible to serve the people." By coordinating the relevant departments, he has helped build greenhouses for relocated residents in Sangan of Qamdo, ensuring their access to fresh produce in winter. To date, Xizang has instituted 772 "homes of deputies to people's congresses", covering all cities/prefectures, counties/districts, and townships/towns/sub-districts in the region. Some villages have set up deputies' functional centers. These facilities enable deputies to perform their duties on a more regular basis in the intersessional period, which has helped regulate and institutionalize the dual-contact system.

The unique advantages of socialist consultative democracy have been further highlighted. Xizang has exercised consultative democracy throughout the process of socialist democracy. It gives full play to the role of the Chinese People's Political Consultative Conference (CPPCC) as a major channel for consultative democracy and its committees as specialist consultative bodies. CPPCC members are encouraged to offer workable suggestions to address major issues related to economic and social development and resolve the people's immediate concerns. The CPPCC is open to representatives from all social sectors and ethnic groups, including those of religious circles, intellectuals who are not CPC members, and people from New Social Groups. There are 440 members on the 12th CPPCC Committee of the Xizang Autonomous Region, 59.3 percent of whom are not CPC members. CPPCC organizations have been established in all the 74 counties/districts in the region. There are more than 8,000 CPPCC members in the whole region; ethnic minority members account for 85.7 percent. Between 2013 and 2022, the CPPCC Committee of the Xizang Autonomous Region received a total of 4,356 proposals, all of which were processed with feedbacks. The CPPCC organizations have urged its members to earnestly perform their duties in political consultation, democratic supervision, and participation in the deliberation and administration of government affairs.

Democracy has been translated into extensive, pragmatic and vivid actions at the grassroots. Grassroots democracy in Xizang has been gradually enriched. The system of villagers' representative meetings has been established, and community residents' congresses or residents' committees have been instituted in urban areas, providing a satisfactory organizational guarantee for grassroots self-governance. In 2019, the Measures of the Xizang Autonomous Region for Transparency in Village Affairs was issued. So far, more than 90 percent of the villages in the region have set up "transparency" bulletin boards, to ensure the right of local people to be informed, to participate in the deliberation of village affairs and in the decision-making process, and to scrutinize the exercise of power.

In 2015, the Regulations of the Xizang Autonomous Region on Workers' Congresses (for Trial Implementation) were promulgated. There are now 8,821 trade unions in the whole region, with 607,000 members in total. Employees in enterprises and public institutions can fully exercise their democratic rights in the decision-making process regarding important matters that concern their immediate interests through democratic management systems such as workers' congresses.

– Full implementation of regional ethnic autonomy

More measures have been adopted to reinforce the system of regional ethnic autonomy. The regional autonomy system ensures the region's right to development in the political, economic, social, cultural and other fields. The People's Congress of the Xizang Autonomous Region and its Standing Committee have also formulated implementation measures for a number of national laws, which have become an important supplement to state legislation. Preferential financial policies have been introduced, such as policies to give the autonomous region the right to retain all its revenues, to receive increasingly higher subsidies from the central government, and to allocate funds earmarked for special projects. The Xizang Autonomous Region relies on its hard-working spirit while benefiting from the caring policies of the central government and support from other parts of the country. It makes judicious use of its own fiscal revenues. To keep pace with the times, Xizang fully implements the autonomy system, regularly updating specific measures and means to exercise autonomy.

The exercise of rights conferred by the Constitution and other laws is fully guaranteed. The offices of chairperson or vice chairpersons of the Standing Committee of the People's Congress of the Xizang Autonomous Region are occupied by Tibetans, as is the office of the governor of the Xizang Autonomous Region. A total of 89.2 percent of the 42,153 deputies to people's congresses at four levels in the autonomous region are from the Tibetan or other ethnic minorities. Of the 24 deputies of the Xizang delegation to the 14th NPC, 16 were from ethnic minorities, including ethnic groups with small populations such as the Monba people and the Lhoba people. There are 29 members of the CPPCC national committee from Xizang, 25 of whom are from ethnic minorities. The proportion of females among deputies to people's congresses at all levels or members of the CPPCC at all levels has risen considerably. Efforts have been intensified in the training and appointment of ethnic minority officials, which has significantly contributed to prosperity, stability, development, and progress in all respects in Xizang.

– Marked progress in the governance of Xizang in accordance with the law

Significant progress has been made in the development and improvement of the legal framework. Since the 18th CPC National Congress, guided by the strategy that stability in Xizang is paramount in the governance of the border areas and the country as a whole, the autonomous region has formulated and implemented a number of local regulations, government rules and other normative documents, establishing a complete and sound legal system. The region has endeavored to advance the rule of law in terms of both government administration and social governance, by introducing institutions, standards and procedures in the management of regional affairs. As of 2022, the People's Congress of the Xizang Autonomous Region and its Standing Committee had formulated and implemented 160 local regulations and statutory resolutions and decisions of a regulatory nature. They ensure that the rule of law contributes to maintaining stability, facilitating development, protecting the eco-environment, safeguarding the borders, and organizing other matters involving social governance and the people's wellbeing. The People's Congress of Xizang and its Standing Committee have focused on practical issues in light of local realities and features. Based on the region's important role as a national and ecological security shield, the congress has formulated and implemented Regulations on the Establishment of Model Areas for Ethnic Unity and Progress in the Xizang Autonomous Region and Regulations on Developing Ecological Highlands in the Xizang Autonomous Region. Starting from 2021, all the region's cities with subsidiary districts have been accorded local legislative powers. More local legislative bodies and the improved local legislative system have provided legal guarantees for stability and prosperity in Xizang.

Fresh progress has been made in law-based government. The business environment has been steadily improved. The Work Plan of the Xizang Autonomous Region for Building a Sound Administrative Environment and the Implementation Plan of the Xizang Autonomous Region for Promoting the Inter-Provincial E-Government in the Five Southwestern Provinces have been formulated and released. To keep the exercise of power under effective restraint and supervision, several local regulations, government rules and other normative documents have been formulated and released, including the Regulations of the Xizang Autonomous Region on the Supervision of Administrative Law Enforcement, the Regulations of the Xizang Autonomous Region on Discretion over Administrative Law Enforcement and Interim Regulations of the Xizang Autonomous Region on Major Administrative Decision-Making Procedures. Transparency in government affairs in accordance with the law has been promoted, with most government services available online now. These efforts have further optimized government services for the convenience of the people.

New breakthroughs have been made in the building of a law-based society. The General Office of the CPC Central Committee and the General Office of the State Council jointly issued the Measures on Accelerating the Building of a Public Legal Service System, further boosting the public legal service system. All judicial administrative offices at the county level and above have launched public legal service entity platforms, gradually extending to the primary-level communities. In 2021 alone, legal aid institutions in the region provided consultation services to people on more than 27,300 occasions and accepted 7,626 legal aid cases, which helped legal aid recipients recover financial losses of RMB98.47 million. The Regulations of the Xizang Autonomous Region on the Awareness-raising and Education on the Rule of Law have been promulgated, and an extensive education campaign has been carried out to raise awareness of the Chinese socialist legal system with the Constitution at the core. Effective public education on the rule of law has been conducted in rural areas, at schools, and in religious facilities to create a culture of respect for the rule of law across Xizang. The region has carried out a vigorous project to encourage villagers to learn about the law, set up WeChat groups for legal services in rural areas, and provided legal advisers to all villages. A campaign to bring legal knowledge and services to the countryside has been executed, in which real-life cases have been used to explain and interpret laws. National pilot villages and communities for democracy and the rule of law have been established. Interpreting laws with vivid cases motivates more people to learn the law, respect it, abide by it, and apply it.

Conclusion

Since the 18th CPC National Congress, Xizang has experienced a period of unprecedented development and huge change, bringing more tangible benefits to the people. The social and economic progress of Xizang epitomizes the nation's outstanding achievements in development, created on the roof of the world through the Chinese path to modernization.

The region's achievements have proved that to ensure long-term stability and high-quality development in the region, the Party's guidelines on the governance of Xizang in the new era must be fully and thoroughly implemented. The region's development must serve to benefit ethnic unity and progress, to safeguard national unity and oppose separatism, and to improve people's lives and build social consensus, so that people of all ethnic groups in Xizang will have a greater sense of gain, fulfillment and security. To ensure long-term stability, prosperity and high-quality development in Xizang, the four main tasks of ensuring stability, facilitating development, protecting the eco-environment, and strengthening the borders must be successfully and effectively fulfilled.

The Report to the 20th CPC National Congress stated that the central task of the CPC is to lead the Chinese people of all ethnic groups in a concerted effort to realize the Second Centenary Goal of building China into a modern socialist country in all respects, and to advance the rejuvenation of the Chinese nation on all fronts through a Chinese path to modernization. This has set a new goal for Xizang, and will encourage the people of all the ethnic groups in the region to follow a Chinese approach to ethnic issues, and fully implement the Party's policies on the governance of Xizang in the new era, underpinned by a strong sense of the Chinese nation as one single community. Applying the new development philosophy in full, to the letter and in all fields, they will promote ethnic unity and progress on all fronts, and open a new and splendid era of long-term peace and stability and high-quality development in the region.

责任编辑：刘敬文

图书在版编目（CIP）数据

中国政府白皮书汇编. 2023 年 / 中华人民共和国国务院新闻办公室著. -- 北京 ：人民出版社，外文出版社，2025.1. -- ISBN 978－7－01－027017－3

Ⅰ. D62

中国国家版本馆 CIP 数据核字第 2025JE1565 号

中国政府白皮书汇编（2023 年）
ZHONGGUO ZHENGFU BAIPISHU HUIBIAN（2023NIAN）

中华人民共和国国务院新闻办公室

人 民 出 版 社
外 文 出 版 社 出版发行

（100706 北京市东城区隆福寺街 99 号）

中煤（北京）印务有限公司印刷 新华书店经销

2025 年 1 月第 1 版 2025 年 1 月北京第 1 次印刷
开本:889 毫米×1194 毫米 1/16 印张:35
字数:371 千字

ISBN 978－7－01－027017－3 定价:150.00 元

邮购地址 100706 北京市东城区隆福寺街 99 号
人民东方图书销售中心 电话（010）65250042 65289539